THE SOVIET
COLOSSUS

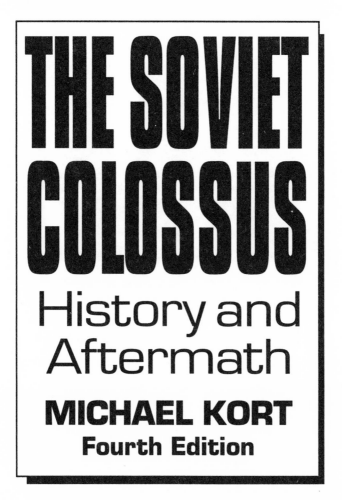

THE SOVIET COLOSSUS

History and Aftermath

MICHAEL KORT

Fourth Edition

M.E. Sharpe

Armonk, New York
London, England

Library of Congress Cataloging-in-Publication Data

Kort, Michael, 1944–
The Soviet colossus: history and aftermath / by Michael Kort.—4th ed.
p.   cm.
Includes bibliographical references and index.
ISBN 1-56324-662-7 (cloth). — ISBN 1-56324-663-5 (paper)
1. Soviet Union—History.
2. Russian—History—Nicholas II, 1894–1917.
I. Title.
DK246.K64   1995
947—dc20
95-38318
CIP

Printed in the United States of America

The paper used in this publication meets the minimum requirements of
American National Standard for Information Sciences—
Permanence of Paper for Printed Library Materials,
ANSI Z39.48–1984.

BM (c)   10   9   8   7   6   5   4   3   2   1
BM (p)   10   9   8   7   6   5   4

for
Eleza and Tamara
and
in memory of
Victor Kort

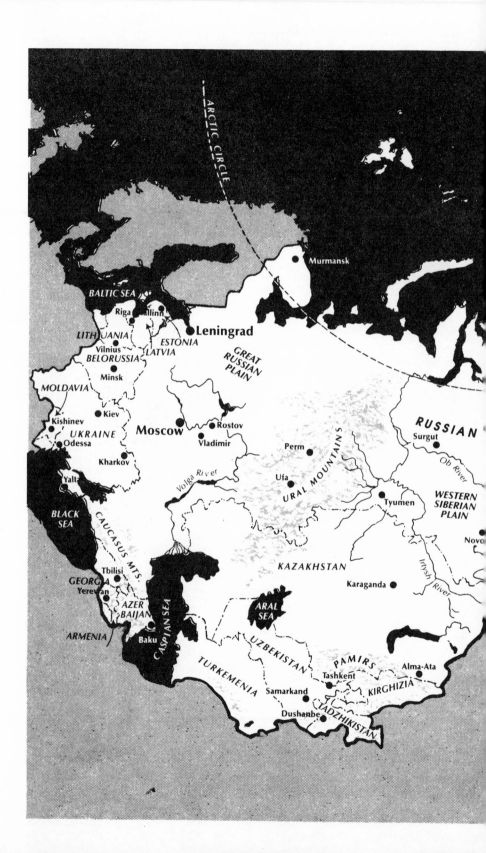

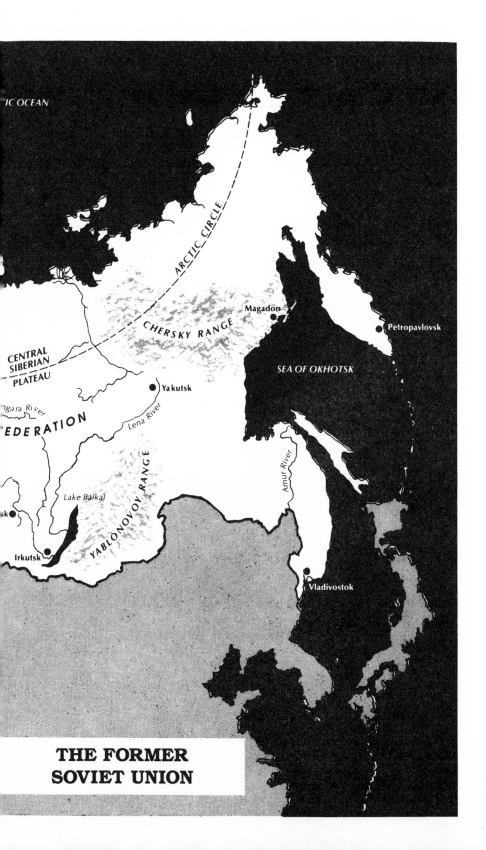

IC OCEAN

ARCTIC CIRCLE

CENTRAL
SIBERIAN
PLATEAU

CHERSKY RANGE

Magadon

Petropavlovsk

SEA OF OKHOTSK

ngara River

Yakutsk

Lena River

FEDERATION

Amur River

YABLONOVOY RANGE

Lake Baikal

sk

Irkutsk

Vladivostok

THE FORMER
SOVIET UNION

Contents

Preface to the Fourth Edition

When the first edition of *The Soviet Colossus* was completed in 1984, the USSR stood imposingly as a troubled but immensely powerful and seemingly durable military superpower. By the time the second edition of the book appeared in early 1990, the USSR, after five years of perestroika and democratic reforms, had undergone change beyond what anybody had expected a few years earlier. However, while badly shaken by the pace and extent of change, the country itself still seemed likely to survive, even if in a drastically altered form.

The third edition of *The Soviet Colossus* appeared as a witness to the shocking collapse of the Soviet Union, which at one time and all at once was the flagship of international Communism, the world's largest empire, one of the planet's two nuclear superpowers, history's first and mightiest totalitarian state, and a huge and complex society whose social system was based on an ideology that at the peak of its influence governed the lives of one-third of the world's population and commanded the adherence of numerous intellectuals the world over. Yet this colossus ultimately crumbled within a few short years and meekly ended up being proclaimed out of existence. Just how and why all this occurred will provide years of work to legions of expert analysts who failed to predict this development in the first place.

The fourth edition of this book, now titled *The Soviet Colossus: History and Aftermath,* continues the methodology of the earlier editions, which focused first on the historical background that shaped Russia before the Bolshevik Revolution, and then on pivotal turning points that led in turn to the establishment of the Bolshevik dictatorship, the development of Stalinist totalitarianism, the reforms and counterreforms under Khrushchev and Brezhnev, the dramatic changes that swept the country under Mikhail

Gorbachev, and, in 1991, the end of the great experiment Lenin and the Bolsheviks so confidently began in 1917. The new edition contains many minor revisions throughout the text. It also contains a new chapter, "Yeltsin and the Birth of Post-Soviet Russia," that covers the period from January 1992 to the fall of 1995. The new chapter features an overview of the problems Russia has faced in attempting to make the transition to a free market economy and democratic political system and an assessment of the extent to which that effort has been successful. Making that assessment has been particularly difficult. To say that there is profound disagreement among specialists about where Russia stands four years after its emergence from the Soviet system is to reaffirm that Russia, in any incarnation, remains, as Winston Churchill succinctly put it, "a riddle wrapped in a mystery inside an enigma."

In writing the first edition of this book, I received invaluable help from Robin King, who read the entire manuscript and helped me rework large parts of it. I benefited from the expertise of Norman Naimark and Jeremiah Schneiderman, and from the support and skills of Alex Holzman, my editor at Scribners. I relied heavily on what I learned from William L. Blackwell, who guided me through my graduate studies at New York University. My colleagues who helped me with either the first or subsequent editions of this book included Jay Corrin, John Zawacki, Michael Lustig, Stephen Frank, William Tilchin, and Brendan Gilbane, the Dean of the College of General Studies at Boston University.

No editions of *The Soviet Colossus* would have been written without the constant support and encouragement of the late Frederick M. Koss, for many years the chairman of the Social Science division at the College of General Studies, a wise and humane man, and a warm and protective mentor and friend. In preparing the third edition, I am grateful to Patricia Kolb, my editor at M.E. Sharpe, who brought to this project her vast knowledge of Soviet affairs as well as her sound judgment, patience, and sense of humor. Elizabeth Granda and Ana Erlić capably shepherded the fourth edition through the labyrinth that lies between writing and publication. I will always owe my parents, Paula and the late Victor Kort, far more gratitude than I can ever express. My daughters, Eleza and Tamara, who have grown up through the writing and rewriting of this book, remain the projects of which I am by far the proudest. My wife Carol, through all editions of every book and for twenty-seven years, has been my essential source of joy and common sense in everything I do.

MICHAEL KORT
Brookline, Massachusetts
December 1995

THE SOVIET COLOSSUS

PART ONE

The Fundamentals of Russian History

1

Prologue

*There was a dreadful time, we keep
still freshly on our memories painted;
and you, my friends, shall be acquainted
By me with all that history:
A grievous record it will be.*

—PUSHKIN

For seven decades, the Union of Soviet Socialist Republics was the colossus among the nations of the world. It sprawled over 6,000 miles from Central Europe across the breadth of Asia to China and the Pacific shore, from the semitropical Asian heartland in the south to frozen Arctic wastes extending toward the North Pole. Its influence stretched yet further into Europe, Asia, Africa, and even the Americas. Like the Russian Empire it succeeded, which an enthusiastic Russian nationalist once called "a whole world," the USSR, whatever one thought of it, surely was more than just another country. It stood like a giant astride the frontier between Europe and Asia, and although at its core European, was geographically and culturally a part of Asia as well. By the 1980s, over 280 million people lived within its vast borders, about 51 percent of them ethnic Russians, or "Great Russians," as they are sometimes called. The Russians are the most numerous of a group of peoples known as the East Slavs, who have lived in the region that eventually became the European part of the USSR for well over 1000 years. Aside from the Great Russians, the USSR was populated by the two other East Slavic peoples, the Ukrainians and the Belorussians (Belarusians), by Latvians, Lithuanians, Estonians, Armenians, Georgians, Azeris, Moldavians (Moldovans), Jews, and others in Europe; and by Uzbeks, Kazakhs, Kyrgyz, Tajiks, Tatars, Turkmens, and many others in Asia, well over 100 distinct ethnic groups in all. Its expanse was well over twice that of Canada, its nearest competitor: over eight and a half million square miles comprising one-sixth of the world's land surface. And the USSR's power dwarfed even this. Armed with a hydra-headed nuclear arsenal, it was the second greatest military power in history, possessing an ability to annihilate that, while calculable, was unimaginable.

The USSR's core, like that of the fallen empire upon whose foundations it was built, was Russia and the Russian people, and its size and strength in many ways were a tribute to the Russian people's ability to endure and survive an almost endless gauntlet of hardships. Nature has imposed the most constant and inescapable of these. Most of Russia lies within the central and eastern portion of the great Eurasian plain. It is the largest such feature on the globe, stretching from Western Europe deep into Asia and Siberia, broken only by a low mountain range—the Urals—that is more of a landmark than a barrier to human or natural forces. The plain's major geographic feature is an extensive river system that for centuries was the region's main highway. Along the rivers laced between the Baltic and the Black Seas, the East Slavs, ancestors to the Russians, Ukrainians, and Belarusians, first developed their civilization and national life.

To the north of the Eurasian plain are Arctic wastes whose winters winds annually sweep over the land to freeze most human activity no less than they freeze the rivers and lakes. A succession of mountain ranges—from the Caucasus in the west to the ranges of central and eastern Asia—demarcate the plain's southern boundary. To the east lie the highlands and mountains of eastern Siberia. Here some of the coldest temperatures in the world have been recorded. The plain itself is divided into three main vegetation zones: the frozen, scrubby tundra in the north; the largest forest in the world, amounting to 20 percent of the world's total timber resources, in the center; and the steppe, the windy, often dry prairie containing Russia's richest soil, in the south.

Overwhelming in size and potential, this is a hard land, a northern land too distant from the Atlantic Ocean to benefit from the moderating Gulf Stream breezes that grace the western fringes of the plain inhabited by other nations. The resulting climate is as severe as it is extreme. Winters are a long, frigid ordeal. Summers are short and hot. The resulting short agricultural season is made even more precarious by other natural idiosyncrasies. In the spring the accumulated winter snows melt rapidly and run off as flood waters, inundating rather than benefiting the farmer and his fields. Rain falls most plentifully on the poor, thin soils of the forest zone, while the rich, black earth to the south must rely on sparser and often unreliable or ill-timed allotments. Though blessed with an uncalculated treasure-trove of natural resources, like most treasures these resources have been for the most part out of reach, either too remote or too poorly located to be put to use. Only modern technology has made them exploitable. All this has forced the Russian people to expend their energies to produce a precarious existence that in the best of times generally meant a tolerable poverty. Bad times often have forced them to endure the intolerable.

Nature has placed at least one other crushing hardship on Russia. The

Eurasian plain has no natural borders to separate its rival peoples or block invaders from the east or west. Russian history therefore is scarred with wars and invasions, either when the Russians fought each other, attempted to expand at the expense of their neighbors, or themselves were the victims of intruders. The period after the founding of the first East Slavic state—the tenth through the twelfth centuries—witnessed a cycle of ebb and flow, with the East Slavs cast both as aggressors and as victims. The next era was harsher: from the middle of the thirteenth century to late in the fifteenth century no formally independent East Slavic or Russian state existed. By contrast, between 1700 and 1900 Russia was on the offensive in a large majority of its wars.

Most other nations, at least those that have survived, have enjoyed greater respites from the battlefield. Western Europe suffered through waves of invasions, but each wave was comparatively short-lived. By the eleventh century they had subsided, leaving most major European nations to develop in relative safety sheltered by a semblance of natural boundaries and their own balance of power. The most favorably located were the English, whose ability to develop institutions of self-government owes a considerable debt to the narrow but stormy channel that insulated them from their neighbors.

Most fortunate of all were the ex-Europeans and their descendants who had become citizens of the United States. America and Russia did have one thing in common: an open frontier. The American West and Russian Siberia were both sparsely populated lands inhabited by backward, poorly organized peoples unable to offer serious resistance to colonization. But here the similarity ends. No powerful enemy lurked behind America's western frontier or her eastern border; thousands of miles of oceans protected it during its early stages of development. The frontier and the riches it contained meant only opportunity, and if conquering it demanded hardships and sacrifice for those who settled it, this was only a price that individuals had to pay in order to exploit the new land. One may not agree with the famous thesis of historian Frederick Jackson Turner that the frontier created American democracy, but it is hard to deny an important link between the nature of that frontier and the economic, social, and political achievements of the American people.

How different was the Russian experience. No oceans protected it, nor for long periods could its various rulers. The road was always open for invaders from Asia and Europe, and it was often taken. The invasions from the east reached a macabre and ferocious crescendo with the Mongol conquest of the thirteenth century. The descendants of these conquerors—whom the Russians called Tatars—settled on the southern portion of the steppe and made the Russian southern frontier a source of unrelieved misery. For centuries the Tatars ravaged the land and its people. Not even Moscow in the distant northern woods was safe. As late as 1571, when Ivan the Terrible, one of Russia's most powerful rulers, was at the height of his power, his capital was sacked.

Even after Moscow was made safe from the Tatars the conflict with them did not end. The struggle against the Tatars and later the Turks for control of the rich black soil of the steppe consumed 300 years. Meanwhile, in the west there were other formidable foes, including the Poles, Lithuanians, Swedes, and Germans. Between the mid-thirteenth and fifteenth centuries, besides forty-five wars with the Tatars, Russia fought forty-one wars with the Lithuanians, thirty wars with the German crusading orders, and a total of forty-four more with Swedes, Bulgarians, and other enemies. The approximate total of foreign invasions during this period was 160. In the 200 years that followed, fully eighty-five were spent in six wars with Sweden and twelve with Poland.

All this the Russians endured, and more. In doing so they saved more than themselves; they helped save the centers of Western civilization that so frequently ignored or despised them. Even at the dawn of Western culture and before there were Russians—in 512 B.C.—the inhabitants of the Eurasian plain made the region's first contribution, however reluctantly or unwittingly, on behalf of the West. Then the Scythians—a nomadic people that controlled the steppe for about 500 years—indirectly helped a struggling Athens when the armies of Darius the Great of Persia pursued them deep into the endless plain. In the intervening centuries, much of the fury of invading Asian nomads was spent in Russia, sparing the luckier Europeans to the west. Russian endurance and the terrible winter of 1812 destroyed Napoleon's Grand Army and helped restore the balance of power fundamental to the European state system. In 1914, the Russian thrust into eastern Germany forced the Germans to transfer troops to the eastern front and left them unable to mount sufficient force in the west to take Paris. And in World War II, once Hitler finally turned his Nazi war machine against his former Soviet ally, the hard-pressed Western democracies received important help when a large part of the German army first bogged down, and then was bled, frozen, and eventually crushed in the heart of Russia.

Russia had to build its state and institutions during centuries of conflict and calamity. Those who are critical of the form these took are missing the point; it is a tribute to the Russian people's courage and tenacity that they had the time and energy to build anything at all. Russia by its very setting was a land of extremes. No less than the extraordinary precautions they take as individuals against the weather, the Russians as a group had to take extreme measures to survive as a people. The institutions they eventually created for this purpose extorted a terrible price from the nation they preserved: the political, civic, and economic freedoms that Westerners have come to take for granted.

Russia, then, was different from the West in many important ways. Among the critical developments Russia missed were the Renaissance and the Reformation, both so important in shaping Western culture. All subsequent Western achievements were regarded in Russia with a mixture of fascination and fear, stopped at the border, so to speak, and searched for possible subversiveness. Even in the periods when some Western ideas and institutions were embraced by certain Russians, the impact was limited. Russia's traditions remained dominant, transforming imports, sometimes beyond recognition, to conform to local conditions.

The great Bolshevik Revolution was supposed to fundamentally change Russian life. But any revolution, no matter how drastic its ends or means, inevitably reflects the historical legacy of a nation's culture, customs, attitudes, and institutions. In Russia that harsh legacy undoubtedly shaped, molded, and, some would argue, deformed the Bolshevik Revolution, even as the revolution so painfully uprooted and contorted Russia itself. That is why, before examining the history of the USSR, we turn to a brief survey of the historical legacy inherited by the nation—or world—that was Russia before 1917.

2

The Autocratic State

*The Tatars were unlike the Moors; having conquered
Russia, they gave her neither algebra nor Aristotle.*

————PUSHKIN

In modern times Russia has been thought of as a monolithic colossus, weighted down by its oppressive social structure and autocratic government and therefore forever lagging socially, politically, culturally, and technologically behind Europe. It was not always so. During the ninth century the first East Slavic state developed along what was called the river road, a web of rivers forming a natural link between the Baltic and Black Seas. A rather loose association of principalities with its center at Kiev on the southern reaches of the Dnieper River, Kievan Russia, as that state is usually called, flourished by virtue of its control of what had become the major trade route linking Europe with the East. This path became a thoroughfare after Arab expansion in the Mediterranean cut Europe's traditional means of access to the Middle East and the lands beyond. By the eleventh century Kiev was the largest city in Eastern Europe, a city of sufficient size, culture, and beauty to rival Constantinople, the glorious capital of the Byzantine Empire.

Because of the importance of foreign trade, Kievan culture was, for the day, relatively cosmopolitan and urban. Most of the population, of course, earned its living from subsistence agriculture, and although there was a large number of slaves in Kievan Russia, the bulk of the peasantry was free. Kiev was only one of numerous well-developed East Slavic towns that, like their European counterparts, had developed organs of self-government. Called *veches,* these councils shared power with assemblies of nobles and the princes of Kievan Russia. There were some significant regional political differences. Non-princely authority was strongest in the more developed areas of Kievan Russia: the *veches* enjoyed their greatest influence in the northwest and the nobles theirs in the south and southwest. In the northeast, a less-developed frontier area, princely authority predominated. This regional division became important later when foreign invasions shifted the center of gravity in Russia to precisely those areas where centralized princely government was strongest.

Religion was another factor that eventually assumed political importance. Late in the tenth century, Kievan Russia adopted Orthodoxy, the eastern branch of Christianity imported from the Byzantine Empire to the south. Most of Europe at that time followed Roman Catholicism. Those countries, like Russia, that were Orthodox found a major barrier separated them from their Catholic neighbors.

Whether measured by economic development, cultural achievement, or political institutions, Kievan Russia compared favorably with most of Europe. Although a frontier between Europe and Asia, Kievan Russia was not a backwater. Its culture carried most of the same seeds for growth as the European states. But in Kievan Russia these still-tender shoots were under the constant pressure of the nomadic peoples pushing into the steppe from central and eastern Asia. By the twelfth century the disunited Kievan polity, weakened by internal feuding and warfare between contending princes, was unable to stem the invaders. They swept across the southern steppe, rendering both the trade route to Constantinople and the farming population of the southern steppe increasingly insecure. Trade and the cities dependent on it declined and the population itself began to migrate to the relative security of the northeast. Another blow to Kievan Russia was the opening of a more direct trade route to the east via the Mediterranean Sea, a process that began as early as the eleventh century and accelerated after the Fourth Crusade of 1204.

Catastrophe followed decline. After an exploratory campaign, the Mongol armies, the invincible conquerors of China, burst out of Asia in 1237 to deliver to the Russians the worst blow they would ever receive. It would take them over 200 years to recover their independence.

The actual conquest lasted five dreadful years. In Riazan, the first city to fall, a witness recorded that "not an eye was left open to weep for those that were closed." Six years after Kiev was burned to the ground a papal envoy found only 200 houses standing in that once magnificent city. Many other cities suffered a similar fate. As much as 10 percent of the entire population may have been enslaved. The region's best craftsmen and artisans were deported to Central Asia to serve the Mongol ruler, the dreaded khan. At home the quality of crafts and buildings dropped precipitously.

The Mongol conquest played a role in several long-term developments. Battered by the wholesale destruction of the conquest and bled by generations of subsequent exploitation, the Russian economy fell behind the economies of the West. Since the thirteenth century Russia has labored with a legacy of economic backwardness. Once independence was regained in the fifteenth century, a fundamental task of the state has been to catch up with a rapidly advancing Europe. It has been a centuries-long chase that has not yet reached its end. The Mongol conquest also cut many of Russia's ties with Byzantium and, more significantly, with the West. While the West was enriched by Humanism and the Renaissance, Russian cultural development was stunted and considerably brutalized by poverty, oppression, and isolation. Another important development was the threefold division of the East Slavic people. Those who lived in the northeast and paid tribute to the Mongols came to be known as the Great Russians. Eventually they accounted for just over 70 percent of the East Slavs. In the west two groups subject to the Lithuanians and the Poles emerged: the White Russians, or Belarusians, and the Ukrainians, or Little Russians. The former would comprise about 5 percent of East Slavs, the latter slightly under 25 percent. Although these groups generally had as much to unite as to divide them, their differences at times have loomed large and emerged as powerful centrifugal forces in their history, strong enough, in the post-Soviet era, to divide them into three independent states.

Most important, the Mongol conquest had a major influence on the development of the Russian state. The next centuries would be the incubation period for a new political phenomenon—the Russian autocracy. The Mongols, to be sure, were not the only force behind this development. The old Kievan princes had enjoyed a great deal of power, especially in the northeast. Kievan Russia had also inherited the concept of Caesaro-papism—the idea that the monarch should exercise both temporal and spiritual powers—from the Byzantines. But these phenomena had been balanced by the power of the nobility and the city *veches,* particularly in certain western and southern cities. The extreme pressures during two centuries of Mongol domination virtually destroyed the *veches* and gravely weakened the power of the nobility in most of Russia. The field was largely left to the princes, and eventually to only one prince.

Although the Mongols ruled Russia indirectly, their state provided a model for its Russian princely puppets to follow. Power was centralized far beyond anything that had existed in Russia or would be achieved by the so-called absolute monarchies of Europe. The ruler, or khan, was in fact an absolute sovereign. All of his subjects were bound to serve his state. He was the sole owner of all land; all others held land on condition of service to the state. A grotesque form of equality was realized by the denial of freedom to all. The state's job was to maintain order and security and collect taxes necessary for those purposes. The state did not serve society; the state dominated it.

As agents of the Mongol khan, the Russian principalities tended to adopt their master's administrative methods. They also competed for the khan's favor, a critical factor in the struggle for survival. The most successful in this treacherous political roulette proved to be the princes of a small state in the remote northeast. A minor village during Kievan times, refugees from the endemic violence in the south had swelled its once insignificant population. Its favorable location near the sources of the Volga and Oka Rivers aided its economic growth. Blessed with a line of princes who were long-lived, intelligent, ruthless, and—perhaps most important of all—lucky, this tiny state grew and became stronger during the dark days of the fourteenth and fifteenth centuries. It proved best able to adapt to the conditions of Mongol rule and incorporate the basic tenets of Mongol government. Outstripping its more venerable and often more cultured rivals, it became the core of the new Russian state and society. It unified and eventually recast Russian society; its history became Russia's history. This was Moscow.

Muscovite society took shape under the most severe conditions. The state lived under the constant threat of foreign enemies: the Tatars to the south and southeast, the Lithuanians to the west, and the Swedes and German knights to the northwest. As if this were not enough, the Russian princes fought ninety wars among themselves between the mid-thirteenth and mid-fifteenth centuries. Survival meant the full mobilization of scarce resources in order to extract the maximum for state use. The affliction that would torment Russia into the twentieth century—the discrepancy between what Russia needed to compete with powerful rivals and the re-sources that were available to do the job—plagued Moscow from the start. With access to only scarce resources and primitive tools, its princes were impelled to resort to compulsion to meet the state's needs. The enormity of the problems and the extreme measures used to solve them gave birth to the two fundamental institutions of Russian life: autocracy and serfdom.

To do its Sisyphean task, the Moscovite state grew until it could muster more power than its enemies, including the dreaded and hated Tatars. In the process it grew stronger than the society it was obliged to protect, finally acquiring the power to mold that society to serve state purposes. This meant in practice the destruction of all competing centers of power within the realm and the regimentation of most of the population. It meant taking control of every aspect of Russian life, leaving virtually no scope for private activity. Through sheer energy and force, the state became the owner of most of the nation's wealth. As the distinguished Russian historian Vasily Kliuchevsky put it: "The state waxed fat, while the people grew lean."[1]

Control was even extended to people's minds. Absolute author-ity required avoiding unfavorable and therefore dangerous compari-sons with life elsewhere. Russia had to be quarantined from subversive ideas, the most dangerous of which came from the West. Russia be-came highly insular and xenophobic; the few foreigners admitted to the country were forced to live apart from the native population. Foreign travel for Russians was extremely restricted; it was not the Communists but the regime they overthrew that first employed the technique of forcing Russians who traveled abroad to leave their families behind. Ever suspicious, the Russian state became the proprietor of an increasingly active political police and a pioneer in the use of terror to control society.

The Russian autocratic state coalesced in the fifteenth and sixteenth centuries, especially during the reigns of Ivan III, the Great (1462–1505), and Ivan IV, the Terrible (1533–1584). Ivan the Great earned his title from Russian patriots because he completed the job of unifying Russia under Moscow's leadership and, in 1480, reestablished the nation's independence from the Tatars. Ivan also began the job of destroying the power of the old nobility, known as the *boyars,* the last remaining genuine obstacle to absolute autocratic power in Russia.

By the time Ivan the Great declared Russia's independence from the Tatars, all potential challengers to autocratic power other than the *boyars* had been eliminated. The Russian Orthodox Church, consistent with its Byzantine inheritance of Caesaro-papism, endorsed the state's expanding power. The loss of their independence had eliminated the princes as rivals to Moscow. Ivan's conquests also had destroyed the powers of the few remaining town *veches.* The somber finale came in 1471 with the annexation of the city-state of Novgorod, home of Russia's most powerful *veche,* and the removal of its bell, for generations its symbol and clarion, to permanent exile in Moscow.

The *boyars* were undermined by the creation of a new class of nobles. Unlike the *boyars,* who held their titles and estates on the basis of heredity, the new nobles held their estates—called *pomesties*—and their titles solely on the basis of service to the state. The *pomestie* nobles became the backbone of autocracy's huge military establishment and of the state apparatus. In some cases, creating *pomestie* nobles simply required parcelling out newly conquered lands to loyal functionaries. But the process often became sticky—and bloody—involving forcible evictions and mass deportations. This did not deter Ivan in the least—having conquered Novgorod, he dispossessed over 8,000 landlords of their hereditary estates, and deported and resettled them on *pomesties* in outlying reaches of his expanding realm. Their old estates went, again on a conditional basis, to Ivan's reliable servants from Moscow. Ivan repeated this process several times as the few remaining independent Russian principalities fell under his control.

Ivan IV, the Terrible, finished what his grandfather began. Early in his reign Ivan modestly promoted himself from Grand Prince of Moscow to Tsar (Caesar) of all the Russians. But tsar or not, the *boyars* still remained a powerful force in Ivan's dominions. His grandfather's methods having proven only partially successful, Ivan IV resorted to even more violent measures. He launched a legendary reign of terror that, with varying severity, lasted almost a quarter of a century. One of its victims, by the tsar's own hand, was his son. Another of Ivan's notable outbursts occurred in Novgorod where thousands of people were slaughtered and the once-proud city leveled. Ivan also gave Russia its first political police —the fanatical and deadly Oprichnina.

The *boyars* were decimated. The new nobility that emerged was a pliable tool of the state. Ivan had granted the nobility hereditary title to its estates, but at a price: an equally hereditary lifetime state service obligation. Genuine local self-governing bodies had been replaced by state institutions that were part of a centralized administrative structure. The country's enormous size and primitive communications, of course, limited the state's control, but Ivan the Terrible had largely made good his claim to being an absolute ruler. Barely a century after the Mongol conquerors had finally been cast out, Russia had been resubjugated by its own autocracy.

It is important to realize how different this state of affairs was from what has ever existed in Western Europe. European travelers in Russia continually were struck by the absolute and arbitrary nature of the tsar's powers compared to that exercised by European monarchs. The early-sixteenth-century ambassador of the Holy Roman Empire, hardly a bastion of democracy, had a typical reaction when he reported: "In the sway which he holds over his people, he surpasses all the monarchs of the whole world." In Europe the monarch's political power and property were separate; no such distinction existed in Russia. The tsar ruled the land as if he owned it, a claim no European monarch dared make. Unlike Europe, the rule of law did not inhibit the Russian state. In short, in Europe even those with "divine" right to rule shared power with some of their subjects; in Russia they did not.

The Russian state, with its gargantuan military and administrative establishments to feed, had a voracious appetite that the primitive Russian economy could not satiate. This imbalance gave birth to the "grim monster, savage, gigantic, hundred mouthed, and bellowing" called serfdom. These words of Alexander Radishchev, the eighteenth-century writer credited with being Russia's first revolutionary, aptly describe the most important social institution in Russia's history. Serfdom ended the peasantry's ability to take advantage of Russia's open plain, where new land and escape from Moscow's authority lay just over the eastern or southern horizon. The serf was confined to the place of his birth and was subject to the authority of his landlord. He therefore was readily available to serve the state's needs, whether to pay it taxes, serve in its army, or work on its building projects. Enserfing the peasant alleviated an urgent labor shortage that had forced landlords to compete for peasants. The *pomestie* nobility was guaranteed a stable labor supply for its estates, thereby freeing it to render its service to the state.

Serfdom developed gradually, more or less parallel with the rising power of the autocracy. Over about 150 years Russian peasants were reduced to virtual slavery, subject, at the whim of their landlords, to being sold (sometimes without their families), tortured, jailed, exiled, forced to marry, forbidden to marry, removed from the land, and a host of other deprivations. The Russian serf, unlike the medieval European serf, enjoyed almost no enforceable rights. If he was better off than a slave, as some claim, the Russian serf still suffered from burdens a slave did not endure. Slaves, at least, were spared the obligations to pay taxes and to serve in the military.

The only compensation, if one assumes that misery does indeed love company, was that the serf was not alone. The Law Code of 1649, which governed Russia for almost 200 years, froze the nation into three basic groups. The service nobility, distinguished by its ability to abuse others even as the state abused it, headed the pathetic parade. Seven categories of townsmen and four of peasant serfs followed. Less significant were a shrinking number of free men and several varieties of slaves. The situation then and 200 years later was best summed up by Michael Speransky, himself the compiler of a later law code and the close advisor to two tsars: "In Russia I find only two estates: the slaves of the sovereign and the slaves of the landlord."

Whatever its internal conditions, Russia was not to be confined to lands occupied by the Russian people. Independence for Russia meant subordination for other nations. On the borderless Eurasian plain, there was no logical place to stop once a nation had acquired more power than its neighbors. The lack of natural frontiers meant that any area conquered immediately required yet another annexation to protect its security. Russia therefore quickly became a multinational empire, and eventually so many peoples were overrun that the Great Russians comprised less than half the empire's population. Russia came to be called, with some justification, the "prison house of nations."

Expansion was really nothing new for Russia; it was a basic component of the nation's history. Since Kievan times the Russians' East Slavic ancestors had been colonizing the empty or thinly settled regions of the forest and steppe beyond their own territory. Even when nomadic hordes were driving them from the southern steppe, the Russians were expanding into the forests of the northeast. By the 1560s, a more powerful Russia was aggressively on the move. The road westward was still blocked by powerful European states, while to the south the mighty Ottoman Empire held sway, but in the east the old Tatar states were decaying rapidly. During Ivan the Terrible's lifetime, Russians established themselves in western Siberia; within barely sixty years they had reached the Bering Sea. Later Russia accumulated the power to surge westward as well, so that while ominous it was not entirely an exaggeration to claim, as a Russian newspaper did on the eve of World War I, that "after a thousand years, [Russia] is still on the march to its natural boundaries."

The Russian people benefitted as little from their nation's rise to empire as the people they subjugated. The demands of governing a sprawling empire and alien peoples reinforced the state's autocratic tendencies. The new lands provided estates for additional legions of *pomestie* nobles who served the burgeoning needs of the state. But destruction of non-Russian power on the eastern steppe removed the main obstacle that had hemmed in the restless Russian peasantry. The nobility thus faced a ruinous loss of already scarce labor essential for farming its estates. The state reacted by tightening restrictions on the peasantry's freedom of movement. In a bitter reversal of the American frontier experience, available and accessible free land resulted in less, not more, freedom for those who actually farmed it. As their country's power rose, the Russian peasants sank deeper into serfdom. Somehow, even when Russia won, the Russian people lost.

By the seventeenth century Russia was master of its own house and increasingly master of parts of Ukraine in the west and its more backward neighbors to the east. The autocracy had survived a dangerous succession crisis when the old royal line degenerated and died out shortly after Ivan the Terrible's death. It had expanded the ranks of its *pomestie* nobility and imposed state service upon it, and its new law code issued in 1649 had frozen in place the entire population, including the hapless serfs.

But Russia was not secure. Even in the sixteenth century, before the runaway advances of the industrial revolution, Russia lagged far behind the West in technology and organization, and therefore in power. Even her most formidable rulers met defeat when confronted with Western strength. Ivan the Terrible was beaten in his exhausting twenty-five-year campaign to expand westward to the Baltic Sea. Peter I, the Great, was routed by a numerically inferior army of Swedes on the shores of that same Baltic in 1700. Competing with the West—geography and the nature of the international state system left the Russians no choice but to compete—required first learning from the enemy. Learning required contact of all sorts, thereby enabling Western ideas about everything from philosophy to politics to penetrate Russia. The state's great unsolved dilemma after 1700 was how to import the Western technology that could be used to build up the autocracy while excluding the influences that might corrode and eventually destroy it. As the West developed its technology and produced new political and social ideas, Russia's difficulties worsened.

The impact Western Europe had on Russia has become known as Westernization. It has since become a world-wide phenomenon in the wake of the spectacular rise of European power after 1600; Russia was one of the first societies to face its consequences, and the necessity of formulating a response. Westernization in Russia has meant different things to different people. To liberal-minded Westerners who feared the Russian autocracy and to some idealistic Russians who hated it, Westernization should have been an all-encompassing process that would transform and democratize Russian society. To the Russian autocrats and their supporters, Westernization meant science and technology only. Any ideals or values potentially subversive to the autocracy would be filtered out, like so many pollutants.

This was the attitude of Peter the Great, Russia's first systematic Westernizer. Peter spent much of his time learning from Europe, and he made his country do the same. His grandiose goals made this imperative. Like Ivan the Terrible, Peter was determined that Russia become a major European power. He therefore began a military build-up. The bloated armed force Peter created strained Russia's already arthritic fiscal, administrative, and social structures beyond their capacities. But despite its size, that force proved initially to be inadequate against the Europeans to the west or, for that matter, the Turks to the south. Russia clearly needed thorough modernizing.

The attitude of most of Russian society was an equally difficult problem for Peter. Steeped in its own traditions, Russia had no desire to change. Not inclined to persuasion in any case, Peter used the Russian state's traditional methods of force and repression to accomplish Westernization objectives. He decided what was necessary and made sure that it was done; after a rebellion early in his reign the youthful tsar served as his own chief executioner. The ironic and terrible truth is that under Peter, Russia's first experience with modernization called forth cruelty that even exceeded Ivan the Terrible's madness.

Westerners were imported to provide the knowledge and skill for Peter's many projects; the Russians supplied the sacrifices. Russia's first modern industries were built and staffed by thousands of conscripted state peasants who were attached to the factories for life, as were their descendants. The Russian people benefitted little from these modern marvels. Peter's factories and mines served his war machine. The state was their chief promoter, either as the direct owner, or through loans, subsidies, tariff protection, and—frequently—coercion designed to encourage private entrepreneurs. The state, with its burgeoning military sector, also was the main market for the new products. A new levy—the soul tax—was instituted to exploit Peter's subjects more efficiently; only the nobility and the clergy escaped this heavy new burden. Serfdom now bore down more uniformly and even more cruelly on the Russian peasants. Russia's upper classes were hounded into submission by the *Preobrazhenskii Prikaz*, Peter's dreaded and deadly political police. The central government's administrative apparatus was rationalized on Western models so that it could better implement Peter's arm twisting and bone breaking, while a brand new navy and a modern army were shaped from the inchoate Russian military mass. Spiritual matters were attended to by stripping the Orthodox Church of its independence. It simply became part of the state apparatus.

The payoff came quickly in battlefield victories that established Russia on the Baltic coast. It is a proper tribute to Peter that when he built his capital there on pilings sunk into disease-ridden swampland, the new city rose on the corpses of thousands of conscripted serfs who died laboring for their tsar. Peter quite logically called his city St. Petersburg; others, just as logically, called it "the city built on bones."

Peter the Great accomplished much of what he intended, pushing Russia's boundaries westward and erecting an efficient absolutist state in place of the rickety older model bequeathed to him. He established Russia's first industrial base and did more than anyone to develop the nation's industry prior to the late nineteenth century. Russia's first experiment with Westernization had dramatically strengthened the autocracy, better enabling it to control the country while resisting Western social and political influences. Peter had served the Russian state, if not the Russian people, well. The state had a political police force and even directly controlled the nation's spiritual affairs. It now was the world's most formidable entrepreneur, its largest landlord, employer, and capitalist. Peter certainly never intended it, but he provided an example for those who 200 years later would murder his descendants, destroy Tsarism, and, by imposing sacrifices that not even he had demanded, give Russia more power than he could ever have dreamed possible.

Yet Peter's accomplishments soon began to erode. Insulated Russia could not keep pace with its intellectually more vibrant neighbors in the freer West. Merely borrowing technology meant that after a generation or two Europe was ahead again and the borrowing process had to be repeated.

Westernization also created new problems while it solved others. No matter how hard the state tried to prevent it, a thin layer of Russian society was exposed to and transformed by Western thought and culture. Members of this Westernized elite, whether they supported or opposed the autocracy, thus became alienated from the vast majority of the nation. Russia was being split into two unequal and mutually uncomprehending parts.

How to compete with Europe without becoming like Europe was a dilemma the Russian autocracy never solved. The horns of this dilemma fatally gored or crippled most significant reform plans when their inevitable implications—placing limits on the power of the autocracy—became clear. As a result of this, no reform of serfdom was undertaken for much too long. But during the nineteenth century the pressures on Russia intensified as the pace of European progress quickened. However selectively Russia modernized, subversive European influences were slipping in and corroding the autocracy and the social structure upon which it rested. By the middle of the century, fundamental changes could no longer be put off. By the end of the century it was clear that the reforms adopted had not been enough. In order to understand how Russia did change and, more importantly, how it failed to change, it is necessary to glance at a few developments in the nineteenth century, the last century that the crisis-ridden autocracy and the society it had spawned managed to survive.

NOTE

1. Vasily Kliuchevsky, *Kurs russkoi istorii* (Moscow, 1937), vol. III, p. 11.

3

The Nineteenth-Century Crisis

One more century of the present despotism will destroy all the good qualities of the Russian people.

———ALEXANDER HERZEN (1851)

The amazing thing about nineteenth-century Russia is that the country changed so much while remaining fundamentally the same, with the old problems left unsolved. During the course of the century Russian culture would flourish, serfdom would be abolished, and major reforms would overhaul the legal system and rural government. Economic development would make the empire the world's fifth-largest industrial power. Yet Russia's population remained overwhelmingly rural. The peasantry found its new freedom limited by an atavistic web of legal limitations and by wretched poverty. The traditional chasm between the ignorant masses and the educated elite widened rather than shrank, Westernization having created in Russia two separate cultures and societies. Meanwhile, although in 1762 Tsar Peter III freed the nobility from its obligation to serve the state, the autocracy retained a monopoly on power that it exercised through an ever-expanding bureaucracy. Tsarism was housed in an elegant capital city with an opulent court, but Russia remained poor and exhausted from her struggle to match the power of more advanced and prosperous European competitors.

Russia moved forward in spite of an autocracy that expended most of its strength in a quixotic and often fanatic crusade to contain the winds of change blowing in from all sides. All of the men who sat on the throne, whatever their differences in personality or style, were committed autocrats. One, Alexander II, instituted unprecedented reforms, including the abolition of serfdom. These reforms contained the potential to set Russia on the course of development that had occurred in the West. But in the end even he remained a loyal disciple of his heritage, like the Alexander and Nicholas who preceded him and the Alexander and Nicholas who succeeded him.

It is probably not unfair to say that Russia, faced by mounting challenges and weighted down by an increasingly obsolete social and political structure, wasted the first half of the nineteenth century. The country's rulers were the logical products of a senile order and refused to consider social change as a solution to the nation's difficulties. Alexander I (1801–1825), the conqueror of Napoleon, talked of reforms, but instituted few. Eventually he became an unbalanced mystic, and he died without an heir. His death was the signal for what is known as the Decembrist uprising, a rebellion led by army officers from the nobility, who wanted to make Russia a constitutional monarchy. Unlike the blindly violent peasant uprisings that had dotted the centuries, this was revolutionary upheaval with a number of modern programs for political change. It was a forerunner and inspiration of things to come. The immovable autocracy finally had a serious rival, a revolutionary movement that, if not irresistible, at least proved irrepressible. The rest of the century and the first part of the next one would be punctuated by an intermittent but unending duel between these two uncompromising forces.

The Decembrist uprising permanently stained the reign of Alexander's successor, Nicholas I. Nicholas suppressed the rebellion and spent the next thirty years trying to keep the clock from moving. Commentators have not been kind to Nicholas. His nickname was the "knout." While there were signs of life, especially regarding economic development, the satirist Saltykov-Shchedrin captured a central aspect of his country's reality when he glumly described it as a "desert landscape, with a gaol in the middle. . . ." Even Nicholas's supporters despaired of him, including one who lamented that "the main failing of the reign of Nicholas Pavlovich was that it was all a mistake."

Mistaken or not, Nicholas was determined to restore stability to Russia. He had good reason to be not only determined, but also frightened. Many of the Decembrists belonged to some of Russia's most venerable noble families. In 1826, only one year into his reign, Nicholas's fears found their institutional expression in the Third Section of the Imperial Chancellery, the innocuous name for what became Europe's most feared and pervasive secret police. Although Russia had known secret police organizations before, the scope of the Third Section's activities was something new. During previous reigns, the secret police had largely limited itself to searching out political enemies of the monarch, and for years at a time had been abolished by one ruler or another. The Third Section was far more durable and probed the work of writers, journalists, historians, and others for the slightest deviation from what the government considered the acceptable norm. This created an atmosphere and suspicion in Russia unlike anything found elsewhere in Europe at the time.

Nicholas gave Russia a model for the modern secret police that became a permanent fixture of Russian life. He also gave Russia its first comprehensive censorship code and a criminal code containing fifty-four pages of political crimes. Historian Richard Pipes has called this code "a veritable charter of an authoritarian regime . . . to totalitarianism what the Magna Carta is to liberty."[1] Between organizing the Third Section and compiling the new criminal code, Nicholas also found time to proclaim a catechism of beliefs for his subjects. Called "Official Nationality," this new formula defined loyalty to Russia on the basis of three principles: autocracy, orthodoxy, and nationality. Autocracy reaffirmed the absolute power of the throne. Orthodoxy asserted the role of the Russian Orthodox Church as the nation's official religion. Nationality stressed the special nature of the Russian people and devotion to the nation's traditions and the status quo. To make sure the people got the message the government sponsored its own corps of journalists,—the despised "reptile press"—to extol Russian virtues and condemn the subversive liberal and democratic notions filtering in from Europe. Meanwhile, the complex demands of controlling an enormous nineteenth-century empire not permitted to govern itself fed the already overgrown bureaucracy.

But time would not stand still, not even for a tsar. Capitalism was taking root in Russia and beginning to tear fissures in the agricultural economy based on serfdom. The spread of education and European ideas overwhelmed even the efforts of the Third Section to keep Russia ideologically pure. By the middle of the century a new class of intellectuals had been created, an extraordinarily brilliant group that initiated the "golden age of Russian literature." Pushkin, Lermontov, and Gogol wrote their major works during Nicholas's reign, and Turgenev, Dostoevsky, and Tolstoy made their first appearances on the literary horizon. Some of Russia's writers, led by literary critics like Vissarion Belinsky, produced a less artistic, but still important, creation: a tradition of opposition to the autocracy. Hounded by the Third Section and the censors and denied the right to a meaningful role in Russian political life, a significant part of the educated elite turned against the autocracy and made literature and art vehicles to express that opposition. The inability of the Russian state to win the loyalty of a large portion of its educated citizens was a critical factor in undermining the autocracy and the social order it was committed to defend.

Nicholas's obsession to repress liberal or reformist ideas did not stop at Russia's frontiers. It led him to intervene in European affairs, earning

Russia the epithet "the Gendarme of Europe." The apparent growth of Russian power finally led the Western powers to oppose by force Russian schemes against the Ottoman Empire. As a result, the Crimean War, which broke out in 1853, ended in disaster for the backward Russian army. Nicholas himself did not survive the war; neither did many of his policies. The lost war was concluded in 1856 by his son, Alexander II. Russians were shocked by their nation's inability to defend itself against the small but modern forces the Europeans had sent against it. Russian backwardness had again led to military defeat, and the realization that drastic reform was necessary reached even the tsar and his advisors. Russia had to modernize in order to compete with Europe, something it could not do so long as serfdom continued to stifle economic development. No less important, the extent and seriousness of peasant discontent threatened the entire social order. These imperatives produced the era of the Great Reforms.

On February 19, 1861, Alexander II abolished serfdom in Russia. Whatever the shortcomings of his edict, and there were many, it remains the greatest single act of emancipation in history. Over 20 million serfs on private estates were freed from the authority of their landlords, five times the number of slaves liberated by Abraham Lincoln in the United States two years later. The Emancipation Edict was followed by several other major reforms, the most important of which were the establishment of organs of rural self-government called *zemstvos* and the reform of the legal system. The latter created for the first time in Russia an independent judiciary on the Western model. Other important measures reformed town government and the system of military service.

The Great Reforms opened an era of Westernization unique in Russian history prior to the Gorbachev era of the 1980s. Russia had "Westernized" before, primarily under Peter the Great, and would again under the Communists, but in both those cases, "Westernization" meant only physical modernization: new factories, industrial techniques, administrative techniques, and the like. The relationship between the people and the state remained the same. The Great Reforms were different, perhaps not in their intent, but definitely in their results. Although the peasants remained subject to numerous legal disabilities, the abolition of serfdom did make the economy more flexible and hence helped promote industrial and commercial development independent of state control and interference. The establishment of an independent judiciary put a small dent in the arbitrary nature of the state's authority. One of the main differences between Russian and Western societies had been that in the West—even in the "absolute" monarchies—citizens were protected from the state by legal norms and rules. In short, those societies were governed by the rule of law. Naturally, the development of the rule of law varied from era to era and state to state, but the situation in Europe stood in dramatic contrast to the untrammeled, arbitrary, and virtually absolute authority of the Russian state. For the most part this remained the case even after the judicial reform, but a crucial seed for change had been planted and had begun to germinate. The question was whether it would have the proper climate in which to grow. Complementing this development was the limited self-government introduced in the towns and in the countryside. Again, actual self-government as known in the West remained a distant star, but for the first time since the days of the *veches* it was visible on the local horizon.

Nonetheless, it is essential to remember that however large the reforms loomed against a background of centuries of inertia, the autocracy had no intention of seeing their democratizing potential realized. Alexander II may have been called the "Tsar-Liberator," but he was a tsar first, determined to maintain all of his autocratic powers. His goals were economic development and the strength it produced, not democracy. In this he was no different from Peter the Great. His response to a group of nobles who shortly after the emancipation petitioned him for an elected national assembly was typical of his outlook; Alexander threw the lot into prison. Hopes that the tsar would "crown" his reforms with a constitution and make Russia a genuine constitutional monarchy were to be disappointed. After a Polish rebellion in 1863 and an attempt on his life in 1866, Alexander began to chip away at his reforms. Hope turned to disappointment and then despair, feeding the revolutionary fervor among Russia's educated youth. That fervor cost the Tsar-Liberator his life; in 1881 he was assassinated.

His son, Alexander III, was the perfect successor to preside over a policy of reaction. Alexander III illustrated his political flexibility when he issued a manifesto declaring he would discuss his empire's destiny only with God. When the latter was not available, Alexander relied on Konstantin Pobedonostsev, a fanatic reactionary who denounced democracy, a free press, public education, and even inventions with remarkable vigor. His advice included telling the tsar that a bloody rebellion was preferable to a constitution.

Guided by Pobedonostsev, Alexander III weakened or gutted many of the Great Reforms. His "counter-reforms" included drastic restrictions in the authority and representative nature of the *zemstvos* and on the independence of the judiciary. The tentative steps taken toward self-government and the rule of law were now rapidly retraced in a race back to bureaucratic and police rule. At the same time, in an attempt to unify his multinational domains, Alexander intensified the pressures on millions of non-Russian minorities through a policy of forced Russification. Poles, Ukrainians, and others suffered, as did religious minorities, but the most victimized were the Jews. They now were caught in an inexorably tightening vise of deep-seated anti-Semitism and the state's readiness to exploit it by making it governmental policy. The main fruit of this policy was that the revolutionary movement, until Alexander's time an almost exclusively Russian enterprise, received a massive dose of new non-Russian recruits. Several of the men who helped bring Vladimir Ulyanov (Lenin), himself a Russian, to power in 1917 and who staffed his government were non-Russians—including Lev Bronstein (Trotsky), the Jew who organized the Bolshevik coup and the Red Army; Felix Dzerzhinsky, the Pole who became the first head of the new secret police; and Joseph Dzhugashvili (Stalin), the Georgian who eventually emerged as Lenin's successor.

Alexander III fastened on Russia a bureaucratic and police rule more intense than the country had ever known. The most important vehicle for this was the notorious Law of August 14, 1881. This "Statute Concerning Measures for the Protection of State Security and the Social Order," an allegedly temporary measure that remained in force until 1917, immediately subjected large parts and eventually most of Russia to regulations very similar to martial law. The authorities and police now were specifically permitted to arrest, imprison, fine, and exile citizens, close down businesses, ban public meetings of all kinds, and turn people over to military courts. No trial or other legal proceedings were necessary. Public employees could be fired without cause and under certain circumstances, elected officials dismissed and the *zemstvos* closed down. As if this were not enough, the next year the police received even more power. Now people placed under what was blandly called "open surveillance"—and it could happen to anyone—became virtual police prisoners, their every move and activity subject to police approval. The long list of disabilities ranged from being barred from several fields of employment to being forbidden to move without permission or join a private organization. These people could be searched at any time and denied their mail. Meanwhile, the secret police was reorganized and renamed the *Okhrana*, a term that would become synonymous with the most sinister and sophisticated secret police machinations.

Thus, at a time when most European nations were broadening popular participation in the political process, a development deemed essential for mobilizing national strength, political life in Russia in effect was rendered illegal. At the dawn of the twentieth century, more than ever before, the bureaucracy and police ruled in Russia.

Alexander III did enjoy some successes. He managed to reign without a foreign war, and his economic policies promoted impressive industrial growth. Yet his repression had only stalled, not destroyed, the revolutionary movement. At his death in 1894, a new revolutionary generation already had debuted. Left to deal with this and other mounting problems was the tragicomical figure of Nicholas II. At his coronation as the ruler of one sixth of the world's land surface he confided, "I know absolutely nothing about matters of state." When his reign was brought to its sudden end in 1917, he could have made the same statement without fear of contradiction.

The reign of Nicholas II marked the final failure of the autocracy to reform adequately in the face of increasingly rapid social and economic change. Out of that failure came a political struggle between a huge reactionary state and a tiny revolutionary minority. The question that immediately arises is why these two forces—a rotten autocracy and a motley collection of revolutionaries—dominated the political stage between 1825 and 1917, with the rest of Russian society serving as little more than so many set pieces. Why, unlike in the West, was there no powerful counterweight in the middle to the combatants at the extremes? What were the different classes of Russians doing while the battle raged that would decide their fates?

NOTE

1. Richard Pipes, *Russia Under the Old Regime* (New York: Charles Scribners Sons, 1974), p. 295.

4

The People

*Your majesty has 130,000,000 subjects. Of them
barely more than half live, the rest vegetate.*

———SERGEI WITTE TO NICHOLAS II (1898)

Most Russians, it turns out, were just trying to survive. In the second
half of the nineteenth century five-sixths of the Russian people were
still peasants. Very few of them had managed to rise above the level of
bare subsistence. During approximately the previous 140 years of serfdom
most of the peasantry fell into two major groups: serfs and state peasants.
Serfs were bonded to land owned by private landlords and were subject
to their authority. The serf therefore served two severe masters: the state
and the landlord. The major obligations owed the state were high and
often confiscatory taxes and, if the serf was unlucky, what amounted to
a lifetime of military service. The debt to the landlord was paid either in
labor in the landlord's fields or by a payment in kind or in money. The
state peasants, created by Peter the Great in the eighteenth century from
the approximately 20 percent of the peasantry that somehow had avoided
serfdom, lived on state-owned land. They also were bonded to the land,
but serving only one master, and a more distant one at that, were somewhat
better off than the serfs. Because of government policies and better overall
economic conditions, the state peasants increased in number faster than
the serfs and actually slightly outnumbered them by the last decades of
serfdom. Aside from his interminable struggle with the elements, the
state peasant's major worry was that he might lose his modest status. Until
emancipation, state peasants could be given to private landlords, in which
case they became serfs, or conscripted as laborers to industrial enterprises.
This fate frequently was worse than enserfment. The conditions of their
emancipation under a separate law issued in 1866 left them better off
than the ex-serfs in several important respects, but as time went on the

overall problems and misfortunes the two groups shared dwarfed these differences, making them little more than varying degrees of misery. Most peasants, both before and after emancipation, also shared the obligatory status of being members of village communes, institutions of limited self-government that primarily assisted the state in regulating peasant life and guaranteeing tax collections.

By the time serfdom finally was abolished it had brutalized most of the Russian people and disfigured Russian life. To appreciate the extent of the damage, the reader who understands the festering and lingering effects of slavery on American society more than a century after the Emancipation Proclamation need only recall that serfdom was for centuries the most pervasive institution in Russia, not a "peculiar institution" confined to one region and ensnaring only a minority of the population. Slavery had been the major cause of the American Civil War and the problems left unsolved by emancipation and Reconstruction contributed directly to a racial problem that still exists in the United States. Similarly, emancipation in Russia was incomplete and left unsolved many of the worst problems associated with serfdom. As historian G.T. Robinson has noted, " . . . the Emancipation of the 'sixties contributed powerfully to the making of the Revolution of 1917. . . ."[1]

The problem with the emancipation was its narrow scope: it simply freed the serfs from the authority of the landlords without addressing the gap between the peasantry and the rest of Russian society. The emancipation was limited because the government feared the peasantry and continued to concern itself primarily with the interests of the landed nobility. Post-emancipation peasants at best were second-class citizens. They were still subject to the authority of special courts and to corporal punishment. The individual peasant could leave the land only with great difficulty. He was forced to remain a member of his commune and remained subject to its authority.

The most damaging aspect of emancipation was its economic short-comings. Emancipation took a primitive, unproductive, and inflexible rural economy and actually exacerbated some of its problems. In 1861, the landlords' estates were divided between the landlords and the peasants, the former getting about two thirds and the latter the rest. But the land came at a high price. Peasants were sold land that they were unable to choose at inflated prices they were unable to negotiate. The landlords retained the best land. Because the ex-serfs did not have the available cash to pay for their land, the government paid the landlord and peasants were given forty-nine years to repay the government. The installments were called redemption payments. This arrangement, combined with high taxes, turned virtually every ex-serf peasant family into bad risks unable to meet their obligations. The arrears mounted each year until, in 1905—two famines, innumerable rural riots, and one unprecedented revolutionary upheaval later—the government finally got the point and abolished the redemption payments. The former state peasants were given larger land allotments at lower prices. They at least initially were able to satisfy their basic needs.

Another serious problem was the failure to change the inefficient system of peasant land tenure. In most parts of Russia, land was still owned and controlled by the commune. Each peasant household held an allotment consisting not of a unified plot, but a series of strips, often as many as twenty or thirty and as narrow as six feet in width, scattered over the countryside. The impossibility of farming efficiently under such conditions was increased by the custom of periodically redistributing the land. This eliminated the incentive to make any long-term improvements. But the commune was a time-tested instrument for controlling and taxing the peasantry, and so it was kept after 1861 and given the additional critical job of assuring that the redemption payments were met. The commune remained an albatross around the neck of the peasantry, choking attempts to increase rural productivity.

In some respects emancipation actually made things worse. As serfs, the peasants at least had access to the forest and the meadowland of the landlord's estate. This provided essential supplements to what the peasant could earn from farming, including such important products as firewood. These benefits were lost when the landlord was granted most of these lands in the 1861 settlements. Meanwhile, the population of Russia increased rapidly during the second half of the nineteenth century, turning what already was a land shortage into a crisis. The average peasant land allotment dropped by almost a quarter in the last twenty-five years of the century. Additional hardship resulted when the growth of industry undermined the cottage industries that provided a margin of survival for many peasant families. Finally, harsh government tax policies squeezed the peasants even further. The rural standard of living declined until, in 1891, when the harvest failed with so many families living right at the subsistence level, Russia experienced one of the worst famines in its history. More than peasants died this time, however; so did patience with the autocracy. Disgust and shame swept large sectors of educated Russian society. Many members of the younger generation turned to revolutionary groups sprouting up in the universities.

Emancipation, then, had not materially helped the majority of the peasantry. As the twentieth century was about to begin, the peasants still lived "worse than cattle . . . they were coarse, dishonest, dirty, and drunken." Anton Chekhov, the great playwright and author who provided this unkind but accurate description in 1897, did not blame his countrymen for their crudeness. Their lives, he explained, were dominated by "crushing labor that made the whole body ache at night, cruel winters, scanty crops, overcrowding; and no help and nowhere to look for help." Such miserable people were hardly likely to concern themselves with common political matters or issues of governmental reform. "For the peasant," historian Richard Charques observed, "all the constitutional government in the world mattered less than an acre of land."[2]

No less absorbed by the struggle to survive was the Russian nobility. Even before losing its serfs in the emancipation, the nobility, unable to manage its own affairs, became totally dependent on the autocracy. Ivan the Terrible had shattered its political power in the sixteenth century. Peter the Great had debased the nobility even further, and a temporary rise in its fortunes in the second half of the eighteenth century, when it had freed itself of state service and received a charter enumerating its rights from Catherine II (1762–1796), had not lasted long. Catherine's successor, her mad son Paul, revoked much of what his mother had granted, proving that charter or no charter, the nobility was incapable of protecting itself from the tsar. It was equally incapable of protecting itself from the lowly peasantry, a point driven home by the great rebellions led by Stenka Razin in the seventeenth century and by Emilian Pugachev in the eighteenth century. Even in quiet times, the nobility knew only the autocracy stood between it and the sullen and seething serfs.

Even more debilitating, most of the nobility, its titles notwithstanding, was poor. Primogeniture—the passing of an estate intact to the eldest son—did not exist in Russia. Estates therefore were continually divided between an ever-increasing number of noble sons. The government estimated that ownership of at least 100 serfs was necessary to live like a gentleman, yet fewer than 20 percent of the nobility had that many. Historian Richard Pipes has concluded that 98 percent of the nobility lacked an income from its estates adequate for a "decent living."[3] The backwardness and low productivity of the countryside had impoverished not only the peasantry but the nobility as well. Its only recourse to supplement its income was bureaucratic work provided by the government. Even this did not help enough; by 1861 the nobility had mortgaged over 75 percent of its serfs. It had a fitting symbol: Ilya Ilych Oblomov, the novelist Ivan Goncharov's fictional character who wakes up in the morning and spends most of the day deciding whether to get out of bed.

After emancipation, the nobility was totally unprepared to cope without its serfs. Despite governmental attempts at resuscitation, it just became sicker and sank deeper into debt. By the end of the century it had sold one third of its remaining land and mortgaged much of the rest. During the new century the decline became more rapid.

In Europe the decline of the landed nobility was accompanied, and in fact hastened, by the rise of the middle class. The growth of the European middle class in turn had been promoted by the increase in trade and the relative security and freedom that existed in the European cities. In Russia few of these conditions existed. The country's isolation had retarded its economic development, and what economic opportunities did exist had been hoarded or closely regulated by the omnipresent Russian state. Not until after the Emancipation Edict did the Russian economy develop to the point where a genuine commercial and professional middle class began to emerge. It grew quickly during the period of rapid industrial growth in the 1880s and 1890s. But the Russian middle class was only a speck relative to society as a whole. Like the nobility, it faced an overwhelmingly powerful state that blocked its attempts to exert political influence. And like the nobility it was dependent on the state for protection, in this case from foreign competitors and from another class it had created through its own efforts: the small but militant Russian proletariat. Westerners and certain Westernized Russians who wanted Russia to follow the European capitalist and parliamentary path of development pinned their hopes on Russia's middle class. These hopes proved to be too heavy a burden for this young and weak class, caught between the unyielding autocracy and the angry masses.

"The working class? I know of no such class in Russia," Pobedonostsev commented less than twenty-five years before Lenin and the Bolsheviks would seize power in the name of that class. At the time Pobedonostsev spoke the working class, several million strong, certainly existed, but barely. It labored under incredibly oppressive conditions. The working day at the close of the nineteenth century often ranged from twelve to as many as eighteen hours, the legal limit of eleven and a half hours notwithstanding. Many workers lived in rotting tenements so crowded that people had to sleep in beds in shifts; others made their homes on the floors next to the machines they tended. Labor unions were illegal. For their efforts, the workers watched their real wages fall during the entire period between 1860 and 1900.

The ex-peasants who suffered so much in Russia's factories did have one advantage over their rural compatriots. Russia's late start in developing industry meant that when the factories finally were built, often with European capital and expertise, they reflected the latest in technology and economy of scale. Therefore, although small in number around 1900 —about 3 million—the Russian proletariat was concentrated in large factories clustered in a few industrial regions. These workers, accessible to and often influenced by university students ready to enlighten them about revolution and socialism, developed a surprising cohesiveness and solidarity. Because everything was so concentrated, a well-organized strike could spread very quickly and become extremely disruptive. And because the proletariat was so wantonly exploited and had so little to lose, it responded to calls for drastic action and change.

Finally, centuries of Russian expansion had created an empire that by the late nineteenth century was only one-half Russian. Many of this vast collection of peoples, some closely related to the Russians and others totally alien from them, opposed not only the tsarist regime but Russian imperial control over their lands and lives. Intensified repression during these years only increased ethnic consciousness and inflamed discontent across the non-Russian parts of the empire. All of these problems played into the eager and passionate hands of a tiny group of secular crusaders who called themselves revolutionaries.

NOTES

1. Geroid Tanguary Robinson, *Rural Russia Under the Old Regime* (Berkeley: University of California Press, 1967), p. 65.
2. Richard Charques, *The Twilight of Imperial Russia* (New York: Oxford University Press, 1958), p. 27.
3. Richard Pipes, *Russia Under the Old Regime* (New York: Charles Scribner's Sons, 1974), p. 295.

5

The Intelligentsia: Strangers in a Strange Land

Is this normal? Everything is abnormal in our society. . . .

———DOSTOEVSKY

The revolutionaries emerged from a new segment in Russian society created by the spread of education and Western ideas. Called the intelligentsia, this was a group with no real counterpart in the West. The intelligentsia should not be confused with what are called intellectuals —well-educated and cultured people who may but do not necessarily have any particular interest in politics. The intelligentsia's main concern, by contrast, was politics. It is probably best defined as that group of Russians that combined a certain level of education and awareness with a social conscience and a commitment to making significant changes in Russian society. It was also true that those who fit this description were odd men out in nineteenth-century Russia: "Foreigners at home and foreigners abroad," in the words of Alexander Herzen, one of their number. Their education and political commitment had made the members of the intelligentsia strangers in their own land, cut off from the ignorant and superstitious masses by their expanded horizons and stifled and hounded by an autocracy that would not let them implement their ideas for improving their country. These conditions and the resulting alienation did not exist in the West, where, whatever the social imperfections, the gap between educated elite and the general population was smaller and the opportunity to participate in the political process was greater. Aside from what it reveals about Russia's difficulties, this alienation was of fundamental historical importance because it created in Russia the first significant group independent of the autocracy and therefore able to challenge it.

The intelligentsia was a polyglot group that varied within a given generation and from one generation to another. It therefore espoused a variety of solutions to Russia's problem. Russia's earliest modern revolutionary thinker, Alexander Radishchev, called in the 1790s for the abolition of serfdom and for a republic that would guarantee individual rights. The Decembrists, Russia's first active revolutionaries, split into two main groups. The majority wanted some sort of constitutional regime on the Western model, while others advocated a centralized dictatorship. In the 1830s and 1840s, some of the intelligentsia wanted change based on old Russian traditions, others called for a democratic federal republic, and a small minority urged a conspiratorial revolution or a vast peasant upheaval. Beginning in the 1860s, opinion was split for several decades between those putting faith in the peasants and those trusting only members of the intelligentsia itself as capable of making a revolution. Of course, this debate over the type of change needed and the means of accomplishing it went on for so long and shifted ground so many times because for decades *nothing* seemed to work.

Nevertheless, over time, the intelligentsia underwent important changes that intensified the frustration and alienation of many of its members, and therefore its determination to make a revolution. Its history really begins in the 1830s and 1840s. Its members then were predominantly nobles whose exposure to Western society made them ask searching and subversive questions about their backward, poverty-stricken, and repressive homeland. These nobles were divided into two categories. A conservative group called the Slavophiles wanted reforms to be based on what it believed was Russia's indigenous traditions. Opposed to this was a liberal group called Westerners who felt that Russia had to follow the European model of development. As education spread, the intelligentsia expanded and changed. Beginning in the 1840s and particularly after 1860, the noble intelligentsia was reinforced and eventually engulfed by elements from the nonnoble classes. These new recruits included, among others, the sons of priests, who abandoned dedication to God for dedication to society; the children of lower-level civil servants; and, later, the sons and daughters of the Russian middle class. The Russian word for these people—*raznochintsy*—literally means "people of various ranks." This new generation, the "sons" of Ivan Turgenev's classic novel *Fathers and Sons*, often had known poverty and physical deprivation as well as alienation and tended to be far more radical and uncompromising than its elders—Turgenev's "fathers"—in both its political goals and the methods by which it proposed to achieve them. The "sons," who came to the fore in the 1860s, and the generations that followed them, constituted what may be called the revolutionary intelligentsia.

The theories and programs developed by the revolutionary intelligentsia tended to be absolutist, unrealistic, or both. This happened because for decades the intelligentsia lived and worked in a vacuum. At no time prior to the 1890s did it have any meaningful contact with a broader audience. The peasants were beyond reach and, unlike in the West, there was no substantial middle class to provide an interested and active public. The result was that theory remained untempered or modified by the necessity of winning widespread support or by the opportunity of being put into practice. These theories were further hardened by the repression to which the intelligentsia was subject. In short, nineteenth-century Russian conditions made for political abstractions, not practical politics.

At no point did the revolutionary intelligentsia make up more than a small portion of Russia's educated elite. But the minority that did belong, like Gideon's army, made up for its lack of numbers by an indefatigable courage born of faith. It was appalled by the poverty, inequality, and injustice that pervaded Russian life and was driven by a passion to rectify everything that was so terribly wrong. Split into factions, divided by ideological disputes, isolated by distant places of exile and prison walls, the revolutionary intelligentsia was united by an iron determination to do good. Somehow it would make a revolution that would destroy the old society and replace it with one without fault. In the face of seemingly impossible odds, the revolutionary intelligentsia persisted, and, after several generations marked by poverty, imprisonment, exile, hard labor, and sometimes untimely death, it made its revolution and seized power. Then, like the bee whose very act of attacking and stinging its victim is suicidal, the revolutionary intelligentsia found that its success soon sealed its own doom.

The intelligentsia, revolutionary or not, faced two critical problems: deciding what the ideal Russia should look like and devising the means to implement the desired changes. During the 1830s and 1840s, the Slavophiles and Westerners debated the first issue. Influenced by German idealism, which stressed the uniqueness of each individual nationality, the Slavophiles looked backward into Russia's history. They felt that Russia had once been a much better place, a spiritual and harmonious society that was disrupted by the reforms of Peter the Great. The spiritual and cooperative instincts of the people had been reflected by their religion —Orthodoxy—and by the peasant commune. The latter supposedly had been a spontaneous creation of the peasants themselves. Russia's problems could be traced, the Slavophiles argued, to Western influence in general and to Peter's reforms in particular. Soulless Western rationality had to be driven out of Russia and the old national spirituality restored to its proper place. Serfdom had to go, but not tsardom. Instead, the pre-Petrine benevolent and paternal monarchy had to be restored. A benevolent autocracy, not a legalistic constitutional or parliamentary regime, was the most suitable form of government for Russia. And once Russia had returned to its moral ways, the Slavophiles added, it could teach the world how to live.

The problem was that this Slavophile vision was a fantasy. The key Slavophile/Westerner battles were fought over the history of the peasant commune, and the Westerners produced convincing evidence that the commune as it existed in the nineteenth century was largely a mechanism of taxation and social control connected with the evolution of serfdom. The Westerners, however, had problems of their own, best illustrated by the difficulties encountered by Alexander Herzen, possibly the most brilliant of the generation that entered the political stage in the 1830s. Herzen was an ardent Westerner—until he learned about the West firsthand. Like the other early Westerners, he was strongly influence by French socialist thought and himself espoused a vague sort of socialism. After going into exile in Western Europe in 1847, Herzen witnessed the revolutions of 1848 that swept large parts of the continent before collapsing. Herzen was demoralized by these failures. Socialism had not triumphed. Capitalism and all the exploitation associated with it now seemed entrenched in Europe. To Herzen, the Western path of capitalism and materialistic bourgeois values was as unacceptable as what existed in Russia.

It was at this point that Herzen took a leaf from the Slavophiles and rediscovered the Russian peasantry and its commune. Unlike the Slavophiles, however, Herzen did not want to use the commune to recreate a version of Russia's idealized past. Instead, it was to become the springboard for Russia to leap over the wilderness of capitalism into the promised land of socialism. Russia's backwardness, once a curse, now became a virtue because it had preserved the venerable commune. In the process, the Russian peasant—brutal, miserable, superstitious, and grasping—was transformed into an instinctive socialist. Some of the ease with which Herzen executed his theoretical gymnastics is perhaps explained by his virtual ignorance about how the Russian peasant really lived. At any rate, the belief that socialism in Russia could be realized on the basis of peasant collectivist instincts and the commune without going through the horrors of capitalism later acquired a more elaborate theoretical framework and a name: populism. It became and remained the dominant political creed of the intelligentsia for the rest of the nineteenth century. For a long time, until its spectacular but Pyrrhic victory of assassinating Tsar Alexander II, populism had the stage all to itself, an era long enough to stamp the revolutionary movement with important characteristics it never really lost.

Having opted for a socialist Russia, Herzen faced another problem. How would the new social order be put into place? What would move the heretofore immovable autocracy, and what form of government would take its place? A fellow nobleman, Michael Bakunin, put his faith in the creative power of a nation-wide violent peasant upheaval. Other Russian socialists issued similar calls, but not Herzen. A basically humane and moderate man, he saw little that was positive in mass destruction and warned his comrades that "whenever somebody's blood is spilled, somebody's tears will flow." He had the same reaction to those who were ready to resort to a revolutionary dictatorship once the autocracy had been overthrown. These people, Herzen complained, were guilty of "Peter the Greatism," a reference to the tyranny and suffering that occurs when the power of the state is used to impose "progress" on an unwilling people.

Herzen never found a means for realizing the revolution and socialism, and the search was continued by revolutionaries who followed him. But a critical change took place. Some important members of the new generation discarded Herzen's reservations and scruples and replaced them with a pitiless, unflinching outlook known as nihilism. Nihilism rejected all existing values and institutions as being hopelessly corrupt or useless. Conventional standards of behavior or ethics were abandoned in favor of a redefined moral code that justified any means to help achieve the end of revolution. Because all existing institutions were condemned as rotten, destruction for its own sake was transformed into a creative act. Nihilists did believe in progress, placing enormous faith in the ability of modern science and the scientific method to solve social problems. Yet in fact they recognized as valid only those scientific discoveries and theories that seemed to support revolutionary political goals. Finally, nihilism emphasized the crucial revolutionary role of a self-appointed elite that had mastered these revolutionary tenets.

It is true that very few of the revolutionaries from the 1860s on called themselves nihilists, but the nihilistic code developed during that decade put its brand on an important segment of the Russian revolutionary tradition. The linchpin of the new attitude was that everything could and should be subordinated to the revolution, morality included. Traditional values and standards of behavior had to give way if they interfered with the imperative of revolution, regardless of the pain involved. Nicholas Chernyshevsky, the single greatest hero for two generations of revolutionaries, including a Marxist named Vladimir Ilyich Lenin, warned his fellows that their path was not a pristine one:

This highroad of History is not a sidewalk of the Nevsky Prospect. It passes all the way through open fields, dusty and muddy; at times it cuts across marshes or forests. If one shrinks from getting covered with dust and dirtying one's boots, then one should never enter into public activity. This is a salutary occupation if one is really inspired by the idea of the good of mankind, but it is not a particularly clean occupation. *However, there are different ways of defining moral purity.* (ital. added)

Chernyshevsky and many of his comrades defined moral purity as anything promoting the revolution, even if terrible suffering resulted. If the people had to sink even deeper into misery to get them to act, so be it. In discussing the Emancipation of 1861, Chernyshevsky commented that "it would have been better if the extreme reactionaries had their way over the reform and liberated the peasants without land: there would have been an immediate catastrophe." And once the revolution came, what if certain roadblocks required that the new progressive rulers employ even greater oppression than had the reactionary autocracy? "Does it really matter?" Chernyshevsky asked. After all, peaceful and calm development is impossible, for "without convulsions there could never have been a single step forward in history."

The revolutionary imperative caught more than morality in its net. Art and beauty also had to do their part. In the 1840s, Vissarion Belinsky— "furious" Vissarion, as he justifiably was called—formulated the thesis that literature was obligated to carry a progressive message. Because in Russia writers were the "only leaders, protectors, and saviors from the desolation of the autocracy," a writer could be forgiven an "inferior" book that was poorly written, but never a "harmful" one that carried the wrong political message. Chernyshevsky insisted that it was the responsibility of all writers to address the proper social and political issues; art for art's sake, in his opinion, was "useless." A leading literary critic of the next generation, Dmitry Pisarev, went further, declaring that literature was a waste of time. "I utterly reject the notion of art having in any way promoted the intellectual or moral advancement of mankind," he intoned.

The ultimate manifestation of the intelligentsia's deification of the revolution was its subordination of the Russian people, supposedly the reason for all this trouble, to that end. The peasantry might be idealized as the instinctive carrier of socialism, but was in reality credited with little more than instinct. It had to be led and molded by the self-appointed elite. Chernyshevsky was convinced that "the mass of the population knows nothing and cares about nothing except its material advantages. . . ." This indifference, he added, was what created the possibility for an effective leadership to institute change. Chernyshevsky summed it all up in a sentence Peter the Great or Pobedonostsev might have used: "The mass is simply the raw material for diplomatic and political experiments. Whoever rules it tells it what to do and it obeys."

Chernyshevsky was not alone in his beliefs. Before him, the Decembrist Pavel Pestel proclaimed his intention to organize a centralized revolutionary police state, and Vissarion Belinsky endorsed the brutal methods of Peter the Great, whom he characterized as a "hero and demigod." After Chernyshevsky, Peter Tkachev insisted that a revolutionary minority had to do the job of changing Russia because if the people were allowed to do what they wanted, "you will soon discover that they won't do anything new." The people, Tkachev warned, "can never save themselves." Therefore the revolutionary minority, by virtue of its "superior intellectual and moral development," had to hold power. A generation later Vladimir Lenin echoed these sentiments when he insisted the professional revolutionaries had to lead the working class to socialism because on their own, the masses could only develop reformist, or what he called "trade union," consciousness.

Chernyshevsky also provided the model of what a revolutionary life should be, a contribution that won him the adoration of several generations of revolutionaries. He created that model in an artless and tendentious novel called *What Is To Be Done?*, a book Lenin admired so much that he used the same title for his first major political pamphlet. Chernyshevsky's book is filled with heroes and heroines ready to endure anything for the cause. One of them, Rahkmetov, engages in constant exercise and eating regimens to prepare himself for his destiny. Not even sleep gives him pause, for this magnificent revolutionary specimen sleeps on a bed of nails. These were not ordinary people, Chernyshevsky stressed. They were "superior beings, unapproachable by the likes of you or me." His "New Men" were "as the caffeine in tea, the bouquet of noble wine, they give it its strength and aroma. They are the flower of the flower of men, the motor of motors, the salt of the salt of the earth."

Beneath the purple prose, Chernyshevsky's "New Men" emerge as a caste of new revolutionary supermen saving the downtrodden and hapless masses. As such, why should they not be permitted to employ any and all means to achieve their noble ends? Chernyshevsky had no problem with this; neither did many of the activists of the 1860s and 1870s who strove mightily to become in reality what Chernyshevsky could only write about. Others did object, of course. Many influential revolutionary thinkers, such as Herzen and after him Peter Lavrov and Nikolai Mikhailovsky, strenuously warned against the dictatorial implications of such an attitude. In fact, the ultra-elitist tendency exemplified by Chernyshevsky and Tkachev was a minority opinion in every phase of the Russian revolutionary movement, as it was in the 1870s, when Lavrov's influence was paramount. But it remained a powerful undercurrent, its failures notwithstanding, in the wake of the majority's own failures and the unsuppressible gnawing fear that something had to be done soon lest Russia follow the capitalist-parliamentary path of the West.

Rejection of the West, even by men like Herzen and Lavrov, turned out to be extremely important. Russian history provided no example of how to keep the state under control. Western Europe did, but Herzen, Lavrov, and so many other Russian revolutionaries rejected Western parliamentary and legal institutions as being tools of bourgeois exploitation, just as they rejected the capitalist economic institutions with which they were associated. Mikhailovsky came closest to advocating a constitutional regime; he even discussed the matter with some prominent liberals in 1879. But these discussions reached no agreement. In short, the prevailing attitude among the revolutionaries of all stripes was opposed to the political system spawned in the West no less than it was to the one spawned in Russia. Presumably there was a third possibility for governing a large modern society, but finding it turned out to be a puzzle the Russian revolutionary movement never solved, a failure that had momentous and terrible implications for the Russian people.

By the 1860s, after a quarter century of writing and reading, the intelligentsia finally was ready to act. Its revolutionary crusade had begun, but for a long time it would be a lonely crusade. The revolutionary intelligentsia may have been ready for action, but the peasantry, the class whose mass strength was to supply the revolution's power, was not. Its horizons bounded by poverty, ignorance, and superstition, the peasantry remained loyal to its "Little Father," the tsar. The first phase of the active struggle against tsarism has a neatly defined beginning and end: 1861, the year Tsar Alexander II liberated the serfs; and 1881, the year revolutionaries assassinated the Tsar-Liberator. What occurred in between was less tidy, as the revolutionaries waged a fruitless and frustrating struggle to spark their upheaval.

It might seem incongruous that the emancipation itself pushed the intelligentsia to active struggle, but it was precisely that edict's limits and the burdens that it put on the peasantry that extinguished the last flickering hope that satisfactory change could be accomplished from above, a hope held until 1861 even by men like Herzen and Chernyshevsky. Subsequent events brought further disappointments, driving some revolutionaries to extreme theories and desperate measures.

During the mid-1860s many revolutionaries were arrested, an experience that convinced those still in the fray that only the most tightly organized conspiratorial party could succeed against the autocracy and its political police. This elitism also received a boost when the people failed to answer the revolutionary clarion. Peasant disturbances that occurred between 1861 and 1863 in the wake of disappointments related to the emancipation soon faded. In 1866, the peasantry responded to an assassination attempt against Alexander II, by a group calling itself "Hell," by choosing to believe a rumor that the attempt was a plot by landlords angry over the loss of their serfs. Instead of rebelling, peasants demonstrated in support of the tsar and even beat up a few students.

Among the new leaders who emerged after this debacle were two men who further promoted the revolutionary movement's elitist and conspiratorial disposition: Sergei Nechaev and Peter Tkachev. Although they briefly worked together, they are important for different reasons. Nechaev carried the concept of revolutionary morality with its logic of the ends justifying the means to its ultimate and scandalous conclusion. To promote the revolution, Nechaev was quite willing to use blackmail, extortion, and, in one case, even murder, not against the oppressors but against his fellow revolutionaries. Among the victims of his lying and deceit were Herzen, Michael Bakunin, and the populist Mark Natanson. There also was an unlucky agricultural student named Ivanov, whose murder Nechaev arranged because Ivanov openly doubted him. Nechaev had proclaimed that the revolutionary was a "lost man," a person with "no feelings, no attachments, not even a name of his own." When he wrote these words his fellow revolutionaries did not react adversely; when he lived them they were horrified and ashamed. But it was easier to repudiate the man and his individual actions than to deal with the problem of revolutionary zeal leading to amoral and corrupting actions, a problem that haunted the Russian revolutionary movement long after Nechaev was in his grave.

Peter Tkachev was a populist without any faith in the peasantry's ability to consummate the revolution. His great fear was that a delay in the revolution would force Russia to follow the European path of development and lose its chance to skip capitalism and jump directly to communism. He therefore focused on the specifics of how the intelligentsia could seize power as quickly as possible.

Tkachev developed, to a far greater degree than had yet been done, a program for a revolution organized and led by a centralized, disciplined party of revolutionaries that would implement communism by means of a minority dictatorship. First and foremost, he emphasized that only the most tightly organized party could have any chance of success:

If organization is necessary for a large and strong party, it is undoubtedly even more indispensable for a weak and small party, for a party which is only beginning to be formed. Such is the position of our social revolutionary party, and for it the problem of unity and organization is a problem of life and death. . . .

The masses would be involved and their support would be sought, but only as followers being told what to do. Finally, once power had been seized, the party would keep that power for itself and use force, if necessary, to set up its utopia since, as Tkachev saw it:

> . . . the revolutionary minority must be able to continue its work of revolutionary destruction in those spheres where it can hardly reckon on the genuine support and assistance of the popular majority. That is why it must possess might, power, and authority.

All this plotting and scheming about setting up conspiratorial parties and revolutionary dictatorships did not escape criticism, especially after the scandal caused by Nechaev's sinister and bloody machinations. In Peter Lavrov, the revolutionaries of the 1870s found a more restrained counsel. Lavrov echoed Herzen's criticism of reliance on an omnipotent state to build a new society. Russia had had more than enough of overpowering states, Lavrov argued. Russia's revolutionaries should rather base their actions on moral and ethical principles that recognize that the revolution had to be made *by* as well as *for* the people. A dictatorship, regardless of what it called itself, would be "hostile to a socialist system of society." It would corrupt "even the best of people" and leave the basic problem in Russia unsolved. "Dictatorship," Lavrov warned, "is torn from the hands of the dictators only by a new revolution."

Lavrov's critique of revolution by conspiracy and dictatorship swept an intelligentsia chastened by the Nechaev episode. So too did his call to "go to the people," to go into the villages and turn the peasants into revolutionaries by propaganda that addressed their everyday needs. The assumption was that the peasants were socialists by an instinct that simply had to be awakened by enlightened emissaries.

In 1874, without the benefit of any central organization or direction, 2,000 students descended on the countryside armed with their revolutionary fervor and faith in the socialist potential of the peasant. What these youths found instead during their "Mad Summer" were desperately poor farmers suspicious of the intruders from the universities and overwhelmingly convinced of the goodness of their tsar. They had no interest in or instinct for socialism. Rather they aspired to acquire more land and become prosperous capitalists in their own right. Adding injury to insult, the peasants proved quite willing to betray the students to the police. For many young revolutionaries the summer that began so full of hope proved to be a way station to years in prison.

The disaster of 1874 was followed by a smaller and equally unsuccessful revival in 1875. Faith in the peasants' socialist instincts received a justified blow from which it never fully recovered. As early as 1876, a group of revolutionaries in the Chigirin district in southern Russia was discovered to be inciting revolution, not with a socialist program, but with a forged manifesto in which Alexander II allegedly called on his people to rise against the evil nobility and bureaucracy. The Chigirin affair was doubly embarrassing to the revolutionary movement, both for what it said about the new lack of confidence in the peasantry and, more importantly, for what it said about the ethics of the revolutionaries involved. They were, after all, using fraud and deceit against the very people they were supposedly leading in a noble cause.

The defeats in the countryside in 1874 and 1875 were followed by defeats in cities in 1875 and 1876, when the police succeeded in destroying revolutionary organizations in Moscow and the southern port city of Odessa. These organizations had represented the first effort to radicalize Russia's small but growing factory working class. The final blow dealt to the revolutionaries of the 1870s was a series of trials in 1877 and 1878. These resulted in harsh sentences for many of the young idealists who had been swept up by the ubiquitous tsarist police net.

All of this revived conspiratorial tendencies and engendered a new cynicism among the revolutionaries concerning the ability of the people to act for themselves. The trauma of 1874 and 1875 ran deep. More and more revolutionaries were becoming panicked by the realization that they had to succeed before the natural course of events transformed Russia into a capitalist society with a strong bourgeoisie. This terrible prospect would end the still-flickering hopes that Russia might leap directly from backwardness into socialism. Once the bourgeoisie was entrenched, a socialist revolution, the populists felt, would be far more difficult to achieve.

The new weapon employed to avoid the spectre of capitalism was terror, specifically the assassination of selected state officials. Terror eventually became the main political tactic of a newly formed secret party, Land and Freedom, organized in 1876. The hope was that assassination could disrupt the functioning of the state and cause its collapse. For a while the government seemed genuinely stymied and confused by the new turn of events. Repression was increased. In 1879, the country was divided into what amounted to six military districts, but still the terrorists could not be stopped. Nevertheless, the primacy of terror as a political weapon was not universally accepted and Land and Freedom split over the issue in 1879. One faction, calling itself Black Repartition, remained committed to propaganda; it soon metamorphosed into Russia's first Marxist group. The other, the People's Will, reaffirmed the use of terror and decided to go for broke: it would assassinate Tsar Alexander II. Presumably, with its head cut off, the entire tsarist system would collapse.

The People's Will, a small sect rather than a political party, was a laser beam focused on the tsar. Despite its name, the People's Will maintained that the "downtrodden state of the people" necessitated its acting in their place. It accepted as permissible any means that led to its revolutionary ends. An attempt on the tsar's life had been made in April of 1879, a few months prior to the party's formation. In 1880, the People's Will blew up the tsar's dining room in the Winter Palace, but Alexander was not present when the explosion took place. Then, on March 1, 1881, decimated by the arrests of its top leadership, the remnants of the organization threw two bombs at Alexander. The second, thrown at his feet where he was more accustomed to seeing his subjects bow down, fatally wounded the Tsar-Liberator.

The assassination of Alexander II brought two eras to a close. The first was the period of reform initiated by the autocracy. Alexander II may have vacillated and even undermined some of his own reforms, but they were still momentous. The new tsar, Alexander III, instituted an era of repression and reaction reminiscent of the reign of Nicholas I. Progress toward broadening the political process in Russia came to a screeching halt for twenty-five years.

The assassination also marked a turning point in the revolutionary movement. The members of the People's Will who had survived to kill Alexander II did not long survive their triumph. They were quickly rounded up and hanged. The police-state measures introduced in 1881 and 1882 kept things quiet for the rest of the decade. Yet silence did not mean the absence of meaningful activity. A new generation of revolutionaries was thinking about what had gone wrong. Some of them began to look beyond the peasantry and conspiracy by isolated groups of revolutionaries to a changing society that was producing new agents and possibilities for revolution. They spoke about dialectics, historical materialism, and the proletariat. Marxism, the quintessence of revolutionary thought, had come to Russia.

PART TWO

The End of the Old Order

6

Capitalism Comes to Russia

I . . . shall preserve the principle of autocracy as firmly and as unflinchingly as did my late unforgettable father.

———NICHOLAS ROMANOV.
Tsar of Russia, 1895

The Romanov Dynasty will end with Nicholas II. If he has a son, the son will not reign.

———VASILY KLIUCHEVSKY.
Russia's leading historian, 1895, upon hearing Nicholas's comment

More than just a century was drawing to a close in Russia by the 1890s. The iron tentacles of Western Europe's industrial revolution finally had reached eastward into Russia, taken hold, and torn irreparable fissures in traditional Russian society. Although many Russians refused to acknowledge what was happening—from revolutionary populists who dreamed of a peasant socialist Russia spared the ravages of capitalism, to arch-conservatives and reactionaries who remembered Russia's hallowed traditions—their visions and memories were helpless to stop capitalist development. The old dreams and days were numbered, the countdown having begun several decades earlier with the emancipation of the serfs.

Two crucial factors shaped the development of Russian capitalism: the disproportionate role played by foreigners and the direct involvement of the state. Foreigners played such a pronounced role because Russia lacked the capital resources and technical skills necessary for extensive industrial development. Foreign investment eventually accounted for one-third of the total industrial investment in Russia, with a particular concentration in such basic industries as iron, coal, chemicals, and oil production. Foreign loans to the Russian government also provided the capital the state needed when it took over the job of building Russia's railroad network in the 1880s. As always in Russia, the state mobilized the nation's resources because no institution or social class was able to do the job. In fact, despite the gradual development of a Russian bourgeoisie after 1860, the state's role in the national economy increased with each passing decade between 1861 and 1900.

Actually, Russia's military and strategic priorities, not economic development per se, determined the state's policies. After 1862, the autocracy actively began to encourage railroad construction. The Crimean War had made it clear that a modern railroad network was needed to move Russian troops and supplies quickly to future battlefields. It also would tie the sprawling empire together, thereby promoting both the government's authority and economic activity. Unfortunately, the cost put an intolerable burden on the already strained state treasury. Foreigners would not risk investing in Russian railroads unless their debts were guaranteed by the state, and since the autocracy barely managed to cover its normal expenditures, it was forced after 1862 to rely heavily on foreign loans to meet its expanding obligations. These loans further compounded Russia's financial troubles, since more foreign investment and loans could only be lured into Russia if the government were solvent and the local currency reasonably stable. The government therefore had to balance its budget and, to protect its currency, maintain a favorable balance of trade. When in the 1880s the government decided that the empire's strategic and economic needs would be better served if it built the necessary railroads itself, the huge costs of direct railroad construction made balancing the budget still more difficult.

The difficulty of balancing the budget was compounded because agriculture, still the main source of wealth in Russia, had progressed only a little in the decades immediately after the emancipation of the serfs. Some progress had been made in raising Russia's chronically low agricultural productivity, as a few landlords managed to modernize and raise the productivity of their estates. Grain exports tripled by the end of the 1870s. Yet the agricultural landscape as a whole remained a bleak patchwork of backward estates and inefficient allotments, and the value of the grain exports themselves was reduced by abundant crops flooding the international market from new foreign sources, particularly the United States.

The state's financial tangle therefore became a noose around the necks of the Russian peasantry, the group that still bore most of the tax burden. First the soul tax was raised by 80 percent. Later, when that tax was abolished, the government placed taxes on most things the peasants needed or wanted, including matches, tobacco, and alcohol. The continuing quest for a favorable balance of trade resulted in an unrelenting export of grain. Even in a *famine* year, 15 percent of the grain harvest might be exported. It is hardly a wonder that the public unlovingly dubbed these shipments "starvation exports." One Minister of Finance, Ivan S. Vyshnegradsky, who deserved more credit for candor than compassion, summed up the policy when he observed that "We must export though we die." Russian peasants did both.

Still, the statistics looked reasonably good. Along with railroad construction, Russia's coal and iron industries registered impressive growth. Banking and credit institutions prospered. Russia's factory working class grew at an unprecedented rate.

None of this helped the autocracy. It staggered from financial crisis to financial crisis. Each finance minister in the first three decades after the emancipation—Mikhail Reutern (1862–1878), Nicholas Bunge (1882–1886), and the quotable Mr. Vyshnegradsky (1882–1892)—ended his tenure in failure. By the end of Vyshnegradsky's term, it was clear that only a far stronger economy than Russia had been able to build could generate the productivity and revenues needed to remain a great power. Vyshnegradsky had been working toward that end when in 1891 he had enacted a high tariff designed in part to protect and foster the growth of Russian industry. But Vyshnegradsky's taxes left the peasants with virtually no reserves. In 1891, the year of his tariff, the harvest failed in large parts of Russia. Bereft of its grain reserves, the country experienced one of the most terrible famines in its history. Aside from the horrors of the famine itself, Russia and the world were treated to a sordid side show when the government tried to limit its bad press and protect its credit rating by minimizing the seriousness of the situation. For a time, the government prevented private relief efforts, insisting that they were unnecessary. Reality soon forced the regime to relent. It also moved the autocracy to resort to the most vigorous industrialization policies since the days of Peter the Great in an effort to break the chain of backwardness and poverty that kept Russia bound to constant crisis.

The man who led that effort was the new finance minister, Sergei Iulevich Witte. Witte was the outstanding Russian statesman of his generation and among the most competent that tsarist Russia managed to produce during its last century. Yet his career as finance minister ended as it began, with Russia in deep crisis. Russia was starving when he assumed office in 1892. In 1903, when he was dismissed from his post, southern Russia was experiencing a massive series of strikes, parts of southwestern Russia had undergone peasant riots in 1902, and the entire country stood less than two years away from a full-fledged, though ultimately unsuccessful, revolutionary upheaval. Paradoxical as it might

seem, from the point of view of social stability and the survival of the
autocracy he served, it was not only Witte's failures, but his very successes,
that made things worse. Nothing better illustrates the difficulties Russia
faced than Witte's successes and debacles as finance minister between
1892 and 1903.

Witte, as Peter the Great before him and Joseph Stalin after him, was
driven by a sense of the urgent need to industrialize. The new finance minister felt that Russia faced far more than a military or financial problem.
Despite the progress of the past thirty years, Russia in 1892 was still predominantly an agricultural, peasant country. Its rivals in Western Europe,
by contrast, were modern industrial powers, and although Russia was
politically independent, its economic relationship with Western Europe
was of the classic colonial type. Russia served Europe as a market for
industrial goods and a source of raw materials. "International competition
does not wait," Witte warned. If Russia did not overcome its backwardness and awaken from its "economic slumber lasting two centuries,"
it would be overwhelmed by its more advanced competitors. Russia's
military situation would become untenable, because in an industrial age
the ability to produce modern machines translated directly into military
power. Beyond that, the increasing foreign ownership of Russia's economy
"may gradually clear the way also for the triumphant political penetration
by foreign powers." In other words, Russia easily could become another
India or China—colonialized or carved up by the industrialized West.

Although Witte hoped that ultimately private initiative and enterprise
could be stimulated to the point where it could guarantee Russia's further
progress and prosperity, he felt that for the moment only the autocracy had
the resources to take the initiative. Industrialization, Witte insisted, could
best be promoted by massive railroad construction. This would stimulate
the metallurgical and fuel industries, and these would stimulate light industry, a pattern that already had occurred in Western countries. Such a
chain reaction would give Russia an industrial base sufficient to compete
with Western industries and, by dramatically expanding Russia's productivity, would generate enough revenue to end at last the state's chronic
deficits.

Railroads were the basis, not the totality, of Witte's program. He also
implemented a broad series of supporting measures. These included subsidies and credits for key industries, building technical and engineering
schools, promoting banking, using the state's purchasing power to support certain industries, protecting Russia behind the tariff of 1891, and
putting the Russian ruble on the gold standard, to name only a few. The
last measure, by guaranteeing the stability of Russia's currency, enabled
Witte to attract large amounts of foreign capital to Russia in the form of
new industrial investment. It also enabled him to borrow more than ever

before and thereby balance his budget, now stretched to the breaking point by his railway building projects and the growing needs of Russia's military establishment.

The results were spectacular by any standard. During Witte's tenure as finance minister, Russia's industrial production doubled, growing at an annual rate of over 8 percent, the highest rate of growth of any of the major powers. Oil production almost tripled, propelling Russia to first place in the world. Coal production more than doubled, pig iron production tripled, and total railroad track mileage grew by 73 percent. Most of European Russia's rail network was completed, as was most of the Trans-Siberian Railroad, then, as now, the longest railroad in the world.

The problems associated with this rapid growth and change were hardly less imposing. The treadmill of borrowing more and more to meet skyrocketing expenses moved even faster, and running to keep up with it meant higher taxes on the peasantry, even higher than those of the pitiless Vyshnegradsky. Witte admitted that the exports squeezed from the peasantry came "not out of excess but out of current needs." In 1897, his export program finally earned Russia enough gold to enable him to put the ruble on the gold standard. However, the next year Russia again experienced famine. The famine passed, but not the problems that had caused it. Despite these periodic famines, the population had increased fifty percent during the past thirty years. Most of that increase took place in the countryside, correspondingly increasing the misery there. Continued low productivity meant that the average peasant family earned barely half of what it needed to survive from its land allotment. Witte, despite some small gestures, had done nothing of consequence for the peasantry. This failure left the overwhelming majority of Russians in an ugly mood.

Added to peasant discontent was a rapidly growing and utterly miserable urban proletariat. The Russian proletariat of the late nineteenth century was exploited in the classic fashion of factory workers in the early stages of industrialization, but conditions were even worse in Russia than they had been during corresponding stages in the West. The few laws on the books protecting workers were rarely enforced. Workers were denied the right to form trade unions or to strike. Nobody could doubt where the government's sympathies lay, least of all the workers, whose strikes increasingly included political as well as economic demands. The strikes hit a peak in 1897, the year Witte triumphantly put Russia on the gold standard. The government's response, aside from an ill-enforced law mandating an eleven-and-a-half-hour day, was repression. The use of troops to suppress strikes and demonstrations was *twenty-seven* times greater than ever before during Witte's tenure. His success in building Russian industry, it turned out, had created in the growing proletariat a volatile element that was all the more dangerous because, unlike the peasantry, it was concentrated at the centers of power in Russia—including St. Petersburg and Moscow. This enabled the workers to organize, often with the help of eager members of the revolutionary intelligentsia. Witte's failures in the countryside, combined with his successful industrializing works, helped bring Russia's social problems to a boil.

Against all of the turbulence stood the autocracy. Although the social instability resulting from the emancipation had magnified the autocracy's weaknesses, this antiquated institution in a modern world remained the most important factor holding Russian society together. A satisfactory understanding of what happened to that society therefore requires an examination of how the autocracy functioned—and malfunctioned—as the old century waned and the new one dawned, bringing with it new and greater challenges.

Perhaps the most noteworthy characteristic of tsarism during these years was how it embodied two normally exclusive features: extreme centralization and chaos. Far too much depended on the tsar himself. Although he was advised by an appointed body called the State Council, the tsar alone could make laws. While such centralization might be expected to produce order and consistency if nothing else, such was not the case. The tsar's ministers, who carried out his orders, were rival free-lancers more than colleagues. Each reported individually to the tsar, where he did his best to defend his turf. A Western-type cabinet, where consultation and cooperation might produce coordinated policy directions, simply did not exist in Russia.

Because the tsar had so much power, the qualities of the individual who wore the crown were of vital importance. Alexander III, who reigned from 1881 to 1894, had few virtues, but at least he was a strong ruler able to stick to and enforce his reactionary policies, however misguided they might have been. His son, Nicholas II, had most of his father's faults and none of his strengths. Nicholas's reign began in disaster, marked its mid-point in 1905 with catastrophe, and closed in 1917 with the annihilation of tsarism. The pattern of ineptitude was set when hundreds of people were killed during a riot by an enormous crowd celebrating his coronation. At a time when rival foreign powers were broadening their political bases, Nicholas dismissed the idea of sharing political decision making with popularly elected representatives as "senseless dreams." Having inherited his father's generally narrow-minded advisors, Nicholas added to this group a coterie of misfits and charlatans that included his unbalanced wife Alexandra and her confidant and spiritual masseur, the drunken, debauching, and ignorant, but hypnotically compelling "holy man," Gregory Rasputin. As a rule, Nicholas continued his father's policies, whether they were constructive, as in the case of Witte's industrialization program, or destructive, as with the notorious Russification programs that embittered so many of his subjects. Where Nicholas deviated from Alexander's path, it usually was for the worse. Alexander III at least had followed a cautious foreign policy that kept Russia out of war. Nicholas's more aggressive policies led Russia into two wars. The first —the Russo-Japanese war—shook the autocracy to its roots and forced it to institute major reforms; the second—World War I—tore Russia apart and cost Nicholas his throne and his life.

As Nicholas had promised, there was no deviation on the issue of sharing the autocracy's power with its subjects. On this question there was considerable agreement among Nicholas's advisors, from the reactionary Pobedonostsev to the forward-looking Witte. Pobedonostsev wanted to preserve the autocracy's prerogatives so that it could beat back progress; Witte wanted to use those same powers to promote progress. In this regard Witte, again, was a worthy successor to Peter the Great and a harbinger of Joseph Stalin. He argued forcefully that the spread of *zemstvo* self-government eventually would subvert the absolute power of the autocracy, failing until 1902 to see the wisdom of political reform. Secure in his conviction that industrialization would solve all of Russia's difficulties, Witte had ignored the country's political problems even longer than he had ignored its agricultural crisis. Even Witte, the best the old system could produce, a man who had vision and realized that the twentieth century had arrived, was not prepared to modernize Russia's dangerously deficient political institutions.

By the time Witte did see the need for reform, his tenure as finance minister was coming to an end. An international economic slump beginning in 1899 had slowed Russian industrial expansion. In 1902, large peasant disturbances rocked the Ukraine, while the next year a massive wave of strikes swept the south. All of this was grist for Witte's many enemies, including fellow bureaucrats he had brushed aside and powerful landlords whose interests he had ignored. Witte was further weakened by his opposition to Russia's aggressive Far Eastern policy, which he feared might lead to war and disaster. In August 1903, Nicholas II dismissed his most competent advisor.

Witte's departure from the scene was soon followed by the first sustained appearance at center stage of a group with another approach to modernizing Russia, an approach that required the destruction of the autocracy and most of what Witte was trying to preserve. After frustrating and painful decades of enacting morose melodrama in underground shadows, the revolutionary intelligentsia, acknowledged at last by some of the aroused masses, finally would get its chance to perform great drama in the sunlight.

7

The Revolutionaries Regroup

. . . it is more pleasant and useful to go through the experience of revolution than to write about it.

——VLADIMIR LENIN

Don't be too hard on Lenin. I think that much of his strange behavior can be simply explained by the fact that he totally lacks a sense of humor.

——GEORGE PLEKHANOV

The revolutionaries got their chance to strike at the autocracy because the economic and social developments that took root during the 1890s also allowed their movements to regenerate and mature. The famine of 1891 had provided the impetus to reorganize. The next several years witnessed a slow revival of activity flowing in two distinct political currents. The old populist force was being replenished by new recruits. By 1901, this new generation of believers in peasant socialism had organized a new party, the Socialist Revolutionaries (SRs). At the same time, the growth of industry and a factory proletariat led other revolutionaries to organize around Marxism, a new theory imported from Western Europe that proclaimed socialism would be achieved when the proletariat, not the peasantry, rose in revolution. Like their colleagues in Western Europe, these people called themselves Social Democrats (SDs).

Economic and social changes meant that the revolutionary intelligentsia no longer was completely alone in its desire to change Russia. A growing and militant proletariat, a peasantry exposed to subversive ideas by a rising level of literacy and improved communications, an angry and restive collection of non-Russian minorities antagonized by Russification, and a growing number of liberal-minded professionals both in the cities and the rural *zemstvos*, all enabled the revolutionary message to reach a broader audience. That disparate audience, if unified, held the potential to become the decisive political force in Russia.

The SRs were worthy heirs to Russia's native revolutionary tradition. The terror campaign by their fearless "combat section" against the government after the turn of the century claimed more victims than the legendary efforts of the People's Will. Aside from directing their message to the peasantry—the largest and traditionally the most troublesome group in Russia—the SRs also had some success organizing among the small but growing factory working class. But here the SRs had serious weaknesses. Their program was more relevant to an agricultural Russia than to one that was rapidly industrializing. Like the peasantry itself, the party was diffused and disorganized. Still, it had the largest following in Russia of any political party in 1905 and again in 1917, so that whatever its limitations in being able to act decisively, its reputation in both revolutionary and police circles was a formidable one.

Although populism was enjoying a rebirth, it no longer had the revolutionary field to itself. By the 1880s the Russian intelligentsia had discovered Marxism, the revolutionary theory that was to become, in one or another of its multiple permutations, the central article of faith for twentieth-century revolutionary socialists all over the world. Marxism's great appeal to the Russian revolutionaries was that it opened a new road to revolution and socialism. Back in the 1840s, Karl Marx postulated that society passes through certain stages of economic organization as the human race develops its technology and increases its ability to produce what it needs to live. Focusing on Western Europe, Marx traced societal evolution from ancient slavery through medieval feudalism and modern industrial capitalism. In each phase of development, there was a struggle between those who controlled the wealth of society and those who did not, what Marx called the "class struggle." When combined with improvements in technology and the resulting changes in the way goods were produced, the class struggle eventually led to the destruction of a given social order and the birth of a new, more advanced order.

It was under capitalism that something unprecedented happened—the development of the technology and productive capacity sufficient to give every person a high standard of living. Of course, under capitalism the haves (the bourgeoisie) were still exploiting the have-nots (the factory working class, or proletariat), so that although technically possible, the universal good life remained an unfulfilled promise. But because the proletariat worked in huge factories where hundreds and even thousands of workers had to cooperate, it was learning from its day-to-day experience about the collective nature of the process that produced all of society's wealth. Eventually, led by a vaguely defined group called "communists," it would unite and overthrow the exploitative bourgeois minority. Society would then go through a transition period guided by a "dictatorship of the proletariat," a form of government Marx mentioned several times but never concretely defined or described. It would soon reach socialism, a nonexploitative society in which the ownership of social wealth, like the productive process itself, was collective. Then communism, a system that functioned so smoothly that each person could work "according to his ability" and be remunerated "according to his need," would be achieved. With this process would come the end of human misery and strife.

The good news about all this, aside from its rosy prediction of harmony and well-being, was that Marx and his lifelong collaborator, Friedrich Engels, claimed that their predictions rested on a scientific study of history. This study demonstrated that the human race was inexorably moving toward socialism. The bad news was that there were no shortcuts to the promised society. It was necessary to go through all the preliminary stages. This meant Russia would have to go through capitalism, something that all populists, including the SRs, desperately wanted to avoid. For years they had devoted much of their time trying to prove that Russia could skip capitalism and jump directly into socialism. Yet Russia's Marxists, or at least some of them, had a problem as well. Russia, after all, was at best in the early stages of capitalism, which meant that Russian Marxists were in for a long wait as capitalism ran its natural course. That Marx had ambiguously suggested that Russia, under certain circumstances, might skip capitalism only added fuel to a multisided debate that raged well beyond the November 1917 revolution that supposedly brought socialism to Russia.

A large part of Marxism's appeal in Russia resulted from frustration among certain populists. They felt that two generations of failure were enough. The peasants, from their hostility to the "going-to-the-people movement" of the 1870s to their negative reaction to those who tried to help them during the famine of 1891–1892, seemed hopeless as a revolutionary force. Terror had produced some sparks and corpses, but little else. On top of that, by the late 1880s and certainly by the 1890s, it was becoming clear that capitalism had come to Russia. Dreams of peasant socialism were fading against a background of railroad lines and factory smokestacks, while in the countryside such capitalist practices as production for the market and renting increased economic differentiation among the peasantry. Meanwhile, new dreams were born as the fledgling Russian working class began to discuss revolutionary socialist theories in the 1870s. By the 1880s, these workers were starting to rattle their factory walls with strikes. Far more massive strikes followed during the next decade. All of this lent even more weight to the impressive Marxist scholarly works detailing and analyzing the development of European capitalism.

Russian Marxism was born in the 1880s among the Russian emigre community in Switzerland. Its godfather was George Plekhanov, a former populist of aristocratic background. Plekhanov marshalled impressive evidence demonstrating the growth and spread of capitalism in Russia and, based on that evidence, maintained that Russia would have to go through a capitalistic phase before reaching socialism. This would require the overthrow of the reactionary autocracy and its replacement by a regime run by the bourgeoisie. As it had in Western Europe, capitalism would create the essential preconditions for socialism, including the proletariat, a genuine revolutionary class. Populist dreams of jumping directly from backwardness to socialism were just that, dreams, Plekhanov maintained.

Plekhanov issued a warning to those who would jump over historical stages, a warning sounded before him by Engels. He cautioned that if a minority seized power before historical developments had prepared the ground for socialism, either it would have to watch the economic equality it decreed erode in the face of economic scarcity, or it would have to assume control of all aspects of the economy. This would require dictatorial methods and would result in what Plekhanov called "Inca Communism," a society in which an all-powerful elite controlled the lives of a mass of slaves. When Plekhanov wrote these words in 1883—the year Marx died —his warning was directed at his conspiratorial populist opponents. It is unlikely he imagined that a generation later some of his fellow Marxists would warrant the same criticism.

Until the turn of the century, Plekhanov was the recognized leader among Russian Marxists. Then practical control of the movement began to pass to members of a new generation schooled in underground work inside Russia during the 1890s. Slowly the movement grew, but as it grew it began to crack. The most important fissure emerged because of the gap between Russia and Europe and, consequently, between the political approaches available in each area. At bottom the question was whether Russian Marxism would be cast in a traditional European or a native Russian mold. At first Plekhanov had done most of the molding. After 1900, a new leader would emerge to take over the job: Vladimir Ilych Ulyanov, better known as Lenin. It is impossible to understand the Russian Revolution and the society that emerged from it without first understanding Lenin and his political incarnation, the Bolshevik Party. While Leninism, like any other political movement, went through different phases, its unchanging foundation may be discerned by examining the personality of its founder, his use of Marxism, and his debt to the Russian revolutionary tradition from which he sprang.

Vladimir Ilych Ulyanov was born in 1870 in Simbrisk, a town on the

Volga River in central Russia. He was the second son in a family of six children. His mother, of German, Swedish, and Jewish descent, grew up in a prosperous and cultured home. She spoke German, English, and French and was an accomplished singer and piano player. His paternal family had risen from serfdom to hereditary nobility in three generations and was a mixture—not unusual for that part of Russia—of Russian and Asiatic (mainly Kalmyk) lineage. Ilya Ulyanov, Lenin's father, was a respected official in the ministry of education whose rise through the ranks had earned his noble status. His well-educated and intelligent wife added yet another element of culture and refinement to what was a comfortable middle-class home.

Although Lenin was not born to be a revolutionary, as his Soviet biographies would have it, a family crisis and his own personality certainly prepared him for the profession. When Vladimir was seventeen, his older brother, Alexander, was executed for complicity in a plot to assassinate Tsar Alexander III. This tragedy exposed Vladimir to his brother's illicit world and began to loosen the moorings linking him to tsarist society. The social ostracism his family suffered, a difficulty aggravated by his father's untimely death several years earlier, embittered and further disoriented the teenager.

Lenin's personality was marked more than anything else by an iron determination and ability to concentrate. As a youth he gave up skating because it interfered with his studies. Later "addictions" he would attempt to overcome—although not entirely successfully—were chess and music, the former because it was too time-consuming and the latter because he thought it weakened his will. He once told a friend, "I can't listen to music too often. It affects your nerves, makes you want to say stupid things and stroke the heads of people who create such beauty while living in this vile hell."

Fellow revolutionaries, themselves fiercely motivated, were struck by Lenin's overpowering will. One told Lenin that in contrast to "the greyhound" Plekhanov, ". . . you are like a bulldog: you have a deadly grip." Lenin never let go because he was convinced that he knew best, that the only possible road to socialism in Russia was the one he had charted. In a tightly knit world populated by many people who were sure they were right on any given issue, Lenin's conviction of his infallibility stood out. One unsympathetic colleague concluded that he was "constitutionally incapable of digesting opinions different from his own." Plekhanov eventually became so exasperated with his former protege that his advice to fellow delegates at a party congress in 1906 simply was "on all issues, vote against Lenin."

Leninism probably is best summed up as an adaptation of Marxism to Russian conditions accomplished by fusing traditional Marxism and the

Russian revolutionary tradition. Lenin never accepted the model and political approach of contemporary Western European Marxist parties, the strongest of which was the German Social Democratic Party. Those parties operated in countries with parliaments and constitutional protections and were able to function legally. They were allied to and supported by powerful trade union movements. While they ultimately stood for socialism, Western Social Democratic parties generally made concessions and deals associated with parliamentary politics, avoided an all-or-nothing attitude, and devoted their energies to achieving democratic reforms and step-by-step improvement of the working class's economic conditions. In short, traditional Marxist rhetoric about revolution notwithstanding, Western Social Democratic parties in practice worked for evolutionary change.

In Russia, a group of Social Democrats called "Economists" adopted an analogous approach. The Economists contended that Social Democrats could best advance their cause by focusing on the proletariat's specific economic demands rather than on political revolution. After 1903, when the Russian Social Democrats finally managed to organize a functioning political organization, a faction of that organization—the Mensheviks—continued the tendency of basing political actions in Russia on Western formulas. But unlike the Economists, who believed socialism would evolve through incremental reforms, the Mensheviks still believed that a revolution was necessary to establish socialism. However, the traditional Marxist scenario called for a long capitalist period in Russia, and therefore they were not concerned with the immediate problems of seizing and holding power.

Lenin, of course, accepted the basic Marxist tenets regarding historical stages, the progressive role of capitalism, its overthrow by the proletariat, and the establishment of communism. He was, however, more than just a Marxist; first and foremost, he was a revolutionary. Throughout his career, he demonstrated his determination to let nothing, including Marxist theory, come between him and the revolution he craved. As he put it, Marxism should not be a "dogma," but a "guide to action." Lenin recoiled from anything that might postpone the socialist revolution, be it economic prosperity, social reform, or Marxist theory. Like Peter Tkachev before him, Lenin's worst nightmare was that given a chance, Russian capitalism might become stabilized. The chances for a socialist revolution then would be severely damaged or even lost. Lenin therefore, while still professing Marxism, wound up trying to circumvent the Marxist tenet that Russia had to have a bourgeois revolution and a subsequent period of capitalist development before it would be ready for its socialist revolution. His career after 1900, in fact, is best understood as a quest for a shortcut to a socialist revolution in Russia. Although intellectually a Marxist, Lenin was temperamentally the heir to the populist tradition of Chernyshevsky, Tkachev, and Nechaev.

In order for Russia and its revolutionaries to avoid the long trip through a capitalist purgatory, Lenin had to develop a practical political vehicle able to undermine the autocracy and secure political power. He also had to make adjustments in Marxist theory to compress the waiting period between the bourgeois and socialist revolutions. Lenin's vehicle was what he called his "party of a new type." He described it and made it a viable institution, as will be seen, between 1900 and 1904. Both his concept of that party and the way he operated it quickly made Lenin the focus of bitter controversy. His adjustments to Marxist theory, likewise a source of controversy, took longer. In fact, for a long time Lenin was not sure exactly where Russia could make its shortcut to socialism and how it could be justified in Marxist terms, and his theoretical juggling therefore continued even beyond the Bolshevik seizure of power in 1917.

Lenin's revolutionary career began in earnest in 1893 with his arrival in St. Petersburg. A short trip to Europe in 1895 to meet Plekhanov and other leaders of Russian Marxism in exile was followed the next year by arrest, and then by exile to Siberia from 1895 to 1900. Since conditions of imprisonment and internal exile for political dissidents under tsarism were not remotely as harsh as they were to become after 1917, Lenin was able to study, write, and maintain contact with his comrades in Russia and Europe. When he emerged from his cold Siberian cocoon in 1900, Lenin had matured into a political leader ready to make his mark on international Marxism and the Russian revolutionary tradition.

Shortly after his release from Siberia, Lenin went to Switzerland to begin an exile that would last, with the exception of a few months from 1905 to 1906, until 1917. The Russian social democratic movement was in disarray. An attempt to set up a nationwide organization two years earlier had failed when most of the participants in what is deferentially called the party's "First" Congress were arrested before they could accomplish anything concrete. After 1901, many young members of the intelligentsia flocked to the newly organized Socialist Revolutionaries, whose spectacular terrorist acts satisfied a youthful urge for action. Others were attracted to an evolving liberal movement. The Russian working class was producing some leaders of its own, practical-minded workers more concerned with wages and working conditions than with political revolution. What was worse, the Economists agreed with them.

Lenin, along with Plekhanov and many others, was horrified by Economism. He and his colleagues claimed that by focusing excessively on the proletariat's immediate economic needs, many of which could be satisfied by moderate reforms, the Economists were denying the essence of what Marxism, supposedly a revolutionary doctrine, stood for. If Economism were not stamped out, Lenin feared, the emphasis on piecemeal economic improvement and gradual reform would blot out the goal of revolution. Russian Social Democracy then would undergo a transformation from a revolutionary movement into a reformist political party, much like what had happened to German Social Democracy.

Lenin's fears about the dangers Economism posed to the revolutionary movement reflected deeper fears about Russian society and the overall prospects for a socialist revolution. In contrast to Marx's overall optimism and faith in the historical process, Lenin has been called a revolutionary pessimist who lacked faith in those forces. In 1900, he certainly had good reasons to be pessimistic. He could see no class capable of making a socialist revolution in Russia. As a Marxist, Lenin rejected the populist conception of the peasantry as Russia's revolutionary force, but while other Marxists had turned wholeheartedly to the working class, Lenin's revolutionary temperament was frustrated by that class's emphasis on wages and working conditions at the expense of explicitly revolutionary goals. He was further distressed when the Economists gave the workers' attitude their theoretical blessing. Also, the liberal movement in Russia was growing stronger, and although it opposed the autocracy, it opposed socialism at least as much. To save the revolution from its enemies across the breadth of the political spectrum, Lenin proposed his "party of a new type."

Lenin felt his new party would have to overcome two obstacles in order to succeed. The first was the Russian state, which still denied its subjects the right to political activity. In this case, Lenin, like all Russians, was the victim of his country's autocratic tradition. The second obstacle, oddly enough, was the Russian people, specifically the proletariat. Here Lenin's difficulties arose not because the proletariat wanted to put any limits on his political activity, but precisely because Lenin wanted to control *their* political activity. In this case, Lenin was the heir to the elitist tradition of the Russian revolutionary intelligentsia. Lenin's solution to both problems was to advocate a tightly organized, conspiratorial, and hierarchical party, one that could avoid police spies and, perhaps more importantly, contamination by insufficiently militant political ideas.

Lenin was on solid ground when it came to surviving in the face of the autocracy and ubiquitous police:

> Against small groups of socialists seeking shelter up and down the broad Russian underworld stands the gigantic machine of the powerful contemporary state . . . in order to carry on a systematic struggle against the government we must bring our organization to the highest point of perfection. . . .

Any political organization, Lenin went on, that could not protect itself against infiltration by the police would quickly be destroyed. It went without saying that a broad-based, open political party on the model of the German Social Democratic Party, as favored by many Russian Marxists, was unequipped to survive in Russia's rigorous political climate.

No less dangerous to Russian social democracy, Lenin believed, were the workers and the Social Democratic leaders themselves. The problem was that both were untrustworthy. While Marx and Engels had believed that the proletariat would develop naturally a socialist and revolutionary outlook, or "consciousness," as a result of the conditions it faced, Lenin had far less faith that the workers would see the light. The workers, he warned, if allowed to follow their "spontaneous" inclinations, inevitably would forsake revolution for "petty bourgeois" reformist objectives such as better wages. The proper "social democratic consciousness"— as opposed to the unrevolutionary and therefore dangerous "trade union consciousness"—that made the proletariat revolutionary was not a product of its own thinking, but of the intelligentsia. It was a harsh and gloomy assessment, to Marxist ears at least, to pronounce that the class allegedly destined to save the world could not think for itself, but Lenin simply had no use for the workers if they did not enlist in the revolutionary struggle as he defined it. The workers, Lenin's good friend Maxim Gorky once observed, "are to Lenin what minerals are to the metallurgist."

Lenin also found that many members of the intelligentsia were no more helpful than the politically unaware workers. In their willingness to give priority to the workers' economic demands, even if only in the short run, Lenin's erstwhile colleagues were guilty of "subservience to spontaneity," in other words, of allowing those who were unqualified to dictate policy. Page after page of Lenin's major work on how to organize a Russian Social Democratic Party, *What Is To Be Done?*, denounced the Economists for that error.

The key to saving the movement lay in organization. Harking back to his Russian revolutionary roots, Lenin stressed that what was needed was not an organization of workers on the Western European model—which to Lenin meant an organization limited to reformist objectives—but a conspiratorial, centralized phalanx of revolutionaries, a party cut from Chernyshevsky's cloth and sewn together according to Tkachev's pattern. Lenin's own conduct as a revolutionary, his total professional dedication, his readiness to sacrifice his personal life, or anyone else's, to the cause, and his demand that others do the same, was pure Chernyshevsky. As Lenin himself put it, Chernyshevsky's *What Is to Be Done?* taught him "what a revolutionary must be like, what his rules must be, how he must go about attaining his goals, and by what method and means he can bring about their realization." Lenin's model for his party closely resembled Tkachev's; it is not for nothing that Lenin frequently told his followers to study populism's leading theorist of a conspiratorial, elite political party.

Lenin's party was to be composed of professionals, people "who shall devote to the revolution not only their spare evenings but the whole of their lives." Of course, this formula excluded the type of armchair socialist Lenin loathed. It also excluded most proletarians who, after all, spent the greater part of their lives making a living in the factories.

Lenin's professional revolutionaries were to be organized in a conspiratorial, centralized, and hierarchical network. All authority was to rest with a central committee. It would not only issue policy orders to be carried out without question by local committees, but would have the power to organize and disband those committees, as well as to select and, if need be, remove their leaders. Those at the lower levels were to consider themselves as "agents" of the central committee, "bound to submit to all its directives, bound to observe all laws and customs of this army in the field into which they have entered and which they cannot leave without permission of the commander." The military metaphor was hardly accidental. Lenin was determined to create an organization capable of waging—and winning—a war for political power.

It must be emphasized that although the party was to be made up primarily of intellectuals, Lenin totally rejected the idea that the party could function without the proletariat. As both a Marxist theorist and revolutionary tactician, Lenin recognized that such isolation in an era of mass politics would doom his party to failure. The party had to make every effort to organize in the factories and to win influence in whatever groups the proletariat might be able to form. But the party, not the working class, would determine the proper doctrine and make all the decisions. Bertram D. Wolfe has aptly summed up the relationship between Lenin's party and the proletariat, noting that "it [the party] is to use that numerous and closely packed class as its main battering ram in its struggle for power, but is itself to supply the doctrine, the watchwords, the purposes, the commands."[1]

If the party was to tell the working class what to do, and the party's central committee was to govern the party, the logical question was how the central committee itself was to make its decisions. Lenin's problem was how to reconcile two divergent and often contradictory imperatives: the need for absolute discipline and unity of action and the desire to maintain democracy within the party. Unity and discipline were vital if the party were to overcome the heavy odds facing it. Internal democracy was a tradition and commitment that no self-respecting Marxist of that era could openly flout. Marxism, after all, still drew its primary strength and leadership from countries where democratic values held sway among both workers and intellectuals. Lenin called his solution to this problem "democratic centralism." Under democratic centralism, unlimited debate could precede any decision, but once the majority decided every party member was bound to obey, regardless of his personal views. By the same token, all decisions made at the center were binding on all other party units. Democracy in this case was assured because, presumably, those at the center had been elected from below and because genuine debate preceded all decisions.

Democratic centralism turned out to be far more centralist than democratic. Rarely was there a shortage of debate under Lenin's leadership, but in a party whose leaders lived either in exile or underground in Russia, these debates took place within a tiny circle. In reality membership in the central committee, supposedly determined by elections at the lower levels or by party congresses, generally was determined by cooption: the standing committee simply selected new members whenever necessary. The discipline and unity Lenin demanded was yet another powerful regimenting force on an already centralized power structure.

None of this lack of democracy bothered Lenin. The exigencies of survival meant that fineries like elections simply would have to wait for a more auspicious time. Anyhow, the party had "more than democracy"; it had the "complete comradely confidence among revolutionaries." Lenin did not worry that the lack of democratic controls would lead to corruption. Good revolutionaries, he pronounced, "feel their responsibilities very keenly." He was quite sure, in any case, that the working class would understand that the cause was more important than the "toy forms of democracy."

Other revolutionaries, no less dedicated or radical than Lenin, disagreed. Julius Martov, Lenin's friend and collaborator in the 1890s and subsequently the leader of the Mensheviks, called his old friend a dictator. Paul Axelrod, a veteran Social Democrat of impeccable credentials—he was one of the few leaders of working-class origins—denounced what he called Lenin's "theocratic" party. He compared it to the Jacobin party of the French Revolution, the party that had attempted to impose a minority dictatorship on France by means of its notorious Reign of Terror.

Even foreign revolutionaries joined in the assault. Rosa Luxemburg, a passionate revolutionary active in the movements of three countries, known for both her unquestionable radicalism and her devotion to the working class, attacked Lenin in an article written in 1904 called "Leninism or Marxism." She deplored the "pitiless centralism" in Lenin's thinking that recalled the elitism of the premarxist Russian revolutionary movement. Lenin's party, she warned, would stifle, not educate the Russian working class, exactly the opposite of what Marxists should want for the class upon which all hopes for socialism rode. What good was it to have the central committee be the "only thinking element in the party?" Socialism could only be realized on the basis of a working class able to think for itself. Lenin's party, Luxemburg complained, would "enslave" the young working-class movement in a "bureaucratic straitjacket"; the movement would become an "automaton manipulated by a Central Committee."

> Let us speak plainly [Luxemburg concluded]. Historically the errors committed by a truly revolutionary movement are infinitely more fruitful than the infallibility of the cleverest Central Committee.

This was damaging criticism, coming as it did from such a respected colleague. The most devastating criticism, however, came from the pen of a brilliant young firebrand named Lev Davidovich Bronstein, later known as Leon Trotsky:

> Lenin's methods lead us to this: the party organization first substitutes itself for the party as a whole; then the central committee substitutes itself for the organization; and finally a single "dictator" substitutes himself for the central committee.

These words, written in 1904, left Lenin unmoved, but after his death they would haunt his successors. Trotsky's criticism turned out to be a chillingly accurate prediction of the history of Lenin's Bolshevik Party and, therefore, of doom for so many of its most devoted members. Among them was Trotsky himself.

Although it would take several decades for Lenin's methods to lead to the end that Trotsky predicted, they did lead to an immediate split in the fledgling Russian Social Democratic Party. In 1903, fifty-seven delegates representing various Social Democratic groups met at what they called their party's "Second" Congress in deference to the ill-fated 1898 meeting. During the course of the sweltering three-week summer affair that began in Brussels and ended in London, the newly organized party split into two factions. One, led by Lenin and committed to his view of party organization, called itself the "Bolsheviks," or "majority." The other, enjoying the adherence of a number of brilliant Social Democrats but in fact led by none of them, accepted the label "Mensheviks," or "minority." Its most prominent member and the closest thing it had to a leader was Martov. Lenin's claim to the "majority" label was based on a series of votes taken at the Congress after a number of delegates sympathetic to Martov's faction had walked out to protest an earlier decision. Until then Lenin's supporters had been in the minority, as they would be within the party for much of the period from 1903 to 1912, at the end of which the two factions finalized their split and became separate parties. Lenin's Bolsheviks nonetheless kept the "majority" designation they had appropriated at the Second Congress and the prestige it yielded, providing a measure of both sides' political instincts and of the reliability of the titles politicians and political parties give themselves.

Despite the patch that seemed to cover it for nine years, the fissure that had emerged between the Bolsheviks and Mensheviks in 1903 was unbridgeable. The initial dispute—over the requisites for membership in the party—revealed that there were two diametrically opposed concepts of what the party should be. Martov's relatively loose requirements reflected his vision of a mass Western-type party composed of sympathizers and workers, not just of the stalwarts manning the party machine. Lenin's strict, narrow definition pointed to the elite revolutionary phalanx he had outlined in *What Is To Be Done?* After his defeat on this issue at the start of the Second Congress, the subsequent walk-out of delegates transformed Lenin's forces into a majority, an advantage he used without pity or compromise to pass rules mandating a centralized party organization staffed, as far as possible, with his allies and supporters. Lenin's tactics shocked not only Martov, who protested about "martial law within the party," but many others, including Trotsky and even Lenin's mentor, Plekhanov. The Congress, convened amidst tears of joy after decades of waiting, ended in bitterness and division.

Lenin's outlook reflected a critical difference between himself and the Menshevik leadership. His conduct was the practical realization of the Russian revolutionary tradition's drive for power at any cost. Lenin accepted the concept that the ends justified the means. Echoing Chernyshevsky, Lenin wrote that there were no absolute standards governing revolutionary activity. Allegations that such standards existed were a "deception" and a "fraud." "Everything that is done in the proletarian cause is honest," Lenin insisted. His ferocious verbal and written attacks against fellow Social Democrats shocked many Russian and European Marxists. So did a series of dirty tricks that included extortion and fraud. Nor did Lenin shrink, as did many Social Democrats, from such out-and-out criminal activities as robbing banks to fill party coffers, or from associating with criminal elements helpful in executing these projects. Lenin labeled the rejection of what he called "expropriations" as "petty bourgeois snobbery." Besides, he added, in response to the queasiness many felt in consorting with less than honorable elements: "Sometimes a scoundrel is useful to our party precisely because he is a scoundrel."

Before the seizure of power in 1917, such tactics got Lenin into trouble with his Social Democratic colleagues, who even set up a special court to investigate his conduct. Lenin survived this, but many would say he did less well when dealing with the consequences of his actions after 1917. In any case, barely a decade after his death, one of the men who rose to prominence by organizing some of Lenin's "expropriations," a taciturn Georgian named Joseph Stalin, launched a bloodbath that claimed almost every one of Lenin's associates still alive at the time. Another of Stalin's victims, at least according to many revolutionaries and observers with some sympathy or respect for Lenin, was Leninism itself.

The Mensheviks were different. Their interpretation of Marxism affirmed that Russia would follow directly in the footsteps of its Western neighbors. The coming revolution therefore was to be what Marxists called a bourgeois revolution led by Russia's small but growing middle class, the group that was the basis of Russia's liberal movement. The role of the proletariat and its representative, the Social Democratic Party, would be to support the liberals in their struggle against the autocracy and permit them to take power. Then, while the bourgeoisie ran things, the proletariat would go into opposition. Since Russia's bourgeois regime-to-come was to mirror the capitalist societies in the West, the Russian Social Democratic party should begin to organize a broadly based party on the Western model. The Mensheviks recognized the necessity of maintaining an underground organization as long as the autocracy survived, but for them this was just a temporary necessity that would disappear when the Russian body politic became like the capitalist democratic regimes in the West.

While the Mensheviks were preparing for a bourgeois democratic regime in Russia, Lenin was building a party capable of seizing power. Yet, as a Marxist, how could Lenin justify this approach when accepted Marxist wisdom mandated that backward Russia first pass through its bourgeois democratic historical phase? Eventually he made three adjustments or additions (some have uncharitably called them distortions or revisions) to Marxism. First, in *Two Tactics of Social Democracy*, written in 1905, he postulated that Russia's peasantry, a social class Marxists traditionally rejected as hopelessly reactionary, would be the proletariat's ally in the coming revolution. Since a revolution in a Russia still 80 percent rural could not be successful without peasant support, Lenin's new strategy was a brilliant political stroke. At the same time, Lenin disagreed with the Mensheviks regarding any compromise or cooperation with Russian liberalism, the political movement of the bourgeois class enemy, whose success would strengthen capitalism and indefinitely postpone the socialist revolution.

Second, Lenin decided that special conditions arising both in Russia and abroad had made it possible for Russia to begin its revolution before the socialist revolutions broke out in the industrialized countries of the West. In *Imperialism: The Highest Stage of Capitalism* and other articles written during and after World War I, Lenin explained that capitalism had become a global system that survived by exploiting the entire world. As such, it was most vulnerable in the relatively backward capitalist countries, where social and economic problems were most acute. According to what Lenin called the "unevenness of economic and political development," which he proclaimed as an "ineluctable law of capitalism," this meant that the international capitalist system might first crack in backward, and therefore brittle, Russia. A revolution in Russia, even one led by the Bolsheviks, would not guarantee the victory of socialism. Russia still lacked the industrial base and technical skills to build a socialist society. The help Russia needed would require a socialist revolution in Western Europe, exactly what Lenin expected would follow once the Russian proletariat showed the world how to get the revolutionary ball rolling.

The final theoretical guidepost to Lenin's shortcut to a socialist revolution in Russia was his analysis of the state. His major work on this topic was *State and Revolution*, written during 1917 but not published until after the Bolshevik revolution. This pamphlet has a distinctly utopian cast unique among Lenin's writings. Large parts of it are devoted to demonstrating how easy it would be for the proletariat to run major institutions once the capitalists were overthrown. Because so much of the job consisted of "watching and bookkeeping," Lenin envisioned the bulk of the transition being accomplished within twenty-four hours. For a man with a reputation of being a pessimist, this certainly was an upbeat picture.

Lenin's concern with theory, while sometimes intense, always remained secondary to his concern for action. In this crucial respect, Lenin was radically different from most of his colleagues in the revolutionary intelligentsia. "Theory, my friend, is grey, but green is the everlasting tree of life," he once said. While others theorized, Lenin practiced. Where others were ready for noble sacrifices, Lenin struggled to survive and fight again. If circumstances dictated a change in strategy or tactics, Lenin adjusted, however painful that adjustment might be. Leon Trotsky, his right-hand man in the great days of 1917, summed up Lenin's genius when he observed that the essence of Leninism lay in "revolutionary action."

A word must be said about Lenin and power. Lenin did not want power for its own sake or as a trophy to satisfy his vanity. Other than his conviction that he was always right, Lenin was devoid of vanity. After 1917, he continued to live in modest circumstances, even continuing to wear an old coat bearing a bullet hole from a 1918 assassination attempt. He derived no pleasure from seeing his name in lights. At large public meetings and party congresses he cut an inconspicuous figure when he was not on the rostrum. A typical photograph finds a rumpled Lenin surrounded and almost obscured by other disheveled delegates. He had no desire to have monuments to himself or cities named after him. Even his detractors admit that he would have been horrified by the cult of adoration his successors built after his death, an enterprise that resulted in his body being mummified and used as a sort of holy relic for communist pilgrims and believers. Lenin had no time for anything but revolution. His goal was the destruction of capitalism and the building of socialism. His monument was to be his good deeds.

For most of the years before 1917 it looked as if there would be no socialist monuments in Russia. For years the debates between Russia's revolutionaries were so many tempests in a teapot. Their political parties were little more than frightened mice, forever hiding in the shadows and crevices of Russian society, occasionally emerging to lead a strike or demonstration before being chased underground again by the police claws of the tsarist state. Tsarism continued to have its problems, but it hung on and even managed a few reforms in the bargain. If any forces were gaining strength, they were the forces of capitalism, not socialism. And of all the revolutionary parties, for years the smallest and least significant was the Bolshevik Party. To any objective observer, it must surely have seemed that only a totally unpredictable and massive historical accident would enable Russia's various revolutionary parties to realize even their most limited dreams.

Lenin therefore was justified in fearing that he would be denied a chance to build socialism in Russia. Hopes were raised during the great upheaval of 1905 to 1907, but the upheaval was crushed, chasing Lenin and most of his colleagues back into exile and leaving those revolutionaries who remained buried further underground and farther removed than ever from their goals.

NOTE

1. Bertram Wolfe, *The Russian Revolution and Leninism or Marxism?* (Ann Arbor: University of Michigan Press, 1961), p. 13.

8

The Final Years and Last Stand

In politics there is no vengeance; there are only consequences.

————PRIME MINISTER PETER STOLYPIN (1906)

He will leap over history; and great will be the tumult when he does so. He will leave the earth: the very hills will crumble from the fear assailing them, and this fear will make the native plains arch themselves into hills . . . and Petersburg shall sink.

————ANDREY BELY (1913)

Russia's 1905 Revolution took almost everyone by surprise. Hindsight reveals that perhaps it should not have. Russia had been staggering from crisis to crisis ever since the economic slump that began in 1899 slowed Witte's development program to a crawl. In 1902, a wave of peasant disorders shook the Ukraine, and in 1903, strikes in the oil-producing city of Baku on the Caspian Sea spread at an unprecedented scale across southern Russia. These strikes were particularly disturbing to the authorities because they shattered what had been an extraordinarily sophisticated attempt by the autocracy to control and direct industrial discontent. Beginning in 1901, under the leadership of a police official named Sergei Zubatov, the government actually had been organizing workers into worker associations controlled by the police. Zubatov, a revolutionary turned police official who envisioned himself serving both the workers and the state that oppressed them, somehow had convinced his superiors that his "police socialism" could direct the proletariat's energies away from dangerous political concerns to a less-threatening concentration on wages and working conditions. The old order would then be left intact. Zubatov enjoyed considerable success in organizing his associations and, for a time, instilling them with patriotic feeling. Once he collected 50,000 workers to lay wreaths at a monument of the Tsar-Liberator Alexander II. Unfortunately for Zubatov, the workers had ideas of their own about liberation. They exploded out of control in 1903, making police socialism and Zubatov's career their first casualties.

While the workers and peasants were striking and rioting and the revolutionaries were spinning their new political webs, a liberal movement, a new force in Russian politics, was growing. Unlike the Socialist Revolutionaries and Social Democrats, the liberals' main goals were a constitution and a parliamentary regime similar to those in the capitalist West. The liberal economic program, far from endorsing one or another form of socialism, envisioned the further evolution and expansion of capitalism as well as social reform. The liberals drew their strength from the country's growing number of professionals and industrialists—Russia's long-awaited bourgeoisie—and from a small but active group of progressively minded landlords. In 1902, an influential liberal journal, *Liberation*, began publication. Organizing efforts quickened during the next two years and in 1905 produced two new political parties: the Octobrists, the more conservative of the two, and the Constitutional Democrats (Kadets), the larger and more militant party.

The liberals did not want a revolution in Russia. On the contrary, they feared that revolution would sweep them away along with the tsar. Their problem was that they were caught in a political vise. The liberals represented very few Russians. On one side, the peasants and workers, poor and hungry, had little sympathy or patience with liberal preoccupations with moderate reform and orderly, legal, and often excruciatingly slow parliamentary workings. Many revolutionaries, including Lenin, bore them a deep-seated hatred and contempt. On the other side, the autocracy refused to accept even the most moderate limits on its power, a posture that not only forced the liberals to resort at times to extra-legal means, but also brought the nation closer to the revolution that meant the end of all their hopes.

By 1903, Russia was in turmoil. The government's response was increased repression, exploitation of popular bigotry, and, finally, a blunder into war. Repression included the increased use of troops against strikers and protesters. In its attempt to direct popular discontent away from itself, in 1903 the government resorted to the old and vicious ploy of exploiting the endemic anti-Semitism of the Russian people. It instigated a pogrom (a riot in which Jews were beaten, robbed, and murdered) in the town of Kishenev. Forty-five Jews were killed and over 1,500 houses and businesses sacked. Dubbed an "anti-revolutionary counter action" by the anti-Semitic Interior Minister V. K. von Plehve, the pogroms neither stopped the revolution nor subsided when it broke out. Just as the disturbances of 1903 were a prelude to the upheaval of 1905, the earlier pogroms were only a harbinger of the horrors 1905 would bring for Russia's Jews. A one-week reign of terror that year engulfed 600 Jewish communities, leaving 1,000 dead, at least 7,000 wounded or crippled, and millions of rubles lost to vandalism. In the Black Sea port of Odessa alone, 300 Jews died, several thousand were injured, and 40,000 left economically destitute.

Von Plehve had one other scheme for avoiding revolution: a "small victorious war." Russia was pursuing an aggressive foreign policy in the Far East designed to win control of a large part of northern China and the Kingdom of Korea. Here the Russians ran into the rising power of the Japanese Empire. War broke out in January, 1904. The fighting resulted in a string of Russian defeats, while at home the war produced privation and hardship. The only arguably good news of the disastrous year 1904 was von Plehve's assassination after six months of defeats in his "small victorious war."

The autocracy's obvious incompetence, now thrown into even higher relief, spurred new demands for reform. Liberals and moderates, including distinguished members of the nobility, pressed their demands for meaningful political changes, including some form of national legislative assembly. The campaign culminated in a series of public meetings transparently disguised as banquets, held in defiance of governmental orders. All these efforts met with rejection from the tsarist authorities.

The scales finally tipped in 1905. Russia's factory workers, short of food in any case, were not inclined to banquets. Because of a rather bizarre situation that could only have occurred in tsarist Russia, the proletariat's ability to organize in St. Petersburg had been given a boost by, of all things, a police agent: a handsome, eloquent, egotistical, and highly emotional Orthodox priest named Father George Gapon. Gapon's credits eventually included associations with numerous revolutionaries—including Lenin—as well as dealings with government officials and police. In the spring of 1904, he managed to get von Plehve's support for a Zubatov-type police union in St. Petersburg. By late December the union had become involved in a strike that soon became citywide. At this point Gapon decided that his flock, wives and children included, should make a direct appeal to the tsar at his Winter Palace. On January 22, 1905, an enormous crowd, armed with religious icons and a humble petition for relief that Gapon personally planned to deliver to Nicholas II, approached the Winter Palace. It was met not by Nicholas but by mounted Cossacks and armed infantrymen. A terrible slaughter ensued. January 22, 1905, justly went down in history as "Bloody Sunday."

Bloody Sunday ignited what became the 1905 Revolution. While the tsar's armies continued to lose battles to the Japanese in the Far East, the empire was engulfed by strikes, riots, meetings, peasant rampages, assassinations, and mutinies in the armed forces. New organizations, from a Peasant Union to an umbrella liberal group called the Union of Unions, sprang up. The cries for a constitution and legislative assembly swelled and were not silenced by either the tiny concessions the tsar was willing to make or the end of the war in September 1905. Russia remained locked in turmoil, and by October the pressures became too great. A series of strikes that began in Moscow spread to St. Petersburg and ballooned into a general strike. On October 20 the workers of St. Petersburg organized a Council— or Soviet—of Workers' Deputies. The Soviet, led by Mensheviks, soon included representatives from all over the city. It also included members of the revolutionary intelligentsia, the most notable of whom turned out to be Leon Trotsky. Cornered by encroaching chaos and pressured by key advisors, Nicholas II finally reached what he called his "terrible decision." On October 30, 1905, he issued the "October Manifesto," promising his subjects basic civil rights and a parliament with genuine legislative powers. The autocracy, that centuries-old immovable object, at last had been budged.

Although tsarism teetered on the brink that October, it managed to survive. The October Manifesto won it some allies among progressives and liberals, although most of them, now organized into the Kadet Party, demanded even more concessions. But a significant minority, including a number of leading landlords and industrialists, were satisfied with the manifesto and formed their own "Octobrist" Party as a demonstration of their support. In early December the government already was strong enough to arrest the entire St. Petersburg Soviet. At the end of the month it successfully crushed a Bolshevik-led uprising in Moscow. Restoring order throughout the vast empire took longer, but the job was done, brutally and efficiently, by troops returned from the Far East. The government also enlisted the aid of reactionary gangs of thugs, called the Black Hundreds, to attack selected targets and mount pogroms against its old scapegoat, the Jews.

On the political front, the generalities of the October Manifesto were made concrete by the empire's new "Fundamental Laws," issued by Nicholas on May 6, 1906. Many liberals were extremely disappointed by the tsar's narrow interpretation of his manifesto. He retained the great majority of his traditional powers. The tsar still appointed all government ministers and they continued to be responsible only to him. He maintained complete control over foreign policy and the military part of the state budget and could veto all legislation. Under Article #87 of the Fundamental Laws, the tsar could promulgate emergency laws while the parliament—called the Duma—was not in session, although such laws required the Duma's eventual approval to remain in force. The tsar also could dissolve the Duma and call new elections at his pleasure. The Duma was elected according to a formula that discriminated heavily against the working-class and urban population, a safeguard that could not prevent the elections to the first two Dumas from producing a majority hostile to the autocracy. After disbanding them each in turn, the government in June 1907 used Article #87 to drastically revise the electoral law in favor of the empire's most conservative elements. In addition, the Fundamental Laws established a second legislative chamber above the Duma called the State Council. Half of its members were appointed by the tsar and half elected by various privileged groups, such as the clergy and the *zemstvo* nobility. The State Council could block any Duma legislation and was, in essence, another client serving the throne.

In short, the political system created by the new Fundamental Laws fell far short of Western conceptions of a parliamentary system. Russia was, as historian Richard Charques aptly put it, only a "semi-demi-Constitutional Monarchy,"[1] but even that was a dramatic change. A legislature with limited but real powers did exist, populated by representatives from various political parties enjoying legal status for the first time. In the Duma, along with reactionary parties committed to their tsar and his goal of reversing his "terrible decision," liberals of various stripes mingled with Mensheviks, Socialist Revolutionaries, and, among others, even Bolsheviks.

Hitched to a hesitant and hybrid political system, Russia still made dramatic strides forward between 1906 and the outbreak of World War I in 1914. A law enacted in 1908 committed the empire to achieving free, compulsory education by 1922. Strides also were made in expanding secondary and higher education. Russian industry grew rapidly, although at a slower rate than during the boom days of the 1890s. Despite uneven progress, by the outbreak of World War I, Russia ranked as the world's fifth-largest overall industrial power.

The most significant developments during this period occurred in agriculture, and the man behind them was Peter A. Stolypin, chairman of the Council of Ministers from mid-1906 until his assassination in 1911. His job was not an enviable one. When he took office, Russia was still gripped by peasant disorders and revolutionary activity. The Socialist Revolutionaries alone assassinated over 4,000 governmental officials between 1906 and 1910. In response to the crisis Stolypin unleashed what amounted to an official terror on the countryside. Special courts tried and executed people within twenty-four hours of their arrests. These "field courts-martial" claimed over 1,000 lives between August 1906 and April 1907, and this represented only a fraction of the executions carried out by the government between 1905 and 1908. Combined with the imposition of martial law wherever it was deemed necessary, these instant trials and the hangings that followed, the so-called Stolypin neckties, did their job. Order was restored and Stolypin was then free to get on with an even more difficult charge: overhauling Russian agriculture in a generation.

The Stolypin Reforms were an attempt to complete, as rapidly as possible, what the emancipation had begun over forty years earlier. Despite some progress in certain areas, almost two generations after the emancipation rural Russia remained poor, inefficient, volatile, and a threat to the dynasty. Land hunger remained the hallmark of the Russian peasant, still bound to backward farming techniques and his commune. Stolypin hoped to solve all these problems by turning the commune-bound Russian peasant into an independent farmer on the Western European or American model. If the autocracy, he reasoned, helped peasants to acquire their own independent, consolidated farms, they would become far more productive, and—equally important—the peasants would become conservative supporters of the tsar's regime. The monarchy, for the first time in generations, would have a broad, solid base of social support. Some peasants, many in fact, would fail once they were cast out on their own. Stolypin nonetheless felt that the potential gains in productivity and support from the successful peasants would far outweigh any difficulties that might arise from those who failed. Russia and the monarchy, he emphasized, could be strengthened only if they relied not "on the drunken and the weak, but on the sober and the strong."

The heart of Stolypin's "wager on the strong" was legislation that released peasants from membership in their communes, allowed them to claim their land allotments as private property, and finally, permitted them to consolidate their scattered parcels into one plot. Other reforms promoted peasant resettlement in sparsely populated regions of central Asia and Siberia, eliminated the remaining legal disabilities on the peasantry, and provided financial help to buy land. When he began his program in 1906, Stolypin asked for twenty years of peace, after which, he promised, Russia would be "unrecognizable." This was a bold boast, but there were many who believed that this tough, able, and single-minded servant of the tsar might succeed where so many others had failed.

A decade after Stolypin began his work the Russian countryside was indeed changing. About one half of the households in European Russia held their land under individual titles. Approximately 10 percent had consolidated their plots. It was a good start, but the race already was being lost. By 1916 Stolypin had been dead for five years and Russia was two terrible years into World War I and falling apart.

The outbreak of the war was not the only limit on the Stolypin Reforms. Like Witte before him, Stolypin had to contend with entrenched reactionary forces. Reactionary nobles and bureaucrats tried to thwart Stolypin's attempts to extend the *zemstvos* to Russia's western provinces. Their constant harassment undermined the prime minister's authority, both with the population at large and with the tsar. At times, however, Stolypin had only himself to blame for his troubles. A devoted nationalist and advocate of Russification, Stolypin carried out repressive and discriminatory policies that antagonized, among others, millions of Finns, Poles, and Ukrainians. Russification was hardly conducive to the twenty years of peace Stolypin said he needed.

Another source of Stolypin's difficulties was his failure to enlist the support of moderate, progressive political elements. The Kadets were determined to turn the Duma into a genuine parliament with powers far beyond those specified in the Fundamental Laws. Led by the distinguished historian Paul Miliukov, the Kadets' attitude placed them in direct confrontation with Stolypin and the government. The more moderate Octobrists accepted the limits on the Duma and initially hoped to be able to cooperate with the prime minister and even join with him in governing the empire. In return they insisted that a number of ministerial seats be reserved for individuals from outside the tsarist bureaucracy. This Stolypin refused to do. The Russian government continued as before to be based on nothing more representative than the corrupt and despised bureaucracy.

This failure to broaden the regime's political base created problems for Stolypin, but he was still able to govern, albeit with more difficulty. In 1907, he simply dissolved the Duma and rewrote the electoral law. The new Duma was sufficiently conservative and pliable to enable the government to work with it. The real losers were the liberals and moderates. The autocracy, having used small concessions to win breathing space and recover its footing, now became as unmovable as before 1905. There were some differences of opinion about what to do. The Octobrist leadership clearly feared the Russian masses more than the Russian autocracy. More militant politicians, such as Miliukov, were ready to flirt with the revolutionaries. He hoped that the revolutionaries could be used to batter down the autocracy, after which the liberals would govern in a parliamentary and republican Russia. (Later, Miliukov became more fearful of revolution and was willing to settle for a genuine constitutional monarchy.) The liberals' dilemma and their inability to function as an independent force was a direct function of the weakness of the Russian bourgeoisie, an observation made many times by political pundits of varying leanings. As Nicholas Berdyaev, a former Marxist turned conservative religious philosopher, put it: "In Russia it was not the communist revolution but the liberal bourgeois revolution that proved to be a utopia."

In the aftermath of the 1905 defeat, however, the prospects of any revolution seemed, if not utopian, at least remote. During the period of upheaval the Socialist Revolutionaries had enjoyed some success in organizing peasant uprisings, but army troops had crushed them. Subsequently, unable to agree on a new revolutionary strategy, the party split into two parts. The Social Democrats, already divided, attempted to learn some lessons from the revolution's defeat. These lessons are important because of what they reveal about the Bolsheviks and Mensheviks and because they turned out to be the difference between success and failure when, much to everyone's surprise, the revolutionaries were given a second chance in 1917.

During 1905, the Mensheviks, insisting that they were involved in a "bourgeois" revolution, tailored their activities to fit that revolution. They welcomed the formation of the St. Petersburg Soviet, declaring that it was the nucleus of a broadly based workers' party. The Mensheviks readily cooperated with other socialist groups inside the Soviet and with liberals outside the Soviet. They had, for example, joined in the liberal "banquet" campaign of 1904 and, at the Social Democrats' Fourth Congress in 1906, they advocated an alliance with the Kadets. In their view, the defeat of the 1905 Revolution proved that the proletariat still had to bide its time and build its strength. Russia's next revolution still would have to be "bourgeois." Only afterwards, as Russian capitalism matured and the proletariat grew, would the proletariat's chance for power come.

Lenin and the Bolsheviks also had a lesson to learn. Their performance during the 1905 Revolution was not impressive. Lenin did not even make it back to Russia until November. During the early months of 1905, when it seemed possible that the tsarist regime might collapse, Lenin had doubted the chances of achieving a socialist revolution. Later he equivocated about the St. Petersburg Soviet. On the one hand, he went beyond the Mensheviks and asserted that the Soviet could be the embryo of a transitional revolutionary government. On the other hand, Lenin distrusted any mass, spontaneous institution that he and his Bolsheviks could not control. The Bolsheviks, in fact, played a relatively minor role in the St. Petersburg Soviet. They were more active in the Moscow Soviet, especially in leading it into an armed uprising in late December 1905. But that bloody failure hardly added to the Bolsheviks', or Lenin's, luster.

Amidst the rubble of the 1905 failure, Lenin honed his two weapons: Marxist theory and revolutionary technique. Out of the realization that the Russian proletariat alone was too weak to make a revolution arose Lenin's idea of a proletarian-peasant alliance (led by the proletariat, of course) and a concerted effort to develop a platform that would appeal to the peasantry. Lenin also worked hard on practical matters. Originally, he favored boycotting the Duma elections, but he reversed himself when he concluded that the Duma, whatever its weaknesses, was an excellent soapbox. In 1906, a variety of pressures, including strong sentiment for unity among the rank and file of both factions, forced him to agree to heal the Bolshevik-Menshevik split. Lenin went through the motions, all the while maintaining a separate Bolshevik organization. When he finally engineered a formal party split in 1912, he seized the organization's funds and records. Finances, always a problem during the dark days after 1905, were seen to by a variety of questionable measures including fraud, extortion, counterfeiting, and a famous series of bank robberies. These activities got Lenin into trouble not only with the Mensheviks, but with the entire European socialist movement, which in effect censured him for conduct unbecoming of a revolutionary.

Lenin remained undeterred. Neither these activities nor his faction's association with the criminal elements sometimes required to carry them out embarrassed him. Nor was he disturbed when those who could not accept his leadership left the party. During the difficult years between the 1905 Revolution and the outbreak of World War I in 1914, the Bolsheviks shrank in size and remained isolated on the political fringe. Yet through it all Lenin never lost sight of his goal. At the outbreak of the war many Marxists forgot their revolutionary priorities and rallied instead to their respective national colors. Others opposed the war from a pacifist perspective and worked to restore the peace. But it was Lenin and a few others who called for turning the conflict into a revolutionary war. This was the message of his book, *Imperialism, The Highest Stage of Capitalism*.

The calls by the left for a negotiated peace or a revolutionary war—depending on which group was making the call—fell on deaf ears. Like battered boxers who refuse to fall, the belligerent powers remained on their feet, and the war dragged on. Even Lenin became demoralized. "We of the older generation may not see the decisive battles of the coming revolution," he told a Swiss audience in January 1917. Within two months the Russian autocracy collapsed.

Because of the momentous changes that were to overwhelm Russia after the revolutionary year of 1917, historians have tried to fix the causes of tsarism's collapse. Pared down to its essentials, the question is whether Russian society was headed for a new stability or toward disintegration in the decade prior to World War I. In other words, did the war destroy a viable society or simply hasten that society's inevitable collapse?

Certainly there had been progress. In the half-century since emancipation, Russia's entire social order had begun to change under Western influences. This was an unprecedented development for a country that historically had done everything it could to exclude all Western influences except for technology. After 1861, serfdom was swept away, local government and the judiciary were reformed, education created a vast new reading public receptive to Western ideas, capitalism sank deep roots, and entirely new classes similar to those in Europe developed. The pace of change quickened in the 1890s. In the generation between 1890 and 1914, Russia experienced one of the highest industrial growth rates in the world. On the eve of World War I, only the United States, Germany, Great Britain, and France stood ahead of Russia as industrial powers. Additional progress marked the decade prior to the war. In the countryside, the Stolypin Reforms began to shape a new, independent, and prosperous peasantry whose conservatism might have become a vital new prop for the monarchy. Even the monarchy itself changed. After 1905, Russia finally had a parliament of sorts with real, if severely limited, powers. Censorship was eased.

The generation before World War I also witnessed a flowering of Russian culture, the "Silver Age" that ranks second in Russian history only to the glorious "Golden Age" of Pushkin, Dostoevsky, and Tolstoy. Although the "Silver Age" produced no equal to those giants, it did create for an unprecedentedly broad audience a great diversity of superb literature, music, and art. Regardless of the empire's other difficulties, Russian culture, studded with such talented artists as novelist and poet Andrey Bely, poet Alexander Blok, composer Igor Stravinsky, dancer Vaslav Nijinsky, and painter Vasily Kandinsky, to name only a very few, stood with the best Europe had to offer.

But this impressive new social landscaping rested astride deep and shifting societal fault lines. Russian industry progressed, but only by producing a very poor proletariat along with its goods and, until the Stolypin Reforms, by living off governmental policies that worsened conditions in the countryside. Trade unions, legalized in 1906, still labored under severe restrictions and remained weak. Meanwhile the workers remained dissatisfied. After a decline in labor militancy and strikes between 1906 and 1910, the tide of unrest began to rise again. Strikes doubled in 1911. In 1912, the country again trembled with shock and anger when workers at the Lena gold fields in Siberia, on strike to improve their miserable wages and shorten their 5 A.M.-to-7 P.M. workday, had their strike broken by troops at the cost of 170 dead and almost 400 wounded. More than 725,000 workers struck in that year. In 1913, 887,000 workers went out. And 1,250,000—out of a *total* work force of barely 3 million—struck in the *first half* of 1914 to back up their demands both for economic improvements and for potentially much more dangerous political reforms.

There simply had not been enough progress to assuage all the pain. When measured on a per capita basis, Russia was losing rather than gaining ground relative to its European competitors. In the fifty years between 1860 and 1910, Russia was unable to overtake even Spain or Italy, much less the real industrial powers, in that vital measure of industrial progress.

In 1900, Russian per capita production had been one-eighth that of the United States and one-sixth that of Germany; on the eve of the war those figures were one-eleventh and one-eighth, respectively. In 1913, Russia produced only one-tenth as much coal and barely half as much steel as Great Britain, a country with less than half Russia's population. Over half of the empire's industrial equipment still had to be imported.

In agriculture the situation was no better. The Stolypin Reforms produced poor peasants as well as more prosperous ones by removing the protective cloak of the commune. Agricultural production rose significantly between 1900 and 1913, but the average Russian could hardly have noticed. Exports of grain were on the average 50 percent higher in the last several years before the war than during the first years of the century, and a rising percentage of the crops that remained in Russia were industrial crops, like cotton, that fed machines rather than people. In fact, it is likely that the average Russian in 1914 had no more to eat than his counterpart had in 1860.

Other problems plagued the empire. Millions of its non-Russian subjects hated the regime. So did many Russians who felt the weight of state oppression because they chose to practice a form of Christianity other than the officially endorsed Russian Orthodoxy. The dangerous cleavage between the educated few and the uneducated masses still remained unbridged. Most of the elite continued to be alienated from the official political process. All Russians also still chafed under the dead weight of the ubiquitous Russian police.

All the while the government teetered on an eroding foundation. In 1914, its largest source of revenue was the state liquor monopoly, with the intoxication of the Russian people producing 30 percent of what were understandably dubbed "drunken budgets." The men Nicholas appointed to head his council of ministers during the war were ignorant, incompetent, senile, or all three. One, J. L. Goremykin, a senile man in his mid-seventies, was labeled by a colleague as one of the "worst products of the Russian bureaucracy." His successor, Boris Sturmer, suffered a lack of intellect that one colleague felt "prevented him from directing anything." Tsarist Russia's last prime minister, N. D. Golitsin, actually begged Nicholas to find somebody else for the job. That probably was the best advice Golitsin ever gave, considering that he was, as the economist and historian Michael Florinsky has noted, "entirely without experience in state affairs."[2] As bad as these men were, they were better than Rasputin, whose influence over the empress and her weak-willed husband increased with each crisis-packed year.

It was with such leadership that Russia entered the inferno of World War I. Although the causes of the war are complex and are still debated, much of the blame must go to the rivalries between the Great Powers and the frustrated nationalist sentiment in Central Europe and the Balkans. Russia's involvement in the war is one thing for which Nicholas II and his government cannot be blamed. It is difficult to imagine how any Russian government committed to traditional interests could have avoided the fatal plunge that claimed all Europe's Great Powers, each of them seemingly gigantic lemmings rushing to a raging sea.

The war began, as wars often do, with a patriotic rally to the colors. Soon, however, twentieth-century warfare began to exact its price. The war strained even Europe's most advanced industrial economies to their limits, and Russia now paid dearly for its backwardness. To the two colossal burdens the old regime had borne before 1914—the unequal competition with the highly industrialized Western Powers and the immense strain caused by rapid social and economic change in the face of limited political change—was added the supreme test of World War I. Russia's semi-industrialized economy, pushed beyond its limits by the skyrocketing demands of modern warfare and the demoralization caused by military defeats, began to fall apart. Economic dislocation immediately generated tremendous social discontent and turmoil. The political system, still an antiquated bureaucratic relic despite the limited reforms of the past fifty years, was woefully overmatched.

It took about a year for Russia's economy to falter seriously. Russia was unable to export to Germany, once an important customer but now a deadly enemy, and at the same time was compelled to increase imports to feed its hungry war machine. The resulting enormous trade imbalance produced severe inflation. Yet all the imports were not enough to meet Russia's needs. Geography and history seemingly had conspired again by placing Russia's enemies—Germany, Austria-Hungary, and Turkey— between itself and its allies in Western Europe. The partially successful enemy blockade caused Russia to suffer grave shortages of raw materials and vital industrial machinery that could not be produced at home. Production fell in several key industries. The eventual mobilization of 15 million men disrupted both industrial and agricultural production, while the enemy's occupation of Russia's economically advanced western regions added to the economic difficulties and also created a massive refugee problem.

Distributing those resources that were available became another unsolvable problem. Russia's railroad system, inadequate in peacetime, was swamped by the vastly larger wartime burden. Eventually it began to deteriorate as worn-out equipment was not replaced. Equally serious, consumer goods disappeared in the wake of industry's conversion to military production, and the peasantry, unable to find goods to buy, began to hoard the food it produced. Eventually the unavailability of manufactured goods and farm machinery caused agricultural production to decline. The cities began to lack food. As it turned out, it was a food shortage in Petrograd (as the capital now was called, instead of the Germanic St. Petersburg) that sparked the crisis that brought down the monarchy in 1917.

The government's almost unbelievable incompetence exacerbated the crisis. Russia was unprepared for war. One year after the outbreak of fighting, one general lamented that "No amount of science can tell us how to wage war without ammunition, without rifles, and without guns." To enforce sobriety, Russia in August 1914 became the world's first country to enact a national prohibition. Liquor, of course, continued to flow illegally. The only documented results of the prohibition were pointed out by an exasperated member of the Duma budget committee who complained, "Never since the dawn of history has a single country, in time of war, renounced the principal source of its revenue."

All the while Rasputin's influence grew. When Nicholas went to the war zone to take over direct command of the army (a blunder that directly tied him to every military failure), the empress and her wild-eyed "holy man" made important decisions of state back in the capital. By 1916, Rasputin controlled most important ministerial appointments. Men who could barely help themselves now were chosen to lead Russia in its moment of dire emergency. The empress, meanwhile, displayed her lack of political acumen by calling for the exile to Siberia of leading Duma members. Not surprisingly, both she and Rasputin were widely accused of treason.

Support and sympathy for the monarchy was evaporating. Rasputin's assassination in December 1916 eliminated him, but not the leadership vacuum. The tsar's refusal to consider reforms proposed by leading Duma moderates and liberals embittered and alienated many would-be allies. During January and February of 1917 strikes and demonstrations rocked Petrograd. Disorder increased nationwide as well. Prophecies of doom and rumors of upheaval were everywhere.

Yet Nicholas remained unperturbed. He was oblivious both to the immediate crisis and to historical developments that dictated that by 1917 even the Russian tsar would have to respond to his people's needs and demands if he were to win their support and survive. When warned by a foreign diplomat that he had to regain his people's confidence, Nicholas rejected the well-intentioned warning. The problem, he indicated, was that the people had to regain *his* confidence. The tsar, trapped in a changing and unfriendly world he did not understand, chose to live instead in a world of his own.

The remarkable thing about the revolution that put an end to the 300-year-old Romanov dynasty and the even-older Russian autocracy is how quickly and quietly it all finally happened. In March 1917 the exhausted and exasperated Russian people did little more than riot for several days in their capital city and the old political order collapsed. A labor dispute that erupted at Petrograd's Putilov works quickly ballooned into a series of strikes involving over 200,000 workers. On March 8, large crowds of hungry strikers clamoring for bread were joined by demonstrators celebrating International Women's Day. Nicholas commanded that order be restored, but troops sent to do the job, sickened by having to shoot down their countrymen, soon mutinied instead. The mutiny spread quickly; suddenly there was no authority in the capital loyal to the tsar. On March 11, the day the troop mutiny began, Nicholas dissolved the Duma. This time a defiant Duma refused to comply. The next day, March 12, a group of its leading members set up a "Provisional Committee" to cope with Russia's crisis, as the tsar obviously could not. (On March 14, that committee reconstituted itself as Russia's "Provisional Government.") Also on March 12, in the very same building that had housed the Duma and now housed the Provisional Committee, a self-appointed contingent of workers, soldiers, and members of the revolutionary intelligentsia organized what they soon called the "Petrograd Soviet of Workers' and Soldiers' Deputies," an institution recalling the renowned 1905 St. Petersburg Soviet, but whose purpose was still unclear. Nicholas II, stranded on his royal train because nobody would follow his orders, stood completely alone. Everyone he spoke with, including his most trusted military officers, told him that his time was up. On March 15, the tsar bowed to the inevitable by abdicating on behalf of himself and his hemophiliac son in favor of his brother, the Grand Duke Michael. When Michael refused the throne, the Romanov dynasty, which had begun just over 300 years earlier with a luckier Michael, came to an end. The autocracy that had guided Russia's destiny for so long was gone.

NOTES

1. Richard Charques, *The Twilight of Imperial Russia* (New York: Oxford University Press, 1958), p. 30.
2. Michael Florinsky, *The End of the Russian Empire* (New York: Collier Books, 1961), p. 90.

PART THREE

Lenin's Russia

9

1917: Russia's Two Revolutions

Surely some revelation is at hand;
Surely the Second Coming is at hand; . . .
And what rough beast, its hour come round at last,
Slouches towards Bethlehem to be born?

———WILLIAM BUTLER YEATS

The events of March 1917 ended a heretofore unprecedented phase in Russian history. The fifty-six-year period between 1861 and 1917 was the only era under the tsars when Western influence was pervasive in Russia and not confined to economic development projects, technological and scientific imports, or a sampling of Western intellectual delicacies by the elite. The society as a whole was changing as Europe seemingly was pulling Russia, inch by inch, across the Urals in a social, cultural, and economic sense. The March Revolution opened up new vistas for change along Western lines by eliminating the autocracy, the greatest obstacle to that process. Yet it also created opportunities for long-suppressed forces working in completely different directions. In the middle of a world war, the main battle for the Russian people suddenly shifted to the home front, where the central issue was not the country's relations with foreigners, but how Russians would relate to each other.

The revolution that toppled Nicholas II and ended the Romanov dynasty was relatively quick and painless, lasting about a week and claiming only about 1,500 casualties. But the removal of the autocracy did not eliminate the myriad of problems that had precipitated the revolution. Russia remained trapped in an unsuccessful and unpopular war that had bled the nation and left its battered army barely able to fight.

The economy was dangerously close to collapse. In the cities and towns food was scarce. Industrial production was declining dangerously. Peasant land hunger remained unsatiated. And the autocracy's collapse, even as it solved one problem by eliminating a derelict system of government, added a new one in its place—what form of government should Russia now adopt?

The removal of the Romanovs created a tremendous power vacuum. In the wake of the collapse of a political order of 300 years standing, no group had a legitimate claim to govern. The result was a peculiar and unstable situation that came to be called "dual power." Two institutions shared political authority, in so much as any authority existed at all: the Provisional Government—Russia's self-proclaimed interim government—and the Petrograd Soviet. The Provisional Government was the creature of leading Duma moderates and liberals. As such, it lacked any enthusiastic support from the bulk of the Russian people. Because of its commitment to establishing a Western-type parliamentary system in a country inexperienced with and suspicious of representative government, the Provisional Government faced long odds from the beginning. Its indecisiveness and mistakes quickly lengthened those odds.

The Provisional Government's chances of success were further diminished by the presence of the Petrograd Soviet of Workers' and Soldiers' Deputies. The Soviet was a hybrid political species, combining the trappings of a government, a political convention, and a mob. Composed of representatives from the factories and military units in and around the capital, the Soviet lacked both a consistent formula for selecting its membership and a defined area of responsibility or jurisdiction. Nonetheless, its strategically placed popular support gave it more power than the Provisional Government. The Soviet's status was further complicated by the attitude of the Mensheviks and Socialist Revolutionaries, the two socialist parties that controlled it from March to September. According to their thinking, the Soviet could not aspire to political power because Russia was going through its "bourgeois" revolution. The Soviet's historically mandated task was to permit the bourgeoisie to govern while it served as a nongovernmental guardian of the revolution and the interests of the working masses.

Because of support from the workers and soldiers of Petrograd and from soviets that soon sprouted up all over the country, the Petrograd Soviet soon made its influence felt, mainly at the expense of the Provisional Government's credibility and its efforts to set Russia's house in order. The Soviet itself accomplished little that was constructive. "Dual power" really meant the Provisional Government had very little power.

Meanwhile, the bulk of the population—the land-hungry peasants, the exploited and hungry factory workers, the oppressed and agitated national minorities, and the weary and demoralized soldiers (themselves largely peasants)—confronted the Provisional Government with demands for reforms that they hoped would improve their lives. Many of these the government could or would not meet, while what it could do satisfied very few people. It did, for example, abolish all religious, national, and class discrimination, eliminate many of the oppressive aspects of military discipline, and guarantee a wide range of civil and political liberties. These were significant advances, and even a cynic like Lenin admitted Russia had become the "freest country in the world." Yet none of these decrees raised anybody's standard of living. The peasants still did not have their land. The workers still faced inadequate wages, ruinous wartime inflation, employer lock-outs and food shortages. The national minorities still lacked the autonomy or independence they craved.

This was bad enough, but besides their demands for immediate measures to improve their lives, Russia's masses were raising more fundamental and dangerous issues. Their hatred for those above them went far beyond the tsar, his bureaucracy, and the nobility; it encompassed all of Russia's economic and social elite, including those who staffed the new government and the intellectuals who ran Russia's various political parties, whatever their protestations or political orientation. The average peasant or worker did not trust any government and saw a plot where often there was mainly hesitation or inaptitude. Thus, when elections to the promised Constituent Assembly were postponed, largely because of technical difficulties, many people were sure that the delay was an upper-class conspiracy. Many local soviets even openly opposed the Provisional Government and its attempt to establish some central authority in Russia to replace the fallen tsar.

For the bulk of the Russian people, freedom meant an escape from their crushing poverty and the governmental authority that always had perpetuated their misery. It meant the right finally to take what they wanted and needed without regard for the priorities of any government, irrespective of whatever well-intentioned gentlemen staffed it or what noble ends it proclaimed. As historian Marc Ferro has observed, Russia's masses seemed to want " . . . not a better government, but no government at all."[1] In such a context, there was no popular mandate for representative government as it existed in the West. The peasants frequently did not even know what the various political parties stood for.

In order to understand the complexity and chaos that followed the March Revolution, it is helpful to focus on three divisions that marked Russia's political life. The first divided Russia's privileged classes into two camps: moderate/liberal and socialist. This split was reflected by the tense relationship between the Provisional Government as originally constituted and the Petrograd Soviet. By making it more difficult for anyone to govern, this cleavage helped leave open the door to further upheaval.

The second division was the old dichotomy between Russia's privileged elite—including those elements running both the Provisional Government and the Petrograd Soviet—and the masses. In 1917, however, this division had a new and crucial dimension; the masses finally had the means to become politically articulate. During the course of the year, the Russian people, for the first time in their history, established a great variety of mass organizations in which they participated directly and through which they projected considerable political power. These organizations—local soviets, factory committees, soldier committees, peasant committees, the Petrograd Soviet itself, and the like—activated and mobilized enormous numbers of people at the bottom of Russia's social pyramid. The nature of the resulting tension was fairly straightforward. The Russian masses increasingly demanded far more radical social changes than the Provisional Government or the Soviet's leadership were willing to sanction. This inevitably weakened the Provisional Government and discredited the Socialist Revolutionaries and Mensheviks, the parties that controlled the Soviet, exposing them as insufficiently revolutionary to lead the aroused masses. This division also furthered the likelihood of another upheaval.

The third division was between those parties that had a viable response to the increasing turmoil and those that did not. As the masses became more frustrated and radical during 1917, most of the major political parties, including the Kadets, the SRs, and the Mensheviks, attempted to restrain them. Only the Lenin-led Bolshevik Party, which until 1917 had been relegated to the fringes of Russian political life, was prepared to go along with and encourage the angry masses. The gulf between the Bolsheviks and the other socialist parties was therefore crucial, for the Bolsheviks were not swamped, like those who tried to contain the revolutionary wave; they were in a position to ride it to power.

The Provisional Government that the Bolsheviks eventually overthrew was more provisional than a government. Because it shared the stage uneasily with the upstart Soviet, the Provisional Government was called the "half power." Yet even that pejorative term was overly generous. The new government drew most of its support from Russia's professional classes and the progressive elements of the nobility and business community, a thin and fragile layer of Russian society. It drew no strength from what were increasingly the real arbiters of power in Russia: the crowds of workers and soldiers in the capital who had first attacked the autocracy, the army that had been unwilling to come to the old regime's rescue, and the peasants.

Moreover, the new government's leading members were ill-suited to swim in a revolutionary tide. Prince George Lvov, the prime minister, was a *zemstvo* notable but not a vigorous leader on the national level. He was overshadowed by members of his cabinet from the start. Among them was Foreign Minister Paul Miliukov, a man who understood the rules of parliamentary procedure better than he understood the masses banging at the gates. The minister most closely identified with the masses was the SR lawyer Alexander Kerensky, who held the justice portfolio. He unfortunately was far better at talking to the masses than at listening to them. Kerensky also was a member of the Soviet's executive committee. As the only person during the early days of the revolution who sat on both the Provisional Government and the Soviet, Kerensky provided an initial, though ineffectual, link between the two bodies. Later, when more SRs and Mensheviks from the Soviet joined Kerensky in the government, this link became a chain that dragged down these socialist parties when the Provisional Government went under.

The Provisional Government's haplessness was established at the very beginning by the Soviet's famous "Order Number One." At a time when anarchy threatened to engulf Russia and powerful enemy armies occupied large parts of her western provinces, Order Number One effectively destroyed the government's control over its army. The Soviet was concerned lest the army be used by conservative forces to crush the revolution. Order Number One therefore stipulated, among other things, that all military units elect their own soviets to deal with nonmilitary matters. It also made the Soviet rather than the government the ultimate authority to which the army was responsible. Order Number One eliminated what was left of the army's fighting ability and shackled the new government before it took a single step. Barely a week after Nicholas's abdication, the man who was supposed to be in charge of the armed forces, Minister of War Alexander Guchkov, summed up his problems and those of his government:

> The Provisional Government possesses no real power and its orders are executed only in so far as this is permitted by the Soviet of Workers' and Soldiers' Deputies, which holds in its hands most important elements of real power. . . . It is possible to say directly that the Provisional Government exists only while this is permitted by the Soviet of Workers' and Soldiers' Deputies.

The Provisional Government bore other burdens as well. The moderates and liberals who initially staffed it wanted Russia to embrace a legal and parliamentary order similar to those found in the West. They therefore insisted that major social reforms await the convocation of a nationally elected Constituent Assembly. It was felt that only such a body would have the proper mandate to both establish a permanent government and promulgate fundamental social reforms. The impatient peasants therefore were told they would have to wait for their land. The national minorities, aside from the Poles, who were promised independence, were informed that their autonomy likewise would have to wait. To make matters worse, while the Provisional Government antagonized the overwhelming majority of the population, it tainted its own legitimacy. According to its legalistic logic, a Constituent Assembly had to confirm any permanent government. That left the government stuck with its ethereal "provisional" status. Topping matters off, the Constituent Assembly itself was postponed because it proved to be difficult to arrange the elections. When it finally did meet, in January 1918, the Provisional Government had been overthrown.

The Provisional Government made another grave error when it reaffirmed Russia's commitment to the Allied war effort and aims. By 1917, while there was no clear national consensus on the war, the nation clearly was war-weary, and the Soviet's call late in March for a peace "without annexations and indemnities" probably represented what the largest number of Russians supported. Sentiment was different in the government, where the leadership was highly nationalistic and sympathetic to the Allied cause. These leaders, particularly Miliukov, assumed that the masses shared their enthusiasm for a vigorous new war effort to secure Constantinople and the Dardanelles in the Ottoman Empire and spheres of influence in China. The disturbances that followed Miliukov's announcement of his foreign policy forced his resignation. The government did not learn from Miliukov's fate. Instead, it began planning an offensive against the Germans and Austrians, which resulted in a disastrous defeat.

Finally, while it planned to fight the mighty Germans, the Provisional Government could not ensure order at home. It was too weak to replace the old tsarist administrative apparatus, which had disintegrated. At the same time, the new government's policies made a difficult job even harder. The police, for example, were replaced with a voluntary militia, which neither helped restore order nor strengthened the regime. It only made things easier for the government's enemies.

While the Provisional Government was stumbling along, the Petrograd Soviet had problems of its own. It was a chaotic body, made up of about 1,500 deputies elected by factories and military units in and around the capital. Constant elections in the factories and military units meant that the Soviet's composition was always in flux. Many of those in attendance at any given meeting were not elected by anyone, but, as in the case of members of the revolutionary intelligentsia, simply were admitted by the Soviet or even self-appointed. In this chaos, real decisions could only be made by the Soviet's executive committee, a body dominated not by workers or soldiers but by members of the politically more experienced intelligentsia.

From March to September the Soviet was controlled by a coalition of

Mensheviks and Socialist Revolutionaries. The Mensheviks and SRs, like the liberals in the Provisional Government, while free from tsardom, were still prisoners of their own ideology. The loosely organized SRs—their leader Victor Chernov once referred to his party as a "herd"—generally deferred to the Mensheviks. They, in turn, deferred to their dog-eared Marxist revolutionary blueprints, which defined the current revolution as being "bourgeois." Therefore, the socialists and their political instrument—the Soviet—would not take power, regardless of the ineptitude and weakness of the Provisional Government. Practical considerations reinforced this conclusion among the Mensheviks, particularly the fear of a violent reaction by the propertied classes and the army against any socialist bid for power. So the Soviet contented itself with supporting the Provisional Government in its efforts to implement social reform, while at the same time, as it did with Order Number One, making sure that neither the government nor any other potentially unfriendly actor could threaten the working masses.

Russia thus lingered in a political vacuum. As Prince Lvov observed, a government possessing "authority without power" faced a Soviet representing "power without authority." That situation was too unstable to survive for very long; it created an opportunity for any politician perceptive and ruthless enough to exploit it. That politician was Lenin. Although he certainly was not expecting the revolution when it occurred, and at first assumed it was merely an Allied-orchestrated plot to preclude a separate Russian-German peace, he quickly realized his chance had come. Yet he could only gaze at it from afar, for March 1917 found Lenin in Switzerland. After several frustrating weeks he managed to reach Russia, courtesy of the German High Command, which decided to grant him and several other revolutionaries safe passage in the expectation that such people would further disrupt things in Petrograd and drive Russia from the war. In the short run Lenin did not disappoint them; in the long run he astounded not only his unwitting benefactors, but many others as well.

One of the reasons Lenin was in such a hurry to get back to Russia was that his Bolsheviks on the scene, his years of effort to set them apart from the other socialist parties notwithstanding, were behaving like everyone else. Led by Lev Kamenev and Joseph Stalin, the Bolsheviks had accepted the prevailing view that the current revolution was "bourgeois" and that socialists consequently should abstain from power. Worse, the Bolsheviks actually were discussing reunification with the Mensheviks, a prospect that threatened the political machine Lenin had been building for fifteen years. The day he set foot in Russia, Lenin repudiated any thought of cooperation with the Provisional Government. The next day, in a dramatic speech that left even his most avid supporters stunned, Lenin spelled out his position in what are known as his "April Theses."

The April Theses were designed to restore the Bolsheviks' ideological insulation and militancy and set them apart from their rivals. Lenin's major points were: no support for the "imperialist" war effort; no support for the Provisional Government; the transfer of "all power" to the Soviets as soon as possible; confiscation of the landed estates for the benefit of the poor peasants; and no reconciliation or reunification with the Mensheviks. Lenin's program, whatever its failings in terms of traditional Marxism— he was, after all, closing down Russia's bourgeois revolution after barely a month—was closer to the popular pulse than that of any other political party. Certain refinements made it even more so. These included support for what was called "workers' control," a vague concept that to some meant worker participation in management decisions in the factories and to others meant a complete takeover of those factories, a contradiction Lenin did not bother to clarify. The Bolsheviks also unequivocally endorsed the right of national self-determination for all of Russia's ethnic groups.

Along with a program that had an immediate appeal to so many, the Bolsheviks had slogans the people could understand: "Land," "Bread," "Peace," and "All Power to the Soviets." They also translated the sympathy these slogans aroused into concrete support by organizing more effectively than anyone else in such key mass associations as the urban soviets, the factory committees, and the soldiers' committees. With Lenin at the helm, the Bolsheviks also had the Russian politician who proved best able to navigate in the treacherous and unpredictable revolutionary rapids.

Against a background of government ineptitude, the vacillation of the Mensheviks and the SRs, the continued decline of living conditions, and their own organizing efforts, Bolshevik strength began to grow. In March they had fared very poorly in the elections to the Petrograd Soviet, winning only about fifty of approximately 1,500 seats. By June, at a meeting of representatives from soviets all over the country, the First All-Russian Congress of Soviets, the Bolsheviks had a fairly impressive 15 percent of the delegates, although the SRs and the Mensheviks still had an overwhelming majority.

The Bolsheviks also were doing well in the streets. Ironically, they, the alleged elitists, were proving to be the best practitioners of the new art of mass politics. The Bolshevik leadership had scheduled an antigovernment demonstration to take place while the Congress was in session, but had been forced to cancel it under pressure from the Congress's Menshevik and SR majority. The Congress then proceeded to stage a demonstration of its own, only to find that slogans on the placards indicated that the more than 400,000 workers and soldiers who showed up strongly supported the Bolsheviks. Bolshevik strength grew in the urban soviets, the burgeoning trade unions, the factory committees set up in the plants and shops, and the military units. The soldiers were particularly important —the Bolsheviks remembered that the 1905 revolution failed when the army remained loyal to the tsar. This time Lenin intended to have the army on his side, or at least to neutralize it, and the concerted Bolshevik effort among the troops reflected this concern. Overall, between March and July the Bolshevik party grew from 25,000 to about 250,000 members, an increase of over 1,000 percent.

Credit for the Bolsheviks' success must go to Lenin; since 1902 he had worked to create an elite political organization that would stand apart from Russia's other socialist parties. It had not been an easy task, as his troops several times had drifted toward reconciliation with the Mensheviks. In 1917, Lenin again faced that old problem as well as poor discipline in the ranks. His April Theses, in fact, initially had been rejected by the party because most Bolsheviks considered them too radical; it took Lenin almost a month to get his way.

Once Lenin got the party on course it was a continual struggle to keep it there. After he had to flee Petrograd in July to avoid arrest, controlling his party was like steering a kite in a swirling wind. For example, he was sometimes unable to control his Central Committee. Ironically, though, Lenin's struggle to maintain party discipline reflected a source of Bolshevik strength. The party was not yet, as it would become and remain, a monolithic and bureaucratic automaton. The tremendous growth of membership during 1917 had changed it from an exclusive, insulated elite into something of a mass party, with many new and expanded local committees and cells often operating quite independently. Decisions in these local bodies often reflected actual feelings of the rank and file. At times this mass base was even more radical than Lenin himself. Thus in June the party leadership, fearing it might lose influence among militant workers and soldiers, nearly staged an armed demonstration that would have been a direct challenge to the Congress of Soviets. In short, the party's new mass base gave Lenin a direct touch on the pulse of the nation. As spring wore into summer, that pulse was beating faster.

The situation was equally vibrant at the top levels of the party. Because Lenin made the Bolsheviks into what was clearly the most revolutionary party in Russia, it attracted numerous talented and impatient revolutionaries from other parties. These were not yes-men; if they had differences with Lenin they did not hide them. They thereby added not only their skills to the party's resources, but an element of awareness and flexibility.

By far the most important of these newcomers was Lenin's long-time critic, Leon Trotsky. His resources included not only his extraordinary organizational and oratorical skills, but his theory of "permanent revolution." According to Trotsky, the peculiar characteristics of Russia's development and the possibility of spreading the revolution to Western Europe meant that Russia, despite its backwardness, could flash right through the "bourgeois" revolution to a socialist revolution. This, of course, was basically what Lenin was trying to do. Trotsky, who jumped from being one of Lenin's most caustic critics to becoming his unabashed admirer, wrote that without Lenin there never would have been a Bolshevik revolution. He certainly was correct, but it is also hard to imagine how Lenin could have succeeded without Trotsky, the man who actually organized the Bolshevik seizure of power and then created, "out of nothing," as Lenin put it, the Red Army that successfully defended the Bolshevik government in a long and terrible civil war.

As 1917 wore on, "permanent revolution" changed from a political dream to a real possibility. The spring of 1917 had been both literally and figuratively the springtime of the revolution, a time of relative optimism and good will. Most people seemed willing to give the new government a chance to prove itself. Even the peasantry, in part because increased demand for food had benefitted many of them economically, and because they expected that the government would soon sanction their takeover of the landed estates, generally held back from violent action. By the summer, hopes and optimism, like spring flowers, were beginning to wilt. The mood in Russia had changed.

The failure to respond to that change was fatal, both to the Provisional Government and to the Mensheviks and Socialist Revolutionaries. After Miliukov's resignation, those two parties entered the government because they hoped to forestall collapse and the threat of civil war. They thereby unintentionally tied their fates to that shaky regime. While the Provisional Government was embarrassed and bruised in May and June, beginning in July it suffered debilitating wounds. Ever since May, Kerensky had been preparing an offensive against the Central Powers, in the hope that military victories would both further Russia's national interests abroad and rally support for the government at home. A man whose reputation owed more to his hyperbolic language than to any political or military acumen, Kerensky went to the front to rally his troops with such cogent advice as "Forward to liberty! . . . Forward to Death." The Russian troops, devoted to their country through it all, amazingly were still ready to try again for the fatherland, moved forward—briefly—into the German machine guns and death. The army then mercifully began to crumble; 700,000 men deserted during the summer and fall. As Lenin put it, the soldiers "voted with their feet" for peace.

Some troops expressed their feelings in other ways. The fear of being transferred to the slaughter at the front led to a mutiny of the army garrisoned in Petrograd. These troops were joined first by militant, pro-Bolshevik workers and then, after some hesitation, by the Bolshevik leadership. The mutiny became a Bolshevik-led uprising against the Provisional Government.

Considering the Bolsheviks' later triumph, the immediate results of these "July Days" were deceptive. The government succeeded in bringing loyal soldiers to the capital to defeat the uprising, and was then able to turn on the Bolsheviks. Several top leaders were arrested, the party newspaper closed, and Lenin, a warrant out for his arrest, was forced into hiding. His reputation was further tarnished by revelations that his party had accepted money from the German government. Lenin, of course, as earlier "expropriations" had demonstrated, did not care where his money came from. Lenin was no more in the Germans' debt than he was to the banks from which his party had once "expropriated" funds. At any rate, intervening events would cause this embarrassment to be largely forgotten by autumn, while the German money helped the Bolsheviks regain their strength.

The Provisional Government and its Menshevik and SR ministers survived the July Days, but the military offensive cost them much public support. In late July Kerensky succeeded Lvov as Prime Minister, with little noticeable effect on the government's effectiveness. As for the Mensheviks and SRs, their commitment to the government now placed them more than ever against the rising tide of popular revolutionary feeling. The Soviet probably could have taken power in July and formed an all-socialist coalition government. Such a move quite likely would have ended Lenin's hopes for an exclusively Bolshevik seizure of power. Yet despite the urging of the respected Menshevik leader, Julius Martov, the Soviet did not act, much to the chagrin of the workers and soldiers roaming the streets of the capital. A famous scene that took place during the July Days in front of the Soviet's headquarters illustrates how out of step with the popular mood the Mensheviks and SRs were becoming. When a mob appeared to demand that the Soviet take power, Victor Chernov, the SR leader and current minister of agriculture in the Provisional Government as well as a leading member of the Soviet, tried to calm the crowd. One demonstrator shook his fist in Chernov's face and screamed: "Take power, you son of a bitch, when it is offered to you." Chernov was saved from injury and possible death only by Trotsky's intervention.

The Bolsheviks' recovery from the July Days was almost as rapid as their eclipse had been. By late July, in fact, the party's Sixth Congress, held in the capital, testified to a growing and well-managed organization, even during its leader's imposed absence. The overall situation in the country during the late summer increasingly favored those who stood for change. The food shortages in the towns and industrial centers continued unabated. Factories closed, unable to obtain supplies. Sometimes owners closed them because of labor unrest, much of which was instigated by Bolshevik-led factory committees. The summer also witnessed the sprouting of peasant committees in the countryside, leaving much of rural Russia in a state of upheaval. The wait for land was over. Peasants, afraid of missing their chance if they did not act, and reinforced by deserters coming home from the army, now seized the landlords' land and property, sometimes killing them in the process. The Bolsheviks also benefitted from the backlash to the July Offensive. Workers, peasants, and soldiers frequently demanded an immediate peace, something the government, with its commitment to the Allies, could not deliver.

All of this naturally frightened the middle and upper classes. As the masses moved to the left, the propertied classes moved to the right. Many people now became sympathetic to the idea of a military dictatorship as the only hope of restoring order and preventing a complete social upheaval. Kerensky also determined that order had to be restored if his government were to survive. To do this he turned to his newly appointed commander-in-chief, a brave but politically inept Cossack named Lavr Kornilov. But Kornilov, the general with "the heart of a lion but the brains of a sheep," marched to a different drummer—the whispers of frightened Russian conservatives and moderates, and worried Allied diplomats. He decided to suppress all the revolutionary forces, from the relatively moderate socialists in the Soviet to the militant Bolsheviks in the streets. Early in September, after a confusing and somewhat comical series of moves and countermoves by the bumbling general and the hysterical prime minister, Kornilov marched on the capital to take charge. Kerensky managed to win this clumsily fought bout, but only by turning to the Bolsheviks for help. Their leaders were released from prison. While the "Red Guards," the Bolshevik militia newly armed by the desperate Kerensky, mobilized in the capital, emissaries sent to agitate among Kornilov's troops succeeded in destroying their morale and provoking a mutiny. Crucial help also came from other sources, including the pro-Menshevik railway workers.

The Provisional Government was saved, but hardly safe. On top of all its old unsolved problems, it had incurred the wrath of many army officers who previously had been willing to take its orders. Additional trouble came from the areas inhabited by non-Russians, from the Baltic Sea to the Ukraine to Central Asia, where nationalist sentiment and impatience were building. By September, the Provisional Government existed by an apparent act of political levitation, for it was impossible to discern its means of support.

Prime Minister Kerensky remained as ineffectual as ever. The best he could do was organize a monthly series of conferences and large meetings: the Moscow State Conference in late August, the Democratic Conference in late September, and the Pre-Parliament in late October.

Kerensky's performance at the Moscow State Conference exemplified his weaknesses as a political leader. His opening speech, as historian William Henry Chamberlin has observed, "conformed to a familiar pattern: loud phrases which covered up feeble and irresolute actions."[2] Despite warnings about Bolshevik intentions, Kerensky did nothing to stop them after the Kornilov affair. He did little about governing Russia, now sinking into chaos in the wake of rioting, looting, and a host of criminal activities. In his closing speech to the Moscow State Conference, the prime minister became so emotional that he almost collapsed.

Bolshevik strength was meanwhile approaching a critical mass. In September, the party won a majority in both the Moscow and Petrograd soviets. With the victory in the capital, Leon Trotsky, the man who had led the revered 1905 St. Petersburg Soviet in its final days, became the president of the Petrograd Soviet. As in 1905, Trotsky's ascension was quickly followed by dramatic events. This time, however, those events would carry him not to prison, but to power.

While Trotsky was the visible star during October and early November, the hidden force was Lenin. Lenin, like Trotsky, felt that a golden opportunity had arrived with the rapid decay of the Provisional Government and the political paralysis of the Mensheviks and SRs, an opportunity that might not come again. Only Lenin could convince the party leadership that the time had come to seize power. This job was much harder than one might have expected, for the party's Central Committee remained, as it would for a few more years, one that could achieve a genuine consensus only through debate and persuasion. Lenin's political genius in 1917 and in the crises of the next four years lay not only in his ability to choose a viable course of action, but also in carrying his party along with him. He probably had a more difficult time convincing his central committee to take power than the party had in seizing power. He observed, after all, that the latter was like "picking up a feather"; controlling a central committee of willful men was more like wrestling with an octopus.

Lenin's campaign to win support for a seizure of power began in late September. It was made more difficult because he and his associates still felt it wise for him to remain in hiding in Finland. His opening salvo was a letter to the Central Committee sitting in Petrograd. "History will not forgive us if we do not assume power now," Lenin warned. The Central Committee, to put it mildly, was not convinced. Rather than prepare for an uprising, it decided to forestall any violent actions by workers and soldiers. It also burned Lenin's letter.

The battle dragged on for a month. The opposition to Lenin was led by two previously loyal lieutenants, Grigory Zinoviev and Lev Kamenev. They doubted that the country would follow the Bolshevik lead, noting that while a majority of the workers and many of the soldiers would support the party, "everything else is questionable." They wanted to wait for the upcoming Second Congress of Soviets, where a Bolshevik majority was expected. The party then could take power without resorting to an armed coup.

However, far more was at stake than the question of when to take power. The underlying issue was how that power would be exercised. Zinoviev and Kamenev did not expect the Bolsheviks to rule alone, but to lead a socialist coalition commanding the support of a majority of the Russian proletariat and peasantry. By predicating a Bolshevik government on winning the support of a majority in the Second Congress of Soviets, Lenin's dissident lieutenants injected a democratic component into their conception of Bolshevik power. Lenin, in contrast, wanted the party to seize power alone and to rule alone. By choosing to rely on his claim that the Bolsheviks represented the best interests of Russia's toiling masses and by his insistence on using force to come to power, regardless of any electoral results, Lenin made dictatorship the basis of his proposed regime.

Lenin succeeded in swinging the Central Committee to his side late in October, though he did not convince Zinoviev and Kamenev. They both promptly protested the decision to the party at large and actually leaked the news of the planned coup to the press. That Lenin, shortly after the seizure of power a few weeks later, was willing to forget this outrageous breach of party discipline and accept the two recalcitrants back into the party's good graces is testimony both to his ability to put practical politics above vindictiveness or spite, and to the give and take that characterized Bolshevism in 1917. That the Provisional Government reacted barely at all to the advance notice of a plot to destroy it is testimony to its advanced state of decay. No wonder seizing power was as easy as "picking up a feather."

The final debate—over the precise timing of the coup—Lenin actually lost. He wanted immediate action. "We must not wait! We may lose everything!" he moaned. Yet even his supporters demurred this time, led by Trotsky. In what historian Alexander Rabinowitch has called the "clearest example of the importance and value of the party's relatively free and flexible structure, and the responsiveness of its tactics to the prevailing mass mood,"[3] Bolshevik leaders on the scene in Petrograd insisted on a delay until the convening of the Second Congress of Soviets in early November, where they expected to have a Bolshevik majority. They cited considerable evidence that the masses in the capital, as well as the peasants, soldiers, and the mass organizations, would oppose a coup by the Bolsheviks acting alone.

While Trotsky agreed with Lenin that the Bolsheviks should seize power, he disagreed on how this should be done. Trotsky reasoned that if the Bolsheviks waited for the Congress to convene and endorse their overthrow of the Provisional Government, the coup would win an important measure of legitimacy. He felt such an endorsement was essential if the Bolsheviks were to avoid strong popular opposition, particularly from the soldiers in Petrograd. At the same time, acting in concert with the Congress satisfied the consciences of those Bolsheviks still wedded to the democratic traditions of European Marxism, men who were loath to seize political power without some kind of expression of support from the working class, whose vanguard they claimed to be.

The Bolsheviks actually had no detailed plan for a coup until Kerensky forced their hand. On the evening of November 5, he proclaimed a state of emergency. He ordered that the Soviet's newly formed Military Revolutionary Committee be dissolved, an eminently reasonable demand since Trotsky was using that committee to organize the Bolshevik coup, as well as the closure of two Bolshevik newspapers and the arrest of several party leaders. A few hours after midnight Kerensky dispatched what loyal troops he had to occupy strategic positions in the capital and close down the Bolshevik printing plant.

Kerensky's moves did little more than provide Trotsky with an excuse to strike under the pretext that the Petrograd Soviet was in "direct danger." On the night of November 6–7, Bolshevik detachments, including sailors from the Kronstadt naval base, had no trouble in seizing most of the key points in Petrograd. So smoothly did the operation proceed that nobody really noticed. As historian Lionel Kochan notes:

> Petrograd's *dolce vita* was not interrupted. Guards officers clicked their spurs and engaged in gay adventures. The sound of wild parties burst from private salons of elegant restaurants. The electric current was switched off at midnight but heavy gambling continued by candlelight.[4]

The only real fighting, and it was minimal, occurred the next night when the Bolsheviks seized the Winter Palace, seat of the Provisional Government, and arrested the deposed ministers. It had taken only twenty-four hours and a few hundred casualties to depose the government and launch the most influential social experiment of the twentieth century.

The Provisional Government's collapse marked the failure of the effort to establish Western democratic political life in Russia. That effort, as has been seen, was severely handicapped from the start by Russia's historical legacy. Only a shallow layer of Russian society—the professional middle class, the business community, and progressive elements of the nobility—had any interest in or inclination toward parliamentary democracy. That was too fragile a foundation to support a political system during the turmoil of 1917. Most Russians had little interest or confidence in democratic institutions. The peasants wanted land, the proletariat wanted workers' control, the soldiers wanted to go home, the national minorities wanted autonomy, and none of them cared how they achieved their respective goals. When the Provisional Government could not deliver right away on crucial issues, the people turned against it.

The Provisional Government failed because, aside from the burdens imposed by history, it also was limited by nationalistic obsessions, legalistic and democratic inhibitions, and unimaginative leadership. Because of nationalism it locked itself into a war it could neither win nor end, with disastrous results. It refused to decree precisely those reforms most urgent to the bulk of the population because that would have violated presumed legal norms. Staying in the war made it impossible to arrest the spreading economic collapse. This, in turn, left the Provisional Government incapable of controlling Russia's masses who, liberated at last from their tsarist fetters, were running wild. Nor could the Provisional Government cope with the Bolsheviks and their determined will to power.

Will, of course, hardly explains the Bolshevik triumph. In ordinary times, the Bolsheviks would have remained where they were before March 1917, isolated and irrelevant, on the fringes of Russian political life. But the Bolsheviks were the political party best suited to a revolutionary environment that demanded flexibility, ruthlessness, and an instinct for the new phenomenon of mass politics. In Lenin the party had a leader ready to exploit any opportunity and flexible enough to adapt to changing circumstances. The Bolsheviks tailored their program to appeal to the masses—the peasants, workers, soldiers, and non-Russian nationalities—especially as those groups became more militant and impatient during the summer and fall. Superior organization enabled the Bolsheviks to build their strength and ultimately win control of key urban soviets and worker and military committees. Because of Lenin's concern for the nuts and bolts of seizing power, the Bolsheviks also organized their own armed units, the famous Red Guards, who were essential to the November success. Finally, because new local Bolshevik organizations sprang up and grew too fast to be dominated by the party's central apparatus, those organizations reflected the sentiments of their rank and file, and therefore kept the leadership abreast of and responsible to the popular mood.

The Provisional Government's fall and the Bolshevik seizure of power was a momentous historical watershed—the end of the broad social, economic, and political process of Westernization that, particularly since 1861, had been recasting ever greater parts of Russian society. The Bolshevik Revolution reversed Russia's direction, and the country embarked on a new path that would widen the gap with the West to the greatest extent since the time of Peter the Great. Perhaps the most important consequence of the Bolshevik victory was that it marked the end of the effort to establish parliamentary democracy in Russia. That effort, to be sure, was a struggle against the odds from the start. During its short life the unsteady Provisional Government legalized all political parties, ended censorship, abolished the secret police, guaranteed freedom of the press, legalized the right to join trade unions and to strike, and took many other progressive steps. However, lacking a broad social base on which to ground their parliamentary edifice, the new government's supporters, devoid of experience and deficient in skill, were forced to navigate stormy and treacherous political seas, driven by the winds of war and social turmoil, that lay between the Scylla and Charybdis of the anti-democratic extreme right and left, only to be swamped within months by the latter.

Still, while political democracy lost out in Russia in 1917, the subsequent triumph of totalitarianism was not inevitable. Most of the country, if not committed to Western-style parliamentary democracy, wanted some kind of multiparty government based on the soviets. The Bolsheviks owed much of the support for their November coup to their ability to wrap themselves in the Soviet's mantle. When their intent to rule alone became clear, many of those who supported the new regime turned against it. Once these elements added their weight to the others opposed to a Bolshevik dictatorship, the stage was set for a bitter struggle, one that brutalized the country and gravely worsened the odds for sparing the Russian people the misery of a regime harsher than anything they had ever known. In light of the suffering that would follow during the next seven decades, the debacle of the first of Russia's two revolutions in 1917, and the resultant failure to establish a parliamentary regime in the land once ruled by the tsars, can be counted as one of the great disasters of the twentieth century.

NOTES

1. Marc Ferro, "Aspirations of Russian Society," in *Revolutionary Russia*, Richard Pipes, editor (Garden City, N.Y.: Doubleday, 1969), p. 196.
2. William Henry Chamberlin, *The Russian Revolution*, Vol. I (New York: Grosset and Dunlap, 1963), p. 203.
3. Alexander Rabinowitch, *The Bolsheviks Come to Power* (New York: W. W. Norton, 1976), p. 313.
4. Lionel Kochan, *Russia in Revolution 1890–1918* (London: Granada Publishing Ltd., 1970), p. 276.

10

Into the Fire: The Civil War

There is nothing unhappier than a civil war, for the conquered are destroyed by, and the conquerors destroy, their friends.

————DIONYSIUS OF HALICARNASSUS

The November Revolution was very different from the upheaval that unseated the autocracy in March. The March Revolution erupted spontaneously among the Petrograd workers and soldiers; as it flowed out from the capital it became a nationwide movement involving millions of people. The November Revolution, by contrast, was a *Bolshevik* revolution, a planned coup d'etat executed by a single political party. The Bolsheviks certainly had considerable support in Russia, particularly among workers and military personnel, and few Russians were saddened to see the Provisional Government fall. Still, most of that support was for the Bolsheviks in their apparent role as defender of the multiparty soviets, not for their ruling alone as dictators of Russia.

The new regime's policy during its first few months had several general objectives. The most urgent need was to relieve some of the immediate pressures threatening it, specifically those caused by the unending war and rising peasant discontent. Hardly less urgent in terms of survival was the need to bring some order to the chaos engulfing the nation, a situation the Bolsheviks themselves had done much to foster between March and November. In effect, this meant containing and even in part reversing the revolution that had been spreading for eight months. Finally, the Bolsheviks were anxious to use their newly acquired power to make some drastic changes; they had come to power, after all, not simply to rule, but to remake Russia into a socialist utopia.

Whatever the Bolsheviks' eventual plans, the odds were stacked heavily against their staying in power. Until they made peace with the Germans, they faced a powerful armed force that occupied Russia's western territories and was capable of marching on Petrograd and unseating them. Nationalism and the desire for independence were rampant, particularly in the west, among the Finns and Poles, in the southwest, among the Ukrainians, and in the south, among the people of the Caucasus. Even where ethnic Russians lived, near-anarchy prevailed. Peasant discontent had boiled over in the countryside. The economy, ravaged by war and revolution, was in a shambles. Serious shortages of necessities, including food, continued unabated. In short, Russia's Bolshevik government was surrounded by hostile capitalist powers, and soon faced domestic opposition across the political spectrum.

These multiple crises demanded something dramatic, and the Bolsheviks responded. On November 8, the same day Lenin presented his all-Bolshevik government—called the Council of People's Commissars or *Sovnarkom*—to the newly convened Second Congress of Soviets, he also offered two decrees for its approval that announced what millions of Russians were waiting desperately to hear. The Decree on Peace called for immediate negotiations to end the war and made it clear that the Bolsheviks were prepared to negotiate with the Central Powers if the Western Allies did not respond to their call. The Decree on Land abolished all private ownership of land; the land turned over to the use of those who tilled it. The peasants' centuries-old dream of getting all the land finally had come to pass.

Although these decrees may have created the impression that the new government had a well-thought-out program, the reality was quite different. Subsequent events were to demonstrate that Lenin, the man who had sought power for so long, actually had no concrete plans once he got it. Efforts to plan ahead, of course, had been complicated because Lenin came to power in a country that met none of the traditional Marxist prerequisites for a socialist revolution. Years earlier Lenin had theorized that something like this might happen, and he had therefore postulated that any advance toward socialism under a Marxist regime in backward Russia would depend on two crucial factors: support from Western Europe after the expected socialist revolution there, and a proletarian-peasant alliance in Russia. Trotsky thought along similar lines, although he ignored the peasantry and staked everything on the "direct state support of the European proletariat." Yet these minimal conditions were not fulfilled. There was no successful socialist revolution in Western Europe and serious problems arose in Russia with both the peasantry and the proletariat.

Still, the November victory bolstered Lenin's somewhat dormant faith that in a revolutionary situation "the people are capable of performing miracles." Lenin was convinced that his party was about to fulfill its historic role as the spark for a world socialist revolution, and with that in mind, he was not about to let some unexpected difficulties in Russia get him down. A key component of his faith in "miracles," however, was that they could only take place under his scepter, and that conviction led directly to his regime's first crisis. The trouble began when Lenin insisted that the new government had to be exclusively Bolshevik. This clashed with the general assumption among socialists both inside and outside the Bolshevik party that any socialist government in Russia would be a coalition of the various socialist parties. A socialist coalition therefore was exactly what the Menshevik leader Julius Martov proposed to the Second Congress of Soviets immediately after the Provisional Government's fall. His motion was seconded by a Bolshevik, and the congress—whose membership of about 650 included about 390 Bolsheviks and their sympathizers—passed it unanimously. A few days later, at a meeting from which Lenin and Trotsky were absent, the Bolshevik Central Committee added its unanimous endorsement to the idea.

Lenin could hardly have been more upset. While some felt a coalition was the best way to represent the popular will, to Lenin it meant "hesitation, impotence, and chaos." It certainly meant his personal power and influence would be diminished. Lenin's first battle to maintain his Bolshevik regime now began. It was an uphill struggle, for although Lenin had Trotsky's support, he was outvoted on the coalition issue even within his most intimate circle. Additional pressure developed when the Executive Committee (*Vikzel*) of the powerful Railwaymen's Union, one of the key groups that had brought General Kornilov to grief in September, placed itself at the head of the struggle for a socialist coalition. *Vikzel* was responding to widespread popular sentiment that, significantly, came not only from virtually all the socialist parties—including the SRs, Mensheviks, Jewish Bund, and Polish Socialist Party—but from rank and file workers' and soldiers' organizations. Soldiers at the front, wounded veterans at home, and many factory committees all joined to protest against what was viewed as a usurpation of power by the Bolsheviks. Even workers in the solidly pro-Bolshevik working-class districts added their protest.

In an attempt to sabotage the procoalition forces in his party, Lenin was reduced to stalling and negotiating on the basis of demands he knew were unacceptable to the other socialist parties. His tactics did not impress many of his comrades; on November 18, five of them, including Zinoviev and Kamenev, resigned from the Central Committee. So did four members of the government, three of whom had the distinction of having quit both the party's Central Committee and the government. As Lenin's *Sovnarkom* comrades parted company with him, they issued a dire warning to their stubborn leader: "Other than this [a coalition government] there is only one policy: the preservation of a purely Bolshevik government by means of political terror."

At this point his opponents' ineptitude came to Lenin's rescue. On November 8, Lenin had gotten away with forming his all-Bolshevik government in the first place when Martov, instead of staying and fighting, had chosen to lead a walk-out from the Second Congress of Soviets to protest the Bolshevik coup, this *after* his motion for a socialist coalition had unanimously passed a body controlled by the Bolsheviks and their sympathizers. "By quitting the Congress, we ourselves gave the Bolsheviks a monopoly of the Soviet, of the masses, of the Revolution," a leading Menshevik later dejectedly recalled. Menshevik ineptitude was even more apparent in their handling of the negotiations for a coalition. At one point they demanded the exclusion of the victorious Bolsheviks from the coalition. Later they suggested leaving Lenin and Trotsky out of the government. Such empty posturing did little beyond helping Lenin to regain control of his Central Committee. He won the support he needed and slipped out of his political corner on December 1, when he agreed to admit the Left Socialist Revolutionaries, a faction that had split off from the main SR group, as junior partners in his government. This shotgun marriage between unequal partners lasted barely four months. At the same time, the Bolsheviks closed ranks. As was becoming a habit that would be repeated again under far worse circumstances, the defeated Kamenev and Zinoviev returned to the fold ready to atone for their ideological sins.

Although Lenin now had the kind of government he wanted, that government was extremely insecure. Prior to November, Lenin had subordinated everything to seizing power. That accomplished, Lenin focused all his party's strength on holding power. More than anything else, it was this ability to focus like a laser on his target that distinguished Lenin from his rivals and made him a figure of historic importance.

Lenin did not wait for trouble to come to him. Never bothered by democratic niceties, he quickly struck against the new regime's opponents. On November 9, the fledgling Bolshevik government suppressed the nonsocialist press. On December 7, "revolutionary tribunals" were set up to dispense justice, short of the death penalty, for "counterrevolution" or "sabotage." (In June 1918, the tribunals received the right to dispense capital punishment.) Also in December, the Kadets, who were preparing to take their seats in the long-awaited Constituent Assembly, found their leaders under arrest and their party denounced for consorting with alleged "enemies of the people." Most importantly of all, that very busy December was crowned with the establishment of the "Extraordinary Commission for the Defense of the Revolution" (*Cheka*). Thus the Russian secret police, not yet cold in the grave it had occupied since March, was reincarnated, albeit in a revolutionary rather than a reactionary body. It was an event of fundamental importance in the history of Soviet Russia, for it immediately placed the new regime above the law. Finally, beginning with a one-week battle to secure Moscow, the Bolsheviks used the waning weeks of 1917 to extend their control over most of Russia's major cities.

In their struggle to solidify their control, the Bolsheviks had to contend not only with alleged "enemies of the people," but with the people themselves, or at least with the proletariat. The problem, for Lenin at least, was not new. Prior to 1917, in order to make the revolution he wanted, Lenin had deemed it essential to oppose what he called "spontaneity," the proletariat's tendency to concentrate on bread-and-butter issues rather than on the intelligentsia's revolutionary goals. Once in power, in order to preserve the revolution in the form he wanted, Lenin quickly had to find a way to keep the workers from using their new-found strength to satisfy what they considered their own interests at the expense of what Lenin considered the legitimate objectives of the revolution.

During the anarchic months between March and November of 1917, the Bolsheviks had supported the spread of "workers' control." The workers attempted to realize their control through factory committees set up in the plants, usually with chaotic results. Where factory committees attempted merely to participate in decision making, friction between workers and owners often disrupted production. Where workers took over enterprises and tried to run them, they frequently lacked the technical skill to manage them or mismanaged them with an eye only for immediate improvements in their standard of living.

Prior to November, workers' control served Bolshevik interests by adding to the chaos undermining the Provisional Government. Yet even then, Lenin had written that workers' control belonged "side by side with the dictatorship of the proletariat and *always after* it (emphasis added)." Once in power, the Bolsheviks found it vital to restore economic order before the economy collapsed completely and brought them down with it. This meant curbing workers' control, although the new government lacked the strength to challenge the workers directly. So, as historian E. H. Carr put it, the Bolsheviks worked instead to make workers' control "orderly and innocuous by turning it into a large-scale centralized public institution."[1] This was done by setting up a hierarchy of factory committees running from the individual plants up to an "All-Russian Council of Workers' Control." The trade unions, whose leadership felt threatened by the free-wheeling factory committees, enlisted with the government in this effort. At the same time, the government began to manage key industries and to limit workers' control through the spreading branches of yet another new highly centralized bureaucratic institution, the Supreme Council of the National Economy (*Vesenka*), set up in December 1917. Workers' control was giving way to Bolshevik control.

"Bolshevik control" during these early months was not particularly revolutionary, at least from a Marxist perspective. The emphasis clearly was on restoring discipline and stability, not on a rapid rush to socialism. Proclaiming an eight-hour day was hardly a fire-breathing step. The thoroughly non-Marxist land decree of November 8—it did nothing to promote the Marxist goal of collectivized agriculture—was confirmed by a law issued in February 1918. *Vesenka* was given extensive powers over industry, but it took only small steps towards establishing a socialist economy.

Other early measures, to be sure, were more radical. The State Bank was nationalized in November, after its management refused to advance money to the new government. Soon, tsarist debts were cancelled and all banks nationalized. There also was some nationalization of industry, but with the exception of the merchant marine, nationalized in January 1918, and the sugar and oil industries, nationalized in May and June, respectively, such things were decided on a case-by-case basis. Less than 500 enterprises were nationalized through June of 1918, most of them by initiatives on the local level.

All this was consistent with an economic policy that was limited in scope. Lenin felt that the regime's immediate objective should be "state capitalism," a highly centralized economy under strict state supervision, but still largely under private ownership. State capitalism was to be a step toward socialism, but no immediate revolutionary leaps were planned. This made some sense, at least when the guideposts with which the new regime had to work are considered. Marxism offered little practical help when it came to economic planning. As Lenin noted ruefully in 1918, "Nothing has been written about it in the Bolshevik textbooks, and there is nothing in the Menshevik textbooks either." The best guide available —and the one Lenin was using—came from a rather unlikely source: the sophisticated combination of private enterprise and state planning developed in capitalist Germany during World War I.

This relatively moderate economic policy had a political counterpart. Despite considerable repression of other political parties, the Bolsheviks permitted a reasonably free nationwide election, an unprecedented event in Russian history up to that time. The Provisional Government, after several false starts, finally had set the elections to the Constituent Assembly for November 25, 1917. By then, of course, the Provisional Government had been overthrown. Lenin was uninterested in how the people of Russia might want to be governed, and in fact feared that his Bolsheviks would be swamped in an election inevitably dominated by Russia's peasant majority. But his government dared not cancel the long-promised election. As expected and feared, the peasant-oriented Socialist Revolutionaries secured a majority of the votes against an impressive but still losing Bolshevik total of 24 percent. The other parties trailed, splitting less than a quarter of the vote.

When the Constituent Assembly convened on January 18, 1918, its SR majority, bolstered by Menshevik support, made it clear that its vision of a democratic federal Russian republic had little room in it for a Bolshevik dictatorship. The Bolsheviks reacted swiftly. The Constituent Assembly, less than twenty-four hours after its convocation, was dispersed by force in what Lenin bluntly and accurately called a "complete and frank liquidation of the idea of democracy by the idea of dictatorship."

The Constituent Assembly caused hardly a ripple as it went down. Almost nobody in Russia rose to its defense; most people were preoccupied with the immediate tasks of finding personal security amidst the turmoil. For Lenin, extinguishing Russia's only political institution reflecting a nationwide consensus violated no revolutionary principle because "the republic of the Soviets is a higher form of democratic organization than the usual bourgeois republic with its Constituent Assembly." Obviously, lower bourgeois forms had to give way to higher socialist forms.

Although the Bolsheviks disposed of the Constituent Assembly rather easily, their regime probably could not have survived had it not solved the problem of getting Russia out of the war. While many of his most able associates, including his right-hand man, Trotsky, could hardly bear the thought of negotiating with the German emperor and his generals, Lenin knew better. The failure to bring peace had contributed mightily to the Provisional Government's demise, and the virtual disintegration of the Russian army since the summer of 1917 had left the Germans and their allies virtually unopposed at the front. The Bolsheviks, Lenin insisted, had to make peace if they were to survive.

Lenin had almost as much difficulty on this issue with his party as he did with the Germans. Between December 1917, when an armistice was signed, and February 1918, only a minority of the party leadership was willing to accept the harsh German peace terms. One faction, led by the young and brilliant Nikolai Bukharin, favored carrying a quixotic "revolutionary war" into Western Europe, oblivious of the fact that the means for such a campaign did not exist. Another group, led by Trotsky, advocated a bizarre "neither war nor peace" formula, a strategy that salvaged revolutionary pride while leaving everything, including the revolutionary government in Russia, in limbo. Lenin was forced to go along with his comrades' stalling and grandstanding until the Germans ran out of patience in February and began a rapid advance that soon threatened Petrograd and the regime's very existence. With their capital hurriedly transferred to the relative safety of Moscow, the Bolsheviks reluctantly yielded to Lenin, and Russia accepted peace terms worse than what had once been rejected. At the Treaty of Brest-Litovsk signed on March 3, 1918, Russia gave up over 1 million square miles of territory containing over 60 million people and huge hunks of its industrial plant, natural resources, and farmland. Lenin justified these concessions because he expected the coming revolution in Germany to render the treaty null and void. Besides, the Bolshevik regime, the beachhead of the world socialist revolution, had survived.

Although the Treaty of Brest-Litovsk gave the Bolsheviks some breathing room, it also provoked anger and resistance. Its harsh terms caused the Left SRs to withdraw from the government that same month. Still, by the middle of 1918, the Bolsheviks had much to show for their first six months in power. The regime had prevailed despite considerable opposition and had even won a large measure of public acceptance. Important institutions to defend the regime and extend its power had been organized, including the *Cheka* and, after Trotsky's appointment as commissar of war in March, the Red Army. There even had been some significant reforms. Despite all their problems, the Bolsheviks, among other things, had abolished all class distinctions, overhauled marriage and divorce laws, decreed the separation of church and state, taken energetic measures against gambling and prostitution, adopted the Gregorian calendar used in the West, given illegitimate children the same rights as anyone else, and even reformed and simplified the Cyrillic alphabet used to write Russian.

In July of 1918, Russia received a new name, the Russian Soviet Federated Socialist Republic, and its first Soviet Constitution, a document that in one breath condemned all exploiters, extolled the toiling masses, and promised a world socialist revolution. The constitution also had a practical side. It disenfranchised all the old "exploiting" classes. Among those who could vote, some were "more equal" than others: the votes of urban residents, among whom the Bolsheviks were strongest, counted five times as much as votes of rural residents. The constitution also established a new governing structure, a network of soviets beginning with directly elected local soviets and proceeding upward via indirect elections to an All-Russian Congress of Soviets. Whatever its merits or flaws, the new constitution was not implemented. By July the country was on the brink of a new ordeal. As if the cumulative hardships of world war and revolution were not enough, Russia was about to undergo the extreme travail of civil war.

The seeds for civil war were planted when Lenin set up his minority government. They began to germinate during the last weeks of 1917,

when several tsarist generals and conservative politicians began organizing anti-Bolshevik military units in the Ukraine. Fighting between
pro- and anti-Bolshevik forces began by February 1918. Bolshevik repression meanwhile fueled opposition to the regime, especially on the
political left. In April, a massive *Cheka* raid on anarchist headquarters
resulted in hundreds of arrests. On June 14, the Mensheviks and Socialist
Revolutionaries, duly elected by the toiling masses to represent them,
were expelled from the soviets.

In July, the embittered Left SRs attempted to overthrow the Bolsheviks.
The government quickly suppressed the ill-planned revolt in Petrograd
and Moscow. Shortly thereafter it quashed an almost haphazard series
of uprisings in several other towns. The Left SRs did a little better at
their old trade of assassination, much to the misfortune of the German
ambassador to Russia, murdered in July, and Michael Uritsky, the chief
of the Petrograd *Cheka*, gunned down on August 30. Lenin, however, got
away with a bullet wound that same August 30. The Bolsheviks responded
by unleashing the *Cheka* to wage massive political terror. Among its first
victims were the former tsar and his family, executed on July 16 to prevent their liberation by anti-Bolshevik forces. On July 29, the government
proclaimed that "the socialist fatherland is in danger," in effect officially
announcing a state of civil war.

The Civil War would have been bad enough had the Russians been
allowed to fight it out by themselves, but it was made worse by outside
intervention. The Allies, deeply fearful that Bolshevism might spread
westward, intervened when the Bolsheviks made peace with Germany and
thereby left the latter free to concentrate its full military might against the
Allied armies in the west. Initially, the Allied intervention was limited to
protecting military supplies stored in several Russian ports and considered
to be in danger of falling into German hands. Thus, in March and April,
British, French, American, and Japanese troops landed on Russian soil.

In May an extraordinary incident escalated the intervention. While
Russia had still been fighting alongside the Allies, it had organized a large
group of Czech and Slovak prisoners of war, about 40,000 in all, into the
so-called Czech Legion. These former soldiers of the Austro-Hungarian
Empire were switching sides in an attempt to liberate their homeland from
the Hapsburg monarchy. They were in the process of traveling eastward
across Russia via the Trans-Siberian railroad for evacuation at the port
of Vladivostok and transfer to Western Europe when fighting developed
between the ex-POWs, whom the Bolsheviks feared and attempted to
disarm, and the newly organized Red Army. The Czech victories in
these skirmishes were a convincing demonstration of Bolshevik military
weakness and therefore encouraged both anti-Bolshevik Russians and the
Allies. During the summer, French, British, and Japanese troops reached

Russia in larger numbers. They were joined by more American troops, the latter dispatched in part to monitor the troops of the territorially ambitious Japanese in Siberia.

The number of foreign troops actually in Russia was never very large. Their main purpose was to support the various native anti-Bolshevik governments and armies scattered throughout the country. Collectively known as the "Whites," as opposed to their "Red" Bolshevik opponents, these disparate groups had only their opposition to the Bolsheviks in common. They ranged in political outlook from socialist SRs and Mensheviks to monarchists. The Whites never were able to establish a united force; at one point they totaled eighteen governments and factions. The closest they came to organizing a respectable government, a liberal-socialist coalition known as the Directory, was established in November 1918, and lasted barely a month. Conservative forces overthrew it and turned to a former tsarist naval officer, Admiral Alexander Kolchak, as their savior.

Real power among the Whites rested with a series of ex-tsarist officers. The most important were the alleged "Supreme Ruler" Admiral Kolchak, whose supremacy lasted only a year, General Anton Denikin, and General Baron Peter Wrangel. Various other generals ineffectively tried to aid the cause. The Whites' military difficulties often resulted not only because the considerable distances between their different armies prevented adequate coordination, but sometimes because the generals' mutual rivalries and suspicions came between them.

Disunity was only part of the Whites' problem. Poorly disciplined troops and military incompetence helped drag the White cause down. So did the burden of having to fight from Russia's periphery while the Bolsheviks controlled the country's heartland, including Petrograd and Moscow. White armies separated by hundreds or thousands of miles were always trying to link up. The Reds, by contrast, were able to shuttle troops and materials along compact interior lines of communication. Foreign aid did little to redress these disadvantages. The Allies, often divided among themselves and plagued by a war-weariness that produced, among other things, a mutiny among French sailors dispatched to the Black Sea to help the Whites, provided neither reliable nor adequate help. The stigma of being associated with foreigners outweighed whatever aid the Whites received and allowed the Bolsheviks to pose as patriotic defenders of Mother Russia.

Most importantly, it proved impossible for the Whites to win a civil war without popular support, and they offered very little to the Russian masses. Many peasants had grown to hate and fear the Bolshevik government for fomenting class war in the villages and seizing grain by force, but at least the Bolsheviks had solidly endorsed what peasants cared about most—the right to the land they had seized in 1917 and

1918. Meanwhile, some White factions endorsed the new order in the countryside, others equivocated, and still others insisted the estates be returned to their former owners. So the peasants, when they favored anyone at all, opted for the Bolsheviks. The Whites also alienated most of the minority nationalities by insisting their new Russia once again would be a centralized, "united and undivided" state. At key points guerrilla warfare by peasants of non-Russian minorities therefore undermined White campaigns, particularly those of Kolchak and Denikin, the two commanders with the best chances to defeat the Bolsheviks.

Still, the Bolsheviks were not that formidable themselves, and the Civil War therefore dragged on for almost three years. In a country already bled by four years of world war and revolution, the Civil War became, as historian William Henry Chamberlin has written, a time "when hunger, cold, disease, and terror stalked through the country like the Four Horsemen of the Apocalypse."[2] Both Red and White forces spread their terror across the land in a desperate struggle for supremacy—and they did not have the field to themselves. Bands of peasant guerrillas known as "Greens," driven by motives ranging from anarchist ideals to pure banditry, fought both the Reds and the Whites and ravaged both the countryside and towns. Class war raged in the villages, in part fomented by the Bolsheviks, in what Louis Fisher aptly called "a civil war within a civil war."[3] The dissolution of normal restraints also produced violent struggles between the poor and propertied classes in the cities and towns. Among the most victimized were the Jews, who suffered terribly from pogroms at the hands of the Whites and Greens as well as from the political terror of the Reds. The Civil War truly marked, as Chamberlin put it, "one of the greatest explosions of hatred, or rather hatreds . . . ever witnessed in human history."[4]

To this catastrophe the Allies added their troops and, even worse, a blockade that denied relief to the suffering Russian people. Regardless of which side one supported, almost every person in Russia had to fight cold, hunger, and disease. People endured ruthless speculation, corruption, inflation, and merciless competition for what little was available.

> The law of survival of the fittest found its cruelest, most naked application in the continual struggle for food. The weaker failed to get on the trains to the country districts, or fell off the roofs, or were pushed off the platform, or caught typhus and died, or had the precious fruits of the foraging taken away by the . . . hated guards who boarded the trains as they approached the cities and confiscated surplus food from the passengers.[5]

Those who did not starve lived in constant danger of freezing to death because of a lack of fuel. Entire houses were dismantled and used as firewood; wooden pavements met the same fate. When that was not sufficient, people gathered together to warm their living quarters with their body heat. Cold and hunger left many vulnerable to diseases, with medical care and supplies rarely available. Even those taken to hospitals had little to celebrate; inside the hospitals, patients were freezing to death.

In the midst of such misery, it stands to reason that neither the Bolsheviks nor their rivals enjoyed much popularity. Victory went to the Bolsheviks because they were better able to mobilize and organize whatever support they had as well as the few resources available to them. The key to their success was Lenin. His performance during these years was the high point of his career and a tribute to his skills as a political leader. He displayed a highly accurate sense of what was possible and what the Bolsheviks' priorities had to be. Like his colleagues, Lenin was driven and sustained by the vision of exporting the revolution; unlike many of them, he was not blinded by that vision. The first priority was to preserve Bolshevik power in Russia, the international revolution's beachhead. That was why in February 1918, Lenin had insisted that the Bolsheviks accept the onerous Brest-Litovsk treaty, and throughout most of the Civil War he maintained similar restraint. His one serious lapse occurred late in the war when the Reds tried unsuccessfully to carry the revolution into Poland. Fortunately for Lenin, most of the Bolsheviks' organized domestic enemies already had been vanquished and his regime did not become a casualty of that defeat.

Above all, Lenin gave the Bolsheviks unity. That alone was an accomplishment. The tremendous strains between 1917 and 1921 led to heated debates, bitter personal rivalries, and breakdowns in discipline—but not a party split. At critical points Lenin's stature and authority as the party's leader and the organizational structures he developed were indispensable in giving the Bolsheviks the crucial unity their enemies lacked.

Lenin's leadership would have meant little without energetic, devoted, and often fanatical followers. The most important was Trotsky, a man with superb skills as a propagandist and organizer. Also valuable was Jacob Sverdlov who, until his death from influenza in 1919, served brilliantly in a number of vital posts, among them that of party secretary. Joseph Stalin later would use that post to blaze his trail to power. Meanwhile, Stalin was an efficient troubleshooter, not much bothered by the means he used to save the regime. Many others lower in the party hierarchy made impressive and often unlikely contributions—people like Mikhail Tukhachevsky, the former tsarist second lieutenant turned Red Army commander, and Mikhail Frunze, a tough labor organizer whose quick mastery of military science enabled him to best both Kolchak and Wrangel. Other noteworthy men were Felix Dzerzhinsky, a Pole of noble blood who devoted his every fiber to making the *Cheka* a deadly weapon of the workers' state, and

Leonid Krasin, a leading Bolshevik until 1908 and a superb engineer, whose return to the fold late in 1917 brought the Bolsheviks invaluable technical and organizational expertise. At still lower levels the party had dedicated and effective organizers and expert propagandists, anonymous veterans seasoned by years of underground work, able to exploit class antagonism and White mistakes for the Red cause. Although the Bolsheviks certainly had their share of corrupt and incompetent cadres, in a struggle where attrition was high and talent was scarce, they still had a decisive edge over the Whites.

In the end, victory depended not only on superior leadership and personnel, but on the ability to organize and apply force. The Bolshevik regime could not have survived without its Red Army, a fighting force Leon Trotsky conjured up from scratch during the early months of 1918. Building the Red Army required burying some revolutionary principles. It was, to be sure, very different in some respects from traditional armies. Military pomp was eliminated and officers were far closer to their men. In other respects, however, military tradition ruled. Conscription was reintroduced as the Bolsheviks abandoned their ideas about a "voluntary" people's militia. The election of officers, once a Bolshevik slogan, was eliminated, while the death penalty for desertion was restored.

Trotsky added a few wrinkles of his own. He found a creative solution to the Red Army's acute shortage of qualified officers: recycling old tsarist officers. Many of them readily volunteered to serve, but, to prevent any change of heart, Trotsky dogged them with what were called political commissars. These were trusted party functionaries attached to military units to ensure the loyalty of officers and spread propaganda among the troops. Trotsky also took the added precaution of holding as hostages the families of his ex-tsarist officers. This was not to be taken lightly, for in order to save the revolution, Trotsky did not hesitate to use force, even against the soldiers of the revolution. In the summer of 1918, for example, he restored order to a regiment that was disintegrating in the middle of a battle by executing over twenty soldiers, including the commander and political commissar. He also issued orders that the political commissar and commander of any unit retreating without authorization be shot and that any dwelling found sheltering a deserting Red Army soldier be burned to the ground. Although such orders were not always carried out, they served as a powerful deterrent to a Red Army soldier considering either retreat or a permanent farewell to arms.

The Red Army was hardly perfect. Only those units with a large percentage of workers were reliable. Constant conflicts erupted between the officers and political commissars who shadowed them, as well as between Trotsky and various party members who resented his arrogance and highhandedness. Many units lacked even shoes for their soldiers, and desertion was a constant problem. The Reds, like the Whites, lost more troops to disease than to the enemy. Nonetheless, the Red Army grew quickly and learned how to fight well enough to defeat the Whites, the Greens, and the various other groups opposing the Bolsheviks.

In Russia, terror was a time-honored weapon among the revolutionaries. Lenin embraced it many times, both before and after 1917. In a typical pre-1917 statement he advocated a "real, nationwide terror which reinvigorates the country." In the heat of the Civil War battles he even endorsed "revolutionary violence" against uncooperative elements of the working classes. Trotsky, who prior to 1917 was critical of many of Lenin's methods, during the Civil War advocated the "guillotine" for enemies of the revolution, and explicitly justified any means to achieve the party's revolutionary ends, which he insisted represented the apotheosis of human progress. Although some Bolsheviks did abhor political terror, they were in the minority.

Given these attitudes, the conduct of political terror was therefore a logical development for the Bolsheviks. The *Cheka*, set up on December 20, 1917, began modestly; by March 1918, its staff numbered only 120 and had only conducted one execution. The pace then quickened. In April the *Cheka* struck at the anarchists, a group that between March and November of 1917 had cooperated with the Bolsheviks. By the summer, amidst the opening salvos of the Civil War, the restraints on the *Cheka* dissolved. Over 400 people were shot in the city of Yaroslavl after the Left SR uprising there in July, and over 1,000 in Petrograd and Moscow after the August assaults on Uritsky and Lenin. By the end of 1921, after only three short, if admittedly troubled years, the *Cheka* had claimed more lives than *all* tsarist security forces in the previous *century*.

The *Cheka*'s growth between 1917 and 1922 was nothing short of phenomenal. From its 120-man core it expanded to a bureaucracy of over 30,000, with branches throughout Russia, plus auxiliary branches, such as the 125,000 security troops it controlled. More important than numbers, however, was the expanded scope of its activity. The *Cheka*'s original mandate was to root out the regime's enemies—the counterrevolutionaries, saboteurs, enemy agents, and speculators. By 1922, the *Cheka* had penetrated virtually every area of life in Soviet Russia. It was active in assuring the food supply, in maintaining transport, in policing the Red Army and Navy, in monitoring the schools, and in assuring that vital industries continued to function and deliver essential materials to the state. It hunted speculators and hoarders, sometimes cordoning off entire neighborhoods during its massive search operations. It surrounded peasant villages and shot those resisting the forced requisitions of grain that often left the peasants without enough to eat. It even suppressed strikes by factory workers, the presumed rulers of the "workers' state."

When the government decreed compulsory mass labor in 1919, the *Cheka* managed the vast enterprise. Sometimes it prevented workers from leaving their posts. At other times it tore peasants from their farms to do extremely difficult and perilous jobs. At the behest of the government the *Cheka* set up a formidable network of forced labor and concentration camps, some in the frozen Arctic north, that contained not only "exploiters" but workers and peasants, whose appalling death rate was matched only by the steady influx of new prisoners.

The *Cheka* was not merely a secret police. With the Bolshevik regime locked in a struggle for survival and compelled to mobilize a society uprooted and exhausted by war, revolution, poverty, and disease, the *Cheka* and its terror became a major and pervasive instrument of Bolshevik rule. But this was inherently corrupt and corrupting. All sorts of unsavory characters found their way into the *Cheka's* ranks, people attracted by violence and spoils. Even many who began honestly were corrupted by the unrestrained power they wielded at a time when people gave up the accumulated treasures of a lifetime for food or favors. The *Cheka*, in fact, did not even defer to regular party authority; it was responsible only to the highest leadership. Aside from the dangerous leeway this situation gave the *Cheka*, it enabled the party leadership to ignore not only the will of the population at large, but at times strongly felt sentiments within the party itself. Thus the *Cheka* contributed enormously to altering the party's relationship to the working class, a relationship that increasingly was becoming based not on shared interests but on the force the party was able to muster to bend the workers to its will.

The Civil War was not only a military and political struggle: it was an economic one as well. After November 1917, the economy continued to deteriorate. The impact of the harsh winter of 1917–1918 and the disruption of food production caused by the expropriation and division of the large estates intensified food shortages in the months after the Bolshevik coup. As industrial production dropped, in part because of fuel and food shortages and in part because of the disruption caused by workers' control, the peasants found little to buy and began hoarding their produce. The Treaty of Brest-Litovsk cut off food and fuel from the Ukraine, Russia's breadbasket, since it left that vital area under German occupation. The ravages of the initial Civil War battles in the summer of 1918 further limited available supplies and added to the general misery. The deepening crisis threatened to leave the cities and the Red Army without adequate resources, threatening the regime's ability to defend itself.

The Bolsheviks responded by mobilizing the entire economy for the war effort. Their policy had two central components. First, instead of relying on the marketplace to provide the resources necessary to fight the war, the state took direct control over as much of the economy as possible. Second, it used force as the primary means for making this economic system function. Other major characteristics of this policy included the mobilization and impressment of labor on a vast scale, and the attempt, largely unsuccessful, to suppress all private trade and eliminate money as the prime means of exchange. No overall plan or framework ever existed; many drastic and desperate measures were concocted on the spur of the moment. These diverse measures even lacked a collective name; only in retrospect did they come to be known as "War Communism."

War Communism in its essence was an unstable combination of cold and often cruel expediency born of the Civil War crisis and utopian visions of recreating Russian society in the Marxist equivalent of six biblical days. Because of the magnitude of the crisis, expediency predominated. War Communism's first harbinger was the "food dictatorship" decree of May 1918, which called for using force and class warfare in the villages against the wealthier peasants (called *kulaks*, the Russian word for "fists") to assure the delivery of grain to the state monopoly at fixed prices. In June, "Committees of the Poor" were organized in the villages to expand the war on *kulaks* and speculators. They were joined two months later by machine-gun-equipped "Food Requisition Detachments" from the cities. They seized not only grain and other food, but such other necessities as horses and wagons. Bereft of produce to sell, food to eat, tools to work with, and money to buy the necessities of life they could not produce themselves, the peasants were left to fend as best they could. This was hardly the way to preserve the proletarian-peasant alliance Lenin had postulated as essential to building socialism in Russia.

On June 28, 1918, the government issued the decree generally recognized as marking War Communism's unofficial inauguration. In a display of shocking or commendable audacity, depending on one's point of view, the Bolsheviks nationalized all of Russia's industry. By the end of the Civil War, the state had taken control of 60 percent of the nation's industrial enterprises. The unenviable job of managing that unwieldy conglomeration fell to *Vesenka*. Endowed with extensive powers to run and reorganize industry, *Vesenka* grew into a bulging bureaucratic apparatus of over forty departments. The government also created new institutions to mobilize resources, the most important of these being the Council of Labor and Defense.

Besides plundering the peasantry and seizing Russia's industries, War Communism involved subjecting the population at large to various forms of compulsory labor. This concept, first broached in 1918, encompassed the *Cheka's* labor and concentration camps. It also included conscripting peasants to cart wood and clear railroad tracks of snow. Beginning in 1920, all citizens became subject to conscription for "socially useful work in the interests of socialist society." People from all walks of life found themselves building, constructing roads, and doing agricultural work at the state's behest. Little was overlooked; one mobilization called for women aged eighteen to forty-five to do "socially useful work" by sewing underwear for the Red Army. The most controversial measure was Trotsky's short-lived attempt to establish "labor armies" subject to military discipline by shifting to civilian projects army units no longer needed for fighting.

These intensified restrictions of the population inevitably meant a marked deterioration in the workers' ability to defend their interests against the state. Workers' control and the collegial administration of industrial enterprises associated with it soon gave way to one-man management under the eye of the *Vesenka* bureaucracy. One innovation in controlling workers was the introduction of labor books in which all jobs held by a given individual were recorded. Strikes were forbidden, and armed force was used against those who defied the ban. Special disciplinary courts fined workers or sentenced them to hard labor, and sometimes the authorities cut the already meager rations of recalcitrant workers. Under War Communism the trade unions steadily lost much of their independence. All of this was enforced by a swift and severe administration of justice, much of it handled by the ubiquitous *Cheka*.

In a strict economic sense, War Communism at best yielded meager results and at worst was counterproductive. Nationalization, for example, resulted in an enormous bureaucracy rather than increased production. Industrial production, beset by poor management, inadequate food for the workers, and shortages of materials, continued to plunge despite the government's best efforts.

Matters were no better in food production. The peasantry responded to the grain requisitions first by hoarding their food, then by growing enough only for their own needs, and finally by armed resistance. In some regions, the area sown dropped by over 70 percent. Despite the brutal requisitioning of grain, the cities remained woefully short of food. Equally demoralizing, the bulk of the food that was available reached its hungry consumers through the black market at ever-inflating prices. Urban inhabitants responded by fleeing to the countryside. Moscow lost half of its population and Petrograd more than two thirds. For far too many it did not matter where they moved; between January of 1918 and mid-1920, over 7 million people died from hunger and disease.

Still, War Communism had its defenders. Many Bolsheviks considered it the first experimental stage in the transition to socialism. Perhaps to some extent this type of thinking represented coating unpalatable social medicine with ideological sweeteners, but beyond that War Communism definitely appealed to the more impatient advocates of overhauling

Russian society, who liked using nonmaterial incentives, such as "social-ist competition" between groups of workers, to spur production. These militants viewed nationalization of industry, the suppression of private trade, and collectivization of agriculture as measures essential to building a planned socialist economy, and they were happy to see them taken, even under difficult conditions. In a classic example of beauty being in the eyes of the beholder, many party enthusiasts viewed paying workers in kind, a measure necessitated by runaway inflation, as a positive step toward a socialist economy free of the evil of money.

These feelings were widespread. They were reflected in the idealistic party program adopted at the Eighth Party Congress in 1919. They were clearly in evidence late in 1920, when Lenin himself was arguing for yet harsher economic measures, including an unworkable plan to control the sowing and harvesting of over 20 million peasant households. And it was still very much alive in 1921, when Lenin, now convinced that rising popular discontent and rebelliousness meant War Communism had to go, encountered considerable opposition among his colleagues to proposals for new economic policies. Still, whatever its failures as a long-term economic program, War Communism was a success as an emergency measure for scrounging up what little was available to supply the Red Army and cities with enough resources to enable the Bolshevik regime to survive during the worst years of the Civil War.

Along with the military victory they achieved between the summer of 1918 and the fall of 1920, the Bolsheviks enjoyed surprising success in reattaching the non-Russian parts of the old Russian empire to the new Soviet state. The Bolsheviks' policy regarding the non-Russian nationalities was two-sided. Sympathizers might call it dialectical; cyn-ics would call it hypocritical. On November 15, 1917, the Bolsheviks boldly announced in their "Declaration of the Rights of the People of Russia" the equality of all peoples of Soviet Russia and their right to self-determination, including the right to secede. In practice, as il-lustrated by what happened in Finland and the Ukraine, attempts to secede were met with claims that "counterrevolutionaries" were behind such activities. Simultaneous attempts to subvert the new regimes and to invade their territory followed. The pattern was similar elsewhere. As soon as they had the strength, the Bolsheviks tried to assert their control over the non-Russian parts of the old empire. In Finland, Estonia, Latvia, and Lithuania they failed. In the Ukraine (by far the most important prize), in Central Asia, in Siberia, and in the Caucasus they succeeded.

Still, the November declaration never quite lost all of its propa-ganda value, especially against the background of White declarations of "Russia: one, great, and indivisible." The situation that developed mirrored what occurred with the peasantry; the minorities feared and hated the Bolsheviks but dreaded the Whites more.

The serious fighting between the Reds and the Whites lasted from the summer of 1918 until the fall of 1920, although the decisive battles were fought in 1919. By October 1920, Baron Peter Wrangel, the leader of the last significant White force, was defeated; his final task was to evacuate 150,000 White soldiers and civilians from what was to be a Soviet Russia. At this point, the Bolsheviks turned their attention to Poland. Two ancient enemies with new, grandiose plans once again collided on the broad Eurasian plain. The Poles, hoping to detach Belorussia and the Ukraine from their giant eastern neighbor and reduce it to a second-rate power, had attacked Russia in April 1920. By June they had met defeat. A tantalizing vision then began to dance in Bolshevik heads—the possibility of exporting their revolution to the west. This meant pursuing the defeated Polish army westward in the expectation that the arrival of the Red Army would ignite a socialist uprising in Poland, and that this in turn would spread the revolutionary flame to Germany and the rest of Western Europe. But Lenin and his comrades miscalculated. The Poles did not rally to the red Russian banners but to the forces defending their long-suppressed and cherished dream of an independent national life. In August they stopped the Red Army, in a battle few thought they could win, at the gates of Warsaw.

The defeat at Warsaw ended three years of civil war and left the Bolsheviks with half a loaf. There would be no quick export of the revolution. Prior to the debacle at Warsaw, two communist uprisings had failed in Germany while one collapsed in Hungary after surviving for 133 days as the "Hungarian Socialist Federated Soviet Republic." In March 1921, another quixotic uprising quickly sputtered out in Germany. Meanwhile the Bolsheviks still ruled in Russia, solitary but steadfast guardians of the revolutionary flame.

Yet the party, while victorious, was brutalized by the Civil War's ferocity no less than the rest of Russia. The party became accustomed to ruling by fiat or from the barrel of a gun. The worst example of this development was the behavior of the *Cheka*, but the same dictatorial tendency existed in virtually every party institution. The party had placed itself above the law and the wishes of the population. This method of rule, the "War Communism model" as some have called it, did not disappear when War Communism was abolished in 1921; it fused seamlessly with the authoritarian thrust of Leninism and became a part of the party's guiding legacy.

Along with the "War Communism model" came an important group of its practitioners, for the Civil War years witnessed the rise to prominence of a new type of party cadre—the tough, ruthless functionary unencumbered with ideological inhibitions and willing to use whatever measures were necessary to complete his assignment. At best, these men fit the popular image of the gruff, leather-jacketed commissar rushing from emergency to emergency on his motorcycle. At worst, they were thugs and killers. They penetrated all levels of the party; at the top their representative was Joseph Stalin, who had become one of the party's three or four most powerful men by 1921. Thus, while the party began its struggle to reshape Russian society during the Civil War, the war began to reshape the party itself, in a way that would have enormous historic significance.

NOTES

1. E. H. Carr, *The Bolshevik Revolution*, Vol. II (Baltimore: Penguin, 1966), p. 75.
2. William Henry Chamberlin, *The Russian Revolution*, Vol. II (New York: Grosset and Dunlap, 1965), p. 335.
3. Louis Fisher, *The Life of Lenin* (New York: Harper & Row, 1964), p. 356.
4. Chamberlin, *Russian Revolution*, p. 356.
5. Chamberlin, *Russian Revolution*, p. 345.

11

New Policies and New Problems

We have failed to convince the broad masses.

———LENIN, 1921

The end of Russia's Civil War did not end the Russian people's suffering, or the grave problems the victorious Bolshevik government faced. In 1921 the economy hit bottom. Agricultural production was less than half of what it had been in 1913, the last full year of peace before World War I. Industrial output had declined even more, to about a fifth of the prewar level. Coal production stood at 10 percent of its old level, and pig iron production was at 3 percent. Russia's railroad network barely functioned. Very little food reached the cities; in Petrograd workers doing heavy labor received less than 1,000 calories a day, far beneath the 1,600-calorie daily requirement of an average person. During the fighting at least 7 million people had died from hunger and disease; in the first years of the peace, 1921 and 1922, one of the worst famines in Russia's history claimed 5 million more victims. Although finally at peace for the first time in seven years, Soviet Russia, as the distinguished historian Isaac Deutscher has written:

> . . . stood alone, bled white, starving, shivering with cold, consumed by disease, and overcome with gloom. In the stench of blood and death her people scrambled wildly for a breath of air, a faint gleam of light, a crust of bread. "Is this," they asked, "the realm of freedom? Is this where the great leap has taken us?"[1]

The people did more than just ask questions—they rioted, staged strikes, and rebelled. As the White threat evaporated, the peasants vented their bitterness against the hated food requisitions, labor mobilizations, and generally cruel treatment by staging numerous uprisings against the victorious Reds. The Bolsheviks responded by calling in the *Cheka* to help crush the various insurgencies. It operated without mercy, burning whole villages, seizing hostages, and shooting rebel prisoners. Meanwhile, thousands of workers went on strike in the cities, where Socialist Revolutionary and Menshevik influence was again on the rise. The most important strikes broke out in Petrograd in February 1921; they were broken by the Red Army and through denying striking workers ration cards. This wellspring of discontent produced such a steady flow of new worker and peasant prisoners that the *Cheka* was compelled to open thirteen new forced labor camps in addition to the 107 it had operated during the Civil War. Suddenly, the proletarian-peasant alliance Lenin had often hoped for now existed. Unfortunately for the regime, this inchoate association was forged from a common misery and opposition to the Bolshevik dictatorship, hardly what Lenin expected. As he glumly stated early in 1921, "We have failed to convince the broad masses."

Lenin had other worries besides the disorganized masses or, for that matter, the increasingly popular Mensheviks and SRs. The policies and methods that won the Civil War for the Bolsheviks had also reversed the democratizing trends of the period from March to November 1917, and led to organized opposition *within* the party. A key requirement during the Civil War, as in any war, had been rapid decision making, something the bulky nineteen-member Central Committee could not do. Therefore, the Eighth Party Congress meeting during March 1919 set up two bodies subordinate to the Central Committee: the Politburo (Political Bureau) and Orgburo (Organizational Bureau). They joined another recently created arm of the Central Committee—the Secretariat. Although the Politburo was supposed to report to the Central Committee, the presence of Lenin, Trotsky, and Stalin among its five members meant that it immediately became the Party's policy-making body. The Orgburo and the Secretariat implemented those policies. As such, they also acquired considerable power, particularly the Secretariat, whose responsibilities included assigning, promoting, and checking on officials throughout the party. In effect, these three bodies soon supplanted the Central Committee.

Critics at the Eighth Congress had protested that these new bodies would further centralize power and destroy party democracy. Their fears, in fact, were well founded, but the future they feared already had arrived. The three new organs were merely the crystallization of tendencies dating almost from the Bolshevik coup. By 1919, as Robert Service notes in his study of the party during its first years in power:

Hierarchical discipline and obedience were now accepted on a scale and
with a speed which made an amazingly abrupt contrast with the organizational looseness of early 1918. It had taken merely a few months for customs
of collective deliberation and democratic accountability, which had seemed
so solidly entrenched, to succumb to radical erosion.[2]

This did not bother Lenin at all. As the Civil War wore on he became
less and less tolerant of dissent and increasingly disillusioned with the
masses, particularly the proletariat. Their sin was not merely refusing
to give the Bolsheviks wholehearted support—sometimes they actually
opposed the party's plans. The masses' failure to see the light was, in
Lenin's eyes, sufficient cause to deprive them of their right to determine
their own fate. In 1919 he wrote that "we recognize neither freedom, nor
equality, nor labor democracy if they are opposed to the interests of the
emancipation of labor from the oppression of capital." Lenin further explained that the masses' "low cultural level" meant that the soviets could
only be "organs of government for the working people," rather than "*by*
the working people" (emphasis added). Real decisions would be made by
the "advanced elements of the proletariat," which was none other than the
Bolshevik Party.

Lenin was not alone in his disillusionment with the masses. His critics
within the party, however eloquent or angry they became ("Comrade
Lenin," one of them asked him at the Ninth Party Congress in 1920,
". . . do you think the salvation of the Revolution lies in mechanical
obedience?"), remained a distinct minority. The majority, taken aback
by widespread hostility to the party, convinced by their own ideological
passions that they represented the people's best interests, separated from
the masses by the privileges that went with being part of the governing
elite, and entrenched by the party's suppression of any political opposition, also often lost patience with Russia's workers and peasants. Most
party cadres were quite prepared to use the *Cheka* or other armed
forces to suppress independent proletarian institutions such as factory
committees or to ignore the local soviets. At the same time, if the party
could be made more efficient by abolishing elective offices or even entire
local committees, many would not object. The party, in short, was losing
its character as a revolutionary force and becoming an elite dictating to
rather than leading the proletariat, to say nothing of the rest of the Soviet
people.

This was hardly what the people had bargained for in 1917; the uprisings
and strikes of 1920 and 1921 were ample proof of that. Yet nothing seemed
to shake the party's confidence—until Kronstadt. The Kronstadt naval
base, located on an island in the Gulf of Finland near Petrograd, long
had been a revolutionary hotbed and Bolshevik stronghold, the "pride and

glory of the revolution," according to Trotsky. During the Civil War the Kronstadt sailors furnished the Bolsheviks with reliable cadres on every front. Although the war took its toll, and many veteran revolutionaries were replaced by new peasant recruits, Kronstadt in 1921 remained a vivid symbol of both the revolutionary movement as a whole and of the November Revolution in particular.

Symbol or not, Kronstadt was not immune to the distress and disillusionment sweeping Russia. On March 2, 1921, as the Bolsheviks were preparing to meet at their Tenth Party Congress to chart their revolution's future, the Kronstadt sailors broke with them and elected their own Provisional Revolutionary Committee. The garrison's demands for freedom of political activity for all socialist parties, elections to the soviets based on free and secret ballot, and an end to the privileged position of the Communist Party (as the Bolshevik Party officially was called after 1918) amounted to demanding abolition of the Bolshevik dictatorship in favor of a multiparty socialist regime.

The Kronstadt sailors had thrown down the gauntlet. Their program, after all, sounded very much like the promises of 1917 and corresponded closely to the most widely held conception of what Russia's socialist government should be. At the same time, the rebellious garrison was a rallying point for a broad spectrum of anti-Bolshevik sentiment. Fearful that impending warm weather would melt the ice in the Gulf and make the Kronstadt island fortress impregnable to infantry, the Bolsheviks, after five days of fruitless negotiations, attacked the men they still called their "blinded sailor-comrades." A terrible civil war was now succeeded by political fratricide. Historian Isaac Deutscher described the macabre end of the ten-day battle:

> White sheets over their uniforms, the Bolsheviks advanced across the Bay. They were met by hurricane fire from Kronstadt's bastions. The ice broke under their feet; and wave after wave of white-shrouded attackers collapsed into the glacial Valhalla. The death march went on. From three directions fresh columns stumped and fumbled and slipped and crawled over the glassy surface until they too vanished in fire, ice, and water. . . . Such was the lot of these rebels, who denounced the Bolsheviks for their harshness . . . that for their survival they fought a battle which in cruelty was unequaled throughout the civil war. The bitterness and rage of the attackers mounted accordingly. On 17 March, after a night-long advance in a snowstorm, the Bolsheviks at last succeeded in climbing the walls. When they broke into the fortress, they fell upon the defenders like revengeful furies.[3]

Many thousands died; thousands more were sent to living deaths in concentration camps. For the victorious survivors it was at best a bitter memory, and for many of them a lingering nightmare. Lenin, Trotsky, and other Bolsheviks defended their actions at Kronstadt as essential to preserving the Revolution, but many Bolsheviks were deeply shaken by what they had done to save their party's dictatorship. Lenin took the trouble to defend the battle and subsequent massacre on several occasions, almost to the point of protesting too much. As for Trotsky, as late as August 1940, the final month of his life, he was still defending the "tragic necessity" that took place at Kronstadt.

Kronstadt, the graveyard for thousands of men and many ideals, drove the final nail in the coffin of War Communism. In the face of rising peasant disturbances, the Bolsheviks were ambivalent and divided about this policy in any case, and Lenin himself apparently concluded in February 1921 that it had to go. Kronstadt, by making it clear that popular discontent was a threat to the regime's very existence, convinced most Bolsheviks that Lenin was right.

The decision to scrap War Communism was made in 1921 at the same Tenth Party Congress the Kronstadt uprising had so rudely disturbed. The attending Bolsheviks, their victory over the Whites and rebellious sailors notwithstanding, had little to cheer about. Their plans, like their country itself, were in ruins. Neither of the two conditions Lenin had set for building socialism in Russia stood fulfilled. No socialist revolution had occurred in Western Europe, and the expected proletariat/peasant alliance at home did not exist. At least for the time being, nothing could be done about instigating a socialist revolution in Western Europe, but something absolutely had to be done about relations with the peasantry. Above all, Russia's economy had to be revived. First and foremost this meant that food production had to be increased, something only the peasantry could accomplish. Since the use of force between 1918 and 1921 had achieved precisely the opposite results, the only logical alternative was to discard the ineffective stick for the untried carrot. The New Economic Policy (NEP) was the result.

With the NEP, the Bolsheviks abandoned an economic policy based on centralized control and force in favor of one relying primarily on the marketplace and traditional market incentives. Its cornerstone was the abolition of forced food requisitions, which were replaced by a progressive and rather moderate tax, initially levied in kind and later, beginning in 1922, in cash. The peasants were free to consume what remained or sell what they wished on the open market. This system once again made it sensible for the peasant to produce as much as possible, and under the NEP, despite the primitive farming methods and technology, Russian agriculture recovered rapidly. For 5 million citizens the recovery came too late. They died during the dreadful famine of 1921–1922, when sharply reduced sowing, the consequence of years of war and forced requisitions, combined with drought to produce the worst harvest in decades. Not even help from non-Communist Russians and volunteer organizations from the capitalist West, all enlisted by the desperate Bolsheviks, could contain the tragedy.

The NEP also meant that the Bolsheviks could no longer contain the spread of their hated enemy, capitalism. It quickly became the vibrant part of the NEP economy. Marketing the peasant surpluses required private trade, which was duly legalized shortly after the Tenth Congress adjourned. The small traders who immediately sprang up to market agricultural production were unlovingly dubbed "Nepmen." The Communists despised and feared them as so many seeds ready to sprout into full-blown capitalists, and subjected them to all sorts of discrimination; still they proliferated. Soon there were few areas in the Soviet economy where their services were not needed and their influence felt.

The "strategic retreat," as Lenin rather defensively called the NEP, was not a complete turnabout. The regime still controlled the economy's so-called commanding heights. The state managed foreign trade, the banks, the transport network, and the largest industrial enterprises, employing over 80 percent of Russia's factory workers. These enterprises were organized in a series of "trusts." Significantly, state factories soon were expected to show a profit rather than look for state aid and were run by individual managers, not worker committees. Planning continued, particularly under the aegis of *Vesenka* and a new body, the State Planning Commission (*Gosplan*).

None of this could stop the changes occurring in the vast economic valleys beneath the commanding heights. Common sense dictated that nationalization of small enterprises be undone. Thousands of small plants and shops were returned to their former owners or leased to other entrepreneurs. They quickly became the nation's main source of essential consumer goods. The process did not stop there. Free enterprise brought in its wake a free labor market. In the countryside, although the state retained legal title to the land, free enterprise sank deeper roots as a series of decrees eventually allowed individual peasants to lease land in addition to their allotments and to hire wage laborers. Capitalism, not socialism, held sway where most Russians lived and worked. Economic necessity also led the Bolsheviks to negotiate with foreign capitalist governments, which resulted in a trade agreement with Great Britain in 1921 and a broad economic and political pact with Germany in 1922.

The NEP was quite successful as a policy of recovery. It relieved the worst of Russia's economic shortages by 1923 and restored the economy to a semblance of health by 1925. Ironically, its very successes greatly distressed the Bolsheviks. They, after all, had made their many sacrifices to build *socialism*, not a quasi-capitalist society of peasant entrepreneurs and

Nepmen. The party shared Lenin's fear that freedom of trade would lead to the "victory of capitalism, to its full restoration." In order to prevent this and to keep Russia from slipping from their control, Lenin and his comrades tightened the nation's political reins. That effort had begun in 1921 at the famous and fateful Tenth Party Congress.

The Tenth Party Congress was the point at which the Bolsheviks first became caught in their own net of repression. Although the party had preserved its exclusive hold on power, it was sharply divided over the measures it had used and what it should do next. The various strains of discontent had coalesced into two main groups: the Democratic Centralists and the Workers' Opposition. The Democratic Centralists, made up largely of party intellectuals, criticized the party's increasingly centralized and undemocratic structure, including the growing practice of appointing cadres to local leadership posts formerly filled by election. The Democratic Centralists also objected to the stifling of free discussion within party organs. In effect, the Democratic Centralists complained, these developments were turning the party into a governing bureaucracy distinguished by rank and privilege.

More important was the Workers' Opposition, a faction largely composed of working-class party members. It was led by Alexander Shlyapnikov, a veteran Bolshevik of working-class origins, and by an ex-Menshevik and 1917 convert to Bolshevism named Alexandra Koliontai, the party's best-known feminist and somewhat notorious advocate and practitioner of free love. The Workers' Opposition initially had opposed eliminating workers' control in favor of one-man management and appointing "bourgeois specialists"—technocrats or even former owners of nationalized enterprises—to run plants and factories. It soon had something more ominous to worry about: the party leadership's attempts to strip the trade unions of their autonomy and turn them into little more than arms of the state. The Workers' Opposition wanted the trade unions to control industry. Interestingly and importantly, while both opposition groups complained about conditions *inside* the party, neither was overly concerned about democracy *outside* the party. The fates or rights of the Mensheviks or Socialist Revolutionaries, to say nothing of the Kadets, were of little importance to most Bolshevik dissidents. They did not, in other words, question the party's dictatorship; they simply wanted more democracy for the party membership.

Lenin, meanwhile, was concerned only for the party dictatorship. In his years as the party's leader, Lenin, while always allowing debate, was unwilling to accept compromise and unhesitatingly did what was necessary to get his way. His attitude was no different in March 1921. The party had an enormous country to govern—unity clearly was critically important. He therefore told the Congress that the time had come "to put an end to opposition now . . . to put a lid on it, we have had enough of oppositions."

Lenin's majority passed two resolutions to do the job. One, denouncing "syndicalism and anarchism," condemned the Workers' Opposition and its ideas about trade union independence and control over industry. Lenin's efforts in getting this resolution passed were made easier by Trotsky, who independently presented a resolution that would have totally abolished the independence of the trade unions and made them organs of the state. Lenin then was able to pose as a moderate by proposing a compromise which only deprived the unions of *most* of their independence and placed them under tight party control. While some trappings of independence remained, particularly in terms of dealing with private employers, the substance of their independence was eliminated.

A second resolution—"On Party Unity"—was more encompassing. Rather than merely muzzling one specific distasteful opinion, its target was *any* group holding a point of view different from that of the leadership. "On Party Unity" banned the formation of what were called "factions" within the party. Those opposed to the party leaders were proscribed from organizing to present their views. Dissenters could speak, of course, but only as isolated voices in a chorus conducted by the leadership. No "factions," as organized dissident groups were called, were permitted. This resolution was given teeth by a secret amendment permitting the Central Committee to expel anyone guilty of "factionalism" from the party. If the offender in question sat on the Central Committee, expulsion required a two-thirds majority.

Considerable uneasiness attended the banning of factions, a step that went beyond the traditional limits of democratic centralism. The expulsion amendment remained unpublished for two years, hidden from the party as a whole like some embarrassing mutilation that one hopes will become less hideous over time. Karl Radek, an articulate veteran propagandist and organizer, verbalized the doubt that plagued many of the delegates as they voted for Lenin's resolution. "In voting for this resolution, I feel that it can well be turned against us, and nevertheless I support it . . . ," Radek admitted. Trotsky once wrote of Radek that he "exaggerates and goes too far." Unfortunately for both men and for so many of their comrades, in voicing his opinion this time, Radek did not go nearly far enough.

The party's first extensive purge, conducted in the summer of 1921, reinforced the steps taken at the Tenth Congress. Although the purge's expressed purpose was to root out careerists and opportunists who had joined the party for personal advancement and was therefore not officially directed at "factionalism," it also eliminated many dissenters and therefore served to intimidate those who remained.

While political activity inside the party was being circumscribed, outside the party it was eliminated altogether. During the Civil War the Mensheviks and SRs had been allowed a marginal existence; in 1921, both parties were completely suppressed. Twenty-two SR leaders were tried for counterrevolution in 1922. Although the irregular proceedings and the unfair sentences associated with these trials paled compared to what was to come under Stalin in the 1930s, the SR trials, with their trumped-up charges and propagandistic grandstanding by the prosecution, were the direct ancestors of Stalin's judicial mockeries.

Also in 1922 the *Cheka* was officially abolished, only to rise again immediately as the State Political Administration (GPU). Unlike the *Cheka*, the GPU was a regular branch of the state administration, an important boost in status for the secret police as an institution and an important reassertion of the principle that the Bolsheviks would rule without deference to the public will. The GPU, unlike the *Cheka*, had the right to arrest party members, a telling sign of the times and of things to come.

The years 1921 and 1922 mark an important watershed in the development of the Bolshevik Revolution. During those years Lenin and the party by their actions resolved a fundamental question—whether the Soviet regime would reach an accommodation with the people or rule over them. Any genuine accommodation would have required the abolition of the Bolshevik dictatorship, for by 1921 not even the most faithful had any illusions about their popularity. Zinoviev even estimated that 99 percent of the workers were anti-Bolshevik. This estimate certainly was excessively pessimistic, but both Lenin and Trotsky, men of more resolve and self-confidence than Zinoviev, admitted that the party had lost the support of the masses. Trotsky reflected the leadership's response to this problem when he pronounced that the party's historical mission bound it to "retain its dictatorship, regardless of the temporary vacillations" of the working masses. In other words, the party would decide what the proletariat needed and would make and enforce its decisions, regardless of what the workers thought about the matter.

The events of 1921 and 1922 were not by themselves sufficient to decide the course of the Bolshevik Revolution. The point is that a critical mass of repression was building as events unfolded from year to year. Thus 1917 was the year of the torpedoed socialist coalition government, 1918 the year of the aborted Constituent Assembly, and 1921 the year of strangled opposition within the party. These measures in turn created the need for a permanent and pervasive secret police and led inexorably to events like the Kronstadt tragedy. One by one they produced the major building blocks for what was becoming a new autocracy over the peoples of Russia, one far more severe than that of the fallen tsars. The one-man tyranny predicted by Lenin's critics, of course, was still almost a decade away. But the tyrant was close by. In 1922 Joseph Stalin was appointed to a newly created post—general secretary. This gave him control of the Secretariat, with its enormous patronage powers. In addition, Stalin was the only Bolshevik sitting on the Central Committee, the Politburo, the Orgburo, and the Secretariat, the party's four main power centers.

Meanwhile, by establishing its dictatorship, the party painted itself into a political corner. As the debates at the Tenth Party Congress made clear, the party was deeply divided. The Democratic Centralists and Workers' Opposition could not challenge the leadership, but they did raise a disturbing question—would the party dictatorship being imposed on Russia lead to dictatorship within the party itself?

This problem had several difficult aspects. The existing divisions easily could grow and lead to a split in the ranks, a development that would threaten the Bolshevik dictatorship. The Workers' Opposition was particularly dangerous in this regard because of its strong roots among the trade union rank and file. More worrisome was the danger of debate leaking outside the party sanctum. After all, the spectacle of open debate carried out by organized factions within the party would set an example for everyone in Russia. So the Bolsheviks were forced to deny to themselves what they had denied to others. Their dictatorship was coming home to roost. As the party became the dictator of Russia, the party's leaders became the overlords of the party.

Although the authoritarian mood was unmistakable in the political arena during the NEP years, things were more complex and contradictory in other areas of Russian life. Lenin hated religion, but he felt it was too early to undo completely the work of centuries and destroy religion in Soviet Russia. The Russian Orthodox Church and other religions therefore were subject to a war of attrition rather than an all-out attack. That campaign included measures such as confiscating property, forcibly closing houses of worship, banning religious instruction, and arresting and even executing members of the clergy. The Bolsheviks tried to undermine their main religious enemy, Russian Orthodoxy, by such indirect methods as sponsoring an alternative of their own making, the short-lived "Living Church." A broader attack on religion in general came from enthusiasts organized into the "League of the Militant Godless." However, the state's full weight did not fall on religion until the NEP itself was abolished.

The Bolsheviks' education system at first was a curious amalgam of state control, ideological straitjacketing, and progressive reform. Many distinguished educators, damned for their "bourgeois" origins or sympathies, were driven from their posts or chose to leave Russia. The new educational system stressed technical subjects and expertise in order to create skilled cadres for the new order. At the same time, in order to break down old customs and habits, many progressive concepts were introduced, including coeducation at all levels, genuine student self-government, abolition of examinations, and liberalized discipline. The universities became more accessible to every youth over the age of sixteen; at the same time, the universities lost their autonomy and were placed under state control.

The same uneven mix prevailed in cultural life. Many of Russia's leading cultural figures went into exile during the Civil War. Those who remained found the state controlled most artistic outlets. The state also spawned cultural organizations to push its revolutionary line, although sometimes they got out of control and had to be shut down. Such was the fate of *Proletkult*, an organization of ideologues and artists dedicated to creating a genuinely "proletarian" literature. *Proletkult* was intensely intolerant of other tendencies in literature and of artistic freedom in general. Its zeal eventually made it a nuisance rather than a useful tool of the state, particularly when it claimed total authority in its area of interest and demanded freedom from party control. *Proletkult* therefore was disbanded in 1923.

Despite the state's monopoly of all means of communication, the NEP era still was a quite creative and relatively free period, particularly when compared with what was to come. Supporters of the regime and its ideals, the foremost among them being the talented poet Vladimir Mayakovsky, expressed their enthusiasm through genuinely interesting work, in Mayakovsky's case through a wide range of writings and his remarkable propaganda posters. Significantly, certain non-Communist writers initially enjoyed considerable freedom, particularly those known as "fellow travelers" because of their vague though often ambiguous sympathies for the Revolution. Many "fellow travelers" gathered together in a group called the "Serapion Brethren," an organization dedicated to preserving complete artistic freedom. The best known of this talented group was Yevgeny Zamiatin, whose career in a way epitomizes the fate of artistic freedom during the 1920s. As early as 1921, his essay "I Am Afraid" stressed the urgency of opposing official dogma. Far better known is *We*, a brilliant antiutopian novel that anticipated the work of Huxley and Orwell. *We* was denied publication in Soviet Russia and Zamiatin and many of his friends and associates came under increasing attack as the 1920s wore on. While many bowed to the pressure, Zamiatin was among the few to stand firm; in 1931 he was fortunate enough to be allowed to emigrate.

The relative freedom of the early 1920s even lured back some emigres. Among them was Ilia Ehrenburg, who in his long career as a novelist and journalist found himself both out of favor and an apologist for Stalinism, and Alexis Tolstoy, who ended up as a Stalinist hack. Others, like the poets Boris Pasternak and Osip Mandelstam, who did not support the regime, never left Soviet Russia but managed to keep working. Average citizens, however, did not necessarily get a chance to appreciate that work. Most of Pasternak's prose remained unpublished in the Soviet Union until 1982; his great novel, *Dr. Zhivago*, for which he won the Nobel Prize in 1958, waited three decades to be published in his native land.

Considerable creativity survived in the state-controlled theater and cinema, both of which the regime used extensively to deliver its message to a mass audience. The theater's outstanding personality, director Vsevolod Meerhold, was extremely innovative in using the theater to create "proletarian" art and bring the arts to the Russian masses. Sergei Eisenstein was Russia's most distinguished movie director. Two of the films he made in the 1920s—*The Battleship Potemkin*, the story of the dramatic mutiny by sailors on a warship in 1905, and *Ten Days That Shook the World*, an adaptation of the account of the November Revolution by American journalist John Reed—represent a remarkable synthesis of political propaganda and artistic achievement.

Perhaps culture during the NEP years appears to shine so brightly because of the stark contrast with the pitch darkness that followed under Stalin. Repression certainly existed in many areas of cultural life, but it was neither uniform nor overwhelming. Cultural historian James H. Billington succinctly characterized the Lenin years as "something of a chaotic interregnum,"[4] a description that may be stretched to include the first few years after Lenin died. Given the new order that followed, chaos never looked so good.

Bolshevik nationalities policy also oscillated between flexibility and repression during the 1920s. The Bolsheviks were unyielding, their official doctrine notwithstanding, when it came to the question of self-determination. Those peoples formerly subject to the tsars who established their independence after 1917 did so only because the Bolsheviks lacked the power to stop them. However, the Bolsheviks did grant considerable cultural autonomy to the non–Great Russians still within the Soviet state, a group that at the time accounted for about half of the population. Ukrainians and Belorussians, Slavic peoples with their own territory and languages, received opportunities long denied them by the tsars to use their languages and develop their native cultures. Russia's 3 million Jews found that the state harassed their religion as it did others, but the Bolsheviks did make anti-Semitism a crime and permitted a considerable range of cultural self-expression in Yiddish, although not in Hebrew. The Bolshevik regime even helped develop written languages for numerous illiterate tribes scattered across Asia. Finally, when a new constitution was written in 1923, it was based on the principle of federalism and provided for four constituent Soviet republics in a Union of Soviet Socialist Republics: the Russian, Ukrainian, Belorussian, and Transcaucasian Soviet Federated Socialist Republics.

All this consideration given the minority nationalities served a greater purpose. Spreading education, regardless of the language used, spread the new socialist gospel as well. Yiddish, for example, was a weapon used to wean Jews away from their religion, an endeavor aided by mass closings of synagogues and the activities of a special unit of the Communist Party called the *Yevsektsiya*, or "Jewish section." At the same time, Hebrew was suppressed by the mid-1920s because the Communists insisted it was, simultaneously, the language of the Jewish bourgeoisie, of religion, and of Zionism, the last already outlawed in 1919. Soviet Moslems were taught how to write, but in a new Latin rather than an Arabic script, in order to isolate them from Moslems across the border. (Later, in order to link the Moslems more closely to the Slavic majority, a Cyrillic script replaced the Latin one.) Although the Union of Soviet Socialist Republics proclaimed in 1924 supposedly was a federal state with each "union republic" enjoying the right to secede, real power was exercised by the centralized and unitary Communist Party. As for the right to secede, it would only be honored if the initiative came from the "proletariat," a rather unlikely development since the regime automatically classified all such agitation as "bourgeois."

The Bolsheviks' relative success in dealing with the various non-Russian nationalities contrasted with the difficulties they had with the economy. It soon became clear that the party's ambitions for beginning a planned economy and industrial development were faltering. The NEP, no less than War Communism, was a product of dire necessity. Unlike War Communism, which at least looked like socialism to many Bolsheviks, the NEP had little redeeming socialist value. It deeply offended Marxist sensibilities to permit such a widespread revival of capitalism in Russia. Particularly galling was the broad and increasing concessions to the peasantry, the class that to Marxists represented everything that was obscurant and reactionary. Yet there was little choice. Denied the aid from Europe they had hoped for because the anticipated socialist revolution there did not materialize, the Bolsheviks were forced to rely on what the peasantry produced at home. In practice this meant such unpalatable concessions as allowing the more prosperous peasants to lease additional land and hire wage laborers.

In industry the picture was equally demoralizing. Small-scale and light industry had been largely turned over to private entrepreneurs or cooperatives. Only Russia's large-scale heavy industry remained in state hands. Yet this sector, hampered by the loss of foreign skills and capital as well as the emigration of native managerial and technical personnel, showed the slowest recovery rate in the Russian economy. Heavy industry drained the state budget and produced inadequate supplies of goods at excessively high prices in return. Even the light industry that produced consumer goods failed to reach 50 percent of its prewar production by 1923. The result was the so-called scissors crisis (named for a graph Trotsky used to illustrate the problem) of that year, during which the prices of scarce industrial goods soared relative to plentiful agricultural products. The danger that farmers would refuse to market their produce under such unfavorable conditions led the government to compel the state-run industries to lower their prices, even at the expense of industrial wages. On top of that, the decision to close some inefficient plants caused unemployment. When a wave of strikes broke out, the regime called in the GPU. After only two years of the NEP, the "workers' state" was being forced to sacrifice the proletariat's interests and the ability of industry to earn profits to be used as capital for future development to the interests of the despised peasantry. Meanwhile, the Nepmen were looking more and more like a fledgling bourgeoisie. No wonder that some cynics called the NEP the "new exploitation of the proletariat."

The Bolsheviks tended to blame many of their domestic problems on international developments, particularly their unenviable position as the lone socialist state making its way in a capitalist world. Trotsky in 1906 had outlined the problem that some feared had come to pass:

> Without the direct state support of the European proletariat, the working class in Russia will not be able to maintain itself in power and convert its temporary supremacy into a lasting socialist dictatorship. We cannot doubt this for a moment.

Intoxicated by their own success, the Bolsheviks believed the potential for revolution was there and in 1919 set up an organization to cater to it: the Communist International (Comintern). The Bolsheviks called their international the Third International to distinguish it from the reformist Second International, the organization of the world's Social Democratic parties. An equally important distinction was that the Second International was an association of independent political parties; from the start the Third International was dominated by the Russian Communist Party, the only member that was not a newly formed, marginal sect. That control was consecrated by the twenty-one conditions imposed on all member parties at the organization's Second Congress in 1920. Each member party was obliged to organize itself along centralized Bolshevik lines, adhere to ideological positions as defined in Moscow (allegedly by the Comintern's Executive Committee but actually by the Bolshevik Politburo), and stand ready to help the "Soviet Republics" in their struggle against "counterrevolution."

The period between 1919 and 1924 brought defeat and disappointment, not a European revolution. Throttled in the West, the Comintern began considering an end run around the European capitalist bulwark. At its "Congress of Peoples of the East," held in September 1920 in Baku, a city on the western shore of the Caspian Sea, delegates expressed the hope that the European capitalist states could be undermined by nationalist revolutions in their colonies. Baku's Asiatic atmosphere seemed to cast a bit of a spell on the European-bred Soviet leaders who organized the conference. Zinoviev, the Comintern's chairman, issued a call for a "holy war" against British capitalism, while Bela Kun, former leader of the defunct "Hungarian Socialist Federated Soviet Republic," offered the distinctly non-Marxist thesis that communism could be established in an economically backward country that did not even have an industrial proletariat! Aside from the dramatic rhetoric, the conference yielded little for the Bolsheviks or their would-be proteges: the colonial revolt against the West was still a generation away. A "Congress of Toilers of the East" held in Moscow in 1922 did no more than the Baku meeting to change that fact.

Actually, the Bolsheviks did not set a very good example for aspiring European or Asiatic revolutionaries. They made some efforts to foment unrest abroad, but at the same time the failure of those efforts compelled them to enter into normal relations with other nations in a world they seemed unable to change. After years of war and blockade, Soviet Russia desperately needed to trade with the outside world. The Bolsheviks had to accept a sort of diplomatic NEP. This meant that within the Comintern, attempts to establish communist regimes had to yield to the "united front" tactics or cooperation with noncommunist parties having some sort of progressive pedigree in Bolshevik eyes. More importantly, during 1920 and 1921, the Bolsheviks signed peace treaties with Estonia, Latvia, Lithuania, Finland, and Poland on their European frontiers and with Turkey, Persia, and Afghanistan on their Asian borders. These treaties enabled the Soviet regime to secure most of its enormous flank and break the diplomatic isolation that had lasted for the duration of the Civil War.

The Soviets won a far bigger prize on March 16, 1921, when they reached a trade agreement with Great Britain. Until then, hostility to Bolshevism and the Soviet regime's cancellation of tsarist debts and nationalization of foreign property had precluded any commercial, much less diplomatic, relations with the major European powers. Once the British set their example, similar agreements quickly followed.

Neophyte Soviet diplomacy achieved its most dramatic success on April 16, 1922. Both Germany and Russia were pariahs in Europe, the former because it had been branded by the victorious Allies as being responsible for World War I and the latter because it declared war on capitalism in the name of revolutionary socialism. Both nonetheless were invited to attend a major economic conference at Genoa in April 1922. Neither country was able to get what it wanted from the victorious but parsimonious allies, Soviet Russia's unrealized objectives being a loan and diplomatic recognition. So at the nearby resort of Rapallo the two outcasts reached their own agreement, announcing to a surprised world on April 16 that they had established diplomatic and commercial relations and renounced all claims against each other. Aside from the shock this treaty of pariahs produced in the West (where the view somehow persisted that these two former Great Powers could be ignored and abused without catastrophic consequences), the Rapallo agreement facilitated secret military cooperation between Russia and Germany, cooperation which enabled Germany to evade the disarmament strictures of the Versailles treaty and provided Russia with much needed experience in modern military techniques, including armored and aerial warfare.

It took a bit longer, until 1924, for the rest of Europe to fall into line. Then, convinced that the Soviet regime was going to last and anxious for access to the Russian market, most major European states, including Great Britain, France, and Italy, granted the Soviet Union diplomatic recognition. The Soviets meanwhile continued their unique brand of foreign policy. They combined normal diplomatic relations with subversion against capitalist states, although after 1921 the former predominated and even the Comintern was leashed to Russian national interests, as promoting international revolution was subordinated to defending the Soviet state.

A more intractable and important problem, and the one that took the largest share of Lenin's time during his last years, lay much closer to home. By 1922, Lenin was worried that something was terribly wrong with Bolshevism. Perhaps being incapacitated by his first stroke in May of that year and therefore forced to observe from the sidelines gave him a new perspective on his regime. In any case, the founder and builder of the Bolshevik Party sensed that his prized political machine was beginning to run out of control, and used the term "bureaucratism" to describe what bothered him. His concerns were not the growth of bureaucracy per se and things commonly associated with it, such as red tape and an impersonal method of operation, although these tendencies certainly disturbed him. Instead, Lenin was deeply worried about the basic relationship between the governing party and the people it governed. Bureaucratism to Lenin meant the growing gulf between officialdom and the people, the tendency of officials to surround and insulate themselves with privileges and to focus on their own interests rather than those of the public they supposedly served. It meant abusive treatment of the powerless by the powerful, sometimes to the point of physical violence. Simple corruption also fell under the damnable rubric of bureaucratism. In short, bureaucratism was the domination and exploitation of the Soviet people by their Bolshevik government.

All this was a terrible shock to Lenin, who, for all his hard-headed realism, believed in many of the things he wrote about in *State and Revolution*, at least as ideal goals. Bureaucratism to Lenin was one of the most hateful aspects of "bourgeois" and especially tsarist society and high on the list of things slated for extinction after the revolution. Unfortunately, it had not taken long for Lenin's regime to succumb to creeping bureaucratism. In part this reflected the transformation of the Bolshevik Party from a revolutionary phalanx into an administrative apparatus attempting to govern an enormous, poor, and troubled country that did not share the party's goals. One aspect of this was the changing nature of the party's membership as it was flooded by careerists, people not interested in what they could do for the cause, like those who had joined in the old days, but in what the cause could do for their personal careers. But something more fundamental was at work. Because the Bolsheviks were determined to rule alone and considered any challenges to their policies to be sedition, the party automatically cut itself off from the people it governed. As it solidified what was increasingly its arbitrary power, the party became corrupted by that power.

This syndrome was not new to Russia. In tsarist times there had been no political checks on the autocracy; hence the tyranny of the tsarist bureaucracy. In Lenin's Russia there were no checks on the Soviet central government. Therefore, the same phenomenon began to appear, although this time it was a revolutionary rather than reactionary bureaucracy that bore down on the people and enforced the decisions of a ruling clique responsible only to itself.

Lenin's battle against bureaucratism actually began as early as 1919 with the creation of a watchdog commissariat called the Workers' and Peasants' Inspectorate (*Rabkrin*). *Rabkrin*'s job was to root out corruption and waste in other governmental agencies. Within the Communist Party, a series of "control commissions" headed by a Central Control Commission was assigned the same job after 1920. *Rabkrin*'s chief was none other than Joseph Stalin. This new commissariat, of course, was no more responsive to the will of the population at large than any other part of the state bureaucracy. Stalin actually used it to promote his own political fortunes. By the time this dawned on Lenin in 1921, *Rabkrin* had become one of the most detested arms of the hydra-headed Soviet bureaucracy. Approximately the same can be said for the work of the control commissions, which did more to suppress dissent than to fight bureaucratism and bring the party closer to the masses.

Lenin's offensive against bureaucratism went into high gear in 1922. He focused on several areas of misconduct, all of which, not incidentally, were linked to Stalin, the man initially assigned to fight the scourge. By mid-1922 Stalin had acquired enormous power by placing himself at every key point of Lenin's party, and, although few realized it, was already the second most powerful man in Russia. Lenin attacked him for two major offenses: his unsatisfactory performance as *Rabkrin's* chief official and his part in a shocking episode that occurred in the recently reconquered Georgia, a small country originally absorbed by Russia in the late eighteenth century but independent since 1918.

Lenin had sanctioned the reconquest of that small republic in 1921. This action broke no precedent, but was a part of the process of reassembling most of the patrimony, Russian and non-Russian, once governed by the tsars. Besides, Georgia was governed, and governed well, by, of all people, the Mensheviks, who made no secret of their distaste for Lenin and his Bolsheviks. ("We prefer the imperialists of the West to the fanatics of the East," said Georgia's president, Noah Zhordania.) The reconquest, against courageous resistance, and the subsequent ousting of a democratically elected regime, bothered Lenin not at all. He was, after all, suppressing Mensheviks himself in Moscow. What followed was another matter. The Communists sent from Moscow to oversee the establishment of Bolshevik rule treated their Georgian Communist comrades no better than they treated other Georgians. Local Georgians, whatever their political leanings, were given no real input into deciding how their country should be governed, and were particularly disturbed by the decision to merge their homeland with other Transcaucasian regions into a "Transcaucasian Federated Republic." A long list of abuses, including using physical violence rather than comradely debate as a means of persuasion, reached Lenin. He reacted by condemning the ranking Moscow emissary on the scene, a Georgian named Sergo Ordzhonikidze. Equally important, Lenin strongly criticized Ordzhonikidze's boss, General Secretary Joseph Stalin, himself a Georgian.

With Stalin at so many trouble spots (the two men also clashed over the proposed new constitution and issues involving foreign trade), Lenin's struggle against bureaucratism merged with his attempt to limit Stalin's power. Both efforts were complicated by Lenin's deteriorating health. The last eighteen months of his life resembled the struggles of a drowning man. Three times strokes dragged him down. Twice he struggled up to renewed political activity. His first stroke occurred on May 22, 1922. After a five-month recuperation Lenin was back on the job, although at a reduced level of activity and effectiveness. A second stroke in December left Lenin partially paralyzed and temporarily speechless. Just as his campaign against Stalin seemed to be getting into high gear, Lenin suffered a third stroke on March 7, 1923. This time he remained a virtual invalid until his death in January 1924.

Had Lenin lived, he might well have succeeded in removing Stalin; overcoming political opponents was a skill Lenin knew well. He would have had a far more difficult time with bureaucratism. Not only was this a foe Lenin never had faced before and a phenomenon that far transcended any one man or group of men, but Lenin himself was a central part of the problem. While he was battling bureaucratic tendencies with one hand, he was building them with the other. He approved Stalin's appointment as general secretary in large part because more effective administrative controls were deemed necessary after oppositionists embarrassed the leadership at the Eleventh Party Congress held in March 1922. One of the worst moments at the congress occurred when Lenin defended the Bolshevik dictatorship *over* the working class on the grounds that the Russian proletariat was too weak to rule because it had disintegrated as a class during the recent difficult years. Shlyapnikov's caustic reply must have hurt as only the truth can: "Vladimir Ilich said yesterday that the proletariat as a class, in the Marxian sense, did not exist [in Russia]. Permit me to congratulate you on being the vanguard of a non-existent class." For his efforts to combat what may fairly be called *Lenin's* bureaucratic tendencies, Shlyapnikov was dropped from the Central Committee and saw his views condemned in a special resolution at the Congress. He was not, as Lenin wanted, expelled from the party. That job, as well as Shlyapnikov's subsequent liquidation, was done by Stalin.

Lenin meanwhile reinforced the party's dictatorship over the proletariat in several ways. After the Tenth Party Congress, the trade unions functioned, but with clipped wings. By 1922 the Soviets were purged of Mensheviks and Socialist Revolutionaries and increasingly subject to directives from the Bolshevik leadership. The secret police was alive and active. The number of concentration camps in Russia almost tripled to 355 between 1921 and the end of 1923, in part because of an influx of dissident workers, peasants, and socialists of various types. Not even party members were safe. Many dissidents were expelled in the purge of 1921. Those who remained politically active after their expulsion ran the risk of arrest; some dissidents who were not expelled complained bitterly of house searches, mail seizures, and even attempts at entrapment by undercover agents.

Lenin militantly supported all of this. In February 1922, he urged intensified repression against the "political enemies of Soviet power and the agents of the bourgeoisie (specifically the Mensheviks and SRs)." He wanted what he called "model trials" staged as examples to potential dissidents and for propaganda purposes. Over the long term, Lenin had strict requirements for Soviet Russia's proposed new criminal code: "The paragraph on terror must be formulated as widely as possible, since only revolutionary consciousness of justice can determine the conditions of its application." Defendants, in other words, should have as little recourse as possible to legal rights and guarantees. If Lenin was concerned about bureaucratism, about Soviet life becoming more authoritarian and arbitrary, he certainly had an odd way of showing it.

Still, Lenin did try to do something about the deterioration of the Bolshevik regime. As 1922 wore on, he struggled against both Stalin and bureaucratism while at the same time trying to prevent another crisis—a split and struggle for power among his chief lieutenants. Late in the year he directed two major salvos at Stalin: a critique of *Rabkrin* in August and a denunciation of "dominant nation chauvinism"—in other words, of Stalin's handling of the Georgian affair—in October. Lenin also tried to rally others to his cause. Twice he unsuccessfully urged Trotsky to become vice-chairman of *Sovnarkom*, a post which would have made him Lenin's number one deputy and greatly strengthened his political standing. Lenin also urged that the two men form a "bloc against bureaucracy in general."

Lenin's second stroke, a mild one, hit in mid-December. It was immediately followed by the most important of Lenin's writings during these years, his "Testament," written late in December, to which a "Postscript" was dictated on January 4, 1923 (both kept secret from most party leaders until 1924). The "Testament" was a critique of each of the major party leaders. It implied that Lenin did not want any one man, but rather a collegium, to succeed him. None of his lieutenants were quite fit. Stalin already had too much power and might not use it well. Bukharin was ideologically suspect. Zinoviev and Kamenev had caved in during the crucial days of 1917. Trotsky, still Lenin's apparent favorite, could be too authoritarian. Lenin also suggested enlarging the Central Committee to a total of fifty to one-hundred members. Such a step, Lenin hoped, would help prevent a split among the party leaders, in particular between Trotsky and Stalin.

Lenin's "Postscript" went further than his "Testament." One thing absolutely had to be done, he warned. Because Stalin was "too rude," a characteristic "unbearable in the office of General Secretary," Lenin urged that he be removed and replaced by someone "more patient, more loyal, more polite, and more attentive to comrades, less capricious, etc."

Although already gravely ill, Lenin pushed on. By now he was floating all sorts of ideas to keep the party dictatorship he had built from degenerating into a modernized version of the late tsarist autocracy. "How We Should Reorganize *Rabkrin*," Lenin's instructions to the forthcoming Twelfth Congress, was published on January 15, 1923. Lenin's key point, aside from urging that *Rabkrin* be drastically reduced in size, again was that the party renew its ties with the working class. He modified his plan to pack the Central Committee by suggesting that workers instead be co-opted to the Central Control Commission, which would meet jointly with the Central Committee. In "Better Fewer, But Better," his last article, published on March 4, Lenin went still further. He stressed that the Party not only had to tap the workers' revolutionary spirit, but the skills and culture of Soviet Russia's educated, nonparty people.

Lenin put much of his remaining energy into a speech he planned to give to the Twelfth Congress attacking Stalin. He also sent a note to Trotsky on March 5 urging him to carry the offensive against Stalin at the upcoming congress, and a note to Stalin in reaction to the latter's extremely rude treatment of Krupskaya, Lenin's devoted wife and indispensable aide of twenty-three years. A bitterly angry Lenin threatened to sever all personal ties with Stalin if an apology were not immediately forthcoming. Two days later, Lenin suffered his third stroke.

Lenin's last stand came too late. His Central Committee already was split. The so-called Stalin-Zinoviev-Kamenev Triumvirate was pitted against Trotsky. Stalin meanwhile was using the general secretary's immense patronage power so effectively that he already had more leverage in the party than any other of Lenin's would-be heirs. His supporters, in alliance with those of Zinoviev and Kamenev, controlled the Twelfth Congress in April 1923, which Lenin could not attend because of ill health. Stalin used a reorganization plan that on the surface conformed with Lenin's desire to bring new blood into the party as a means to place his cronies in key party and state positions. By the end of 1923, although Lenin still was clinging to life, Trotsky was isolated enough to put aside his own authoritarianism and demand a return to what he called "intra-Party democracy."

Much more was wrong with Lenin's efforts than timing. His campaign against bureaucratism was as feeble as his health. It focused on individuals or symptoms rather than on the Bolshevik system as a whole. For example, he suggested that only the most dedicated people—"some good people" or "the right people"—should be recruited for the state or party apparatus. To combat inefficiency and intolerable behavior, Lenin felt an enormous education effort was needed to raise the Bolshevik's level of "culture." Initially, even "real bourgeois culture" would be an improvement, although Lenin looked forward to what he called a "cultural revolution."

Unwilling to go to the heart of things—that establishing a dictatorship, even Bolshevik dictatorship, meant oppression, corruption, and hence bureaucratism—Lenin grasped at straws. In 1923, he even turned to the proletariat, the very same mass that since 1902 he had insisted was inept and unconscious and needed his "vanguard" to lead it along. Now it was the vanguard that needed help. That is why Lenin suggested that 75 to 100 genuine workers be elected to the Central Control Commission and that the Commission meet in joint session with the Central Committee. Presumably, the proletariat's very presence in the inner sanctums of power would automatically clear the stagnant air that was suffocating socialism. By a process Lenin did not elaborate on, proletarian honesty and purity would invigorate his dried-up Central Committee.

Lenin's hopes were misplaced. Individuals could not alleviate problems that were rooted in the nature of the regime. For example, thousands of workers were added to the party after his death in the "Lenin enrollment," but their selection and placement were determined by the very people who controlled the levers of the party bureaucracy, thereby strengthening the very forces Lenin opposed. Stalin's interests, not Lenin's objectives, were the beneficiaries of this tactic.

Lenin's dilemma was that he wanted to invigorate the party, but would not permit genuine criticism of his policies from within the party, to say nothing of suggestions from outside it. He wanted the proletariat to improve the party, but would not let it judge the party—it might "vacillate," in Trotsky's words. He would not even let the proletariat have its own independent trade unions, only unions controlled by the increasingly corrupt Bolshevik Party. He wanted to prevent the party from ruling arbitrarily and cruelly, but would not allow it to be subject to laws and legal norms that could have restrained it.

Lenin, in reality, could undertake no genuine reform. To do so would have limited the party's freedom of action and raised the possibility of its being thrown out of office, thereby violating the prime directive underlying everything he had done since the Bolshevik seizure of power in November 1917. Given his commitment to untrammelled Bolshevik power, Lenin was no more capable of reversing the advance of bureaucratism that was killing his dream than he was of stopping the arteriosclerosis that was killing him.

As for Lenin himself, the lion went out like a lamb. In December 1923, the avowed atheist spent an evening with family and friends around a Christmas tree as gifts were given out. On January 19, Krupskaya read him Jack London's short story "Love of Life." It tells of a sick man, dying of hunger and unable to walk, who survives a life-and-death struggle with a starving wolf and somehow reaches safety. Lenin greatly enjoyed the story; possibly he took hope from it. Two days later, not yet fifty-four years old, the living embodiment of Bolshevism was dead.

Lenin's death gave birth to a new secular cult, promoted by his successors, which led to his being revered by millions of true believers. Eventually his career spawned a no less durable debate among serious observers and students of the Bolshevik Revolution, both Marxist and non-Marxist. To what extent, the argument runs, was Lenin responsible for the totalitarian society that developed in the Soviet Union under Stalin? Did Lenin prepare the way for Stalin, or was Stalinism a betrayal of the ideals and practices that have come to be called Leninism?

Some of Lenin's achievements are largely beyond debate. By modifying, some would say mutilating, Marxism, he adapted it to the Russian political environment. His "party of a new type" gave Marxism the protective armor it needed in Russia and provided a model for Marxists in many other countries. To this he added two key political insights: the concept of the peasantry as a revolutionary class allied to the proletariat and his analysis of the revolutionary opportunities imperialism created for Russia. Lenin also had extraordinary gifts of decisiveness, timing, and flexibility. In combination with his ruthlessness and courage these characteristics made Lenin an unsurpassed master at winning and holding power.

Power, however, was not an end in itself; it was a means to an end. While it is difficult to be certain precisely what Lenin had in mind when he talked about "socialism" and "communism," it seems fair to say that he envisioned a collectivistic society with a high standard of living based on advanced technology in which the population at large would actively, willingly, and enthusiastically work toward generally accepted goals. This was the vision contained in *State and Revolution*. It also seems fair to say that Lenin did *not* spend his life working for a revived autocracy bearing down ever more heavily on the Russian people through a new bureaucratic machine. This is the meaning of his struggle against "bureaucratism" and why he expressed his fear about the revival of the old Russian bureaucratic tradition with a "Soviet veneer." It also accounts for his eleventh-hour struggle against Stalin.

Stalin's rise to power resulted in a tyranny over the Russian people far worse than Lenin or almost anyone else could have imagined in the 1920s. Yet the evidence is compelling that Lenin, whatever his intentions, prepared the way for Stalin. Before 1917, Lenin created a political party with an ethos that, in the name of revolution, justified many activities that repelled many other revolutionaries. That ethos also heartily endorsed a regime based on force so long as it was a "proletarian dictatorship" committed to socialism. Lenin's highly centralized party also required all members to subordinate themselves completely to the collective; all members, that is, except the leader.

However, the key to Stalin's rise to power was the interaction between Bolshevik theory and practice and the extreme strains and harsh conditions of the period between 1917 and Lenin's death in 1924. In order to stay in power during those difficult years, Lenin initiated or approved virtually every institutional process that Stalin later used to establish his dictatorship: the authority of the Politburo and the tentacles of the Secretariat; the rule that forming a "faction" within the party was tantamount to treason; the Central Committee's power to expel party members simply for actively disagreeing with the leadership; the party's control of every branch of the state; the party's attempt to control every institution in

Russian life, leaving no room for anything that opposed the Bolshevik dictatorship; and a secret police operating above the law as an integral part of Soviet society. Lenin's government also engaged in brutal and widespread repression, established and expanded a network of concentration camps, staged farcical political show trials, and wrote a criminal code giving the state almost unlimited repressive powers.

A vitally important product of the centralism Lenin infused into Bolshevism and of the harsh measures used to maintain the party's dictatorship after November 1917 was the steady narrowing of the party's decision-making structure. Overwhelming power became concentrated in a tiny group of men holding a few key bureaucratic levers. Because of this, the Bolshevik Party was a pyramid standing on its point rather than on its base and therefore was subject to being upset by sudden jolts. In practice this meant the possibility that after Lenin was no longer there one of the leaders at the top might seize power from the others and impose his will on the party as a whole. This, in fact, is what happened, and there is every reason to consider this development a natural eventuality deriving from the nature of Bolshevism. (Trotsky had predicted as much back in 1904.) That the man who succeeded in doing this was Stalin, a warped individual who committed innumerable criminal acts, including mass murder, both on behalf of and against the party, cannot be seen as an inevitable outgrowth of Bolshevism. But although Stalin was different from the other Bolshevik leaders in several fundamental ways, the key point remains that the political structure Lenin built was made to order for such a horrible historical development to occur. In that sense, Lenin must be judged as responsible for Stalin and what occurred after Stalin took control of the party.

Beyond that, and even assuming someone other than Stalin had won the struggle for power, in establishing a regime based on force rather than on popular consent and the rule of law, Lenin reached a political dead end. Force, expedience, and ruthlessness served him well in seizing and holding power. They were futile and counterproductive for achieving anything remotely resembling the socialist society he described in *State and Revolution*. Ironically, his successful quest for power made his use of it a failure. As historian Rolf H. W. Theen has pointed out, Lenin

> . . . was unable to recognize that he could not manipulate Russian society as he had manipulated his party and at the same time hope to develop the mutual trust between the ruled and the ruler which is the foundation and *conditio sine qua non* of any civilized government.[5]

The idea of a revolutionary state overhauling Russia by force was neither new nor uniquely Lenin's; Russian revolutionaries from Tkachev to

Trotsky had endorsed the concept. Lenin's contribution was to develop the basis for such a state in practice. In doing so, he went beyond what traditional Marxism suggested was possible and ran into the precise dilemma it predicted. Before Lenin was born, Friedrich Engels, writing about Thomas Münzer, a sixteenth-century visionary with communistic notions, commented that Münzer's actions "paved the way to a social system that was the direct opposite of what he aspired to." The same almost certainly was true for Lenin.

If Lenin would be unhappy about sharing Münzer's fate, he might take posthumous comfort in knowing that he played a pivotal role in preventing Russia from sharing the West's capitalistic and parliamentary fate he so hated, at least until the last decade of the century. For the Bolshevik Revolution in the end guaranteed one thing: that Russia's course of modernization would be by a different path than any other nation had taken before. Lenin must be judged on the basis of the burdens that path imposed on the people he promised he would lead to a better world.

NOTES

1. Isaac Deutscher, *The Prophet Unarmed, Trotsky: 1921–1929*, Vol. II (New York: Vintage, 1965), p. 1.
2. Robert Service, *The Bolshevik Party in Revolution* (New York: Barnes and Noble, 1979), p. 110.
3. Isaac Deutscher, *The Prophet Armed, Trotsky: 1879–1921*, Vol. I (New York: Vintage, 1965), pp. 513–514.
4. James H. Billington, *The Icon and the Axe* (New York: Vintage, 1970), p. 532.
5. Rolf H. W. Theen, *Lenin* (Princeton, N.J.: Princeton University Press, 1973), pp. 139–140.

PART FOUR

Steeling the Revolution

12

Bolshevism Without Lenin

It's a struggle for the throne—that's what [it is.]

———STALIN, 1923 OR 1924

If Lenin were alive now, he would be in one of Stalin's prisons.

———KRUPSKAYA, 1927

Lenin's death left the Bolshevik Party politically orphaned. In the past, whatever the problems it faced, the party had known who its leader was. Suddenly, Lenin was gone; only the problems that had sapped his last strength remained. Replacing Lenin would have been extremely difficult under any foreseeable circumstances. Devising coherent policies for dealing with the degeneration of party life and disturbing tendencies in the NEP would have been difficult even with Lenin at the helm. After January 1924, the party faced the herculean task of performing these tasks simultaneously.

Because the Bolsheviks had never before had to choose a leader, the process became lengthy, disorderly, and disruptive. This was not because of any formal arrangements or offices that Lenin held. He had been the chairman of the *Sovnarkom*, but he held no titles within the party that distinguished him from his leading colleagues. His formal status on the Politburo and Central Committee was like any other member's. Neither body had a chairman and both decided issues by majority vote, votes that Lenin sometimes lost.

Nevertheless, the man who listed his party role as merely "member of the Central Committee" was irreplaceable. He was the heart and soul of the Bolshevik Party, its founder and the only leader it had ever known. He also was the linchpin of the Soviet regime; while he was still healthy no major decisions were implemented without him. He wielded almost dictatorial power by persuasion rather than force and was able to do so because his political stature dwarfed that of every other party leader. It loomed so large that many of his colleagues could not conceive of governing without him.

Although Lenin's mystique prevented any of his lieutenants from openly claiming the right to succeed him, this did not prevent several of them from struggling for position and power against each other even while the sick leader still lived. Two men dominated the unofficial battlefield: Leon Trotsky and Joseph Stalin. Trotsky was the best-known Bolshevik after Lenin. The Revolution, and his place in it, was his life. A Jew by birth, Trotsky once responded to an anti-Semitic taunt about whether he was "a Jew or a Russian" by pronouncing himself "a Social Democrat, that is all." A brilliant polemicist and orator, Trotsky also was a superb organizer and administrator and capable of both fearless and ruthless conduct. Revolutionary situations brought out the best in him. During the 1905 Revolution he clearly eclipsed Lenin as a revolutionary leader, rising to the chairmanship of the renowned St. Petersburg Soviet and defending himself heroically at his trial after the Soviet was suppressed. His performance in 1917 was even more spectacular. Again he became chairman of the Soviet in what was then called Petrograd and was instrumental in putting that vital body at the service of the Bolsheviks. Trotsky was Lenin's right-hand man during the Revolution and Civil War. He headed the Soviet's Military Revolutionary Committee that actually planned the Bolshevik coup and, among other things, forged and directed the Red Army. After the Civil War, Trotsky continued to sit on the Politburo and serve as the commissar of war. Until 1923, he seemed to be Lenin's logical successor.

Yet for all his magnificent skills as a revolutionary, Trotsky was an inept politician. A long-time critic of Lenin who did not join the Bolsheviks until July 1917, Trotsky did nothing to assuage the bruised feelings of many veteran party members who resented his meteoric rise to the top. Trotsky could be intolerably aloof and insufferably arrogant. Who else would have read French novels during meetings of the Politburo while his enemies sniped at him? During the Civil War his high-handedness and ruthlessness made him additional enemies in the party, even as his Red Army was defeating the Whites. Trotsky did, to be sure, enjoy wide popularity in the party, but proved unable to organize his supporters into an adequate power base by ensconcing them in strategic places in the growing party apparatus. Thus, after the Tenth Party Congress, several of his supporters were removed from the Central Committee and his loyalists lost control of both the Secretariat and the Orgburo, the two bodies that soon became the fulcrum of Stalin's strength. Trotsky also was hamstrung by his obsession with history and his place in it. He therefore refused to rely on the Red Army during the struggle for power because, in his Marxist eyes, this would have made him a Russian equivalent of Napoleon Bonaparte, the French general (and later emperor) whose coup restored order and protected the interests of the bourgeoisie after the French Revolution. Finally, Trotsky grossly underestimated Stalin. Even after Stalin had banished him from the party and from Russia, Trotsky could do no more than grant his victorious opponent the dubious status of being the party's "outstanding mediocrity." It was Lenin who raised Trotsky up and made him a leading Bolshevik. Without the "old man's" support, Trotsky, his talent, popularity, and immense personal charisma notwithstanding, stood on a shaky political base.

Joseph Stalin was born Joseph Dzhugashvili in a village in Georgia. Stalin (which means "man of steel" in Russian) was the only leading Bolshevik whose class background made him one of the masses. Born into poverty, he was the victim of a particularly brutal childhood, enduring terrible beatings from his drunken father until the latter was killed in a brawl when Joseph was eleven. Despite this, young Joseph excelled in a local church primary school and won a scholarship to a seminary in Tiflis, the Georgian capital. Here he met more mistreatment at the hand of obscurant monks until he rebelled and was expelled in 1899. By then, Stalin's revolutionary career was already under way.

All of this marked Stalin's personality as deeply as his childhood case of smallpox marked his face. As a young man Stalin was intelligent, persistent, and sometimes lively, but he also was vicious, conniving, hostile, and domineering. "Koba," as he was known in the revolutionary underground, alienated many of his colleagues. Years later, in Siberian exile, Stalin made a similar negative impression on several Marxists from other parts of Russia. His reputation also suffered because of his association with criminal elements and activities both inside and outside of prison. His most significant such venture was his role in organizing robberies, with Lenin's approval, to fill the empty Bolshevik coffers. These "expropriations," as their supporters preferred to call them, led Lenin to take his first serious notice of young "Koba." Others were less impressed. Stalin apparently was expelled from the Menshevik-controlled Transcaucasian Social Democratic organization for his troubles. Some of his fellow Georgians referred to him as a "kinto," an insulting Georgian term connoting a combination of street tough and petty thief. He certainly was a man devoid of many usual human sensibilities and restraints and was capable of extraordinary cruelty.

Stalin's background differed from that of the other Bolshevik leaders in another significant way. While Lenin and the others lived as emigres in Western Europe, Stalin spent virtually all of his pre-1917 revolutionary career as an underground worker inside Russia. Lenin, Trotsky, Zinoviev, and the rest, all well-educated, and exposed to European life and culture, tended to be cosmopolitan and internationally oriented. Their lives were not easy, but they were spared much of what the underground workers at home had to endure. Hardened by poverty, hounded by the secret police, betrayed by informers, and tempered by prison and Siberian exile, the "practicals" in Russia were in many ways a tougher breed than their leaders living in Europe. Their lives left them unconcerned with the ideological fineries that so intrigued men able to spend hours in European libraries or cafes. "Practicals" tended to be parochial in their outlook, more concerned with a revolution in the Russia they knew than one that might sweep across countries they had never seen.

Whatever his faults or limits, Stalin nevertheless possessed important talents. He was efficient and tough, a good choice for any difficult or unsavory job. Stalin also was an excellent actor, able to ingratiate himself with people and even charm them when necessary. The list of those he impressed includes not only Lenin, but such men as Winston Churchill and Franklin Roosevelt. In a party of garrulous intellectuals, Stalin knew when to keep silent. He was blessed with an acute sense of political timing and sixth sense for his opponents' weaknesses. Perhaps that is why Nikolai Bukharin, one of the brilliant intellectuals he bested in the struggle for power, called him not only "Genghis Khan" but a "devil."

Stalin tended to side with Lenin in party disputes as early as 1901, and became a steadfast Bolshevik immediately after the 1903 party split. His rise nonetheless was slow until 1912, when Lenin, his ranks depleted by defeats and hard times, promoted the man he called a "wonderful Georgian" to the newly formed Bolshevik Central Committee. This promotion was followed by Lenin's bringing Stalin to Europe for six weeks to write a major pamphlet on the nationality problem in Russia. Shortly after his return to Russia in 1913, Stalin was arrested and exiled to Siberia, where he remained until freed by the March 1917 Revolution. He did not play a particularly visible role in the great Bolshevik triumph in November, but was appointed commissar of nationalities in Lenin's original cabinet. The Civil War, which created such opportunity for clever and ruthless people, propelled him to the top echelon. By 1921, Stalin headed two commissariats—nationalities and state control (*Rabkrin*)—and sat on both the Politburo and Orgburo. Aside from enjoying Lenin's confidence, his party jobs and position at the head of two commissariats gave him considerable clout. Upon becoming general secretary in 1922, Stalin indisputably was the man with the most direct control of the rapidly growing party apparatus. The man once called a "grey blur, which glimmered dimly and left no trace" was beginning to leave his mark.

The struggle for power had several phases. From late 1922 until January 1925, most of the senior Bolshevik leadership united against and defeated Trotsky. The core of this anti-Trotsky conglomeration—it was too diverse and internally divided to call it an alliance—was the "Triumvirate" composed of Zinoviev, Stalin, and Kamenev. From its inception in late 1922, the Triumvirate was the party's strongest organizational bloc. It fell apart as soon as Trotsky was defeated because Stalin was hard at work undermining his partners and they in turn feared his growing power. Their fears were justified; by 1925 Stalin had bolstered his considerable organizational strength by allying himself with three other Politburo members: Nikolai Bukharin, Alexi Rykov, and Mikhail Tomsky. These men were the leading advocates of continuing the moderate NEP policies of tolerating and even encouraging private peasant enterprise and the small-scale capitalist enterprise of the Nepmen. Since Zinoviev and Kamenev attacked these policies, and because they immediately found themselves a minority in the party as a whole, their faction was called the "Left Opposition." Stalin's alliance with the party's moderate or "right" wing easily defeated the Left Opposition and its successor, the "United Opposition," a quickly hatched combination of the Zinoviev-Kamenev and Trotsky forces that rose from the ashes in 1926 only to sink back by December 1927. The final phase was the showdown between Stalin, suddenly emergent as a critic of the Bukharin-Rykov-Tomsky economic policies, and the general secretary's latest ex-allies, collectively known as the "Right Opposition." This phase spanned much of 1928 and 1929 and ended in complete victory for Stalin.

Stalin was aided in his "struggle for the throne" because each of his opponents had serious political weaknesses. Zinoviev, the only man who fought Stalin on his own terms by trying to manipulate the bureaucratic apparatus, had considerable political and oratorical skills and a formidable array of party and nonparty posts. Lenin's closest associate in the decade before 1917, Zinoviev was a Politburo member, head of the Leningrad party organization, and the chairman of the Comintern. He also had the unswerving support of the third triumvir, Lev Kamenev. Kamenev, the powerful boss of the Moscow party organization, so closely and consistently orbited his friend that the two men became Bolshevism's binary star, locked into the same positions and, as it turned out, the same fate. Yet Zinoviev, for all his power and oratorical skills, was a mediocrity. Many of his "comrades" criticized him for his cowardly behavior during the fall of 1917. Once in power, he proved to be eminently corruptible. By 1921 he was not above delaying an entire railroad train to suit his august convenience or ordering railroad cars full of passengers detached to accommodate his personal parlor car (Kamenev raced through Moscow in a Rolls Royce). Like most of the other Bolshevik leaders, Zinoviev and Kamenev underestimated Stalin. However, they both also hated Trotsky for having replaced Zinoviev at Lenin's right hand, a hatred that prevented them from turning to Trotsky to block Stalin until it was too late.

Nikolai Bukharin, the leader of the party's moderate wing, was an outstanding theoretician and highly able economist. He was a member of the Politburo and popular among the party elite. A man whose interests ranged from reading to collecting butterflies, Bukharin was far better suited for the rarefied height of intellectual discourse than for the political trenches, something he demonstrated conclusively in his ineffectual struggles against Stalin in 1928–1929.

These men compounded their individual weaknesses by failing to unite their strengths. Although Stalin's power initially was something of a political iceberg largely hidden in the stormy Bolshevik factional seas, by the summer of 1923 it loomed large enough to worry Zinoviev and several other leaders. They hatched a scheme to limit the general secretary's power by converting the Secretariat from Stalin's personal preserve into a body composed of several of the top leaders. But the plan was stillborn because Zinoviev and his cohorts lacked the resolution to see it through. First they readily accepted an alternative compromise offer from Stalin and then they failed to use the supervisional powers the compromise gave them. After Zinoviev took the lead in attacking Trotsky in 1923 and 1924, Trotsky stayed in his tent while Stalin demolished Zinoviev and Kamenev in 1925. By the time Trotsky and Zinoviev joined forces, they were too weak to stop Stalin. In 1928, a desperate Bukharin was unable to get Kamenev to help him forge an anti-Stalin alliance while, true to form, several important Trotsky supporters joined up with Stalin after 1929 because they agreed with his plans for rapid industrialization. All of this allowed Stalin room to divide, conquer, and destroy his opponents one by one.

Stalin also benefitted from a mystique that surrounded the party. It was rooted in Lenin's conception of a vanguard party that was the only agent capable of blazing a path to socialism. That vanguard therefore required absolute unity, an imperative that gave birth to democratic centralism. The concept of unity, venerated in 1903 and beatified in 1921 at the Tenth Party Congress, was canonized after 1924. It became a devastating weapon the majority could use against the minority or "opposition." The accusation of "factionalism" became a mark of Cain that delegitimized any attempt to criticize the leadership. Thus the Triumvirate used it against Trotsky, Stalin and Bukharin used it against the Left Opposition and United Opposition, and Stalin used it against the Right Opposition. Equally telling, the shimmering party mystique seemed by itself to paralyze oppositionists. The outstanding—but not the only—example of this occurred when Trotsky, a fearless critic of Lenin and democratic centralism before 1917, drew back from the fray with Stalin in 1924 with the proclamation that he accepted his party "right or wrong" because "history has not created other ways for the realization of what is right."

Lenin left behind some handy practical tools that Stalin found useful, including the expulsion provisions of the 1921 resolution, "On Party Unity," the party purge, and the party machine itself. While he made effective use of the first two, the key to his strength was his control of the party machine through the Secretariat. Stalin used the Secretariat to shift opponents to where they could do the least harm and move supporters to where they could do the most good. By "recommending" local secretaries supposedly chosen by free elections, a practice that was increasingly common by 1923, the Secretariat won control of local organizations. This control meant that Stalin's supporters dominated the selection of delegates to the party congresses, and it was the party congress that elected the Central Committee, which in turn elected the Politburo. This meant that although Stalin did not win firm control over the Politburo until late 1929, the power he exercised through the Secretariat made him the Politburo's dominating figure as early as 1924.

The party's transformation from a revolutionary elite into a governing bureaucracy also aided Stalin. It became an organization one joined to make a career rather than a revolution. In 1924 Stalin engineered what was called the "Lenin Enrollment," which brought over 200,000 new members into the party. Because most of them were workers, Stalin was able to present this maneuver as a step to fulfill Lenin's desire to combat bureaucratism. In fact, it allowed the general secretary to pack the party with thousands of raw and malleable recruits. The "Lenin Enrollment" and subsequent recruitment drives literally revamped the party, which grew from 386,000 members in 1923 to over 735,000 in 1924 and over 1.5 million in 1929. At the same time, the revolutionary veterans were disappearing. In 1922, only half of the 24,000 who dated from before 1917 remained; only 8,000 were left in 1929. Indeed, by 1929, barely one quarter of the party's membership antedated the 1924 Lenin enrollment. One old-guard leader summed up the situation when he observed that ". . . I am not exaggerating when I say that the activist of 1917 would find nothing in common with his 1928 counterpart." All of this strengthened the machine politician adept at bureaucratic manipulation and formulating simple or even simplistic formulas at the expense of the idealist who relied on his intellectual brilliance to inspire revolutionary enthusiasm. The mass of new, young, and inexperienced Bolsheviks was a tide made to order for raising a man like Stalin and swamping a man like Trotsky.

The failure to defend the fragile democratic part of "democratic central-ism" gave Stalin another boost. Each of his rivals proved quite prepared to suppress dissent within the party when in the majority, only to redis-cover the virtues of democracy when in the minority. Trotsky militantly supported suppressing the Workers' Opposition in 1921. In 1923, how-ever, he denounced the Triumvirate for authoritarianism in a long article called "The New Course." In 1923, the most avid defender of party unity was Zinoviev. Two years later, when he, too, realized the merits of de-mocracy, he was trenchantly informed by V. M. Molotov, one of Stalin's closest associates, that "When Zinoviev is in the majority he is for iron discipline. . . . When he is in the minority . . . he is against it." Even the comparatively gentle Bukharin was as guilty of suppressing dissent as anyone else, to the point of demanding harsher penalties for the defeated Left after 1927 than even Stalin wanted.

Another important cog in Stalin's political juggernaut was his link with the secret police and his readiness to use them against his rivals. During the Civil War Stalin had worked closely with Felix Dzerzhinsky, head of the *Cheka*, and by 1923, the GPU, as Dzerzhinsky's secret police was then known, already was doing Stalin's bidding. Among its services was to harass and eventually to arrest M. G. Sultan-Galiev, a party leader who opposed Stalin's nationalities policies in 1923, and to fan out across Moscow to collect copies of Lenin's damning "Testament" after it was distributed to delegates attending the Thirteenth Party Congress in 1924. Prior to Lenin's death Stalin already was using his formidable resources to keep party leaders, including Lenin, under surveillance. Stalin, the former "kinto," also used the secret police to beat up members of the opposition in 1927. Enlisting twentieth-century technology in his cause, he even used electronic bugs to overhear the conversations of his colleagues.

Stalin also found strength in unexpected quarters. Five days after Lenin's death, he delivered a speech subsequently known as the "Lenin Oath," which proved to be a stunning success for a man not known as a public speaker. Sounding more like a church litany than a tribute to a revolutionary and atheist, and replete with vows to honor the dead man's wishes, Stalin's long verbal genuflections did not impress many other Bolshevik leaders. But it spoke far more clearly to the less-sophisticated party membership at large and the general public than did those same colleagues' Marxist-laden hyperbole and so became an important stake in Stalin's claim to be Lenin's disciple.

The growing secular cult devoted to Lenin received a further boost when the leadership, on Stalin's initiative, embalmed Lenin's body and dis-played it in a mausoleum in Red Square. Many Bolsheviks were outraged, including Trotsky and Kamenev, who finally found something to agree on. It is fair to say that Lenin, had he had one, would have been spinning in his grave. Petrograd soon became Leningrad in another posthumous honor Lenin certainly would rather have done without.

Stalin also revealed his heretofore unknown theoretical talents. For years Trotsky had been known as the theorist of "permanent revolution," the doctrine that linked any hope for achieving socialism in Russia with the spread of the revolution to the industrialized countries of the West. This doctrine had considerable appeal in 1917, but by 1924, when hopes for a revolution in the West seemed dead, it was not what most party members wanted to hear. They wanted to be assured that their own efforts at home could guarantee success, which is exactly what Stalin did. In 1924, his book, *Problems of Leninism*, outlined his soothing theory of "socialism in one country," the idea that Russia could build a socialist society regardless of what happened in the West. *Problems of Leninism* made Trotsky look like an overly pessimistic prophet of gloom in contrast to the upbeat Stalin. It also established Stalin as a major Marxist theorist, giving him another key leadership credential he previously lacked.

Despite all of his strength, Stalin could have been stopped, especially if Trotsky had acted firmly in 1923 and 1924. Historians remain perplexed as to why he did not. Perhaps it was his failing health—he suffered from a long series of fevers of unknown origin—or his reluctance to declare his ambitions while Lenin was still alive. Perhaps he simply lacked the discipline, will, and stamina required to build a political organization and govern a country. Whatever the reasons, Trotsky let his opportunities pass. He ignored Lenin's wishes and failed to attack Stalin at the Twelfth Party Congress in 1923. Although the Triumvirate controlled a majority at the congress, Trotsky's position was strong. He was still immensely popular with the rank and file and had several excellent issues, including the Georgian affair, the Secretariat's abuses of power, and Lenin's hostility toward Stalin. A concerted attack probably could have won the day, but Trotsky let this chance pass with barely a murmur.

Trotsky let his next chance pass equally quietly. When Lenin died on January 21, 1924, Trotsky was in the Caucasus for a rest cure. Incredibly, he missed Lenin's funeral, because he chose to believe Stalin, of all people, regarding the date of that event. Trotsky thus cast another shadow over his political future while Stalin used the opportunity to seize the spotlight with his "Lenin Oath" speech.

After that, only one real trump remained to Trotsky: Lenin's "Testament." Lenin's wife, Krupskaya, had kept the document secret until the eve of the Thirteenth Party Congress, at which point, on May 21, 1924, it was read to a Central Committee plenum. This was a moment of truth. There was little that Stalin could do; he sat feeling "small and miserable," an eyewitness recorded, while others considered his fate. He offered to resign. Trotsky, once again, did nothing, but the fear of what he might do if Stalin were demoted became the latter's safety net. Zinoviev, still more afraid of Trotsky than Stalin, saved the general secretary. Lenin's fears had proven unfounded, Zinoviev announced; Stalin should be left at his post. So he was. The "Testament" was suppressed; Stalin survived.

Trotsky's defeat was virtually assured after the "Testament" episode. His subsequent attempts to speak against the Triumvirate at the Thirteenth Party Congress itself were drowned in jeers. It was a new species of party congress, run according to the new Stalinist script. Debate and decision making were banished forever in favor of prefabricated speeches, prepackaged decisions, and organized abuse. Even Krupskaya was driven from the podium when she tried to criticize the new leadership. The end of the congress brought no relief; in January 1925, Trotsky yielded his position as commissar of war, his last bastion of power. He now sat only as an isolated lame duck on the Politburo.

With Trotsky relatively powerless, Stalin locked horns with Zinoviev and Kamenev in a short, fierce battle that ended with Stalin's overwhelming victory at the Fourteenth Party Congress in December 1925. The congress was an awesome demonstration of the Secretariat's power. Only the Leningrad delegation escaped its control. For the first time, Stalin was able to move several of his loyalists, including Molotov, into the Politburo in place of demoted oppositionists. The sad saga of the United Opposition followed. In successive waves in 1926 and 1927 its leaders lost all their important posts, including their seats on the Politburo. On November 7, 1927, Trotsky and Zinoviev led street demonstrations in Moscow and Leningrad in a last desperate attempt to bring their case to the workers. A far more formidable and ruthless foe awaited them than in 1917. The demonstrations were broken up and the two men who had been Lenin's closest associates were expelled from the party. Trotsky was even evicted from his Kremlin apartment. At the Fifteenth Party Congress that December, lesser oppositionist leaders were expelled as well; a thorough purge of several thousand lower-ranking dissenters followed. Zinoviev and Kamenev caved in as they had before and would again. After humbly recanting, they were allowed back into the party for more abuse. Not Trotsky. In January 1928, the still-defiant ex-Bolshevik was deported from Moscow in the middle of the night to avoid any demonstrations and shipped into Siberian exile. The next year he was banished from the Soviet Union altogether. Still, Trotsky's trumpet of criticism continued, although from ever more distant shores, until 1940. Then, having already taken almost everything from his hated rival—his power, his homeland, even his children—Stalin sent an assassin to take Trotsky's life.

After disposing of his critics on the left, Stalin wasted little time in undermining those on the right who had provided the balance of power in the just completed battle. As usual, he was calculating and flexible. His latest ex-allies-turned-opponents had considerable strength. But although Bukharin headed the Comintern and edited *Pravda*, the party newspaper, Rykov chaired the *Sovnarkom*, Tomsky headed the trade unions, and all three sat on the Politburo, they could not match Stalin's organization, will power, cunning, and pure ruthlessness. By the end of 1929, the right had lost most of its important posts and was politically decimated. On his fiftieth birthday, December 21, 1929, Stalin had obtained victory in his struggle for power.

Aside from the question of who would lead the party, Lenin's death had left unanswered the equally vexing question of the fate of the NEP. Lenin had frankly called the policy a "retreat," and when it was implemented, it was difficult for many Bolsheviks to see the many concessions made to capitalist enterprise in the name of the NEP as anything else. Given the party's raison d'etre of building socialism, it was clear that the retreat must be a temporary one.

However, in the course of this retreat Lenin's views moderated. He began to think in terms of progress over the long haul. He suggested that peasants be encouraged to form autonomous cooperative institutions and that education had to be a primary means of consummating the "cultural revolution" essential to building socialism. One of Lenin's last articles, significantly entitled "On Cooperation," outlined these new ideas. They clearly complemented antibureaucratic themes Lenin was developing, particularly his criticism of Stalin. But Lenin's death left these matters for his colleagues to unscramble.

By 1925, the discomfiture many Bolsheviks felt about the NEP was increasing. Agricultural production, including the all-important grain crop, was approaching its 1913 levels, and the Soviet people were eating tolerably well. Industrial production also showed progress, with such key industries as coal mining and fabric production at 90 percent or more of their peak prewar levels. Steel and pig iron production, respectively, reached 75 percent and 60 percent of their peak prewar levels. Industrial workers probably enjoyed higher real wages than before the war, in part because of the impressive range of social benefits conferred on them by the Soviet regime. The NEP had done its job.

All this unfortunately was not enough from a Bolshevik point of view since much of the progress had been bought at the price of continued concessions to private enterprise. The most galling measures were the ones granting peasant farmers the right to rent more farmland and hire workers without restrictions. Furthermore, the industrial picture was hardly cause for rejoicing. Recovery was based almost entirely on repairing the old physical plant damaged between 1914 and 1921. Relative to the West, Russian industry was still backward, inefficient, and unproductive. It was unable to meet urban and peasant consumer needs; neither could it produce the necessary profits to finance new capital investment that was needed, particularly in heavy industry, before any real progress could be made toward a highly industrialized economy.

There was no agreement where funds for that investment could be found. Little was available from the agricultural sector, the traditional source of government revenue over the centuries. Its recovery was more complete than that of industry, but its future was hardly inspiring. Russian agriculture was dominated by small, inefficient peasant allotments. The old three-field system and division of allotments into strips subject to re-apportionment still prevailed. Perhaps 20 percent of all peasants used the ancient *sokha*, or wooden plow, causing one demoralized official observer to complain of how often he saw "a wretched wooden *sokha*, dating from the flood . . . often dragged along by a miserable yoke of lead oxen or by the farmer, or even his wife."

The Revolution was in part to blame for this state of affairs. It had expropriated the large estates and even some of the largest peasant hold-ings and redistributed them among peasants with little or no land. This meant that the most modern and productive units, those large and efficient enough to use modern machines and methods and produce a large surplus, had disappeared, and with them much of the marketable grain that had made prewar Russia one of the world's largest grain exporters. By the mid-1920s, slightly *less* grain was being produced by a slightly *larger* rural population divided into *more* and *smaller* allotments, while more of that grain was staying on the farm and being eaten by peasants benefitting from the lower taxes of the NEP. And much of the grain that was marketed went into the private sector of the Nepmen to serve consumer needs rather than state policy interests. So Russia, which in 1913 had 12 million tons of grain to export in exchange for foreign goods, including industrial equipment, had only 2 million tons available in 1925–1926, 2.1 million tons in 1926–1927, and 300,000 tons, or almost nothing at all, in 1927–1928.

In addition, the concessions to private peasant enterprise were pro-ducing a growing class of prosperous peasants called *kulaks*, whose development indicated to some nervous Bolsheviks that capitalism might reconquer the countryside. Though the *kulaks* actually were quite poor by Western standards—one might farm enough land to justify hiring one worker and own all of two horses and two cows—they looked prosperous to the many peasants who had none of either. While the government wanted to see Russian agriculture based on communal principles, the *kulak* was undeniably an incipient capitalist and an example most of the peasantry wanted to follow. He had no love for the Bolsheviks, a party of urban functionaries lacking in any knowledge of or sympathy for peasants like himself. The *kulaks* produced about 20 percent of the marketable grain, which they refused to sell when the government's price was too low, and they exerted a significant and growing influence on their fellow peasants, an unpleasant reality reflected in elections to rural soviets after 1925. In short, the government wanted the peasant to live one way; the peasant generally preferred to live another way. This did not bode well for the *smychka*, the union between the proletariat and the peasantry proclaimed by Lenin as the cornerstone of the NEP.

The core of the problem was that by the mid-1920s the NEP apparently was at an impasse. Socialism required overcoming economic scarcity, and that in turn required a highly industrialized economy. Unfortunately, the capital essential to achieve this was not available. Russia's backward industry could not produce it. The agricultural sector could not either. The government might have found a partial solution by encouraging the *kulaks* to create large-scale capitalist farms, but this would have been an odd posture for a "socialist" regime. The capitalist West was not interested in investing in Soviet Russia, as Lenin had hoped it would. And the failure of the Revolution to spread to the West meant that there was no advanced socialist nation to bail out the local cause, as Lenin had insisted was necessary if socialism were to survive in Russia.

The economic noose slowly began to tighten in 1926 to 1927, partly because unrelenting struggle for power left economic policy in a lurch. Enforced low prices for industrial goods produced by state-run industry (Trotsky wanted them raised) helped create a demand for those goods that Russia's inefficient industries could not meet. This left the peasantry with nothing to buy in exchange for its grain, a "goods famine" that after 1926 became a seemingly permanent part of the NEP landscape. Even worse, to save money the government, though split on the issue, lowered the price it was willing to pay for grain in 1926. The peasants responded by refusing to sell any until the price was raised, leaving the government without the grain it needed to feed the cities, much less use for export. More confusion resulted from another policy change noticeable as early as 1926: the decision to strangle the nonagricultural private sector, which many Bolsheviks continued to view as a potential womb for the rebirth of capitalism. By 1928, that sector was in a tailspin.

All of this lent credence to Stalin's opponent, Leon Trotsky. Trotsky's thinking was based on the theories of a brilliant economist, Yevgeny Preobrazhensky. Preobrazhensky argued that under capitalism the necessary capital for the Industrial Revolution was accumulated by exploiting the working class and forcing it to live in poverty, a process he called "primitive accumulation." He theorized that because socialists had seized power in Russia before a modern industrial base existed, they would have to do something similar. Since it would be done under a socialist regime, Preobrazhensky called this process "primitive *socialist* accumulation."

But who would bear the burden of this accumulation? Not the workers, said Preobrazhensky. There were far too few of them, for one thing. For another, one could hardly expect the "workers' state" to exploit its leading class. The source, as usual in Russia, would have to be the peasantry. Preobrazhensky hoped this could be done through high taxation and a policy that charged high prices for the goods the peasants used and paid low prices for the products they produced. Productivity could be increased by forming collective farms—large units in which farmers would combine their land and resources and work together—able to use modern machines and methods. Since the total number of farms would decrease drastically, the government could oversee peasant activities more closely. It could then drain off peasant wealth and apply it to industrialization, feeding a growing working class in the cities, and exchanging it abroad for necessary industrial machinery. A modern industrial base could be built in this way. At the same time, peasant and Nepman capitalism would be stopped in its tracks, and Russia would cease to be so vulnerable to Western economic and military might.

The Achilles heel of this otherwise perceptive analysis was the question of how to get the peasants to agree to this program. They had shown absolutely no interest in collectivization and would surely object to a drop in their meager standard of living. Trotsky hoped to collectivize by persuasion, but offered little evidence of how to do this. How to implement this program without using massive force, which Trotsky and Preobrazhensky insisted they would avoid, became known as the "Preobrazhensky Dilemma": how is one generation convinced to sacrifice itself for future generations?

At the other end of the Bolshevik spectrum stood the defenders of the NEP led by Bukharin. They insisted it did work and only needed modification. Bukharin believed that the key to success was balanced growth. He suggested that lower industrial prices would encourage the peasants to produce more while their purchases of agricultural implements would stimulate industry. As industry grew, it would provide the peasants with more agricultural implements at lower prices, thereby increasing both the peasantry's ability and desire to produce more. A continuous upward cycle would result. Bukharin also stressed the need to stretch available resources through careful planning.

Bukharin's theory had its own dilemmas. Private enterprise would be tolerated and the rate of economic growth would necessarily be slow. Bukharin's slogans did little to make these facts more palatable to many Bolsheviks. In 1925 he urged the peasants to "Enrich yourselves," a remark he had to repudiate. He suggested that Russia would have to grow at the "speed of a peasant nag," an unedifying prospect for Bolsheviks who considered themselves dynamic revolutionaries, not country-bumpkin teamsters. Still, Bukharin remained confident. The party's control of the economy's key areas—such as large industry and the banks—would enable it to keep small-scale capitalist enterprise within limits. This small-scale enterprise would in turn fill in the gaps left by the socialist sector. Meanwhile, the peasantry, if treated properly, would cooperate and become an ally rather than an adversary.

There was a prophetic urgency to Bukharin's analysis. He certainly was no democrat, as his political tactics against the Left indicate. Still, he desperately wanted to avoid an all-encompassing dictatorship. Bukharin feared that the breakneck industrialization advocated by the Left would lead to a Leviathan-type state that would crush all human freedom. He had written about the dangerous growth of state power in the industrialized West and felt that socialist societies were not immune to that phenomenon. Bukharin was in good company; fear of the state is a thread running through socialist thinking back to Karl Marx, and it was shared by many in the Bolshevik old guard. That is why socialists wanted the state to "wither away."

Preobrazhensky and Bukharin represented only two views in a many-sided "Industrialization Debate" that took place in Russia during the 1920s. The many economists of varying persuasions who took part produced a glittering array of questions and policy suggestions that mark the birth of development economics. Preobrazhensky and Bukharin were the leading lights, but they shone as part of a small galaxy of stars who lit a new path in economics. They were almost all imprisoned, and many executed, during Stalin's reign.

Stalin meanwhile used the Industrialization Debate as a field in which to maneuver. While the others argued principles, he built his organizational strength. Although he sided with Bukharin after 1925, he was careful never to embrace his ideas too closely. He rejected the "Enrich yourselves" slogan and permitted the Fourteenth and Fifteenth Congresses, both of which he controlled, to endorse expanded industrialization efforts. In fact, the same Fifteenth Congress that expelled the Left from the party endorsed a large part of its industrialization program and called collectivization "the principal task of the party in the villages," something that was certainly news to Bukharin. Stalin played his cards so well that even as the Left and Right drew closer together in their theoretical approaches he still was able to play them against each other. By the time Bukharin realized in 1928 where his real enemy lay, he had helped cripple his potential allies.

Between 1927 and 1929, torn by its own internal difficulties and by government policies that made them worse, the NEP fell apart. During 1927 the government had begun a serious attempt to formulate a comprehensive economic plan, a job undertaken by the State Planning Commission (*Gosplan*). At the same time, major new investment projects in mining,

iron and steel mills, railroads, and hydroelectric dams drained resources
from the economy as a whole and intensified the "goods famine." To pay
for all this, the government raised taxes on the peasants and Nepmen,
measures that were accomplished by discriminatory practices that made
it increasingly difficult to do business, and did not help in the crucial area
of grain procurements, where near disaster loomed. By January 1928,
procurements trailed the previous year's by 25 percent (although recent
research suggests that Stalin may have falsified these figures to bolster
the case for collectivization). This Stalin would not tolerate. Since the
peasants were unwilling to sell their grain at the government's price, he
decided to take it. Armed with a newly passed decree against "speculation," Stalin, acting on his own, ordered that peasant stocks be seized by
force. Called the "Urals-Siberian" method because of Stalin's personal
tours to those areas, this virtual reign of terror was applied nationwide.
Roads were blocked, houses searched, and peasants arrested while their
grain was carted away.

During 1928, Stalin still had to compromise with Bukharin and his allies
while he built his own organizational strength. The next year, he felt strong
enough to launch a frontal attack against the moderates, now branded as
the "Right deviation." By the fall of 1929, the Right was finished as a
political force, leaving Stalin free to forge policies of his own.

It is worth noting that the Stalinist denouement of Bolshevism was not
inevitable. The party might well have chosen another economic course. It
had, after all, chosen the NEP after its unsuccessful experience with War
Communism. Furthermore, Stalin's methods certainly were not the only
ones that could have industrialized Russia rapidly. His methods were extremely wasteful, and the Industrialization Debate of the 1920s suggests
that far less violent and brutal methods might have achieved impressive
results. For example, recent research suggests the Bukharin's methods
would have produced much higher production in agriculture during the
1930s than was actually achieved, in part because the tremendous losses of
animal power would have been avoided. According to one computer
model, by *not* collectivizing, the Soviet Union by 1940 would have enjoyed an agricultural output 10 percent higher than what was achieved via
collectivization; that increase in turn would have fed an economy at least
29 percent larger than what was achieved by Stalin's methods. That most
economists working for the party advocated a course far different than the
one Stalin took is by itself significant. Stalin's final triumph in 1929 meant
that Soviet Russia would indeed make spectacular economic advances in a
very short time—but hardly as impressive as they seem at first glance and
only at an incalculable, horrible human cost.

13

The Revolution From Above

No, no, kindness is lost upon the people;
Do good—it thanks you not at all; extort
And execute—'twill be no worse for you.

————PUSHKIN

Although the Bolshevik Revolution took place in 1917, the party did not fully revolutionize Russian society until the 1930s. Despite the extensive changes that took place between 1917 and 1929, on the eve of Stalin's triumph the country was strikingly similar to what it had been on the morrow of Lenin's revolution. In 1929, the Soviet economy was still dominated by small-scale and backward peasant agriculture. Its industrial sector, notwithstanding the socialized "commanding heights," still could not meet the nation's needs and lagged behind the modern industrial establishments in the West. Russia, in fact, had basically the same industrial base that had existed in 1913. In short, in 1929, the majority of the population lived much as they had before 1917.

Ten years later the picture was dramatically different. Collectivization had substantially transformed Soviet agriculture. The Soviets had built a new industrial infrastructure, one that at long last had the potential to be competitive, at least in terms of military power, with the industrial economies of Western Europe. The balance between the rural and urban sectors was changing rapidly in favor of the latter. Soviet Russia also had a largely modernized military force. An unprecedented reign of terror had produced a thorough social revolution of its own. After a decade of what Stalin called his "revolution from above"—sometimes called the "Second" Bolshevik Revolution—very few Soviet citizens lived as they had before.

The economic transformation of that decade is of major historic importance, for Russia's system of economic development, based on a planned, state-controlled economy, would become a serious alternative to the free enterprise Western model for many unindustrialized nations from the 1930s until the 1980s. The economic growth during the decade after 1929 is relatively easy to chronicle and describe. What cannot adequately be described is the catastrophic human cost of the Soviet "revolution from above." Millions of human lives were sacrificed, millions more brutalized beyond endurance, an entire nation terrorized. And what is even more difficult to comprehend is how the building and the dying, the elation and the agony, the glorious and the grotesque, all were locked together in an inseparable embrace, whirling like a surrealistic dynamo to generate a new Russia.

Astride it all stood Stalin, the coldly calculating *Vozhd* (leader) who, like the biblical Pharaoh, hardened his heart to human suffering as he pushed ever harder to build the Soviet pyramids he felt were so vital to the state and the revolution. Yet, while Stalin for almost a generation held power as absolute as any monarch or dictator in history, imposing many of his dreams, fears, and hatreds upon the Soviet Union, it is vital to remember that a larger historical context framed his life and deeds. The Stalin era resulted from a confluence of several broad historical currents. The recent World War had been only the latest of many historical crises to punish Russia for her backwardness, thereby compelling the state once again to undertake a program of crash modernization. Stalin was part of a tradition stretching from Ivan the Terrible to Peter the Great to the twentieth century. At the same time, the unusually severe internal and external pressures of the early twentieth century had shattered the old society, scattered the old elites, and permitted a new elite to come to power, one far more vigorous and with more expansive goals than the ruling class it replaced. Further, the social revolution that brought it to power had broken down many traditional moral restrictions, thereby enabling that new elite to consider and implement more radically intensive measures than ever before to achieve its goals, and to find many allies among the population at large ready to carry out those measures, whatever the suffering they caused. All of these factors were necessary to produce what is now called "Stalinism," one of the several examples in this century, including Germany under Hitler and Cambodia under Pol Pot, of an entire society thrown into a horrible rampage when social disintegration combined in just the right proportions with dynamic—or perhaps demonic—historical forces promoting drastic social change. In the case of the Soviet Union, Stalin's personality certainly loomed large as a catalyst and shaper of events, but he got his chance to play such a major role because greater forces first prepared the historical stage and provided a large supporting cast.

Although there is no formal date that inaugurates the Stalin era, the convenient reference point is the adoption of the Soviet Union's First Five-Year Plan in April 1929. The 1,000-page plan was the first document of its kind, a comprehensive attempt to coordinate an entire economy to promote rapid industrialization and economic growth. The economists produced two serious options, a "minimum" and an "optimum" plan. While virtually all the Soviet Union's economic experts felt that the minimum version's hefty projected increases represented the maximum realizable goals, the Central Committee adopted the optimum version. Not only did the optimum version call for quantum leaps in production —industrial production was to rise by 250 percent, heavy industry by 330 percent, coal, pig iron and electricity by two, three, and four times respectively—but there were also optimistic projections for consumer goods and agriculture. The plan was declared operational as of October 1928, five months *before* it was adopted and several *more* months before it was completely prepared. Its targets were then immediately raised (in the summer of 1929), while the Sixteenth Party Congress meeting in June and July of 1930 declared that the already thoroughly impossible was to be achieved in *four* rather than five years.

In reality, Stalin's economic program was not a plan in the sense of taking what was available, organizing it as efficiently as possible, and striving for realistic goals. Rather it was a series of gigantic mobilization campaigns, often uncoordinated and sometimes in conflict with each other, in which the impetus came partially from the enthusiasm the regime was able to generate and mostly from brute force and terror on a horrendous scale. If the First Five-Year Plan was anything at all, it was a propaganda piece signaling the regime's intention to push the nation ahead at a reckless speed, regardless of the costs involved. The optimum version's original goals were unrealizable. They depended on simultaneously achieving a 110 percent increase in industrial productivity, a 30 percent drop in fuel consumption, and a 50 percent drop in construction costs. They also required ideal weather and optimum agricultural production, high prices for Russian agricultural exports, and low defense spending, among other things. *None* of these prerequisites were met. All kinds of bottlenecks developed after the first year of the plan (1928–1929), the only year the projected production increases were reached. When that happened, Stalin and his Politburo, no longer restrained by any organized opposition and driven by a fanatical desire to transform Soviet Russia in a decade, reacted with a vengeance. They raised, rather than lowered, the goals and intensified the pressures to meet them. "We are bound by no laws. There are no fortresses the Bolsheviks cannot storm," was Stalin's motto. "Objective conditions" could not be permitted to block the party's goals. Bukharin denounced Stalin's program as "military-feudal exploitation," a reference to tsarist policies of old. Or as historian Robert Daniels observed, Stalin's economic policies "accorded more with the economics of Ivan the Terrible than with those of Karl Marx."[1]

It is difficult to say precisely what accounted for the insistence on these impossible goals. The decisive factor certainly was Stalin himself, as his insatiable ego and indomitable will refused to let the petty computations of economists or the picayune desires of the people sabotage his goals. But there was a great deal of support for these goals. Party members, after all, knew how Russia had paid for lagging behind the West. They knew that the West had intervened against them during the Civil War and, as Marxists and Bolsheviks, they felt an urgency to transform Soviet Russia into a proletarian society with an industrial base adequate to support a socialist way of life. Therefore, the party was ready, even eager, to tackle the goals, however difficult, its *Vozhd* and Politburo set.

The first people to find this out were the peasants. Between 1929 and 1932, they were torn from the homesteads and pushed, pulled, driven, and lured into collective farms. Collectivization engulfed the majority of the Soviet people and hence was an enormous revolution in itself. It is important to realize that although the Bolsheviks had been discussing collectivization for years, the actual implementation of the project was not carefully thought out or planned. Stalin and his colleagues simply adopted massive collectivization to remedy unsuccessful attempts to guarantee sufficient state procurements of agricultural products in 1928 and 1929. This lack of planning helped produce the mixture of chaos and brutality that made collectivization such a human and economic catastrophe.

The First Five-Year Plan adopted in the spring of 1929 projected that only about 20 percent of the peasantry would be collectivized—on a voluntary basis without resorting to violence—during the life of the plan. By the fall this no longer seemed enough to the leadership. Stalin's procurement campaigns had helped disrupt agriculture enough so that the 1929 harvest was less than that of 1928. There were severe shortages not only of grain, but of such vital industrial crops as sugar beets and hemp. The peasants' refusal to deliver what they had to the state because of low prices made matters worse. Things became so bad that the government issued a decree in June that threatened peasants with imprisonment, confiscation of property, or even deportation to a remote area if they failed to fulfill certain production obligations.

The industrialization drive begun with the First Five-Year Plan made everything even more urgent. New industrial projects had swollen the labor force more than initially expected, because labor productivity was lower than anticipated and additional workers had to be hired. These workers had to be fed. Another "Urals-Siberian" campaign relieved some of the pressure during the summer, but the unpleasant reality was that Russian agriculture was in a downward spiral. Something had to be done before the 1930 harvest, or the entire industrialization plan would be threatened.

Stalin and the Politburo decided on full-scale collectivization. Incredibly, the gargantuan enterprise of overhauling the lives of most of Soviet Russia's peasants was to be completed in three years. In the key grain-producing areas the target was one or two years. As if that were not enough, the bulk of the job was to be completed "in the months, weeks, and days ahead." Beginning in December 1929, the full power of Stalin's coercive machinery descended on the countryside, spearheaded by the GPU and its heavily armed military units. It also included the regular army and eventually over 100,000 urban cadres. This force was assisted locally by poor peasants who were encouraged to wage class war on their more prosperous neighbors and on those who somehow lacked sufficient enthusiasm for the idea of having their entire lives uprooted. Sometimes a serious attempt was made to convince peasants to join the new collectives, but "no" was not taken for an answer. Villages were invaded by these various government-sponsored gangs, whose persuasive methods consisted of house-to-house searches for seed and supplies. Villages that resisted these intruders were surrounded and machine-gunned into submission. Often the ferocity of the resistance required the intervention of the Red Army. The strongest resistance, and the government's most severe repression, was in the Ukraine. The following eyewitness account is indicative of what happened:

> In 1930, in the Dniepropetrovsk region thousands of peasants armed with hunting rifles, axes, and pitchforks revolted against the regime. . . . NKVD units and militia were sent. For three days . . . a bloody battle was waged between the revolting people and the authorities. . . . This revolt was cruelly punished. Thousands of peasants, workers, soldiers, and officers paid for the attempt with their lives, while the survivors were deported to concentration camps. In the villages of Ternovka and Boganovka . . . mass executions were carried out near the *balkis* (ravines). The soil of this region was soaked in blood. After the executions, these villages were set on fire.[2]

The collectivization campaign quickly ran out of control as cadres, fired by enthusiasm or fear of the party's wrath in the event of failure, strove to outdo each other in reaching or exceeding their targets. By March 1930, less than three months into the campaign, over half of the Soviet Union's peasants had been driven from their homesteads into collective farms. But the resistance was so intense that even Stalin had to give ground. On March 2, he published an article called "Dizzy with Success." Using what was to become a typical tactic, Stalin shifted the blame for what he had ordered to others. In this case, the hapless culprits were party cadres who allegedly exceeded their instructions, having become intoxicated by the great victories the party was winning and, hence, "dizzy with success." Some cadres were singled out for exemplary punishment while many peasants were permitted to leave their collectives. Although those who left did so with nothing, half of those collectivized still chose to depart. They did not do so for long. The government was just catching its breath. Soon the collectivization offensive was on again. By 1932, two-thirds of all peasants were collectivized; by 1936 the figure reached 90 percent. Stalin and the state had won the collectivization war.

The price of the victory was high. Breakneck speed and the resultant disorganization, so characteristic of the First Five-Year Plan in both industry and agriculture, added immeasurably to the destruction and dying. Peasants arrived at their new "collectives" to find no one, least of all the urban cadres who had brought them there, knew anything about how to manage this new approach to farming. Production plans or workable remuneration systems did not exist. Frequently, precious farm implements or scarce machinery taken from their original owners were ruined by lack of proper care. Many farm animals died for the same reason. The urban party functionaries caused more havoc when they refused to listen to the "backward" peasants. Sometimes waste or meadow land was sown or ill-conceived agricultural experiments undertaken. Forced sowing campaigns produced careless work by demoralized peasants. Weeds rather than crops soon covered hundreds of thousands of acres, particularly in the Ukraine, the nation's traditional breadbasket.

Overwhelmed by the state's coercive power, peasants resisted as best they could. They destroyed their crops, tools, and animals rather than give them up to the collectives. Sometimes they consumed their slaughtered animals in enormous eating orgies that literally left them sick. This peasant tragedy was an economic disaster. As a result of mismanagement and deliberate destruction, barely half the nation's cattle, less than half its horses, less than 40 percent of its pigs, and barely a third of its sheep and goats survived collectivization and the First Five-Year Plan. It took decades for Soviet agriculture to make up these animal losses and the food and power they provided. Meanwhile, overall production in agriculture dropped by 20 percent and did not reach precollectivization levels until the eve of World War II. In 1953, the year of Stalin's death, grain production was below the level reached in 1913.

Collectivization was made much worse by its companion project, what the regime called "dekulakization," or, in its franker moments, the "liquidation of the *kulaks* as a class." It is not entirely clear why Stalin and the Politburo made this murderous decision. The party, to be sure, had long discussed what to do with the *kulaks*, but liquidation was something new. Perhaps the Politburo reasoned that destroying the *kulaks* would make it easier to bend the rest of the peasantry to the party's will. What is clear is that millions of people died as a result.

In 1929 the *kulaks* amounted to perhaps 5 percent of the peasantry. They included not only the most prosperous and influential peasants, but the best and most efficient farmers, whose skills presumably would have been an asset to the proposed collective farms. Instead, all *kulaks*, from the heads of households down to the infant children, were to be excluded from the new collectives. Some were to be deported to Siberia or the frozen far north, others deported to less distant realms, and some left to become impoverished pariahs where they were. Wherever they were, they were first to be thoroughly broken. These peasant farmers, who had done little more than rise from abject poverty through hard work and thrift, were left with nothing. One police report recorded that *kulaks* were left "in their underclothes, for everything was confiscated, including old rubber boots . . . women's drawers . . . 50 kopeks worth of tea . . . pokers, washtubs, etc. . . . *Kulak* families with small children were left without any means of feeding themselves."

Many *kulaks*, often entire families, committed suicide. Those who chose to try to continue living were deported under inhuman conditions:

> Trainloads of deported peasants left for the icy North, the forests, the steppes, the deserts. These were whole populations, denuded of everything; the old folk starved to death in mid-journey, newborn babies were buried on the banks of the roadside, and each wilderness had its crop of little crosses of boughs of white wood.[3]

Some of the trains were so long and densely packed that it took two locomotives, one to push and one to pull, to move them. Inside the boxcars, those who died of thirst or disease did so on their feet; there was no place to fall down. Once they reached their destinations, the men were separated from their families and sent to labor camps; many never survived the forced marches through frozen wastes to their hellish destinations. Their families did little better, as one prisoner discovered in Siberia:

> At the foot of many slopes something had been dug that looked from a distance like garbage dumps. Out of them black beings emerged, adults and children, it seemed, and followed us with their eyes.
> "What are they? Human beings?" I stupidly asked. . . .
> "These are called . . . special migrants," our new authority on local affairs began to explain. "There are thousands of them, many thousands. For the most part they are forgotten. They are sent here as voluntary deportees.

They won't let them into the camps or barracks. If you want to eat, you've got to work; if you don't want to, you might just as well dig yourself into the earth. There is little difference. . . ."[4]

The *kulaks* were thoroughly liquidated, but they did not die alone. All sorts of peasants were sucked into the maelstrom. Often it was difficult to distinguish a *kulak* from his neighbor, or even to know if one was a *kulak*. Thus the story was told of one peasant busily "dekulaking" on one side of a village while his own homestead was being "dekulaked" on the other side. It was enough to be unenthusiastic about collectivization (or to have the wrong enemy, or to have something that someone else coveted) to be labeled a *kulak*. According to Stalin's own testimony, millions of human beings were uprooted; vast numbers of them died.

Most of the *kulaks* were liquidated between 1930 and 1932. What followed was equally horrible. Bad weather and the raging turmoil combined in 1932 to produce a poor harvest. Despite reduced quantities of grain on the farm, particularly in the Ukraine and North Caucasus, key breadbaskets which traditionally provided half the country's marketable grain, quotas for grain deliveries to the state remained as high or higher than in previous years. Bereft of the food they had grown, the peasants of the Ukraine and North Caucasus began to starve. People ate cats, dogs, field mice, bark, and even horse manure in a desperate struggle to stay alive. ("Yes, the horse manure. We fight over it. Sometimes there are whole grains in it," a peasant woman told a shocked party worker.) They ate animals that had died of disease. Even cannibalism occurred. In some areas infant mortality approached 100 percent; in others entire villages starved. Army units were deployed to keep starving peasants from eating unripened crops in the field, a crime that fell under the expansive rubric of "theft of state property" or "kulak sabotage." Those who managed to get their hands on a few seeds of unripened grain often died anyway, as such seeds were indigestible to weakened and ravaged bodies. Thousands of peasants defied police attempts to keep them out of the towns, where they begged for food, lay listless, and died.

And no matter what they did, they went on dying, dying, dying. They died singly and in droves. They died everywhere—in yards or streetcars and on trains. There was no one to bury these victims of the Stalinist famine.[5]

The best estimates are that 7 million died in the terror-famine of 1932–33, 5 million in Ukraine, one million in the North Caucasus, and one million elsewhere in the Soviet Union, mostly in the Lower Volga area. The government made no effort to stop the famine and every effort to prevent news of it from reaching the nation at large and the West. Grain was used to feed the burgeoning urban industrial labor force; it continued to be exported for foreign exchange, whose value apparently exceeded human life. Far from trying to relieve the famine, the evidence suggests that the government used it as a tool to break peasant resistance to collectivization, particularly in the Ukraine. Stalin called this policy "war by starvation."

From the depths of 1933 there was no place to go but up. The defeated peasants were compelled to accept collectivization. The victorious government likewise yielded a bit in order to make its new system work, if not efficiently, at least tolerably well. It is a system that remained remarkably stable until the demise of the Soviet Union. While some peasants worked as straight wage-earners on huge state-run farms called *sovkhozy*, the majority lived and worked on collective farms called *kolkhozy*. These smaller units supposedly were independent and collectively owned by those who lived and worked there. Actually, the party controlled the *kolkhozy* through party members who controlled the leadership positions on the farms. Each peasant's income was determined according to his share of the collective's profits, each share being determined by the number of "labor days" he earned. The peasants were not paid until the state had taken its share of the farm's production, at a very low fixed price, and resources were set aside for planting, reserves, and other needs. Another institution, the Machine Tractor Station (abolished in 1958) for years also fed at the trough before the membership of the collective. The Machine Tractor Station supplied the *kolkhozy* with heavy agricultural machinery, in theory because it was more efficient for several farms to share the use of these expensive and complex machines. In reality, the Machine Tractor Station was another lever of control, since it took a large percentage of the crop (generally around 15 percent) in exchange for services that often were of questionable quality.

Yet despite all these controls, the Soviet government simply never was able to get the system to work effectively. Instructions and orders handed down from party authorities to the farms often produced confusion, emphasis on the wrong crops or techniques, and apathy rather than increased yields. Even more important, peasants were paid so poorly for their work in the collectives that they frequently did not bother to work very well.

What really have helped the system work better were the tiny private plots left to each peasant family. These Stalin had to tolerate almost from the start. Beginning in the 1930s, despite periods of increased restrictions, the peasants were permitted to raise what they could on these plots and sell whatever surplus they could produce. Given the price the government was willing to pay for what it took from the collectives, a price that for many years was below what it cost the collectives to produce these crops, the peasants never could have survived without their private plots. Neither, in fact, could the nation as a whole have managed, for these tiny plots, amounting to 3 to 4 percent of the Soviet Union's farmland, over the years produced 25 percent of the total agricultural output, including at least a third of the fruit, milk, meat, eggs, and vegetables.

Despite the human cost, from the government's point of view collectivization was a success. It gave the regime the leverage it needed to procure the grain necessary to feed the growing industrial labor force and to export in return for industrial machinery. Beginning in 1930, the regime drastically increased its grain procurement over previous levels and kept them there, despite poor harvests for several years and the unfair and inadequate price it was willing to pay for what it took. Once the peasants were under the heel of collectivization, for example, there was nothing to keep the regime from taking 40 percent of the poor 1931–1932 harvest, thus setting the stage for the famine that followed. The result was that the Bolshevik regime followed the tsarist tradition of putting the bulk of the burden for industrialization on the peasantry's back.

However, agriculture became a drag on the Soviet economy. In 1929, the leadership apparently hoped that collectivized agriculture would soon provide it with one third of the capital needed for industrialization. The subsequent disasters made this impossible. At best, only extreme exploitation of the peasantry kept the agricultural sector from disrupting the industrialization plans. It is also undoubtedly true that during the 1930s all Soviet citizens, not only the peasants, suffered enormously because the peasants produced so little. After Stalin's death, matters improved but nothing enabled the Soviet Union to feed itself. A country that under the tsars was a leading grain exporter was turned into the world's largest grain importer. Collectivization had remained not only a yoke on the Soviet peasantry, but an albatross to the entire country.

Agriculture was so ravaged because it was treated as only a means to an end. The paramount goal of Stalin's revolution from above was industrialization—to build, at any cost, an industrial base capable of supporting a modern military establishment. This meant that heavy industry—iron, steel, coal, machine tools, electric power, and the like— were fed virtually every available resource at the expense of everything else, devouring five-sixths of all investment during the First Five-Year Plan. Consequently, these industries grew tremendously during the 1930s.

The industrialization drive might have been more successful were it not for the excessive speed at which it took place. Reckless haste produced bottlenecks, shortages, and enormous waste. Precious supplies delivered to a given project often lay unused because other vital materials were unavailable. Since heavy industry could not be permitted to lag behind, the nonfavored sectors were squeezed even more to make up for what had been wasted. The Soviet Union did become an industrial giant, but a grossly deformed one, at once heavily muscled to produce armaments, yet too weak to provide many basic human needs, let alone pleasures, for most of the population. Housing, consumer goods, and agriculture were ignored and stagnated.

Stalin's enthusiasm for gigantic projects also added to the general misery. He seemed convinced that bigger was better—one critic complained that Stalin wanted "a canal that could be seen from Mars"—and that human will could be harnessed to overcome any obstacle. Some of the projects eventually succeeded, like the Dneprostroy hydroelectric dam or the construction of the steel center of Magnitogorsk from scratch. Others were expensive and tragic fiascos, like the Baltic–White Sea canal, built in less than two years at the cost of at least 250,000 lives. Triumphantly finished on time, the canal proved to be too shallow to serve its strategic objectives.

Stalin also raised production targets at will. Fairly typical was his tripling a tractor production target to 170,000; less than 50,000 actually were produced. Some grandiose schemes, such as Stalin's dream to change Russia's climate through massive reforestation, mercifully were never begun. At best, these grand schemes tied up valuable resources for excessive periods of time until they became productive and relieved some of the pressures on the nation. At worst, precious resources were squandered. Of less concern to Stalin and his colleagues were the hundreds of thousands of human lives these economic musings destroyed.

All of this—the ravaging of agriculture, the wasteful destruction of resources, the gigantic projects—played havoc with the plans that were supposed to guide the industrial drive. The first two Five-Year Plans actually were little more than propaganda billboards. Real planning was done over one- or at best two-year periods. Even at this level, planners labored under extreme hardships. Resources allotted for one project often were suddenly diverted to a "priority" project or to the most favored projects being built by what were called "shock methods." Since quantity, meeting the designated tons of steel, tons of coal, or numbers of tractors, was the main criterion for judging success or failure, the tendency was to produce large amounts of poor-quality, often useless, goods. Yet if they were produced, they counted toward fulfillment of the plan. Another persistent problem was the poor quality of the work force. Hastily recruited, ill-trained, poorly paid, and constantly browbeaten and threatened, Stalin's new industrial proletariat was so unproductive that many additional workers had to be recruited and trained in a desperate attempt to meet the regime's targets. This inevitably led to budget overruns, increased costs, and greater demands on increasingly scarce social services.

Against this background it should not be surprising that very few major targets were reached during the first two Five-Year Plans (1929–1937).

Nonetheless, the achievements were impressive in the key target areas of heavy industry. Steel production rose from 4 to 17 million tons, oil from 11.7 to 30.5 million tons, coal from 35.4 to 128 million tons, electricity from 5.5 billion kwh to 36.2 billion kwh. Important new industries were created, among them automobile, aviation, tractor, and chemical, as were several entirely new industrial complexes. Many new sources of raw materials were developed, particularly east of the Ural mountains and in Siberia. Transport was significantly improved, mainly by additions to the canal and railroad networks. Some small strides even were made in expanding light industries producing consumer goods, although these remained a very poor relation to heavy industry. Overall, heavy industry grew by 400 percent. The industrialization drive, precisely because it was planned and controlled by a central authority, yielded vital economic and strategic benefits beyond purely quantitative growth. Because a significant proportion of this development was located in the central and eastern regions of the country, it both contributed to the economic advancement of these previously backward regions and made the new industrial plants and resources safer from foreign attack. Planning also yielded economic benefits because industrial installations were located closer to essential raw materials. Soviet Russia, despite the suffering and waste, built a viable modern industrial base in a decade. By 1941, that economic infrastructure was producing a full range of modern weapons, including some of the world's best aircraft, artillery, and tactical rockets. After World War II, it provided the take-off point for even greater growth that made the Soviet Union, until it was surpassed by Japan in the 1980s, an industrial power second only to the United States.

The question that logically arises is how so much was built in the face of such enormous chaos and waste. Several factors help account for this. The narrow focus on heavy industry was a two-edged sword. It caused imbalances and shortages, but it also meant that those projects most vital to a modern industrial infrastructure were completed, even if a great deal was sacrificed along the way. It was much easier to get all those steel mills built if no heed was paid to putting shoes on the steel workers or housing their families in decent dwellings.

The enthusiasm and dedication that Stalin and his propaganda machine were able to generate helped spur production. Many urban cadres gave their best efforts to the collectivization drive, and were capable of extreme cruelty in carrying out their charges, because they believed they were participating in the birth of a socialist utopia. The same enthusiasm was evident at many of the great construction sites, such as Magnitogorsk, where an American engineer somewhat hyperbolically observed how "construction work went on with a disregard for individuals and a mass heroism unparalleled in history," adding that the "battle" to build that great steel complex claimed more casualties then the battle of the Marne. It proved possible to stimulate additional effort through such campaigns as socialist competition of labor, in which rival groups tried to outdo each other, and through the famous (or notorious) Stakhanovite movement. The latter got its name from a coal miner named Alexei Stakhanov who, with help from the management of his mine, organized his team of workers so that in one shift he was able to mine fourteen times his quota of coal. The world's largest propaganda machine turned Stakhanov's effort into a national event in order to inspire the rest of the nation. The honors and material awards that went to overachievers like Stakhanov quickly produced a host of "Stakhanovites." However, although the state glorified these people, the proletariat often did not, since their extraordinary feats were used as excuses to raise the norms and quotas of ordinary workers.

Far more important was what the economist Naum Jasny has called the "strangulation" of consumption. Stalin and his planners could invest—and waste—as much as they did only because the Soviet people were denied the fruit of their excruciatingly hard labor. Jasny estimates that the per capita income dropped by 25 percent for urban workers and 40 percent for rural workers in the generation after 1928. During the worst years of the 1930s, the drop almost certainly exceeded 50 percent. Housing for the rapidly expanding urban working class simply was not built. Instead of the promised consumer goods, the people received rations, shortages, long lines, and high prices. The price system, in fact, was the regime's best revenue-raising tool. All goods were subject to a "turnover tax," a levy collected not just once, but several times as a product moved from its origins as raw material to the state-run retail outlet. This made it possible to exploit both the producer and the consumer at the same time by paying the former next to nothing, adding on a stiff turnover tax, and charging the latter an astronomical price. High prices unfortunately were the least of the average citizen's problems, since low agricultural productivity and the neglect of consumer-goods industries meant that often nothing was available at any price. According to economist Alec Nove, "1933 was the culmination of the most precipitous peacetime decline in living standards known in recorded history."[7]

The industrialization drive also was helped by compromises and concessions made after 1933. These changes came at an opportune time. Collectivized agriculture was in a shambles. Many large and expensive projects stood unfinished and unproductive. The mad rush to create an industrial labor force out of uneducated peasants resulted in enormous losses of expensive and complex machinery that had been operated by unqualified personnel. The regime responded by modifying its emphasis on expansion and quantity; instead, more attention was paid to consolidation and quality. This was manifested in greater attention to the training of workers, efforts to improve technical education, a determined effort to finish the huge projects started during the First Five-Year Plan, administrative reorganizations, and better managerial techniques, including the reorganization of the railroad administration by Lazar Kaganovich, Stalin's chief collectivizer. Concessions made to the peasantry regarding private plots and livestock allowed agriculture within three years to recover to approximately its pre-1929 level. The result was what Jasny called the "three good years" of 1934 to 1936, a period that yielded the most impressive growth rates of the great industrialization drive of the 1930s.

One frequently overlooked contribution to the Soviet industrialization drive came from abroad. As with the Russian efforts to build modern industry since the time of Peter I, Soviet industrialization under Stalin required Western technology and expertise. American firms like Ford, General Electric, and DuPont participated in Soviet industrial projects. American engineers helped supervise construction at the Dneprostroy hydroelectric dam and an American firm provided designs for the Magnitogorsk steel mills, two of the giant showpieces of the first Five-Year Plan. While depression gripped old established industries of the capitalist world, American and European companies and individuals eager for business and jobs provided vital technical expertise to the fledgling industry of the Communist world.

The most important force behind the industrialization drive was compulsion on a huge scale. During the 1930s, the Soviet labor force, largely recruited from the peasantry, was brutally exploited and regimented. With little to hold them in the way of incentives, these workers made a habit of moving from job to job in search of tolerable wages and working conditions. The workers' state therefore made simple absenteeism a criminal offense, stipulating that being twenty minutes late to work constituted absenteeism. Theft of collective farm or state property became a capital offense. After 1932, all citizens excepting peasants had to carry an internal passport, a form of control dredged up from the tsarist past. In 1938 came the notorious labor books. These contained a record of every job an individual held, and it was impossible to get a job without producing one's book. In 1940 all workers were frozen in their jobs.

The proletariat was not alone in its misery. The managers, engineers, and technocrats above them toiled under the same whip hand. Since most of them were of "bourgeois" origin, they were a convenient scapegoat for the many failures that plagued the industrialization drive, failures that were the consequences of the regime's irrational policy decisions. A series of public show trials between 1928 and 1933, complete with executions and long prison terms, blamed the nation's economic difficulties on "wreckers," "saboteurs," and the like. These trials, orchestrated to the drumbeat of a large propaganda campaign, undoubtedly convinced many people that their economic problems could be blamed on these "bourgeois" specialists rather than on the regime's errors. They also deprived that economy of valuable talent and drove many of those not arrested to seek the relative safety of positions with little responsibility, which wasted their valuable skills. Meanwhile, executions of many other "bourgeois" specialists took place in secret, often without the benefit of any trial.

The quintessence of the exploitation and force that fed Stalin's new economic machine was the largest slave labor empire in history. Compulsory labor had a long history in Russia, and it was not abolished after the Bolshevik Revolution. However, under Stalin it reached record proportions, both in terms of size and cruelty. Slave labor had three important advantages. It was cheap, since it cost very little to maintain workers whose lives often were expendable. It also could be used as a substitute for machines, since the workers had no choice about the jobs they did. Finally, the most severe discipline could be enforced to get the work done. These were valuable assets in a country so short of food, machines, and other factors vital to the industrialization drive.

Millions of people, mostly men but also large numbers of women and children, labored in these camps, collectively known as the Gulag ("Chief Administration of Camps"), a special department run by the secret police. The best available estimates put the Gulag population by 1938 at about 7 million, a figure that held steady or even grew over the next dozen years. The area under the Gulag's control was equally astounding. One division, the Dalstroy, which included the notorious Kolyma gold mines in eastern Siberia, by itself governed an area four times the size of France. Smaller Gulag camps were almost everywhere, including in every major Soviet city.

Slave labor built the most difficult and dangerous projects of the First and Second Five-Year Plans. It mined gold, iron, and coal. It built canals and railroads, harvested lumber in the frozen north, built hydroelectric stations, and built an entire port city, the notorious Magadan, from scratch in one of the most inhospitable regions of eastern Siberia to service Stalin's gold mines there. Slave laborers worked on many other types of industrial projects as well, including many in which the Gulag provided the work force for enterprises run by other state authorities. A recent estimate is that slave labor accounted for as much as 25 percent of the entire Soviet economy during the 1930s.

But only at the price of human life. Many prisoners never even survived the trip to the camps. Once a slave ship headed for the Kolyma gold mines, the "land of the white death," became stuck in the Arctic ice; when it finally arrived at its destination, every one of its 12,000 prisoners was dead. In the Pechora region in northern European Russia, no less than 1 million people died between 1937 and 1941 alone. Mortality rates of 10 and 20 percent per year were common in the Gulag and higher rates were not unknown. In certain lumber camps, few prisoners survived for more than two years. The Gulag camps not only killed more people than the regime executed, but may well have taken a toll comparable to Hitler's extermination camps. The working conditions eloquently explain why:

> . . . We were forced to work in temperatures of −40 degrees [F.]. Rain and snow storms were disregarded. We had to cut trees in the forests even when the snow was waist deep. Falling trees hit the workers, who were unable to escape in the snow. In the summer . . . men had to stand knee deep in water or mud for 10 or 12 hours. . . . Influenza, bronchitis, pneumonia, tuberculosis . . . malaria, and other illnesses decimated our ranks. . . . The men continually had frozen extremities and amputation due to frostbite was common. . . . The men were compelled to work by force . . . camp authorities would force the prisoners to work by beating, kicking, dragging them by their feet through mud and snow, setting dogs on them, hitting them with rifle butts, and by threatening them with revolvers and bayonets.[8]

Aleksandr Solzhenitsyn, who spent eight years in the camps, described what he found to be a typical death. After suffering from innumerable diseases and their ravages—the rotting teeth, bleeding gums, ulcerated legs, decaying and peeling skin, diarrhea, and the like—a dying man:

> . . . grows deaf and stupid, and he loses all capacity to weep, even when he is being dragged along the ground behind a sledge. He is no longer afraid of death; he is wrapped in a submissive rosy glow. He has crossed all boundaries and has forgotten the name of his wife, of his children, and finally his own name too. Sometimes the entire body of a man dying of starvation is covered with blue-black pimples like peas, with pus-filled heads smaller than a pinhead—his face, arms, legs, his trunk, even his scrotum. It is so painful he cannot be touched. The tiny boils come to a head and burst and a thick wormlike string of pus is forced out of them. The man is rotting alive.
>
> If black astonished head lice are crawling on the face of your neighbor on the bunks, it is a sure sign of death.[9]

The industrialization drive was the core of Stalin's revolution from above, but it did not define its limits. Bolshevik ideology also demanded a fundamental recasting of Russian society into a new socialist mold. The requisites of the industrialization drive and the ideology of the nation's leadership meant that the state inevitably intruded into virtually all areas of life. While this occasionally had a positive effect (such as education), overall it meant that a suffocating cloud of repression, rote, and uniformity enveloped Soviet Russia's cultural, scientific, and spiritual life for a generation.

The First Five-Year Plan had a far-reaching effect on education. The various liberalizing reforms of the 1920s were largely done away with and replaced with a stress on technical achievement, discipline, and heavy, unrelenting indoctrination. Technical education received the most attention because of the state's burgeoning need for specialists to staff the growing industrial infrastructure. At the same time, the needs of a modernized economy required a broad-based effort, and the spread of free primary education led to a dramatic drop in illiteracy during the 1930s.

If a case can be made that Stalin's education policy produced some progress, his cultural policy was a giant step backward. This was particularly true in what may be called the mass or popular culture. It was dominated by a secularized religiosity recalling some of old Russia's most obscurant traditions. Cultural historian James H. Billington has aptly called this phenomenon the "revenge of Muscovy." As Billington observes, instead of "icons, incense, and ringing bells" Stalin's Russia had "lithographs of Lenin, cheap perfume, and humming machines"; instead of the "omnipresent calls to worship of Orthodoxy" there was the "inescapable loudspeaker or radio with its hypnotic statistics and the invocations to labor"; instead of "priests and missionaries" there were Stalin's "soldiers of the cultural army," all united, as in Ivan the Terrible's time, by "the believer's cry of hallelujah in response to the revealed word from Moscow."[10]

Culture was just another soldier conscripted for the campaign to build socialism. It marched under the banner of "socialist realism." Artists were not to depict things as they were, but as the state wanted them to be. As "engineers of the human soul," artists were expected to produce propaganda that served the ends of the state, not art that expressed their untrustworthy inner feelings. They were to compose patriotic, upbeat music, paint prosperous and plump collective farmers and enthusiastic and heroic factory workers, and write novels extolling the new socialist work ethic. In novels, plays, and movies, heros and heroines acted out positive themes in settings crowded with self-sacrifice, enthusiasm for the Five-Year Plan, and unlimited devotion to the greatest of all leaders, Comrade Stalin. Although Soviet artists produced some worthwhile work, socialist realism suffocated most attempts at genuine artistic expression.

The sciences and social sciences also suffered grievously. History was rewritten to suit the needs of Stalin and the state, from questions concerning the origins of the Russian state to the history of the Bolshevik Party. Interestingly, the traditional Marxist historical school favored under Lenin, which was extremely critical of Russia's tsarist past, was suppressed in favor of an approach stressing selected aspects of the past useful to Stalin. Russian expansionism, for example, suddenly became a progressive historical force beneficial to the people it enveloped, while tyrants like Ivan the Terrible and Peter the Great became great builders and statesmen. The history of the Bolshevik Party was rewritten right down to the participants' memoirs. It emerged unrecognizable to anyone who had lived when Lenin was alive. The entire movement and the Revolution itself became the exclusive work of Lenin and his magnificent right-hand man, Stalin, with occasional input from the masses. All others receded into the background or, like Trotsky, into ignominy.

The sciences also suffered. How could it be otherwise when so many of the best scientists were imprisoned or murdered for having the wrong political outlook, or simply for having the wrong enemies? The worst destruction occurred in biology and genetics, where a charlatan named Trofim Lysenko became the leading authority because his theory that environmentally acquired traits could be passed to succeeding generations meshed with Stalin's desire to create a "new socialist man." Many of Lysenko's critics were dismissed from their jobs, and some of them arrested. Lysenko's theories were never scientifically proven, nor could they be, since they were wrong. But that did not prevent them or Lysenko from wreaking havoc on Soviet biology, genetics, and agronomy from the late 1930s until the early 1960s.

Stalin's policies caused considerable harm to the Soviet Union's non-Russian nationalities. Cultural diversity in any genuine sense was dangerous to Stalin for two reasons. It could easily reinforce the centrifugal forces in the multinational Russian (now Soviet) empire, and it might provide living examples of alternative social systems. The 1930s therefore witnessed intensive and extensive Russification. In Ukraine, home to over 30 million non-Great Russian Slavs, cultural policies included the arrest of leading Ukrainian intellectuals, the Russification of the Ukrainian language, and the required study of Russian in the schools. Similar programs were implemented in Belorussia. The Jewish community, a traditional victim of the Russian state, also suffered. Anti-Semitism resurfaced, Jewish culture was largely suppressed, and Jews were excluded from key positions in the party and state bureaucracies. Overall, although certain forms of non-Russian cultural expression were permitted, everything had to take place within the context of the new "Soviet" nationality, a formula that meant the domination of the Great Russian language and culture. Anything outside that context was "bourgeois nationalism."

The regime's weapons for suppressing ethnic feeling among the minority nationalities were not only cultural. Stalin used his "war by starvation" to break Ukrainian resistance to collectivization and deported many of those who survived. Collectivization devastated the way of life of the Moslem Kazakhs, while colonization by ethnic Russians turned some nationalities into minorities in their own homelands. Russia under Stalin remained a very difficult and often dangerous place for any non-Russian ethnic group desiring genuine self-expression—as it had been under the tsars.

Other vestiges of the tsarist past also reasserted themselves. During the 1930s Stalin reintroduced various forms of hierarchy that had been eroded or eliminated by the Revolution, and Soviet society became as hierarchial as Russian society had been during tsarist times. These hierarchies included a full range of wage differentials based on categories of work and elite classes of workers, such as Stakhalnovites. In 1931, the idea of equal wages was demoted from a socialist ideal to "petty bourgeois egalitarianism." Piece rates frequently replaced straight salaries. Economic differentials began to approach those of the capitalist countries. Whereas an ordinary worker might make 150 rubles a month, an engineer made 500 rubles, a shock worker—someone able to exceed his quota— as much as 2,000, and a high state official more than 5,000. Below the workers stood the peasants, confined to a second-class status reminiscent of serfdom, and below them the slave laborers. Ranks, complete with uniforms, reappeared in the civil service, while military ranks similar to the tsarist pattern returned to the armed forces. Aside from salary and rank, Soviet citizens were distinguished by their access to goods and services. The "new proletarian aristocracy," as some uncharitably but not inaccurately called the Communist Party, enjoyed a wide variety of privileges. Members of the party's upper crust shopped in special stores stocked with goods unavailable elsewhere, sent their children to exclusive schools, and received the best social services, not the least of which was adequate medical care. They enjoyed private cars, country villas, fine restaurants, and even servants. At the other pole, the slave laborers had literally nothing, not even hope.

Personal matters also came under state scrutiny and regimentation, undoing more of the liberalizing reforms of the 1920s. The sudden drop in the birth rate during the 1930s—it fell by one third—was met by reinstating the old ban on abortion. Children and young people were regulated by a pyramid of organizations (Young Octobrists, Pioneers, and the Communist Union of Youth, or *Komsomol*, in ascending order) that supervised and indoctrinated them until they were about thirty and eligible to enter the party itself. Attempts to restore some of the social order disrupted by the industrialization drive included making children liable for punishment as adults from the age of twelve. The ideal child not only joined the appropriate youth organization, but gave it and the state his primary loyalty. The hero to emulate was Pavlik Morozov, a peasant child who turned in his parents to the secret police because they spoke against the regime. Other attempts in this direction included far stricter divorce standards and other attempts to promote more stable and authoritarian family life.

Although it is undoubtedly true that under Stalin a great deal changed, one thing did not. Power, as it always has, continued to corrupt, and when it was as close to being absolute as it was in Stalin's Russia, there was a corresponding degree of corruption. A vast gap opened up between the Communist Party elite and the general population in a society officially committed to socialism. The secret police officialdom enjoyed much of the best housing, medical care, and luxuries Soviet Russia had to offer. Typical of the men at the top was Henrik Yagoda, Stalin's secret police chief during the early and mid-1930s. During the first Five-Year Plan, when there were no funds to build housing for the proletariat and millions had to group together in filthy substandard quarters, Yagoda's apartment was described as "beautifully equipped. . . . One of the rooms was furnished in the Asiatic style, with carpets on the walls, divans, and thick rugs on the floor." Anastas Mikoyan, a top Stalin aide for many years and one of the very few to survive his leader's purges, lived in the mansion of an industrialist against whom he had once organized strikes before the revolution. Stalin's daughter, Svetlana, described it as:

> . . . to this day exactly as its exiled owners left it. On the porch is a marble statue of a dog. . . . Inside are marble statues imported from Italy. The walls are hung with Gobelins, and downstairs the windows are of stained glass. The garden, the park, the tennis court, the orangery, and the greenhouses are all exactly as they have always been.[11]

Many of Russia's new rulers could hardly believe they had achieved so much. Abel Yenukidze, a draftsman before 1917 who came up the ladder with his long-time friend and patron, Stalin (who later had Yenukidze shot), apparently spent much of his time comparing his new life-style with how the tsars used to live. Not even the privations of World War II were allowed to get in the way of the fun, as an American general observed at a luncheon when so many Soviet citizens were starving at the height of their "Great Patriotic War":

> The centerpieces were huge silver bowls containing fresh fruit specially pro-cured from the Caucasus. . . . Beautifully cut glass ran the gamut from tall thin champagne glasses, through those for light and heavy red wines, to the inevitable vodka glass. . . . There were bottles the entire length of the table from which the glasses could be and were filled many times. Interspersed among the bottles were silver platters of . . . fresh large grained caviar . . . huge delicacies. . . . Knives, forks, and spoons were of gold, and service plates of the finest china heavily encrusted with gold. The whole spectacle was amazing and called to mind the banquet scene in Charles Laughton's movie *Henry VIII*.[12]

All this revelling inevitably had a touch of frenzy, for the revellers never knew if and when the secret police would step in and end it all. After the

Great Purge in 1934, people lived for the moment, as the end often came without warning. One prisoner who survived Stalin's camps reported seeing women in prison still dressed in the tattered remnants of their luxurious evening dresses. Apparently, like so many Cinderellas, they did not even make it home before their world disappeared in a flash.

The corruption peaked with the general secretary. No tsar ever lived better. As historian Nikolai Tolstoy observed, "There was no whim, however extravagant or eccentric, which the state budget could not be brought to indulge."[13] Stalin, his simple public image notwithstanding, enjoyed a large number of magnificent estates, a fleet of luxury cars, and enormous public spectacles ranging from operas to films. He viewed some of his favorite films in private, however; they were pornographic movies seized from the Nazis during World War II. When Stalin left the Kremlin en route to one of his nearby country homes, he traveled in a heavily armed convoy along wide avenues specially built to ensure his safe trip.

All of this actually was the lesser part of the corruption, for as historian Roy Medvedev[14] and others have reported, party leaders could and did get away with kidnapping, rape, and murder. It is with good reason that Stalin felt the need to assert that "equality has nothing in common with Marxian socialism." The point is debatable. What is not debatable is that in its uncontrollable power and the moral and material corruption that accompanied it, the Communist party of the Soviet Union had much in common with its presumed ideological opposite, the German National Socialist (Nazi) Party. Corruption, it would appear, knows no ideology.

There was one area in which the Communist Party of the Soviet Union stood alone. Between 1934 and 1938 it became simultaneously both the perpetrator and the victim of what is referred to as the "great purge." Prior to the great purge, terror clearly was the main force behind Stalin's revolution from above. As such, terror was the core of that revolution, the force that held its various component parts—in industry, agriculture, culture, and so on—together. Then something happened deep inside that unstable core. It exploded and became a raging super-nova, expanding in all directions seemingly at the speed of light, enveloping everything in sight as it reached the four corners of the vast Soviet universe that had given it life. By the time the terror ran its course, large parts of Soviet society were seared beyond recognition; others, most tellingly the party's old guard and much of Stalin's new guard, were vaporized almost entirely. New orders of society were created out of the cataclysm as it tore old ones apart. The great purge eventually ran its course, but left large, sometimes enormous remnants, including the burgeoning Soviet system of labor camps, a black hole into which millions continued to disappear until the 1950s. Other elements, including the most fortunate members of Brezhnev-Andropov generation of party cadres, survived beyond the

1950s to become the managers and later the masters of the new society the mighty force of Stalin's terror forged.

"Why? What for?" were the questions of the era, scratched into innumerable prison walls and transport vehicles by the uncomprehending victims. In a sense it is difficult to give a definitive answer to that question. There are only several partial responses to those simple words that became the epitaph for so many.

Terror—the use of extensive, indiscriminate force—was nothing new to Bolshevism: it was built into the new Soviet order from the start. What changed was its scope. Lenin's use of terror was limited to destroying opponents of the regime and to coercing certain elements of the population in the face of a crisis, as was the case during the Civil War. Still, Lenin relied heavily on terror, and most Bolsheviks accepted it as a legitimate political weapon. Equally important, Lenin also institutionalized terror in the form of the secret police. When the party went beyond fighting for power to recasting society in a new socialist mold, terror became not only a logical but a primary tool in the face of an overwhelmingly reluctant population. Because the job of recasting an entire society was so much more massive than simply beating back enemies, the use of terror was exponentially greater after 1929 than in Lenin's day. In fact, the terror employed in the collectivization drive was so dreadful that many Bolsheviks, probably most of them, recoiled from it once collectivization and the great construction projects of the First Five-Year Plan were completed by 1933. As for party purges, they were a periodic occurrence, the latest round having begun in 1933. Still, by 1933 the general hope was that the worst, in every sense, was over. Instead, a far greater terror lurked just ahead.

The Bolshevik legacy was one factor contributing to the great purge. The decisive factor, however, was the nature of the man in power, for just as there would have been no Bolshevik revolution without Lenin, there would have been no great purge without Stalin. Stalin, an incessant plotter himself, seems to have been convinced of innumerable plots against him, plots which in his mind could best be quashed by striking first, not just against the individuals involved, but against entire groups that might produce additional plots. His fears were reinforced by his inability during the early 1930s to secure absolute power. In 1932 Stalin was unable to convince his Politburo to execute a group of party dissidents, partially because of the moderating influence of Sergei Kirov, a tough functionary who had rendered loyal service in both the collectivization drive and as Stalin's appointed boss in Leningrad, but who was also capable of making his own decisions. Stalin may also have opposed the more moderate economic policies of the Second Five-Year Plan. He certainly was disturbed further by the results of the Seventeenth Party Congress in 1934, his hand-picked "Congress of Victors." That congress reflected a widespread desire among party leaders for consolidation and moderation, at least regarding the industrialization drive. Thus Kirov, an excellent orator, a politician with a strong power base in Leningrad, and, unlike Stalin, an ethnic Russian, not only received tremendous ovations from the delegates, but according to credible reports received the greatest number of votes in the balloting for the Central Committee while Stalin received the least. (All candidates were elected, as there was only one candidate for each seat, and the official announcement of the voting results, of course, were falsified to eliminate all but a handful of about 270 anti-Stalin votes.) Several memoirs also refer to an incipient plan to replace Stalin with Kirov as general secretary, although if such a plan did exist Kirov did not encourage it. There certainly was tension between the two men, and reliable witnesses to at least one public incident where Stalin spoke harshly to Kirov. What is clear among all these shadows is that the continued presence of the Bolshevik old guard that remembered Lenin, combined with the general sentiment among many of Stalin's own loyalists that the time had come to moderate the pace and the harshness of the revolution from above, would deny Stalin the absolute power he craved.

If the Bolshevik legacy and Stalin's personality provide some explanation for the impetus of the great purge, they do not explain how such a horror could engulf an entire society. The great purge required the active participation of hundreds of thousands of people. There were, to be sure, many thugs and killers in Soviet Russia, and Stalin made good use of them, but they were not enough to staff the gigantic apparatus that ran the purge. That required many people who in normal times would have been quite content to go about their customary business. But the 1930s in Soviet Russia were *not* normal times. Society had been torn apart by relentless and extraordinary violence that began with World War I and ran through the 1917 revolutions, the Civil War, collectivization, and the industrialization drive. People by the millions were torn from their traditional social moorings and morality. And they were bombarded by a new morality—the revolutionary morality of Bolshevism—that justified extreme measures for the sake of the revolution. These otherwise ordinary people therefore were available to serve as informers, police, administrators, guards, and executioners in the terror apparatus, much as they had been during collectivization. Some did so because they believed they were building a modern socialist Russia, as Stalin may well have believed himself. Others participated simply to better their lives and advance their careers. And of course, many participated out of fear, producing victims lest they become victims themselves. While it is true that the great purge had many unique characteristics, it is also true that this combination of extraordinary social turmoil and ideological extremism has produced comparable horrors elsewhere. In Germany, just a few years later, they produced the Holocaust; in Cambodia forty years later they produced a slaughter that, at least in terms of the percentage of the population killed, exceeded even Stalin's great purge.

In 1934 Stalin began to prepare his new campaign, this time against the very people who had brought him to power and carried out the revolution from above. The secret police, now part of the Internal Affairs Commisariat or NKVD, was reorganized and new personnel brought in. A shadowy but vital organ, the Special Section of the Central Committee, became more active. Headed by A. N. Peskrebyshev, Stalin's personal secretary, the Special Section functioned as Stalin's private secretariat, his personal eyes and ears that spied on all party and state agencies, including the NKVD, and carried out some of his most secret projects. Finally, in December 1934, the Soviet Union was shocked to hear that its beloved Comrade Kirov had been assassinated. Stalin calmed a nervous nation by intervening directly in the investigation, a prudent step since evidence published since his death, including remarks by Nikita Khrushchev, makes it likely that Stalin gave the order to have Kirov eliminated.

A wave of hysteria swept the country as the press filled with stories of legions of anti-Communists, foreign agents, disloyal Communists, unscrupulous Trotskyites, and similar menaces. About 40,000 alleged plotters were arrested in Leningrad alone, while thousands of "Japanese spies" were uncovered in eastern parts of the country. Several hundred thousand people were deported to the Gulag. Draconic new laws made children over twelve liable to capital punishment, and gave almost unlimited scope to the crime of counterrevolution. Zinoviev and Kamenev were arrested (again), tried, and convicted of "moral responsibility" for Kirov's murder. Stalin may also have been involved in the timely deaths of two important Bolsheviks who opposed further purges: V. V. Kiubyshev, a Politburo member who died in 1935; and Maxim Gorky, the famed writer and friend of Lenin, who died in 1936. A tidal wave of denunciations, arrests, deportations, and executions was building.

The great purge reached high gear in 1936, the year of the first of the famous show trials of leading Bolsheviks. Between August 1936 and March 1938, almost every leading member of the surviving Bolshevik old guard went on trial for plotting against Lenin and/or Stalin. To believe such charges one would have to accept the contention that virtually every member of the Leninist leadership, excepting, of course, Stalin, aligned himself with foreign capitalists, counterrevolutionaries, and other enemies of the worker's state. The archvillain in this gallery of Bolshevik rogues was Trotsky, whose evil web at once ensnared Hitler, the emperor of Japan, Zinoviev, Kamenev, and Bukharin, to name but a few, quite a tribute to a man who proved so incapable of building a political organization when it really counted. Thus Andrei Vyshinsky, the prosecutor at these trials, was able to link, in one sentence, the "Rightists, Trotskyists,

Mensheviks, Socialist Revolutionaries, bourgeois nationalists, and so on and so forth. . . ." The language of the trials reflected the quality of the charges and the supporting evidence. The accused, who included the pride of the party and Lenin's Politburo, were a "foul-smelling heap of human garbage," the "scum and filth of the past," "hateful traitors" who "must be shot like mad dogs." They were spared nothing; they were even forced to join the cheerleading against themselves. Hence Zinoviev's remarkable political odyssey: "My defective Bolshevism became transformed into anti-Bolshevism and through Trotskyism I arrived at fascism." This type of statement typified the most remarkable fact about the trials: that every single man in the dock confessed to his crimes.

There were three show trials. In August 1936, Zinoviev and Kamenev were tried with fourteen men of lesser rank. All were executed. In January 1937, seventeen former supporters of Trotsky, all of whom had repented and joined with Stalin after Trotsky's defeat, took their turn in the dock. Thirteen were executed; the rest disappeared into the camps. The grand finale in March 1938 featured Bukharin, Rykov, and Nikolai Krestinsky, all former members of Lenin's Politburo, as well as Yagoda, the former head of the NKVD, and seventeen others of various stature. All but three were shot; the survivors vanished into the camps. In between these extravaganzas, Stalin's police found time to arrest, torture, and execute secretly the cream of his military establishment for treason and spying, including the Civil War hero and chief of the general staff, Mikhail Tukhachevsky.

The linchpin of the Moscow Trials was the confession. Every one of the Bolshevik luminaries brought to trial confessed, often in excruciating detail, to a host of crimes ranging from sabotage to murder to treason. Only one, Nikolai Krestinsky, dared to retract his "confession" in open court, an error he quickly corrected after one additional night with the NKVD. One can understand why Stalin wanted confessions since there was no other evidence of any kind to back up the charges. Also, by getting his once-mighty victims to confess and demean themselves, Stalin totally discredited not only them, but any version of the "truth" other than his own. The confessions gave the trials surprising credibility, not just in the Soviet Union, where the people were under constant bombardment from the state-controlled media, but in the West, where it was possible to know better.

The question, then, is why so many hardened revolutionaries who had once stood up to the mighty tsarist empire broke like eggs and spilled out their confessions to Stalin. A variety of factors were involved. Some old Bolsheviks had lived their lives only for their revolutionary deity and sanctified party, and it was possible to convince them to render the party one more service, even in their disgrace. Many forlornly hoped to save their wives and children if they cooperated. Some, like

Bukharin, apparently hoped that by confessing in general terms while denying many of the specifics of the charges against them they could obliquely make the point that the charges against them were false. If all else failed, the men who confessed were broken under foul and sophisticated torture.

As bad as the show trials were, they were only the smallest tip of an iceberg the size of the Soviet Union itself. The great purge decimated the nation's elites. No group suffered worse than the Communist Party, particularly its old guard. Five members of Lenin's April 1917 Central Committee, aside from Stalin, survived until the 1930s. Stalin killed them all. Nor did any of the seventeen surviving members of the Central Committee elected in September 1917, the Central Committee that made the Bolshevik Revolution, survive Stalin's terror. Stalin's own supporters, the people who had given him victory in 1929, did not fare much better. The purges claimed 70 percent of his hand-picked Central Committee at the "Congress of Victors" and 1,108 of the 1,966 delegates at large. They swept through the middle and lower ranks of the party several times, sometimes wiping out the leadership of a locality three or four times. Estimates of the dead range upwards from a million to several times that, making Stalin the greatest killer of Communists in history. Whatever the exact total, the party was unable to recruit members fast enough to make up its losses.

The armed forces were ravaged because Stalin greatly feared the military leadership, which was critical of the purges, might unite and overthrow him. Three out of five marshals, fourteen out of sixteen top army commanders, all eight admirals, and 131 out of 199 divisional commanders perished. Half of the entire officer corps—over 35,000 men—were shot or sent to the camps. Not even the secret police itself was safe. It was purged several times. Yagoda, its chief since 1929, lasted until 1936. His successor was Nikolai Yezhov, a criminal psychopath by any reasonable standards. He ran the purge during its peak years, so that the entire period came to be called the *Yezhovshchina*. He was eliminated in 1938 in favor of Lavrenti Beria. Down the rathole also poured the Soviet Union's artists and writers, people like Boris Pilniak, Isaac Babel, Osip Mandelstam, Vsevolod Meyerhold, and uncounted others.

And yet even this represents the headlines of a story millions of lives long. The general secretary's drive for absolute power and security meant that the entire nation, not merely the party or an entire social class, like the peasantry, had to be terrorized into complete submission. He had available for this purpose the world's largest secret police organization. By the mid-1930s, fed by the collectivization and industrialization campaigns, the NKVD had grown to behemoth size. It ran prisons, managed and guarded the labor camps, controlled the regular police, guarded the borders, and had its agents planted virtually everywhere people gathered, from factories, collective farms and railroad stations to libraries, theaters, apartment houses and parks to police and terrorize a nation of 170 million people. The NKVD at its peak had an armed force, including units armed with heavy artillery and tanks as well as guards, that numbered in the hundreds of thousands. Its ubiquitous network of informers swelled that number even further so that its administrative expenses may have totaled two-thirds of the amount spent by the rest of the state apparatus put together.

Between 1936 and 1938 nobody could ever feel safe. The nights were the worst, since the NKVD preferred to operate in the shadows, but the days were not much better. Solzhenitsyn has chronicled what Soviet citizens had to expect:

> They take you aside in a factory corridor . . . and you are arrested. They take you from a military hospital with a temperature of 102. . . . They take you right off the operating table. . . . In the Gastronome—the fancy food store— you are invited to the special-order department and arrested there. You are arrested by a religious pilgrim whom you have put up for the night "for the sake of Christ." You are arrested by the meterman. . . .You are arrested by a bicyclist who has run into you on the street, by a railway conductor, a taxi driver, a savings bank teller, the manager of a movie theater.[15]

As with the show trials, there were no objective standards of truth, no standards for guilt or innocence. Most people never knew why they were arrested or, almost as frightening, why their neighbors were arrested and they were not. While still free, people denounced each other without rhyme or reason in order to demonstrate their loyalty.

Once arrested and put through the NKVD's mill, people confessed to anything and denounced anyone in a desperate attempt to win a small measure of mercy; it is not difficult to understand why. Bodies and spirits were damaged and broken beyond repair. The system was good enough to bring most of the main figures to trial and get innumerable others involved in other "cases" to "confess" to virtually anything the human imagination could dream up. Few could resist the notorious "conveyor," a series of continuous interrogations under bright lights that often lasted for several days or, if necessary, for several weeks. Even more devastating was continued interrogation combined with sleep deprivation that often went on for many months. Men were made to stand for ten or twenty hours as their legs swelled up, or until they collapsed, or to sit on hot pipes until their skin was burned. Others were tied under a strip of wood that was then pounded with an axe until the victim's internal organs were destroyed. More direct methods included beatings with rubber truncheons and empty bottles, the breaking of limbs, which were then left unset, and kicking a person's teeth out. If all this failed, and it rarely did, a man's family could be threatened. One witness recorded how women and girls were "beaten to a pulp. . . . Their hair was torn from their scalps, their fingers broken, their toes crushed, their teeth knocked in, temples crushed, skin broken open."[16] Often the beatings destroyed their internal organs. They might also be raped. A prisoner's child could be killed outright. No wonder that one expert interrogator reportedly could brag that "If Karl Marx himself fell into my hands, he'd confess to spying for Bismarck."

Most arrestees wound up in Stalin's labor camps, where they were eagerly awaited, since by the mid-1930s the stream of peasant laborers for the NKVD economic empire had run dry. One reason the police had arrest quotas, in fact, was to assure that the NKVD had enough laborers for its many projects, something that was not at all easy, given the mortality rate in the camps. The purges literally deformed Soviet society. Since at least 80 percent of those in the camps were males, by the 1950s the percentage of males to females of the age groups most affected by the purges was about 35 percent versus 65 percent. The comparable figures for the generation most affected by World War II is about 38 percent versus 62 percent.

The great purges roared ahead until 1938. By then the upward spiral was becoming dangerous even for Stalin. The spreading net of denunciations, as each arrestee had to denounce someone, if not several people, threatened to pull in so many people that Soviet society might have broken down altogether. Stalin therefore ended the slaughter in a typical way. He blamed others for it. The media conveniently announced that Yezhov, the NKVD head since 1936, and many of his subordinates had been committing "excesses." Yezhov therefore was arrested in December 1938 and replaced by Beria, who proceeded to purge the secret police. Stalin thus both deflected the blame for the terror from himself and preempted the possibility that the secret police could threaten him. The system of terror, it should be stressed, was not dismantled. The newly cleansed NKVD remained in place. Under Beria it simply functioned in a more systematic manner, arresting enough people to keep the population under control rather than totally disrupting all life with haphazard arrests. The camps also remained; they were, among other things, a vital part of the state's economic policy. During the war years, they grew to hold as many prisoners as they had during the great purge. The terror, in fact, reached around the world. In 1940 an NKVD agent in Mexico murdered Trotsky as the latter labored to complete his biography of Stalin.

The end of the purges marked the consolidation of Stalin's virtually absolute power. He not only eliminated all real or potential personal rivals, but he destroyed the party as a ruling institution. After 1938, the party was mainly a pliant transmitter enforcing Stalin's personal dictatorship. Much like the nobility under Ivan the Terrible or Peter the Great, the party under Stalin became a caste without any rights; it rendered service to the sovereign in return for privilege. Its status was not fundamentally different from other major Soviet bureaucracies—the army, the secret police, and the state bureaucracy—with which it both overlapped and competed.

The party served Stalin in another way. It provided his personal dictatorship with revolutionary legitimacy. Yet even here the party and the memory of Lenin and Marx were superseded by what amounted to a cult dedicated to the glorification of Stalin. He was pictured as the world's greatest genius, a man whose expertise and ability in every area exceeded anyone else's. Anyone in the Soviet Union who accomplished anything— the pilot who set a speed record, the scientist who discovered something, the production team that set an output record—gave credit to Stalin for inspiring the accomplishment. Stalin's name and likeness were everywhere. Two dozen cities begin the list of places named after him. Coins bore his profile, songs glorified his name, the national anthem paid him tribute. He had a list of titles (Great Leader of the Soviet People, Great Helmsman, Leader of the World Proletariat, etc.) that seemed to go on forever. A statue on top of Mt. Elbrus summed things up by proclaiming "On the highest peak in Europe we have erected the statue of the greatest man of all time." In effect, Stalin legitimized his rule by turning himself into a secular deity. (A typical song gushed that "We give Thee our thanks for the sun Thou has lit.") His cult was a true measure of the extent to which Stalin, rather than the party, ruled in Russia. The Soviet people had been broken to Stalin's will.

Aside from the incalculable suffering they caused, the purges also did a great deal of other damage. They deprived the economy of thousands of invaluable specialists and rendered those who remained free unable to make decisions for fear of the consequences, which contributed significantly to the stagnation that marked the period from 1937 to 1940. They also left the Soviet military virtually devoid of experienced senior officers, which helped the Germans to come close to victory on the Eastern Front during 1941–1942. Finally the purges also marked a revolution in the composition of the country's leadership. The Old Bolsheviks, including such loyal Stalinists as Kirov, were liquidated, as were several layers of cadres that originated after 1924. A few of Stalin's original cronies did survive, the most important being Molotov and Kaganovich, as well as some lesser lights like Mikoyan and Klement Voroshilov. Of them, only Molotov, the soviet premier and later foreign minister under Stalin, had any stature at all when Lenin ran the party. Around them were the new men who earned their spurs during the 1930s: Andrei Zhdanov, Kirov's replacement in Leningrad; Georgi Malenkov, an important member of the Secretariat and Stalin's heir-apparent in 1953; and Nikita Khrushchev, an efficient satrap in the Ukraine and in Moscow, and Stalin's eventual successor. Others who rose from obscurity as the killing opened up so many opportunities were Leonid Brezhnev and Alexei Kosygin, the duo who succeeded Khrushchev, and Georgi Zhukov, Soviet Russia's greatest general in World War II.

The social revolution that accompanied the purges went far deeper than the party's upper ranks. The purging finished the job of decimating the Westernized layers of Russian society, a process that had begun with the Bolshevik Revolution and accelerated during the Civil War and Stalin's revolution from above. They were replaced by people usually of peasant origin, largely untouched by Western culture. The ascendency of these new men—tough, ruthless, either poorly educated or possessing a narrow technical education, and completely loyal to the tyrant who had raised them up—meant that Russia was turning back from Westernization and reverting to many of its earlier, homegrown ways. When one adds to this Stalin's brutal treatment of his servitors, the purges of the 1930s represent a critical point in what economist Alec Nove has called the "revival of . . . the Asian-despotic element in the Russian tradition,"[17] the tradition of Ivan the Terrible and Peter the Great.

Stalin's new men were far better suited to the new (or old) environment than their predecessors. The latter, better educated and more cosmopolitan, were too independent. Although many supported Stalin quite enthusiastically, they recoiled from his worst excesses, as evidenced by the events of 1934 and opposition to the purges in the Politburo as late as 1937. Stalin's new men had no such qualms. They and many thousands below them were in fact the beneficiaries of the purges, which for them were the route to power and privilege. They therefore were loyal to the system. Thus the purges, while doing so much damage to the Soviet Union, provided Stalin and his system with the base of support necessary to survive the great strains that lay ahead in World War II and the postwar period.

Out of the fire and brimstone of the Stalin years there emerged a new phenomenon—a totalitarian society. Totalitarianism could not exist prior to the technological advances of the twentieth century. In such a society, the state to an unprecedented degree is the dominant force. It uses modern technology to control not only the armed forces and all operational weaponry, but all means of communication and every institution of a society's economic, intellectual, cultural, and political life. All human activity and every citizen is considered to be at the service of the state. Stalin's Russia was not a perfect totalitarian society, but it came closer to that ideal than any other contemporary competitor (e.g., Nazi Germany or Fascist Italy) and was more perfectly totalitarian than it was anything else (e.g., socialist or Communist). It was molded by the Soviet party/state that exercised power through terror administered by a secret police. No institutions independent of the state were permitted to exist, nor was the state limited by the rule of law. There was simply no way for the average citizen to oppose or avoid the multiple levels of control the state possessed.

It was a bitter irony that in 1936, at the height of the purges that represented Soviet totalitarianism at its most extreme, the Soviet Union received a new constitution that proclaimed socialism, the crucial stage just before communism had been achieved. The "Stalin Constitution," proclaimed as the world's most democratic, contained an extensive list of individual rights and gave the Soviet Union an elaborate federal structure that seemed to protect the various minority nationalities. It provided for a bicameral legislature called the Supreme Soviet, elected by direct suffrage. The Supreme Soviet was divided into a Soviet of the Union, elected by the population at large, and a Soviet of Nationalities, elected by the different nationalities according to their administrative status (e.g., each "union republic" selected twenty-five deputies, while lesser national administrative units had correspondingly lower representation). There were now eleven, ranging from the Russian SSR, the most populous, to the diminutive Kyrgyz SSR. The point is that the constitution provided no enforcement mechanism to protect all these rights and rendered them all so much window dressing with several crucial disclaimers. Thus, although Soviet society became extremely hierarchical, with enormous gaps between the population at large and the party elite, all Soviet citizens shared the same status of being powerless vis-à-vis the totalitarian state.

Still, Stalinism cannot be understood simply as totalitarianism; that concept must be supplemented by other perspectives to explain some of Stalinism's features and a number of changes that took place after he died. These are best understood by looking at the several historical forces that converged to produce what is referred to as "Stalinism," and by examining the particular components each of those forces gave to the whole. Historian Robert C. Tucker has suggested three major forces: the legacy of traditional Russia, the legacy of Bolshevism, and what he calls the "mind and personality of Stalin."[18]

Marx once wrote that history weighs upon the present like a mountain, and the history and tradition of old Russia certainly weighed heavily on the Soviet system despite the sworn intention of the Russian Marxists to break completely with the past. Backwardness, poverty, and outside threats had produced the old Russian autocracy, a force that mobilized that nation's resources in its struggle to survive. That state developed a tradition of "revolution from above," a process of mobilization and

imposed change regardless of the cost or resistance involved. Its leading
practitioners were Ivan the Terrible, who destroyed the old nobility and
secured the autocracy; Peter the Great, Russia's first industrializer; and
Alexander II, the "Tsar-Liberator" who abolished serfdom. After 1917,
Russia faced many of the same problems as the tsars and the old tradition
of revolution from above, an idea that intrigued Russian revolutionaries
from Pestel to Herzen to Lenin, was a natural model for Stalin. The major
difference between Stalin and the tsars is that Stalin had far more power
at his disposal and a far more comprehensive vision for change. Like Ivan,
only far more thoroughly, Stalin secured autocratic rule. Like Peter, but
again more thoroughly, Stalin promoted industrialization, using force as
his major tool, and imposed state service on all Russians without any
compensatory rights. Like Alexander II, Stalin revolutionized Russian
agriculture, but where Alexander abolished serfdom, Stalin in effect restored it. Stalin also turned to many other relics from the past—the use
of ranks in civilian and military life and internal passports, for example—
not because of nostalgia, but because old cultural habits were not easily
shed and old methods seemed applicable to problems and conditions that
themselves were not new.

Stalin's revolution from above was far more dynamic and comprehensive than anything the tsars attempted. This in large part was due to the
second wellspring from which Stalinism drew—its Bolshevik heritage.
The tsars had only wanted to make certain changes, albeit sometimes
very large ones, in order to keep the basic Russian system intact. Stalin,
drawing from the legacy of Marx and Lenin, wanted to overhaul society
completely. This all-encompassing goal was reinforced by the Bolshevik
morality justifying any measure so long as it served the Revolution. From
Bolsheviks also came the idea of a centralized, dictatorial party, which
both contributed to the establishment of a one-man dictatorship and was
invaluable in the industrialization drive. Although there certainly were
various ways to interpret the Bolshevik heritage, the general thrust of its
ideology and the experience of War Communism created a constituency
within the party receptive to the measures used during collectivization and
the First Five-Year Plan.

Collectivization and the industrialization drive had roots both in tsarist
history and Bolshevik ideology, as did the overall concept of revolution
from above. The purges also had both an old Russian and Leninist pedigree. However, it was because of Stalin personally that these policies took
the shape they did and were pushed as far as they were. As political
scientist Stephen Cohen has put it, Stalinism was "excess, extraordinary
extremism"[19] in every respect, so much so that it was qualitatively different from any and all of its antecedents. Unlike the other Bolshevik
leaders, Stalin truly knew no limits; that is why he had to eliminate them

in order to complete his revolution from above. Beyond that, to keep the revolution on the course he wanted, Stalin had to eliminate most of those who had supported him during the struggles of the 1920s. His personality was the driving force of a social system built on unrelenting terror, and not until that personality was eliminated in 1953 could the system undergo substantial change.

Finally, Stalinism in an important sense was also a product of circumstance. Circumstance in this case was both the consequences that flowed from a dictatorial elite's attempt in the twentieth century to overhaul a society and the relative backwardness of that society. Stalin's revolution from above, particularly the state's takeover of the entire Russian economy, was only possible with twentieth-century technology. The extent of this takeover was unprecedented in Russian history and a critical factor in changing the pre-twentieth-century autocratic state into a twentieth-century totalitarian one. This is precisely what Bukharin feared would happen and why he opposed first Trotsky and then Stalin during the 1920s. Given the enormous job the state had undertaken and the modern technological tools at its disposal, a powerful totalitarian thrust would have existed no matter who was leading it. Also, the level of what could be imposed on the party and the nation was heightened by the particular conditions existing in the Soviet Union during the 1930s. The nation's economic backwardness and the fever pitch of building that resulted from trying to overcome it created an atmosphere in which brutality was excused by the god of progress. These in turn produced institutions (e.g., the Gulag) required to get the job done. To a certain extent they even produced Stalin, for the unsophisticated party cadres drawn from Russia's uneducated population, locked in a battle with the nation, naturally looked almost unquestioningly to their *Vozhd* for guidance, much as their even more ignorant forefathers had looked to their "little father" the tsar. In other words, both the background of these individuals and the circumstances in which they found themselves impelled them to accept the comforting strong hand of an absolute authority or dictator. Thus, as political scientist Severyn Bialer has observed, by creating such a violent and all-encompassing upheaval in a backward society, Stalinism "created its own conditions" that distinguished it from what had come before.[20] However, because the industrialized drive had achieved its basic goals and in the process created an entire new elite of educated and sophisticated people, it became increasingly difficult to sustain certain aspects of the 1930s totalitarian system and major changes became unavoidable. Stalin's very successes, in other words, meant that certain parts of the system of government he built became obsolete, even while he lived and worked feverishly to protect them.

NOTES

1. Robert V. Daniels, *The Conscience of the Revolution* (Cambridge, Mass.: Harvard University Press, 1965), p. 358.

2. Victor Kravchenko, *I Chose Justice* (New York: Scribners, 1950), pp. 99–100.

3. Moshe Lewin, *Russian Peasants and Soviet Power* (New York: Norton, 1975), p. 506.

4. David J. Dallin and Boris I. Nicolaevsky, *Forced Labor in Soviet Russia* (New Haven: Yale University Press, 1947), pp. 42–43.

5. Fedor Belov, *The History of A Collective Farm* (New York: Praeger, 1955), pp. 13–14.

6. Naum Jasny, *Soviet Industrialization, 1928–1952* (Chicago: University of Chicago Press, 1961), p. 9.

7. Alec Nove, *An Economic History of the U.S.S.R.* (Middlesex, Eng.: Penguin, 1969), p. 207.

8. Dallin and Nicolaevsky, *Forced Labor in Soviet Russia*, pp. 37–38.

9. Aleksandr Solzhenitsyn, *The Gulag Archipelago Two* (New York: Harper & Row, 1975), pp. 210–211.

10. James H. Billington, *The Icon and the Axe* (New York: Vintage, 1970), pp. 532, 538.

11. Svetlana Alliluyeva, *Twenty Letters to a Friend*, Priscilla Johnson McMullan, translator (New York: Harper and Row, 1967), p. 27.

12. John R. Deane, *The Strange Alliance: The Story of Our Effort at Wartime Cooperation with Russia* (New York: Viking Press, 1947), p. 14.

13. Nikolai Tolstoy, *Stalin's Secret War* (New York: Holt, Rinehart & Winston, 1981), p. 37.

14. Roy A. Medvedev, *Let History Judge*, trans. Colleen Taylor (New York: Vintage, 1971), p. 368.

15. Aleksandr Solzhenitsyn, *The Gulag Archipelago* (New York: Harper & Row, 1973), p. 10.

16. Nikolai Tolstoy, *Stalin's Secret War*, pp. 65–66.

17. Alec Nove, *Stalinism and After* (London: George Allen Irwin, 1975), p. 62.

18. Robert C. Tucker, ed., *Stalinism* (New York: W. W. Norton, 1977), p. 78.

19. Stephen Cohen, "Stalinism and Bolshevism," in Tucker, ed., *Stalinism*, p. 12.

20. Severyn Bialer, *Stalin's Successors* (Cambridge, Eng.: Cambridge University Press, 1980), p. 47.

14

Trial by Fire: The Great Patriotic War

Millions of men perpetrated against one another such innumerable crimes, deceptions, treacheries, robberies, forgeries, issues of false monies, depreciations, incendiarisms and murders as the annals of all the courts of justice in the world could not muster in the course of whole centuries, but which those who committed them did not at the time regard as crimes.

————LEO TOLSTOY

Although the Soviet Union did not live in a friendly world during the 1920s, it was not a world that posed the direct threats the Bolsheviks had faced immediately after the Revolution. The Soviet Union, to be sure, had no real friends, only acquaintances offering a degree of toleration that varied from country to country and year to year. There also was no shortage of loud ideological opponents to the Soviet system in every Western country. This enabled Stalin to raise the specter of war when it suited him in his political struggles, while in truth, during the 1920s none of the world's military powers was ready for war. The onset of the Great Depression in 1929 and the resulting domestic turmoil in the advanced capitalist powers, if anything, worked to the Soviet Union's advantage. Western businessmen began to knock at the Soviet Union's door to sell the heavy machinery so vital to Russia's industrialization drive. All in all, the decade after the Civil War was a breathing space in which the party leadership was able to go about its business without undue concern for what its critics in the West were planning.

This tolerable, if not tranquil, situation changed during the early 1930s.

The Soviet Union became one of many nations with new security problems. Germany and Japan, the former an industrial giant held down by the dead weight of the Versailles settlement and the latter a rapidly growing military and economic power hamstrung by the European colonial web that covered large parts of Asia, began to challenge the world order they resented. What followed, particularly with regard to Germany, does little credit to any of the world's major powers. Courage and foresight were in short supply everywhere, including the Soviet Union.

Stalin, to be sure, wanted security and peace during the 1930s as much as anyone. However, his definition of national security was skewed, as it focused first and foremost on his personal power and rule. Sometimes, as when he brought the Soviet Union into the League of Nations in 1934, his needs and national interests coincided. At other times, particularly when he purged the army, or when he persecuted and murdered foreign Social Democrats and Marxists of various stripes for fear they might help galvanize opposition to him at home, Stalin's needs were directly opposed to those of the nation as a whole.

Stalin's concern for his own power also played havoc with the Marxist goal of a world socialist revolution. He simply did not want to see a socialist revolution under circumstances he could not control. Such an event, after all, might demonstrate that there was an alternative to his form of socialism and consequently threaten his throne. Stalin could not say that publicly, of course, but the role foreign Communist parties were expected to play was made clear by the Sixth Comintern Congress in 1928. It proclaimed that the litmus test for revolutionaries was their readiness to "defend the USSR," a formula that really meant complete subservience to Stalin's orders and interests. This primacy of Stalin's personal interests is essential to understanding Soviet foreign policy in the 1930s and Stalin's share in the chain of events and blunders that led to World War II and its attendant horrors.

Stalin was most successful in dealing with the Japanese. During the early 1930s, while absorbed in the industrialization drive, he made concessions to them while at the same time working to flank them by improving relations with the United States and the Chiang Kai-shek regime in China. An important success occurred in 1933, when the United States finally recognized the Soviet Union, almost sixteen years after the fall of the Provisional Government. Later Stalin was able to build up his Siberian army sufficiently to defeat the Japanese in a fierce border war, a defeat that helped convince them to sign a nonaggression treaty with the Soviet Union in 1941 and shift their territorial ambitions from eastern Siberia to Southeast Asia.

Stalin's greatest problems were in Europe, where the gears of his private war against independent Marxists ground against the gears of the Soviet

Union's national interests. There is no doubt that Hitler's rise to power was facilitated by Stalin's insistence after 1928 that German Communists make political war on that country's Social Democrats. This strategy, which was linked to Stalin's battles against his opponents within the party, prevented a Social Democratic–Communist alliance in Germany precisely at a time when Hitler's strength was growing in the wake of the Depression. Trotsky's warnings about the Nazi threat in Germany only reinforced Stalin's determination to stay his course. In 1933, with the German Communists still at the throats of the Social Democrats, Hitler became the German chancellor. Within a year he was shipping Communists and Social Democrats alike to his concentration camps. (Some German Communists would have the dubious distinction of rotting in Hitler's and Stalin's camps before both dictators finally passed from the scene.)

The same situation arose during the Spanish Civil War of 1936–1939. During that conflict between the democratically elected republican government and fascist rebels supported by Hitler and Mussolini, the Soviet Union was the only nonfascist nation to give significant help to the republican cause. However, that help soon deteriorated into a search-and-destroy operation that Stalin's NKVD waged against anarchists and especially Trotskyites fighting on the antifascist side. With friends like Stalin, the embattled Spanish republic hardly needed enemies. Despite heroic resistance, it fell to Francisco Franco's fascist legions in 1939. Stalin, meanwhile, having tested some of his new weapons, withdrew his people and material support. He also made sure that none of the potentially infectious Trotskyite or anarchist viruses spread from that end of Europe to the "Socialist Fatherland" by purging and murdering many of the agents he had sent to Spain.

The burning issue in Europe during the 1930s was how the various powers were going to deal with Hitler once he began his efforts to rebuild German military might and reverse the results of World War I. Again, it must be stressed that none of the powers did themselves credit. Britain and France either did nothing, or they attempted to appease Hitler by allowing him to remilitarize the Rhineland in 1936, annex Austria in March 1938, and dismember Czechoslovakia the following September. The last concession, made in Munich, gave the word appeasement a pejorative meaning and added the word "Munich," meaning an unconscionable and unjustified surrender in the face of threats, to several languages. The United States, ever ready to moralize about international aggression, stood by while the Germans and Japanese blithely went about their business.

Stalin, ever cautious and careful, tried to play the diplomatic game both ways. He may have felt more comfortable working with Hitler, a fellow dictator, than with the Western democracies, despite Hitler's unabashed call for creating *Lebensraum* (living space) for Germany by expansion to the east. Stalin continued Soviet-German military cooperation until Hitler ended it in 1933, and there seem to have been secret German-Soviet contacts between police and government officials during 1933 and 1934. Meanwhile, nonaggression pacts signed with several small states on the Soviet Union's western border, in effect small insurance policies against German aggression, remained in force. In 1934, the Soviet Union entered the League of Nations and became an advocate of "collective security." In 1935 the pace picked up. The Comintern reversed itself and called for "popular front" tactics, that is, cooperation between Communists and other nonfascist parties against the common fascist menace. This led to a short-lived socialist government in France the next year. The Soviet Union also signed alliances with France and Czechoslovakia, the latter a small, vulnerable state wedged along Germany's southeastern border. Under these agreements, the Soviet Union committed itself to come to the Czechs' aid in the event of German aggression, provided the French did the same.

The road to war, a four-year odyssey that stretched to 1939, is far too complex to cover in detail here. Suffice it to say that Hitler continued his disruptive behavior and nobody did anything about it. The Soviet Union's position meanwhile generally improved in the east and deteriorated in the west. After 1937, the Japanese became ensnared in their war against China and the Soviets triumphed against them in their undeclared border war by the fall of 1939. In a negative development, Germany and Japan signed the "Anti-Comintern" Pact, an anti-Soviet document, in November 1936. In the west, Hitler annexed Austria in March 1938. In September came the Munich conference, a meeting between Germany, Italy, France, and England from which both Czechoslovakia and the Soviet Union were excluded. Prior to the conference the Soviets offered to honor their 1935 commitments to defend Czechoslovakia against Germany if the French did likewise. This the French did not do, and the Czechs therefore were forced to cede to Germany a strategically vital border area inhabited mainly by ethnic Germans. This left Czechoslovakia militarily indefensible. Further annexations of most of what remained of Czechoslovakia soon followed, as well as a new series of German demands on Poland. At this point, Britain and France, realizing that appeasement could not satisfy Hitler, suddenly found their backbones and threatened to go to war if Germany violated Polish sovereignty.

Darkening war clouds shrouded the diplomacy that followed. Stalin, no doubt, was fed up with the weakness of the West and feared, with some justification, that the Western powers hoped to turn Hitler eastward against the "Bolshevik menace." In May, the Soviet dictator took an important step. He replaced Maxim Litvinov, his urbane and effective foreign minister, who happened to be Jewish, and therefore hardly suited for dealing with Hitler, with Molotov, and himself took over from Molotov as the Soviet Union's head of state. By August the Soviet Union was negotiating with the Germans on the one hand and the British and French on the other. The latter seemed to believe that the Nazis and the Communists, archenemies according to their ideologies and propaganda, could never get together. The two Western powers therefore negotiated with the Russians with a shocking lack of urgency. But Stalin (and Hitler) calculated in terms of power politics, not ideology. A pact with Germany could buy Stalin the time he needed to rebuild his military strength, so damaged by his own purges, while allowing him to wait while the capitalist democracies and the fascists slugged it out and weakened each other.

On August 23, 1939, a diplomatic bombshell exploded. The USSR and the German Third Reich announced a nonaggression pact. Along with the public expression of friendship, the two powers secretly agreed to divide Poland and the rest of Eastern Europe between them. Hitler was now freed from the nightmare that haunted generations of German military strategists—a war on two fronts. His only formidable enemies now lay in the west. Within ten days real bombshells came raining down as German troops crossed the Polish border, and World War II began.

The Stalin-Hitler pact of August 1939 gave the Soviet Union almost two years of breathing space while the Nazis, their eastern flank secured by their new Soviet allies, busily and efficiently conquered most of Western Europe up to the English Channel. Stalin was a good ally. There was tension between the two totalitarian giants, but no more than subsequent tensions between the Soviet Union and the Western democracies in the so called Grand Alliance they hastily forged when Hitler invaded the Soviet Union in June 1941. From August 1939 to June 1941, the Soviet Union supported the German Reich diplomatically, provided it with naval bases, and punctually delivered the raw materials Hitler needed to storm Western and Central Europe. No wonder that Hitler called Stalin "indispensable" and "a hell of a fellow," while Mussolini pronounced Stalin to be a "secret fascist."

Whatever Stalin was, he used his two years of grace to do more than please Hitler. The Soviet Union intensified its military build-up. It developed such major new weapons as the T-34 tank and the Katusha rocket launcher. New defense plants were built deep in the interior, away from the menacing armies in the West. But the build-up was badly flawed. The armed forces, decimated by the purges, were commanded either by Stalin's incompetent old cronies, men like Kliment Voroshilov and Semeon Budenny, or by inexperienced and inadequately trained officers, whose promotions resulted solely from the liquidation of those above them. The military build-up also was hampered because many of the Soviet

Union's best scientists and engineers, including experts in both rock-
etry and airplane design, were sitting in prisons or labor camps. Many
older industrial plants dangerously close to the western border remained
vulnerable. Moreover, Soviet military units in the western part of the
country were left exposed and unprepared for combat, even when hard
intelligence warned Stalin of the precise day the Germans were planning
to attack during the spring of 1941.

In the Soviet Union, the cataclysm known in the West as World War II
is usually referred to as the "Great Patriotic War." The war was a struggle
that, in Hitler, finally produced an opponent who matched Stalin in cruelty, cynicism, and determination. Not only Stalin's regime, but Russian
national life was at stake, and the Soviet Union nearly lost. As terrible as
it was, though, killing millions of Soviet citizens and uprooting tens of millions more, the Great Patriotic War actually changed the Soviet Union very
little. It was not an earthquake that permanently alters the landscape, but
more of a monstrous tornado that sweeps in, does incalculable damage,
and then passes, leaving the survivors to mourn the dead and rebuild in
a manner that resembles as closely as possible that which was destroyed.
By surviving, the Stalinist system was tempered and strengthened, and the
repressive and hierarchial structure of Soviet society was consequently
reinforced.

This surprised many people, who mistook Stalin's various small concessions to rally the nation to the war effort as signs that a period of relaxation
and reform would follow the war. They did not understand that Stalin,
while laboring so hard to avoid a two-front war against both Germany
and Japan, in reality fought two wars between 1941 and 1945, one against
the Nazi war machine and one against the Soviet people. The latter, aptly
dubbed "Stalin's Secret War" by Nikolai Tolstoy, was surreptitiously carried out by the NKVD to assure that the Soviet people could mount no
challenges to their government. Ironically, during the war Hitler was also
fighting his own secret war—his campaign of extermination that some
have called his "War Against the Jews." The great difference between the
two dictators is that while Hitler lost one of his wars—his battle against
the Allies—Stalin won both of his. Hitler's secret war therefore was completely exposed; Stalin's remained a secret. Hitler's brand of murderous
totalitarianism was destroyed; Stalin's survived.

Stalin made better preparations for his secret war than he did for the
Germans. When the Red Army claimed the Soviet Union's share of Poland
in 1939 in accord with the August 23 pact, several hundred thousand
Polish troops were rounded up and deported. This operation included
15,000 officers later murdered in the Katyn Forest near the Russian
city of Smolensk. At least 1 million Poles were deported to the Gulag.
When in 1940 the Soviet Union occupied Latvia, Lithuania, and Estonia,

three small countries on its western border, the NKVD moved in with detailed lists of whom to arrest. The operation was so well planned that the smallest details—when and how to make arrests, what the arrestee could take with him, even how the police should handle their weapons— were covered in the instructions the NKVD agents carried. Over 130,000 people were deported without so much as perfunctory legal procedures.

One aspect of Stalin's preparations, his dealings with Finland, went less well. Because the Finns refused to grant territorial concessions and military bases Moscow wanted, Stalin sent his purge-riddled Red Army into Finland. For months during the winter of 1939–1940 tiny Finnish military forces held Stalin's army, navy, and air force at bay, killing over 200,000 Soviet troops and destroying over 1,000 airplanes, as against losses of sixty-two of their own small aircraft. Eventually the Soviet Union's enormous resources and Stalin's willingness to suffer appalling casualties in frontal assaults prevailed and the Finns were forced to sue for peace in March 1940. Stalin got the bases and territory he wanted. More importantly, he began a massive effort to reorganize and reequip the Red Army, whose inadequacies had glared so brightly in the Finnish winter twilight.

The job was not completed in time, in part because Stalin refused to believe that Hitler would break his word so soon and attack the Soviet Union. When he did, Stalin panicked. Molotov had to break the news to the nation in place of the shattered *Vozhd,* who, once he found out his Politburo colleagues were not going to arrest him, retreated to the solitude of one of his country homes. Stalin did not recover his equilibrium sufficiently to address his anxious people until July 3, by which time the Germans were deep into Russia and the military disaster was well under way. So, too, was the slaughter of Jews, who had no warning about either the impending German invasion or the Nazis' attitude toward them. Still, Stalin could congratulate himself for having survived the first weeks of the war still in power. By June 1941, there simply was no one left capable of thinking the unthinkable—that Stalin could be replaced. The purges had done their job.

Bolstered by the element of surprise, superior generalship, and better equipment, the Germans might have won the Nazi-Soviet war. A combination of factors prevented this, none of which can be credited to Stalin. The Nazis made both military and political errors. At key points Hitler interfered with the military operations, overruling his generals and dissipating advantages his forces held. He weakened his forces poised before Moscow in August 1941 in order to attempt to take the Russian oil wells in the Caucasus, a maneuver which failed and left his forces unable to take Moscow. Equally disastrous was Hitler's conduct of the battle of Stalingrad during the winter of 1942–1943. The Germans could have bypassed Stalingrad, the former Tsaritsyn, where Stalin had served during the Civil War and then renamed for himself. But the Führer was determined to take the "City of Stalin" at all costs. Instead the Germans suffered a crushing defeat, their first on the European continent, a defeat considered by many military experts to be the turning point of the war.

Perhaps more important, the Nazis squandered the support they might have had from the Soviet population. In many places, particularly in the Ukraine and Belorussia, German troops were greeted as liberators from the hated Communist regime. Millions of Soviet citizens suddenly had some hope. The peasants hoped for freedom of religion and the dissolution of the collective farms, the most hated single institution in Soviet Russia. Many ethnic Russians, Ukrainians, and others were ready to fight the loathed Soviet government, if the Germans would only arm them. Among them was General Andrei Vlasov, a captured officer who apparently had both considerable military skill and popular appeal. Many German civilian and military experts urged a policy that would exploit this vast reservoir of good will, but Hitler would hear nothing of such thinking. To him the Slavic *Untermenschen* (subhumans), although better than Jews, were fit only for slave labor, deportation, or repression. The collectives were not dissolved, prisoners of war were brutally mistreated, and the population at large terrorized. By 1942 the Russians under German occupation had learned their terrible lesson and were resisting their would-be conquerors with considerable effect. By the time Hitler recognized his mistake in 1944, it was far too late to do anything about it.

Aided by the Russian winter that helped stall the Germans at the gates of Moscow in 1941 and the effectiveness of newly installed commanding officers (including Georgi Zhukov, brought in from the Far East, and K. K. Rokossovsky, plucked from a labor camp), the Soviet government survived the defeats of 1941 and 1942. Allied Lend Lease shipments also arrived to help stem the German tide. This aid was particularly important in providing the Red Army with motor vehicles needed to match the German army in mobility. Most of all, the Soviet Union and Stalin were saved by the Soviet people. It was the average citizen's stunning heroism and ability to endure that saved Leningrad, where in a 900-day siege over 600,000 defenders died, mostly of starvation. Soviet resistance at Stalingrad during the dark winter of 1942–1943 was equally remarkable, as they yielded 90 percent of the totally destroyed city inch by inch but never broke. Although losses of territory, livestock, and farmland cut agricultural production in half between 1940 and 1943, an inadequately fed, clothed, and housed labor force, further weakened by military conscription, gradually managed to raise industrial production levels after the severe drop caused by the invasion. It was a painful process, but by 1944, largely on the basis of domestic production, the

Red Army was better equipped than the German *Wehrmacht*. This was in large part possible because during 1941 and 1942, under the worst of conditions, the Soviets succeeded in dismantling and transporting hundreds of factories eastward beyond the reach of the Germans.

Although Stalin was to promote himself to "Generalissimo," he showed little talent for military strategy. General Zhukov, the Soviet Union's best general and its overall commander during most of the war, succinctly summed up matters in 1956 when he bitterly complained to several of Stalin's associates and successors: "You people collaborated with Stalin in driving the troops like cattle to the slaughter." Stalin's greatest contribution to the military effort was to stay out of it and let Zhukov run things, a restraint the generalissimo frequently failed to display.

It was as a political leader that Stalin excelled. Once the "man of steel" recovered his nerve (he panicked a second time as the Germans approached Moscow in October 1941 and fled the capital for three days), Stalin gave the nation a focal point. He directed the war effort from the Kremlin. Exhortations for more work and sacrifice were cleverly framed in terms of "Mother Russia" and "fatherland," Slavic pride, and other references to traditional Russian patriotism. Little was heard of the "socialist fatherland" or other aspects of Communist ideology. Stalin reached an accord with the Russian Orthodox Church. It received the right to elect a patriarch for the first time in thirty years, and in return, it blessed the *Vozhd* and his regime in its struggle to defend Russia. In 1942, the army commanders finally were rid of the political commissars, the party functionaries with whom they had shared authority, much to the detriment of military operations. Even the peasants got something; restrictions on their private plots were eased, while higher agricultural prices enabled them to raise their miserable standard of living and even to save a little. These may in reality have been little more than crumbs, but Stalin doled them out so skillfully to his materially and spiritually starved people that they seemed like divinely produced loaves of bread.

Where Stalin really shone was in his dealings with the Allies. He not only impressed men like Roosevelt and Churchill, but it is hard not to feel that he got the best of them in their mutual dealings. Churchill, to be sure, had few illusions about Stalin; the English leader was a long-time anti-Communist crusader. FDR was different. He mistakenly felt he could befriend and maneuver the man he called "Uncle Joe."

Until Stalingrad, Stalin was unavoidably cast in the role of supplicant. He was desperate enough in 1941 to plead for British and American troops to fight the Germans on Russian soil, a plan he quickly abandoned when the first emergencies passed. He was more insistent that the Allies invade Western Europe to open up a "second front" and relieve some of the pressure on the Red Army. This the Allies proved unable to do until June

1944, by which time the Red Army, at appalling cost, had turned the tide in the east and was pushing beyond Soviet borders into Eastern Europe. As a result, not only was Stalin after 1943 able to negotiate from a position of strength provided by his advancing Red Army, but he was able to exploit Western guilt over having been unable to hit the Germans directly while the Russians bore the brunt of the fighting between 1941 and mid-1944. He also earned some good will by dissolving the Comintern in 1943.

Stalin used all of his geopolitical and psychological advantages to extend Russian influence over large parts of Eastern Europe. His Western Allies, of course, resented this. Britain and France had gone to war in 1939 in part because Hitler's gains in those same areas threatened the European balance of power. This struggle over Eastern Europe, which focused initially on Poland, caused tremendous tensions within the "Grand Alliance," whose only real glue, as postwar events were to demonstrate, was the mutual Nazi menace. For his part, Stalin always feared that his allies might make a separate peace with Germany that would deny the Soviet Union what he felt were its rightful gains after the suffering it had endured in turning back the Germans.

Stalin scored his first major victory during his first meeting with Churchill and Roosevelt in Teheran during November 1943. There, despite the embarrassing revelations of the Katyn Forest massacre in April, Stalin won acceptance of the Polish-Soviet border he wanted, one that was considerably to the west of the 1939 border. He also finally got a definite commitment to establish the long-awaited second front the following spring. In return, the Soviet Union committed itself to join the war against Japan once Germany was defeated.

Stalin won further concessions during 1944, as the Red Army swept the Germans out of the Soviet Union and toward Germany. In a famous meeting with Churchill in the Kremlin in October 1944, the British prime minister, hoping to save what he could, proposed a deal that gave the Soviet Union predominant influence in Romania (90 percent) and Bulgaria (75 percent), gave it equal influence with the West in Yugoslavia and Hungary, and gave Britain and the United States predominance in Greece. Stalin accepted that formula without saying a word. Later some of these figures had to be revised in the Soviet Union's favor, owing to the Red Army's rapid advance.

In February 1945 came Yalta, the critical conference of the war. By then the Red Army occupied large parts of Eastern Europe, while the Western Allies were struggling in their arena. The United States, which had not yet tested its atomic bomb, was more anxious than ever for Soviet participation in the war against Japan and in its proposed "United Nations." Churchill headed a totally exhausted nation, while FDR was a dying man with barely three months to live. In return for very small concessions,

Stalin accomplished most of his agenda. The Polish-Soviet border was moved westward, Poland getting formerly German territory as compensation for her losses to the Soviets. More importantly, a Soviet-sponsored group of Polish Communists, diluted ever so slightly with representatives from a British sponsored non-Communist Polish government in exile, was in effect established as the new Polish government. The Soviets were to hold "free and unfettered" elections in Poland, an event that, had it transpired, would have meant the ouster of Stalin's puppet regime. Stalin, who never took this commitment seriously and assumed that no one else did either, naturally did not honor this part of the Yalta agreement. The Polish question soon became one of the key issues that launched the Cold War. Plans for the occupation and denazification of Germany also were made at Yalta. In addition to the substantial territory that was to be turned over to Poland, the Soviet Union received a small slice of Germany for itself and joined the United States, Britain, and France in a four-power occupation of what remained. This arrangement left the Soviet Union in control of Latvia, Lithuania, Estonia, and some other territories annexed between 1939 and 1941 in agreement with the Germans. Yalta thereby solidified Soviet power in the heart of Europe. It also gave the Soviets a de facto veto over any attempt to reunify Germany, a veto that was exercised until 1990.

Germany's defeat in World War II brought the full horror of Hitler's secret "War Against the Jews" to world attention. By contrast, the Soviet Union's spectacular victory over the Nazis created a halo that obscured Stalin's secret war. In truth, however, that war, while different in intent, was no less bloody. There were other parallels as well. Both wars originated in the recesses of the respective dictator's mind. Hitler was driven by his all-consuming hatred for Jews, Stalin by his obsession with potential threats to his power. Both secret wars hurt their respective nation's war effort. Hitler used thousands of elite SS troops, invaluable railroad cars, and other resources needed for the war effort to speed up the extermination campaign even as the Allies closed in. Stalin also used large numbers of troops and guards for various repressive and murderous tasks, including guarding millions of innocent men who otherwise would have been available to fight the Germans.

Stalin's war against the Soviet people was fought on many fronts. When the Germans first invaded, the NKVD murdered thousands of prisoners rather than let them and their potential testimony fall into enemy hands. Millions of others were deported to the Gulag. Aside from those deported from Poland and the Baltic States before June 1941, the NKVD sent at least 1 million Ukrainians to the Gulag after the fighting began. This type of deportation was not new. During the war, however, the Soviet regime broke new ground by deporting entire nations. This was justified by a new legal innovation: blaming an entire nation for collaboration with the enemy on the part of some of its members. Approximately 1.5 million people, comprising all or most of the Soviet Union's Chechens, Ingush, Karachai, Balkars, Kalmyks, Crimean Tatars, Meskhetians, and Volga Germans were deported; perhaps one third of them died. These operations were swift—the Crimean Tatars were given fifteen minutes to collect their belongings—and so well concealed that news of what happened to some of these small nations did not reach the West for years. Thus, to the horror of the deportations themselves must be added the chilling fact that it was possible to drop entire nations, as historian Robert Conquest observes, down a "memory hole."[1]

In the camps themselves, the population swelled to the peak levels of the purge years. Conditions, eased briefly after 1938, sank to the rock bottom levels of the 1930s. When possible, the camps were switched to war production. Slave labor was used for military construction projects, such as border defenses, air fields, and fortifications, including some of those at Stalingrad. At the front, unfortunate people were organized into "penal battalions." These units were used for mass frontal assaults against heavily fortified positions and for clearing mine fields—by marching through them. To push them forward, special NKVD troops followed to shoot anyone who hesitated or tried to retreat. The NKVD troops also killed the wounded. These "barrier troops" also served behind the lines of regular units to prevent any "unauthorized retreats" by shooting anyone who took a step backward without permission.

Adding to the toll of the dead were the prisoners of war and civilians who managed to survive the German labor and concentration camps. To Stalin they were "traitors," and as such were either shot upon repatriation or shipped by the hundreds of thousands to the Gulag. Overall, recent estimates put the Soviet Union's wartime losses over 20 million. The Nazi invaders obviously killed or indirectly caused the deaths of millions of Soviet citizens. Yet the Stalin regime, through its deportations, purges, Gulag camps, military tactics that ignored human losses, and other measures, also killed millions; its toll of Soviet citizens may even compare to that of the Nazis. All this the Soviet people endured, and still they managed to fight their way from Leningrad, Moscow, and Stalingrad to Berlin. It was a collective act of courage and endurance of titanic proportions that lent new truth to the old saying, "Only the Russians can conquer Russia."

World War II, which exacted the greatest human toll of all the calamities in Russia's history, left a wound that was a nation wide and generations deep. Like the painful wounds and scars millions of citizens carried in their individual lives, the war experience became an integral part of the Soviet Union's postwar life. May 9, Victory Day, marked a solemn day of remembrance, but it was only twenty-four hours of what was for many a recollection lasting all year. Almost every town in the western part of the Soviet Union built its war memorial, and for those who did not come to one of these shrines, an endless stream of books, films, theater productions, songs, and reminiscences about the war came to them. This obsession in part was a product of propaganda, as both Stalin and his successors used the victory over the Nazis as vindication of the Communist system and the sacrifices made to build it. But it was no less a reflection of the genuine feeling and emotion of the Soviet people. For millions of them World War II was both the best and the worst of times, an era when Stalin's tyranny abated slightly and the desperate national defense effort created a unity and comradeship that enabled the country to survive the horrors of war and Nazi atrocities.

There was, however, a demon lurking behind the saintly memory of World War II: some of that memory was a lie. A short-lived reevaluation of the war began after 1956 when Nikita Khrushchev criticized Stalin's wartime leadership for having cost enormous unnecessary suffering. A far more thorough and painful reassessment took place three decades later. Soviet citizens then were confronted with, among other things, their country's brutal treatment of returning prisoners of war and costly blunders by military commanders, including even at the legendary battle of Stalingrad. Often the revelations were too much to bear. One war veteran spoke for many when he complained that they "will end with our national values and everything which represents the spiritual pride of the people toppling into the abyss."[2] His complaint, while poignant, ultimately had to be futile, for as a distinguished Chinese writer observed well before Russia fought its Great Patriotic War, "Lies written in ink cannot obscure a truth written in blood."

NOTE

1. Robert Conquest, *The Nation Killers* (London: Macmillan, 1970), p. 67.
2. Cited in R. W. Davies, *Soviet History in the Gorbachev Revolution* (Bloomington and Indianapolis: Indiana University Press, 1989), p. 111.

15

September Songs

I told you that I am becoming a conservative.

——JOSEPH STALIN, 1943

The eight years between the end of World War II and Stalin's death in 1953 witnessed two major developments. On the international scene, the Soviet Union joined the United States as one of the world's two superpowers. Domestically, the postwar years were a period of conservative retrenchment as Stalin battled to keep intact the system he had built during the 1930s.

The war greatly enhanced Soviet power. It destroyed or gravely weakened most of Russia's traditional rivals. Germany and Japan, the great powers on its immediate flanks, were defeated. Britain and France, supposedly among the "winners," were exhausted by their victory. Meanwhile, the fortunes of war carried the Red Army into the heart of Europe. The Red Army drove the Nazis from Poland, Romania, Bulgaria, Czechoslovakia, and Hungary, and controlled a large part of Germany itself. After 1945, it occupied those territories, while native Communist resistance movements controlled Yugoslavia and Albania. A strong Communist movement also existed in China, to say nothing of France and Italy. Soviet power also was magnified because its totalitarian government was able to demand further sacrifices from its people in order to rebuild and expand the nation's heavy industrial sector and pursue the development of new weaponry.

The Soviet Union's enormous new power was not without its pitfalls. It caused great concern in the West, contributed to the dissolution of the "Grand Alliance" that had defeated Nazi Germany, and thus became one of the major factors that precipitated the Cold War. The former allies already were seriously at odds by early 1945. This should not be surprising. The alliance was a shotgun marriage of unlikely partners, born of Nazi aggression. Mutual suspicions between the partners had already been rampant during the war. When the tide had turned in 1943, the British and their prime minister, Winston Churchill, desperately concocted military and political strategies to get British and American armies into Eastern Europe before the Soviets. Their plans ran afoul of geopolitical and military obstacles and America's determination to place strictly military matters, rather than future political considerations, at the head of the wartime agenda. Still, there was growing fear in the American camp of escalating Soviet power. During the war, such considerations were subordinated to the immediate task of defeating Germany and Japan, but they immediately became a major concern once victory was achieved. As for Stalin, he was no less suspicious of the Western powers than he was of anybody else. He lived in fear of a separate Western-German peace and was convinced that delay in establishing a second front was part of a plot to weaken the Soviet Union by leaving her to fight the Germans alone as long as possible.

These tensions, which first surfaced during the wartime conferences, burst into the open at the first postwar conference, held in Potsdam in July 1945. The conferees managed to agree on most issues concerning the occupation of Germany, but disagreed about everything else, from Stalin's failure to hold "free and unfettered" elections in Poland to who would control the Black Sea straits. It is probably appropriate that the atomic bomb, the symbol of the Cold War, was tested by the United States the day the Potsdam conference began. If Stalin needed any more fuel for his fear of the West, America's possession of this awesome new weapon more than filled the bill.

Whatever his fears, Stalin's foreign ambitions after World War II were extensive. To be sure, the Soviet Union was too exhausted to march westward to the Atlantic, as some initially feared. Rather, as Molotov put it, Stalin's policy was "to expand the borders of the Fatherland as much as possible." In 1945 the area of possibility was Eastern Europe. Stalin therefore pushed his armies westward as fast as he could in the last months of the war (taking enormous losses in the process) in order to occupy as much territory as possible as a potential buffer against the West. He was committed both to retaining the territorial gains he had won during the period of the Nazi-Soviet pact and to ensuring that no governments hostile to the Soviet Union could establish themselves in the rest of Eastern Europe. This would enhance the Soviet Union's strategic defensive position and also insulate the Soviet people from the outside world. Beyond that opening position, Stalin was flexible—quick enough first to use the opportunities created by the advance of the Red Army to expand Soviet influence in Eastern Europe and then, when the West began to object to his activities and tensions began to rise, to clamp down on the countries within his grasp while he had the chance.

Some of Stalin's ambitions were thwarted by Western resistance, including his desire for a role in the occupation of Japan, joint control with the Turks of the Black Sea straits, and a permanent presence in oil-rich Iran. Nonetheless, Stalin had a great deal to show for his efforts in the years immediately after the war. Germany, even if the West tried to put her back together, had been permanently weakened by losses of territory and resources to the Soviet Union and Poland. Already in 1945 Stalin had installed what he called a "friendly regime" in historically anti-Russian Poland, the country that twice in half a century was Germany's main invasion route eastward. As pressures built with the West, Stalin, using a combination of treachery, threats, and pure force, succeeded in establishing a series of Communist-controlled states in countries occupied by the Red Army along the Soviet Union's entire western border. Poland, the major prize, was completely under Communist control before the dust of World War II had settled. Hungary, another country with few fond feelings for the Russians, maintained some vestiges of political pluralism until mid-1947; by 1948 Communist control was total. In Romania and Bulgaria the job of eliminating all opposition was finished for all intents and purposes in 1947.

The lone holdout was Czechoslovakia, the only country in the region with a democratic tradition. It also had a powerful and popular Communist party and a tradition of friendship with the Soviet Union. This was not enough for Stalin. Undisguised pressure and the not-so-carefully disguised murder of Foreign Minister Jan Masaryk closed the book on Czechoslovakian democracy and genuine independence in February 1948. Meanwhile, native Communists brought Yugoslavia (a country the Red Army occupied only partially, withdrawing completely in 1945) and Albania into the Soviet camp. Less than three years after German Nazism was driven from Eastern Europe, Russian Communism had come quickly, cruelly, and thoroughly.

These Soviet gains were a bitter pill for the West to swallow. One of the causes of World War II had been the West's determination to prevent Germany from dominating Eastern Europe and thereby upsetting the traditional European balance of power. Now suddenly the Soviet Union, a power considered by many to be a greater threat to Western democratic freedoms than Germany, was firmly in the saddle from which the Germans had been dislodged at such great cost. But Western protests meant little to Stalin. He had not interfered in the areas his 1944 agreement with Churchill allotted to the West—in Greece, for example—and therefore felt free to do what he wanted in what he considered the Soviet Union's sphere of influence. Moreover, the Red Army still occupied the countries from which it had driven the Germans and was not about to leave.

This did not mean that Stalin did not have some very big problems. In Yugoslavia, he caused them himself. Although the Red Army was gone, Yugoslavia was firmly under the control of a local, very pro-Soviet Communist, Joseph Broz, better known as Tito. Stalin, however, was not satisfied with Tito's loyalty; the Soviet dictator wanted complete and direct control. To feel safe, Stalin required puppets, not allies. But Stalin's effort to assert this control ended in complete failure in 1948. As a result of this struggle, Tito in effect was compelled to set Yugoslavia on an independent, though Communist, course. Stalin's response was a series of purges in the satellite nations to extinguish all embers, real or imagined, of "Titoism." The iron curtain, proclaimed by Churchill in his famous speech in Fulton, Missouri, in 1946, clanged down even harder after Tito bested Stalin two years later.

By 1948 Stalin had far greater problems than his ex-"comrade" Tito. The United States, the other superpower, was moving into the power vacuum in Europe. Stalin apparently lived in secret terror of an attack by the United States, the world's only nuclear power until the Soviets tested their first bomb in 1949, keeping Moscow's air raid defenses on twenty-four-hour alert. But the United States had far more than bombs with which to frighten the Soviet Union. It was American strength and the threat to use it that forced Stalin to give way in Turkey and Iran in 1946. In 1947, when the exhausted British indicated that they were no longer able to support the anti-Communist side in the Greek civil war, the U.S. stepped into the breach. It proclaimed the "Truman Doctrine" in March of that year. This declaration committed the United States to aid the anti-Communist governments of Greece and Turkey and to prevent any other Communist takeovers elsewhere. Four months later, an article in the authoritative journal *Foreign Affairs* signed by "X" (American Soviet expert George Kennan) outlined America's overall policy toward the Soviet Union. Henceforth, the United States would undertake a policy of "long-term, patient but firm and vigilant containment" of the Soviets. The United States, in other words, intended to block any attempt the Soviet Union made to expand its influence. In the wake of the Communist coup in Czechoslovakia, the U.S. responded with its Marshall Plan to rebuild Western Europe's war-shattered economy. This was particularly troubling, as Stalin was counting on continued European weakness to give the Soviet Union breathing space and freedom of maneuver in foreign policy. A weak Western Europe, after all, meant a safer Soviet Union. Equally disturbing, by 1948 it was clear that the Western powers were intent on fusing their occupation zones in Germany and permitting that former enemy to rebuild its industrial might.

Aside from his moves in Eastern Europe, Stalin responded to the West in September 1947 by resurrecting the Comintern in a new guise, the Communist Information Bureau (Cominform). In 1948 he responded more forcefully by attempting to discredit Western, and especially American, resolve. His point of attack was Berlin. The former German capital actually was located over 100 miles inside the Soviet occupation zone, but, like Germany as a whole, had been divided into four occupation zones. In June 1948 Stalin blockaded Berlin, hoping to force the Western powers to halt their plans for Germany and to abandon the city. Stalin hoped to convince the German people in both the Soviet and Western zones that they could not rely on the West and therefore should seek whatever accommodation the Soviet Union was willing to offer. That accomplished, he hoped to erode American influence in the rest of Western Europe. The West stood firm. It avoided both an ignominious retreat and the frightening prospect of firing the first shot of a potential third world war by airlifting supplies over Stalin's blockade. War was something a still war-weakened Soviet Union could not afford, so the planes flew without a Soviet shot being fired. When Stalin gave in in May 1949 and lifted his blockade, his problems were worse than in 1948, for on April 4, 1949, the North Atlantic Treaty Organization (NATO), a military alliance of eleven Western nations led by the United States, was formed in Washington.

The chain of events between 1945 and 1949 left Europe divided into two hostile halves, a Soviet-dominated bloc and an American-led bloc. The Soviet bloc even had its own version of the Marshall Plan, the "Molotov Plan," or Council of Mutual Economic Assistance (Comecon), set up in January 1949. If this was uncomfortable, at least by 1949 the situation was relatively stable.

The same was not true in the Far East, where developments were further intensifying the Cold War. In 1949, China, the most populous country in the world, was overrun by Communist rebels led by Mao Zedong. This development did not particularly thrill Stalin. Mao had won his victory without extensive Soviet help, controlled his own party and army, and was quite independent of Stalin—and Tito had given Stalin more than his fill of independent Communist leaders. The Soviet dictator would have preferred a non-Communist China kept weak and divided by a strong Communist presence. Whatever Stalin's preferences, the West, especially the United States, was horrified. In one blow, 25 percent of the world's population "went Communist." The discovery later that year that the Soviets had tested their own atomic bomb well ahead of all predictions did little to calm Western anxieties.

Then came North Korea's invasion of South Korea in June 1950. The former was a Soviet puppet state set up in the part of Korea occupied by the Red Army in 1945, the latter an American-backed dictatorship. The United States flatly blamed the Soviet Union for the invasion—correctly, as it turns out. Stalin had approved the North Korean invasion plans and then provided them with the arms they needed to launch their attack. The Americans, under the auspices of the United Nations (where the Soviets boycotted the crucial session), immediately sent troops to stem the North Korean tide. These included small contingents of troops from several American allies. In November, to stave off a North Korean defeat, the Communist Chinese intervened in force. The war dragged on beyond Stalin's death in March 1953, helping to guarantee that the Cold War, intensified even further by the American-Soviet race to develop a hydrogen bomb, would remain dangerously acute even after Stalin passed from the scene.

Whatever its faults or failures, Soviet foreign policy after World War II was dynamic, even revolutionary. In Eastern European countries he controlled, Stalin imposed entirely new social systems based on the Soviet model. This meant the Communist Party's monopoly of political power, purges, terror, concentration camps, planned industrialization, and collectivization. Significantly, collectivization was pursued much more slowly in the satellite countries than in Russia. Only in Bulgaria was more than half the arable land collectivized by 1953. At the same time, as one of the world's two nuclear powers, the Soviet Union enjoyed a status in international affairs that at least matched that achieved by Russia after the Napoleonic Wars.

By contrast, Stalin's internal policies were conservative, and in a sense, even reactionary. Most of his efforts were directed toward restoring and preserving the system that had evolved prior to 1941. His problems in this regard came from several sources. During the war millions of Soviet citizens—either as prisoners of war, displaced persons, victorious soldiers, or inhabitants of territory overrun by the Germans—had come into contact with foreign ideas, or, even worse, had actually seen the way people lived outside the Soviet Union. The war had forced Stalin to relax certain controls in order to win popular support for the defense effort. More importantly, Stalin's revolution from above had produced a new generation of highly educated specialists, people who wanted the type of security Stalin has never been willing to grant. This new generation staffed the huge and complex bureaucratic machine that ran the country, a machine whose very complexity made it increasingly difficult for its creator to control. Much of what Stalin did during his last years may therefore be explained as variations on an attempt to manage that apparatus, generally by using threatening gestures to keep its most powerful elements off balance and pitted against each other.

There also were very direct challenges to Stalin's way of doing things. In some areas once occupied by the Germans, the attempt to reestablish Soviet control met fierce resistance. This was especially true in Lithuania and the western Ukraine, where thousands of Soviet troops died fighting local partisans. By 1946 the Gulag, brimming with newly deported soldiers, partisans, and nationalists of various stripes, was boiling over.

Several major uprisings involving thousands of prisoners rocked Stalin's slave labor empire between 1946 and 1950. These revolts were crushed, but unrest continued to simmer in many parts of the Gulag into the new decade.

Stalin's defensive measures began with the approximately 5 million soldiers, POWs, slave laborers, and refugees, all of whom had spent part of the war outside the Soviet Union. It was an episode with many victims and no heroes. Hundreds of thousands of people of all types who were outside the Soviet Union when the fighting ended did not want to return to their homeland. They were forced to because the Western powers wanted to assure the safe return of their nationals behind Soviet lines and were still trying to avoid an open split with Stalin. They therefore made every effort to honor the Yalta agreements calling for the return of all displaced persons to their respective countries. Many of the people subject to these agreements committed suicide rather than return to the Soviet Union. Some tore their clothes off in a vain attempt to stay where they were. Allied soldiers had to force others into trains and trucks at gunpoint or with rifle clubs and bayonets. Still others fought with the troops sent to ship them eastward: some begged the troops to shoot them. Between 1945 and 1947 over 2 million Soviet citizens and several thousand who had left the Soviet Union before 1921 and therefore had never been Soviet citizens were shipped back to Stalin's clutches. They were joined by 3 million more people brought back from territory occupied by the Red Army.

These people did not receive a gracious welcome at home. Stalin was determined not to repeat Russia's experience after the Napoleonic Wars, when soldiers returning from their victorious campaign in the West brought back enough subversive ideas to foment the Decembrist Revolution of 1825. To him, anyone's presence in the West, regardless of the reasons, was proof that he was a traitor. So the returnees were quarantined as soon as they touched native soil. Some were executed outright, sometimes behind the warehouses on the docks where they had just landed. Most were shipped directly to labor camps without a question being asked. Of course, there were some collaborators with the Nazis among those shot or arrested, but uncounted innocent people were murdered or sent to living deaths because Stalin decided that they were "socially dangerous."

If Stalin was secretive about what he did to the millions of "returnees," he was quite forthright about many of his plans for the Soviet Union as a whole. When he spoke to the nation on February 6, 1946, many in his audience undoubtedly were expecting their leader to promise them some relief. The end of the war had left the country in ruins. It was literally possible to travel for hundreds of miles in the Ukraine and Belorussia and find virtually nothing still standing. In cold statistical terms, aside from the unspeakable human losses, 70,000 villages, 100,000 collective farms, 40,000 miles of railway, and half of all urban housing had been all or partially destroyed. But although Germany was beaten, there was to be no relief. Soviet Russia still lived in a hostile world, Stalin told his people, and this meant that the traditional emphasis on industrial development and heavy industry would continue. Collectivized agriculture would be preserved. Stalin's goals were as grandiose and oppressive as ever. Steel production would have to reach 60 million tons by 1960 (versus 12 million in 1945) and coal production 500 million tons (versus 150 million in 1945). Other targets for heavy industry were equally ambitious.

Actions followed these words. The lax practices of the war were abolished. Agriculture was the hardest hit; the wartime expansion of private peasant plots was reversed and *kolkhozy* were forced to deliver grain and other produce to the government at extremely low prices, often at less than the costs of production. That was not even the worst of it. Every peasant household, for example, was obligated to deliver 200 liters of milk per year to the state: unfortunately, over half the peasant households had no cow. The number of workdays each peasant owed the collective was raised, as were taxes. To better supervise all this, the state ordered that the *kolkhozy* be merged into larger units, a process that decreased the total number of collectives by more than half. The currency reform of 1947 substituted one new ruble for ten old ones, thereby effectively wiping out the savings some peasants had accumulated during the war. Meanwhile, there was no investment in agriculture that might have boosted the chronic low productivity. Agriculture did manage a slow recovery, reaching its overall 1940 production level by 1949, but considerable hunger still stalked both the city and the countryside. There was a major famine in the Ukraine in 1946. By 1952, agriculture still produced less grain and potatoes, its two major crops, than in 1940. In fact, total grain production was less than it had been under Nicholas II in 1913. Meanwhile, in the cities privation still remained the rule. Workers in the immediate postwar years were burdened with low wages, intensified labor discipline, and devastated and unrebuilt housing. In 1949 real wages were less than half of their 1940 level.

It is extremely unlikely that any other regime could have demanded such sacrifices from its people after the war and survived. Such were the advantages of totalitarianism. Because of their sacrifices the immediate postwar years produced spectacular economic growth. By 1953, steel and pig iron production were about double their 1940 levels. Oil production was up by two-thirds over 1940, coal by 100 percent. By 1960 Stalin's steel and coal targets were reached and those for oil were exceeded. No less important, the Soviet Union managed to rearm with the most modern weapons, particularly after 1949. By Stalin's death in 1953, it possessed not only atomic bombs, but an array of new land, air, and sea weaponry that included guided missiles, and was only a few months away from successfully testing its first prototype hydrogen bomb (the United States had tested a thermonuclear device in 1952). Finally, during the Fourth Five-Year Plan of 1946–1950, some progress was made in producing consumer goods. Although these continued to be in extremely short supply and life remained extremely difficult, the miserably low living standards slowly began to rise. Overall, aided by industrial booty taken from Germany as war reparations immediately after the fighting stopped and by its economic exploitation of its European satellites, the Soviet Union's economy grew rapidly during Stalin's final eight years. It thus was able to support the Soviet Union's superpower pretensions.

No less than Western military or economic strength, Stalin feared Western ideas, which accounts for his treatment of the unfortunate returnees after the war. Yet even with the returnees out of the way, Stalin was convinced that the rest of the Soviet population had been contaminated by Western ideas during the war. He therefore decided to launch an ideological offensive to vaccinate every Soviet citizen against Western intellectual germs. This campaign against Western influence of all sorts has gone down in history as the *Zhdanovshchina*, after Andrei Zhdanov. From the time of Kirov's murder until his own mysterious death in 1948, Zhdanov was Stalin's satrap in Leningrad. He began his comprehensive campaign against Western influence in 1946 with a vicious attack on two of the Soviet Union's leading writers, Anna Akhmatova and Mikhail Zoshchenko. Zhdanov called Akhmatova a combination of a "whore and a nun" because of her concern with inner spirituality and art for art's sake. Zoshchenko, perhaps the Soviet Union's leading humorist, was the "scum of the literary world." The campaign spread to theater and film, and from there to music, philosophy, economics, and beyond. The great composers Prokofiev and Shostakovich were informed that their music was too "bourgeois," while Sergei Eisenstein was compelled to admit that part two of his classic film *Ivan the Terrible* was "worthless and vicious" because it was too critical of Ivan and his murderous police. Eugene Varga, the country's leading economist, was condemned for failing to foresee the impending American depression (which never occurred).

The list goes on. Jazz was banned. Trofim Lysenko flourished as the destructive dictator of Soviet genetics. Everything Russian was extolled vis-a-vis the West. Russian expansion under the tsars was deemed progressive. It was revealed that previously unheralded Russian geniuses invented innumerable things before Western tinkerers falsely received credit for their achievements. Russian, as Stalin himself hinted upon intervening in an academic debate on linguistics, was the language of the future. Zhdanov's death in August 1948 brought relief only to his political rivals. The *Zhdanovshchina*, stripped only of its masthead, forged ahead, its motive power still hatching plots in the Kremlin.

Another aspect of the *Zhdanovshchina* was its relegitimization of anti-Semitism. Stalin seems to have always hated Jews. There were clear anti-Semitic overtones in his struggle against Trotsky. He became furious when two of his children married Jews, and the presence of numerous Jews among the Old Bolsheviks Stalin so loathed and feared did little to improve his toleration of that minority. Many Jews were removed from sensitive positions in the state and party apparatus during the 1930s, a process that culminated in Litvinov's removal as foreign minister in 1939. Still, these elements did not coalesce into a coherent policy for many years. After the war, however, the Soviet government embraced anti-Semitism as closely as had any monarch in the days of the bigoted tsars.

There seem to have been several immediate causes for Stalin's anti-Semitic campaign. Soviet Jews probably had more contacts abroad than most other ethnic groups. In fact, during the war Stalin had even used this resource, sending his hand-picked "Jewish Anti-Fascist Committee," headed by the great Yiddish theater actor Solomon Mikhoels, to drum up support for the Soviet Union in the West. A special attack on Jews, particularly on the community's intellectual elite, therefore grew naturally out of the overall campaign against Western influences. Equally important, if not decisive, the establishment of the state of Israel in 1948 (which Stalin had initially supported in order to undermine the Western powers in the Middle East) and the enormous enthusiasm it evoked from Soviet Jews unnerved Stalin, the potentate of a multinational empire.

The result was a frontal assault on the Soviet Jewish community. The period from 1948 to 1953 is aptly known as the "Black Years of Soviet Jewry." It began with Mikhoels' murder in January 1948. Late in 1948, hundreds of Jewish intellectuals, including the remaining leaders of the "Jewish Anti-Fascist Committee," were arrested. Some were shot immediately, the others sent to prison. Twenty-four of them, some of the greatest names in Soviet Jewish culture, were shot on one terrible night, August 12, 1952. All these people were "rootless cosmopolitans," people whose knowledge and love for Western culture made them un-Russian, unpatriotic, and unreliable. Virtually all the Jewish community's communal institutions—theaters, newspapers, the remaining synagogues—were shut down. Thousands were arrested. The assault climaxed in 1952, when a group of nine doctors, seven of them Jewish, were arrested for allegedly plotting to murder Stalin and key members of the government. No one can tell for sure where the "Doctors' Plot" would have led, but recently revealed evidence suggests that Stalin intended to deport Soviet Jews en masse to Siberia. In his book *The Time of Stalin*, Anton Antonov-Ovseyenko, a dissident with access to some of Stalin's top associates, reported that huge barracks were built to house the deportees. Several years after the plan had been aborted by Stalin's death, the barracks designed for Jews were deemed unfit for storing grain.[1]

During his last years, Stalin's mental state began to deteriorate markedly under the impact of hardening of the arteries and growing paranoia. Milovan Djilas, the Yugoslav Communist, commented that in 1948 the formerly quick-witted Stalin began to act "in the manner of old men." Khrushchev reported that in Stalin's last years, "He trusted no one and none of us could trust him. He would not let us do the work he was no longer able to do." Regardless of his deteriorating health, Stalin still was capable of many things. Among them was keeping everyone around him on the edge of a cliff, including several would-be successors. Prior to August 1948, for example, Zhdanov looked to be Stalin's right-hand man. Yet Zhdanov died under very mysterious circumstances and his death immediately was followed by a massive purge of his Leningrad organization. Thousands died in this "Leningrad Affair," which supposedly involved a plot to turn the city over to the British.

Zhdanov's demise raised the stock of two other top Stalin lieutenants —Lavrenti Beria and Georgi Malenkov, the men who conducted the Leningrad purge. Beria was Stalin's secret police chief and a Politburo member since 1946. By 1951, however, his star was dimming because of his alleged involvement in another of Stalin's concoctions, the "Mingrilian Affair," a fantasy named after a region in Stalin's and Beria's native Georgia. Nor could Molotov, formerly the Soviet Union's prime minister and its foreign minister since 1939, rest easy. Stalin removed him as foreign minister in 1949 and sent his (Jewish) wife to a labor camp. It was, in fact, one of Stalin's long-established practices to arrest immediate relatives of his closest aides, which may explain why Molotov's wife once greeted an acquaintance at a function with the remark, "Ah, Sasha, haven't you been arrested yet." Stalin also publicly called both Molotov and Voroshilov British spies. Other ministers to lose their jobs were A. I. Mikoyan (whose sons had been arrested) and N. A. Bulganin. Nikita Khrushchev, a tough old purger and administrator who served Stalin in the Ukraine and in Moscow and a Politburo member since 1939, seemed to be a rising power. Yet he too ran into trouble, first in 1947, when he temporarily lost his post as first secretary of the Ukrainian party organization, and again in 1951, when his scheme to consolidate the *kolkhozy* into huge "agro-cities" was rejected. The best bet in this thoroughly confusing situation was Malenkov. The youngest of the group—he was only fifty in 1952—his power base was in the Secretariat. The clearest sign of his ascendency appeared at the Nineteenth Party Congress in 1952, when he became the first person other than Stalin to deliver the main report to the Congress since Zinoviev did it nearly thirty years before.

The Nineteenth Party Congress was the first one Stalin had called in thirteen years, party regulations that called for a congress every three notwithstanding. The Congress was noteworthy for three rather contradictory things. Several speeches suggested an attempt to reduce tensions between the Soviet Union and the United States, a theme Stalin had hinted at earlier in a recently published book called *Economic Problems of Socialism in the USSR*. Stalin also seemed to be using the congress to dilute the powers of all his top lieutenants. The congress abolished the old Politburo and Orgburo in favor of a "Presidium." The Presidium was a bulky body of thirty-six members, in contrast to the trim Politburo's eleven. The Secretariat was expanded from five to ten members. The implication of these changes undoubtedly was not lost on Stalin's top aides, since packing party bodies had been one of his most effective techniques in his struggle for power in the 1920s. Stalin also continued his war on the Bolshevik past. In 1946, he had changed the name of the government from the Council of People's Commissars, its revolutionary title, to the more conventional Council of Ministers. Now he changed the party's name from the "Communist Party of the Soviet Union (Bolshevik)" to the "Communist Party of the Soviet Union." The term "Bolshevik" now joined the dreams it once represented and the many human beings who had proudly embraced that label in the huge historical graveyard Stalin built for them all.

Stalin did not long survive the Nineteenth Party Congress, a fortunate development for his nervous lieutenants. In all likelihood he had been planning another purge, one that almost certainly would have engulfed most of them. The "Doctors' Plot," announced to the world in July 1952, accused the doctors of murdering Zhdanov, and of being in the clutches of the CIA, British intelligence, and the Joint Distribution Committee, a Jewish social welfare organization. Aside from what evil they boded for the Soviet Union's Jewish population, these revelations and the enormous security lapses they implied suggested nothing good for Beria and Malenkov, among others. However, except for two doctors who died under torture in prison, everyone survived. The underlings lived because this time it was the boss who died. After suffering a stroke on March 1, 1953, Stalin, who normally had the best of everything, could not be treated by his personal physician. That unfortunate man was under arrest in the "Doctor's Plot." Stalin died on March 5, 1953.

Stalin's death ended what may have been the most murderous regime in human history. The number that died will never be known, because after March 1953 many of the relevant police records probably were destroyed and cemeteries and burial grounds either plowed under or covered with fresh soil. A reasonable guess is that collectivization, dekulakization, the Stalin famine, the purges, the labor camps, the executions, the wartime military policies, and the deportations claimed at least 20 million lives, and possibly even more. It was said in the eighteenth century that

Peter the Great built his city of St. Petersburg on bones; in the twentieth
century Stalin built his socialist society on them. It goes beyond human
reason or sensibility that anything could justify such apocalyptic human
suffering. Yet the student of history must assess and evaluate what the
Stalin regime built and accomplished between 1929 and 1953 against at
least two standards: Russia's historic struggle to catch up economically
and militarily with the West, and the professed goals of Marxism and the
Bolshevik Revolution.

In terms of cold statistics, the economic growth of the Stalin years
(1929–1953) was substantial, even spectacular. After centuries of lagging
behind the West, Soviet Russia in a generation became the world's second
leading industrial power, trailing only the United States. Despite the destruction of World War II, overall production grew by four times and heavy
industrial production by nine times. The gap in the ability to fight modern
warfare was overcome by increasing the funds available to the military by
twenty-six times between 1928 and 1952. All of this translated into enormous power that gave Soviet Russia greater security from foreign attack
than ever before. In short, under the "man of steel," Soviet Russia's position in the world underwent a profound and fundamental improvement.

These gains look less impressive in a broader perspective. Despite
all the *Sturm und Drang*, overall growth under Lenin and Stalin was
no greater on a per year percentage basis than it had been during the
last fifty years under the tsars. Most Western estimates place the annual
industrial growth rate for Stalin's great industrialization drive (1928–1940)
at between 9 and 12 percent, a range that exceeds but certainly does
not dwarf what Witte achieved in the 1890s (about 8 percent annual
growth). Nor can the Soviets boast vis-a-vis the Japanese. Their average
annual rate of growth in gross national product matched Russia's for the
1902–1940 period as a whole, while their annual rate of industrial growth
was close (8.9 percent versus between 9 and 12 percent) for the 1931–1940
period. Between 1950 and 1973, Japan's annual GNP increase averaged 10
percent, a record of long-term growth unmatched in the Soviet Union
before, during, or after the Stalin era. In light of the enormous waste,
inefficiency, and suffering Stalin's methods entailed, as well as the existence of other records of achievement and the alternative methods suggested within the Communist Party prior to Stalin's revolution from above,
there is compelling evidence that the industrial growth achieved under
Stalin could have been made with far less pain by other methods.

If the record in terms of quantity is ambiguous, it is clear in terms of
quality, at least as defined by traditional Marxist and socialist ideals and
goals of the Bolshevik Revolution. The socialist and Marxist vision was
of a classless, egalitarian society held together by voluntary cooperation,
a situation that supposedly would eventually render the old oppressive

state superfluous. That vision promised prosperity, freedom, and the end of human alienation. Under Stalin, the people of Russia were oppressed more than ever before by a state that became larger and more powerful than ever before. Despite economic growth, the standard of living plummeted for most Soviet citizens. A new elite replaced the old. Djilas called that elite the "New Class." Under any name it monopolized the fruit of the nation's labor for itself, much like the old aristocracy or any other ruling class. It is true that capitalism and private property were abolished in the Soviet Union, but this in itself, especially when accompanied by tyranny, did not constitute socialism or communism to Marx. Plekhanov, the father of Russian Marxism, had called this control of the masses by an all-powerful elite "Inca Communism" and had warned strenuously against it. When measured against the traditional Marxist premises of what a socialist society should look like, the Stalinist response would seem to be its political, economic, and social opposite.

Despite its formidable record in terms of heavy industry and military power, the Stalin system was yet another catastrophe, possibly the worst that has befallen the people of Russia in their troubled history. As historian Robert Conquest has noted: "Stalinism is one way of industrialization, just as cannibalism is one way of attaining a high protein diet."[2] In 1953, there was nothing anyone could do about Stalin's methods. What counted was what his successors could do with the impoverished and brutalized society his methods had left them.

NOTES

1. Anton Antonov-Ovseyenko, *The Time of Stalin* (New York: Harper & Row, 1981), George Saunders, ed., p. 291.
2. Robert Conquest, *The Great Terror* (New York: Macmillan, 1968), p. 495.

PART FIVE

The Socialist Superpower

16

Khrushchev: Reforming the Revolution

With determination
We took him out of the Mausoleum
But how out of the heirs of Stalin
do we take Stalin?

——YEVGENY YEVTUSHENKO

Although Stalin's death was welcome news to many, including a large number of his top lieutenants, it also evoked genuine mourning throughout the Soviet Union. Over two decades of unrelenting propaganda had done its work; millions of Soviet citizens loved Comrade Stalin. This mourning was accompanied by fear, for Stalin's passing left a yawning gap in Soviet life in which all that was visible was the dark and foreboding unknown. At the same time, the atmosphere was heavy with relief. Life under Stalin had been unbearably harsh for the millions of ordinary Soviet citizens who had very little, and insufferably tense and dangerous for the privileged elite who had everything but could lose it in a single stroke. This was as true for those at the very top as it was for the tens of thousands of functionaries who managed the governing bureaucratic apparatus. More than anything else, these privileged but insecure people were determined to seize the first opportunity to protect themselves and stabilize their lives and careers. Stalin's last breath therefore became a wind of change that almost immediately began to sweep away parts of the system he had so laboriously built.

This process of change was anything but smooth, for Stalin's death added an enormous problem to the many others left unsolved while he was alive. The dead tyrant's successors knew that they could not govern as he had. Their personal security could not be achieved simply by the end of the terror from above; it also required additional reforms to avoid a possible threat from the abused and oppressed masses. The dilemma that Stalin's death presented was to determine what kind of reform the system could stand without being undermined. At what point would the reforms that were necessary to sustain the system begin to threaten it? No consensus existed on this crucial question. While there was great fear that reform, like terror, might generate its own momentum and run out of control, moves toward retrenchment evoked fears of a renewed Stalinist terror.

This two-sided dilemma immediately evolved into a long-lived hydra that sprouted new heads even as Stalin's successors hacked away at the old ones. It wounded Georgi Malenkov, Stalin's unsuccessful heir-apparent, plagued Nikita Khrushchev, the eventual winner in the post-1953 struggle for power, and nagged Leonid Brezhnev, who led the coup against Khrushchev and his reforms. After Brezhnev it stalked Yuri Andropov and Konstantin Chernenko, and then devoured Mikhail Gorbachev, tearing the Soviet Union itself to pieces in the process.

After March 1953 Soviet political life became a sort of interlocking two-ring circus, with the struggle for power being conducted in the first ring, and a bevy of reform activity in the second. In the first ring Stalin's former Politburo lieutenants moved to reassert the authority they as a group had lost during Stalin's last months; at the same time, as individuals they scrambled to acquire as much personal power as they could. Georgi Malenkov, the number-two leader before Stalin's death, initially cornered both the job of senior party secretary and prime minister, respectively the top party and government posts, to emerge as the apparent number one. Lavrenti Beria, Stalin's long-time secret police chief, took over the newly strengthened Ministry of Interior—it was given control over the secret police—and also became first deputy prime minister. The veteran Bolshevik (one of the very few pre-1917 figures left) Viacheslav Molotov, a Politburo member since 1925 and formerly both a prime minister and foreign minister, now became foreign minister and, like Beria, a first deputy prime minister. These three in effect formed an uneasy triumvirate ostensibly committed to what they solemnly called "collective leadership." A step below them was Nikita Khrushchev, longtime party boss of the Ukraine and subsequently the first secretary of the party's Moscow organization. Along with such other Stalin henchmen as Lazar Kaganovich and Anastas Mikoyan, Malenkov and his partners purged the Presidium (as the Politburo was called after 1952) of the newcomers Stalin had brought in to dilute their power in 1952 and emerged as Stalin's successors, the new rulers of the Soviet Union.

This new ruling order proved to be unstable. It buried Stalin without incident (Beria deployed his secret police troops and tanks around

Moscow to make sure that the population avoided "disorder" or "panic"), but small cracks quickly appeared in the ruling group's "united and unshakable" ranks. On March 14, only nine days after Stalin's death, Malenkov was compelled by his "colleagues" to give up his post on the Secretariat, probably to prevent him, or anyone else, from accumulating too much power and following in Stalin's footsteps. That important job now went to Khrushchev, possibly because the three senior men did not consider him a serious candidate for supreme power. On June 26 the crack widened when Beria, the member of the ruling group most feared by his colleagues because he controlled the secret police, was secretly arrested in his Kremlin office while army tanks surrounded the secret police headquarters. An immediate purge of the secret police, including several executions, followed, as did a public announcement in July that Beria had been a "capitalist agent" and "enemy of the people" all along. His "trial" and execution came in December, while trials of leading secret police officers that resulted in numerous executions continued until 1956.

Beria's removal was followed by a showdown between Malenkov and the rapidly rising Khrushchev. At first Malenkov, who stood senior to Khrushchev both before and after March 1953, appeared stronger, but several inopportune moves, including his attempt to monopolize the top party and government posts in March 1953, hurt his standing with his colleagues. Also damaging was his public promise to raise the standard of living by producing more consumer goods at the expense of investment in heavy industry, a pledge that antagonized powerful vested interests, including the military and party leaders directly involved with heavy industry, and which Khrushchev was able to use against him. Malenkov also was hindered by habits acquired as a result of his past successes. He seemed to believe that behind-the-scenes intrigue in Moscow, which had been sufficient when Stalin's support was the crucial political factor, would still suffice in a new era when there were many more flanks in the huge party bureaucracy to be covered.

Most of all, however, Malenkov lost because Khrushchev won. Blessed with a dynamic and in many ways attractive personality, Khrushchev was skilled at using face-to-face meetings to rally support, both on the collectives and, far more importantly, in meetings with party cadres and officials. He also was skilled at bureaucratic intrigue, using his old contacts from his decade as the party boss in the Ukraine as a base and his new job as first secretary to place his supporters in key positions during 1953 and 1954. Thus, by 1955 Khrushchev people controlled Leningrad (Frol Kozlov), Moscow (Katerina Furtseva), the secret police (Ivan Serov), and the Komsomol (Alexander Shelepin). Khrushchev's replacement of over half of the provincial party first secretaries meant the emergence of yet more of his partisans. Khrushchev also skillfully exploited the poor conditions in agriculture and the discomfiture felt by the moguls of heavy industry and the military over Malenkov's consumerism to discredit his rival. Malenkov was further compromised by his ties to the discredited Beria. By February 1955, he was outmaneuvered. Recognizing his lack of support, Malenkov resigned as prime minister, confessing his overall "inexperience" in local work and industrial affairs and his "guilt and responsibility" for the "unsatisfactory" state of agriculture. Neither Khrushchev nor Malenkov mentioned that it was Malenkov who had successfully oversaw the postwar reconstruction of the aircraft industry and managed the recovery of large areas occupied by the Germans, or that it was Khrushchev, not Malenkov, who had been in charge of agriculture between 1953 and 1955.

It is a measure of the enormous pressure for reform that so much changed even as the struggle for power was being played out. In fact, the struggle for power itself contributed to the reform process. That Malenkov tried to win public acceptance and support in March 1953 by publicly promising the Soviet people more consumer goods was a landmark in itself. An equally significant departure from Stalin's methods occurred in April of that year, when Beria, who apparently was willing to undertake more extensive reforms than any of his colleagues, publicly admitted that the "Doctors' Plot" was a hoax perpetrated by the presumably infallible Soviet government. He then released the seven surviving doctors and sanctioned the arrest of the secret police officials supposedly responsible for the hoax. Of course Beria's own arrest and the subsequent purge of the secret police produced a far greater reform as they helped bring that dreaded institution under the control of the party leadership as a whole for the first time in over two decades. Henceforth, methods other than terror would have to be used both in the struggle for power and to govern the nation as a whole.

This was all certainly welcome news to the long-suffering Soviet public. The events of 1953 seemed to signal that some degree of personal security and an improvement in the material standard of living, two things the Soviet people desperately needed and wanted, were in the offing. There were even hints that the Soviet intellectual community might get a small measure of what it craved: a loosening of censorship. The public therefore had good reason to watch with interest, even if that was virtually all it could do as its fate was decided.

April 1953 brought the Soviet people even more good news. Retail prices were cut by an average of 10 percent. Some foodstuffs, like meat and potatoes and vegetables, were cut by even larger amounts. Though this policy led mostly to longer lines at stores because there were insufficient quantities of these goods, the announcements did represent a new interest in wooing popular support. So did the title Malenkov gave to his economic program in August, the "New Course," in which even the peasants received something. During 1953, among other things, some debts and tax arrears were cancelled, taxes on private plots and compulsory deliveries by the collectives to the state reduced, and higher prices paid for those deliveries. The wind of change reached even to the deepest caverns of Stalin's system. Four thousand political prisoners (a tiny percentage of the total) were released. But because some were people with important connections, they increased the pressures for more amnesties and reform, especially as the number released grew to 12,000 (including some of Khrushchev's associates from the Stalin days) by 1955.

In 1954 an increasingly visible and active Khrushchev initiated the most dramatic economic reform of the immediate post-Stalin years, his " virgin lands" campaign. While Malenkov's attention focused on the "intensification" of agriculture, that is, on the complex and long-term effort to increase productivity on land already under cultivation, Khrushchev, an impatient man by nature, expected to achieve an immediate, spectacular expansion of the food supply (and not incidentally to boost his own political stock), by putting enormous new areas under cultivation. His plan was to farm previously uncultivated land in Central Asia and Western Siberia. These areas had been left unsown for good reason: rainfall there was unreliable and often inadequate. Many party leaders therefore opposed the plan. Still, Khrushchev succeeded in launching the program, and tens of thousands went to work on newly organized state farms. Despite poor planning and considerable hardship, they produced a good harvest in 1954, an important year in Khrushchev's power struggle with Malenkov. A drought in 1955 caused a setback, but good weather and millions of newly plowed acres produced an excellent harvest in 1956 that again helped the program's sponsor. Never a man to rest on his laurels, Khrushchev had also opened another agricultural front in 1955 with a campaign to increase the production of corn, a crop he believed was a key to the agricultural success and consequent high standard of living in the United States, the Soviet Union's rival and nemesis.

The post-Stalin "thaw," as it usually is called after Ilia Ehrenburg's 1954 novel of that name, also extended to cultural affairs. In 1953 Ehrenburg felt emboldened to declare that a writer was "not a piece of machinery" but someone who required autonomy and freedom. Others echoed his sentiments, including author Vladimir Pomerantsev, who attacked the all-powerful Writer's Union by noting that "Shakespeare was not a member of a union at all, yet he did not write badly." A new and more liberal minister of culture, G. F. Alexandrov, was appointed. Writers began to explore a number of previously taboo themes, including corruption in the party and the damage Stalin's policies did to artistic endeavor. It once again became possible to read the works of formerly proscribed authors, such as Isaac Babel and Michael Bulgakov from the Soviet period and Dostoevsky from prerevolutionary times. In science, Lysenko's genetic "theories" came under attack, while contacts with the West were renewed in several disciplines in both the sciences and social sciences during 1954 and 1955. But although optimism for further reform swelled, Alexandrov's dismissal in March 1955 indicated there were limits to change.

Another major area of change was foreign affairs. By the 1950s the United States and the Soviet Union were busily building arsenals of nuclear weapons. Fearing a possible nuclear confrontation, particularly in light of the stalemate in Korea, Malenkov moved to defuse tensions with the West. A Korean armistice was signed in July 1953, and the next year the Soviet Union helped arrange a conference that ended the war between the French colonial forces and communist guerrillas in Vietnam. Relations with the West were further improved when the Soviet Union agreed in May 1955 to remove its forces from Austria and permit the reunification and neutralization of that country. In July Khrushchev and Nicolai Bulganin, Malenkov's successor as prime minister, met with American, French, and British leaders in Geneva. The meeting yielded few concrete results, but it did provide an impetus for the policy Khrushchev was calling "peaceful coexistence." Another conciliatory move was the return to Finland of its naval base at Porkkala.

Although certainly not insignificant, these episodes proved to be islands of cooperation in a sea of contention. They did not prevent hardening of Europe's division into Eastern and Western blocs. Germany remained divided, and West Germany began to rearm after entering NATO in 1955. The Soviet reaction included organizing the Warsaw Pact, the Moscow-dominated military alliance that after 1955 stood opposed to NATO across Europe.

The Soviets also worked to mend their fences with Communist nations in an attempt to reunite the Communist world. A 1954 treaty with the People's Republic of China acknowledged Chinese control of Manchuria, stipulated that Soviet troops would withdraw from Port Arthur, and turned over certain assets to the Chinese. But the bargaining was hard, leaving the Chinese grudgingly satisfied rather than gratefully overjoyed. This was followed in 1955 by Khrushchev's momentous visit to Belgrade, Yugoslavia, where the Soviet first secretary publicly apologized to Tito for the latter's treatment at Stalin's hands. Khrushchev also acknowledged Yugoslavia's, and by implication any nation's, right to develop socialism in its own way, another radical departure from Stalin. Tito, while pleased, remained at arm's length from the Soviet fold.

The Soviet leaders enjoyed greater success in their approaches to the newly independent nonaligned nations of Asia and Africa, an area Stalin had neglected. Unlike Western Europe, where deeply rooted fears and

American power were insuperable obstacles to Soviet advances, or Yugoslavia and Communist China, where the Soviets faced both old fears and new grievances, Asia and Africa represented a virgin and fertile field for the Soviet Union to sow. The United States, despite its great wealth and power, was tainted by its associations with the British, French, Dutch, and Portuguese, whose crumbling empires left a powerful residue of resentment and anti-Western feeling. The Communist regime in Beijing, a potential if not an actual Soviet rival, may have had a "pure" anti-Western ideological pedigree, but it was too poor to offer much more than words to the poverty-stricken emerging nations. The Soviet Union, by contrast, which seemed to provide a glittering practical example of rapid economic progress, was an arch foe of Western imperialism, and even was able to offer some economic and military assistance to any prospective new Asian and African friends.

A signal of this new interest in the Third World was a highly publicized junket that Khrushchev and Bulganin made to India, Burma, and Afghanistan in 1955. Subsequent Soviet efforts bore fruit especially in India and Egypt, two of the most important nations in their respective regions of the world. They became the largest recipients of Soviet aid. Other major recipients of Soviet economic or military assistance were Burma, Afghanistan, Indonesia, and Iraq after a revolution overthrew its pro-Western monarchy in 1958.

These internal reforms and foreign-policy initiatives did not come easy; they took place against a background of instability. Within months of Stalin's death, in fact, the combination of reduced pressures and apparent indecision among the new leadership led to violent anti-Soviet outbreaks in Czechoslovakia and East Germany. The incidents in East Berlin quickly got out of hand and required Soviet tanks to put them down. Even worse, there was trouble in the Gulag. The worst of several rebellions during 1953 and 1954 was a massive uprising in the Vorkuta coal mines that was suppressed only after extensive bloodshed.

Resistance to reform and doubts and hesitation by the would-be reformers themselves further constricted the process of change. Molotov, for example, strongly opposed a conciliatory foreign policy in general and Khrushchev's overtures to Tito in particular. Khrushchev himself circumscribed some of the regime's agricultural reforms by increasing party supervision of the collectives and raising the peasants' work obligations. The first secretary even played the role of antireformer when reform conflicted with his political goals. He spoke against Malenkov's intention to increase consumer goods production at the expense of heavy industry, for example, thereby winning the support of key party elements who favored the traditional economic priorities.

Khrushchev's battle with Malenkov reached its decisive phase in late

1954 and ended with Khrushchev's victory in February 1955. Its bloodless denouement marked a major milestone in political reform. Malenkov was demoted, not liquidated. He even remained on the party's ruling Presidium and in the government as minister of power stations. He was succeeded as prime minister by Bulganin, a technocrat rather than a top-ranking political power.

Although the events of February 1955 seemed to clarify the issue of who was in charge, a great many important issues remained unresolved. The reforms of the past two years were incomplete, to say the least. The basic structure of the economy remained unchanged, with old inefficiencies persisting and productivity still lagging. An increase in wages had produced both long lines for unavailable consumer goods and a rising black-market price for food that remained in short supply. These discrepancies between supply and demand forced the government to raise prices in 1955. A few thousand people had been released from the Gulag, but millions still languished in the camps. Meanwhile nervous bureaucrats at all party levels, including those in the Presidium, feared the consequences of further reform and resisted it. A bottleneck seemed to have been reached.

The stage thus was set for Nikita Sergeyevich Khrushchev, the peasant-born, poorly educated worker from the coal fields, who joined the Communist Party in 1918, supplemented his formal education, and built himself a remarkable career. An early protegee of Stalin's collectivizer and troubleshooter Lazar Kaganovich, Khrushchev was one of the generation that rose to prominence during Stalin's purges. He ran the Ukraine for Stalin, for over a decade after 1938, where he won Stalin's favor by being a skilled Russifier, deporter, and intriguer. In 1949 he moved to the center of power in the Moscow party apparatus. Khrushchev was ruthless and tough, but crude; perhaps it was the latter characteristic that led his rivals to underestimate him after 1953. Whatever the reason, Khrushchev skillfully negotiated the post-Stalin political rapids, emerging as first secretary in September 1953 and as the victor in the struggle for power barely eighteen months later.

His surprising victory accomplished, Khrushchev soon provided other surprises. He was folksy and down to earth (sometimes excessively so, as numerous embarrassing public outbursts, such as pounding his desk with his shoe at the United Nations General Assembly, testify). While others in power remained remote from the population, Khrushchev was known for going out among the people and was often at his best when surrounded by crowds of ordinary workers and peasants. Khrushchev's contact with the people distinguished him from both his dead mentor and his living rivals, despite what he had done as one of Stalin's henchmen. His continual trips to the collectives and factories gave him first-hand knowledge of conditions there and direct contact with the people's suffering. This apparently kept alive in him a spark of sympathy that grew after Stalin's death.

Khrushchev also had been a horrified witness to some frightening consequences of Stalin's methods, especially the mass desertions and surrenders that occurred during the early days of World War II by millions of people desperate enough to seek help from the invading Germans. This experience seems to have convinced him that the regime had to reach an accommodation with the population if it were to survive. Beyond that, Khrushchev was convinced that the Soviet Union could never overcome the inefficiency and incompetence that weighed so heavily on the economy unless public apathy and alienation were overcome. Only with popular support could the bountiful promises of socialism be realized. And Khrushchev, both for reasons of personal vanity and genuine concern for the Soviet people, was determined to deliver on those promises, to see progress in his own time and receive the credit for it. Yet Khrushchev also reflected his Stalinist background and was not a democrat in any sense of the word. Therefore he inevitably undermined his own reform efforts. He wanted the people to participate and contribute, but not to have any real power, and, like Stalin, was determined to bend the party to his will.

The great obstacle to change remained Stalin, since his name still lent important legitimacy to those in the party opposed to further change. To be sure, his reputation had been tarnished slightly between 1953 and 1956, and his name was invoked far less frequently. Lenin's accomplishments were stressed at the expense of Stalin's, and a few of Stalin's victims were, as the euphemism went, "rehabilitated," posthumously. Yet, though tarnished, Stalin's reputation still stood, like the thousands of statues and monuments to him that littered the Soviet landscape.

All of that changed late on the night of February 24–25, 1956. The Twentieth Party Congress, the first since Stalin's death, was nearing the end of its deliberations. Just when most of the delegates thought the congress had finished its work, Khrushchev called them together for a closed session. The congress already had a respectable list of credits. The Sixth Five-Year Plan it approved promised increased investment in agriculture and more consumer goods. Khrushchev endorsed the doctrine of "peaceful coexistence" with the capitalist world, although he added that he expected the process of decolonialization would provide ample opportunity for the spread of socialism and Soviet influence. There was even some criticism of Stalin in a speech by the old veteran Anastas Mikoyan.

Nothing, however, had prepared the delegates for Khrushchev's four-and-one-half-hour tirade. The Communist closet burst open and the skeletons came tumbling out. Khrushchev accused the late *Vozhd* of being a brutal dictator. Stalin, the first secretary revealed, had ravaged the party by murdering thousands of its best people, including over 70 percent of the

Central Committee at his own 1934 "Congress of Victors." The "General-issimo" was a blunderer whose errors during World War II cost enormous losses in lives. His bloodletting and mistakes had damaged vast areas of Soviet life, from governmental administration and economic performance to the nation's very ability to defend itself against the Germans. Adding insult to injury, Stalin had promoted a "personality cult" that glorified him beyond recognition and gave *him* credit for what so many others had done. Khrushchev documented it all with many long horror stories about particular individuals.

Although this sort of criticism was unparalleled, Khrushchev also left out a lot. He ignored the millions of peasants killed during collectivization and the suffering that accompanied the brutalities of the industrialization drive. The party itself, as distinguished from its leader, was left above criticism, as was everything Stalin did prior to 1934. None of Stalin's major opponents of the 1920s were exonerated, nor did the millions of *non*party victims of the purges receive their due. Lenin and all he did emerged as pristine and pure, the party as infallible, and Khrushchev as an avenging hero.

The "secret speech" did not remain secret for long. In the West, its contents were published by the United States State Department. In the Soviet Union, where it was not published until 1989, word of Khrushchev's earth-shaking speech soon spread. It proved to be a many-edged sword, cutting most deeply into Malenkov, Molotov, and Kaganovich, who stood closest to Stalin's throne while the worst crimes were being committed. Khrushchev therefore had helped himself in his campaign to discredit his most formidable opponents and consolidate his power.

Yet the speech also cut dangerously into the system that Khrushchev was determined to save and revitalize. After all, Stalin had ruled for almost twenty-five years with barely a breath of opposition from Khrushchev or anyone else in the leadership. Once Khrushchev cast doubts on Stalin, the party's symbol of truth for so long, he inevitably cast doubt not only on the party's future policy, but on its very legitimacy to rule. Using Khrushchev's speech, a good case could be made for condemning the entire party for permitting such terrible crimes.

Since the evidence and damage from Stalin's "crimes" were visible everywhere, the pressure for more reform built once news of the speech and its explosive contents spread throughout the Soviet Union and its satellites in Eastern Europe. Inside Russia, about 8 million prisoners were released from the Gulag and many of the camps closed down during 1956 and 1957. The reintegration of these people into Soviet life further intensified the pressures for an accounting of what had happened under Stalin and for those still in office to answer for what they had done prior to 1953. Some officials even received light rebukes, for example, I. A.

Serov, who was fired as head of the secret police in 1958. But to accede to such demands in any meaningful way would have been suicidal for the party leadership and possibly for the system as a whole, and Khrushchev quickly found that he had let a tiger loose.

Developments in the satellites were hardly less disturbing. The combination of oppressive, Moscow-imposed Communist dictatorships and nationalist feeling proved to be an explosive compound in the wake of Khrushchev's catalyzing secret speech. Poland and Hungary, two nations with little love for Russia, burst out of control in 1956. In Poland, bloody riots occurred in June. By October the pressures on the old-line Stalinist rulers was great enough to force a major change. Wladyslaw Gomulka, an independent-minded Communist recently released after serving five years in prison for "Titoism," crowned his political comeback by being elected first secretary. Although Gomulka made no attempt to pull Poland out of the Soviet orbit, he was determined that his country enjoy a measure of independence. He stood up to immense Soviet pressure, including an angry visit from Khrushchev and the threat of military intervention, to finally win Soviet acquiescence to his rule and program. A Pole replaced the Russian designated by Moscow to head the Polish armed forces, and Gomulka dismantled most of the hated collective farms.

If the pot boiled over in Poland, it exploded in Hungary. There reform sentiment in late October facilitated the return to power as prime minister of Imre Nagy, a Gomulka-type Communist, or so it seemed. Within a few days of becoming prime minister, Nagy requested that Soviet troops leave Hungary. Then came the real bombshell. Nagy announced that Hungary would cease to be a one-party dictatorship and would leave the Warsaw Pact and the Soviet bloc to become a neutral state like Austria. Khrushchev now revealed some strict limits to his tolerance for reform. He and his colleagues had no intention of letting a satellite state achieve any measure of real independence, a development that could easily set off a chain reaction that might sweep Eastern Europe and possibly cross the Soviet frontiers. On November 4 Soviet troops and tanks invaded Hungary. The West, preoccupied by the Suez Canal crisis in the Middle East, watched helplessly. Thousands were killed in bitter but futile resistance and over 200,000 fled to the West. Nagy and several colleagues, after being promised safe conduct, left their refuge in the Yugoslav embassy and were seized and taken to Moscow. They were executed in 1958.

The Polish "October" and the Hungarian uprising were nearly politically fatal to Khrushchev as well. They provided ample grist for those in the party opposed to his reforms. Whether to strengthen his own position or because his own enthusiasm for reform had cooled, Khrushchev now made it clear to intellectuals at home that he would not tolerate the type of open discussion and criticism that had helped spark the events in Poland and Hungary. But even his new hard line was not enough. On June 19, 1957, a coalition in the Presidium led by Malenkov, Molotov, and Kaganovich, joined by old Stalin cronies like Voroshilov and Khrushchev's own prime minister, Nikolai Bulganin, secured a majority to remove the first secretary. Aside from being upset over events in Eastern Europe, Khrushchev's opponents were opposed to his economic schemes, particularly an administrative reorganization that would have greatly strengthened his political loyalists at their expense. But their seven-to-four majority in the Presidium turned out to be insufficient. Khrushchev, citing party rules, demanded that the dispute be decided by the full Central Committee. There the first secretary was aided by the minister of defense, Marshal Zhukov of World War II fame, who provided the military planes that brought in Khrushchev's supporters from the provinces, where his greatest strength lay. He triumphed in the showdown at the Central Committee.

His opponents, unceremoniously dubbed the "antiparty group," now were scattered to the four winds, as Malenkov, Molotov, and Kaganovich were dismissed from the Presidium and their government posts. Still, they survived. Molotov was sent to apply his diplomatic skills as ambassador to Outer Mongolia and later retired on a pension. Malenkov was dispatched to manage a remote power station in Central Asia. Kaganovich, the ex-hatchet man who after his defeat had tearfully called Khrushchev to beg for his life, was allowed to retire on a pension. Since it would have been awkward to dismiss Khrushchev's own prime minister just yet, Bulganin temporarily remained at his post as window dressing. Zhukov was rewarded with a seat on the Presidium. Thus, just as Khrushchev had triumphed over his opponents, the new, less murderous politics had triumphed decisively over the old. Only four years after Stalin's death things had changed a great deal.

Khrushchev soon followed up his June victory. In October he eliminated a potential rival by removing Zhukov, an ally growing far too powerful for Khrushchev's comfort, from the Presidium. Zhukov was replaced as minister of defense in the bargain with a trusted Khrushchev associate, Marshal Rodion Malinovsky. In March 1958 Bulganin followed his colleagues into political oblivion. Khrushchev now became prime minister as well as first secretary, thereby duplicating Stalin in holding both the top party and government posts, though not matching Stalin's power.

Political victory over his opponents did little to solve Khrushchev's other problems. One major difficulty was that his agenda was much too large. Khrushchev had defeated Malenkov back in 1955 in part because he criticized his rival's emphasis on producing consumer goods and insisted that heavy industry must maintain its traditional priority, an orientation reflected in the grandiose goals of the Sixth Five-Year Plan approved by the Twentieth Party Congress. This plan called for oil and electricity production to double, for steel production to rise by 50 percent, and so on. Yet, Khrushchev was also totally committed to boosting his nation's standard of living until it was equal to that of the United States. Early in 1957 Khrushchev even had promised his people that the Soviet Union would out-produce the United States in milk, meat, and butter within four years, a promise that required a huge increase in agricultural production. Khrushchev intended to accomplish all this while keeping the voracious military machine fed and making enormous investments in space technology. To his sorrow, there simply were not enough resources to realize these herculean ambitions.

Along with his self-imposed tasks, Khrushchev was burdened by his methods. He was in such a terrible hurry that he was given to panaceas, as with the virgin-lands program and his various reorganization schemes. Panaceas, of course, rarely work; moreover, as time went by, Khrushchev's increasingly embarrassing failures eroded his base of support. Khrushchev also did himself little good when he resorted to threats, a tactic that alarmed the governing bureaucracy that so cherished its newfound security. Finally, both nature and foreign adversaries refused to cooperate in the long run. Khrushchev, prime minister and first secretary or not, was left with ever steeper mountains to climb.

Whatever his eventual problems, Khrushchev enjoyed considerable success during his early years in office. He won friends in various ways. The millions released from the Gulag became his strong supporters. Another popular measure was the abolition of Stalin's worst labor laws. It once again became possible in the workers' state to change jobs without permission and be absent from work without being subject to criminal prosecution. A minimum wage was introduced, pensions were raised, and the workweek reduced.

More controversial was the economic reorganization of early 1957, a measure that helped galvanize the "antiparty group" to move against him. Khrushchev's goal was to combat the inefficiency and lack of initiative that resulted from centralizing all planning and economic decision making in Moscow. Since the Moscow planners seldom knew or understood conditions in the provinces, their decisions and targets often were unrealistic and counterproductive. Khrushchev therefore abolished over 140 ministries on both the national and union republic levels. Instead of having individual ministries that dealt with a single industrial sector either throughout the entire USSR or in a single union republic, Khrushchev divided the country into 105 economic units called *sovnarkhozy*, each responsible for the overall economy within its geographic jurisdiction. Presumably decisions made locally would better reflect the available economic resources and requirements and therefore produce more rational policies and better results. Not incidentally, this massive administrative upheaval enabled Khrushchev as first secretary to place and replace thousands of officials and thereby strengthen his political base.

Good weather and bumper harvests in the virgin lands during 1957 and 1958 further strengthened Khrushchev's support. He could also take satisfaction in the expansion of state farms relative to collective farms, a development favored by the party leadership because it facilitated greater state control over agriculture and, presumably, economies of scale as smaller inefficient collectives were amalgamated into larger, more viable units. The year 1958 also witnessed the abolition of the Machine Tractor Stations, which eliminated the burden the collective farms carried in paying exorbitant rental fees for the machines they needed. However, because the collectives were compelled to buy certain machines regardless of their needs or wishes, many were saddled with machines they could not use or repair and debts they could not pay.

Khrushchev also enjoyed other successes. Industrial growth rates, benefitting from the huge investments of earlier years, remained high until the end of the 1950s. The first secretary also managed to double ! using construction from 1955 to 1959, an area vital to consumers. Beginning in 1957, the Soviet Union scored a series of stunning successes in space exploration, a major dividend of a policy of encouraging and even pampering the scientific elite. In October 1957 the Soviet Union launched *Sputnik*, the world's first artificial satellite, and in 1959 became the first country to photograph the moon's "dark side" when one of their rockets circled the moon. Two years later, Yuri Gagarin thrilled his Soviet comrades by becoming the first human being to ride a rocket into space and orbit the earth.

Back on the ground, Khrushchev crisscrossed the country, meeting, encouraging, exhorting, and often charming his countrymen. He was a refreshing change from the remote and foreboding Stalin, holed up in the Kremlin or in one of his country homes.

In foreign affairs, results were mixed. The Soviets tried unsuccessfully to pressure the West to abandon its position in Berlin late in 1958, and to recognize East Germany. Both policies failed. Still, relations with the United States improved enough to allow Khrushchev to visit the bastion of capitalism in 1959. The trip produced little that was durable; the "Spirit of Camp David" that supposedly emerged from Khrushchev's meeting with President Dwight D. Eisenhower at the presidential retreat proved to be ephemeral. Khrushchev nonetheless did very well with the American public and media and added to his prestige at home.

A more lasting development occurred in 1959 when Fidel Castro came to power in Cuba and proceeded to align that island nation, only ninety miles from the Florida coast, with the Soviet Union. Soviet diplomatic initiatives and careful use of foreign aid also won friends in the strategic Middle East. In Egypt, the Soviets profited from the 1956 Suez Canal Crisis. Israel, in retaliation for repeated Egyptian-sponsored terrorist raids against its territory, attacked Egypt in the Sinai desert, while Britain and France landed troops near the Suez Canal in an attempt to undo Egypt's nationalization of that strategic waterway. Soviet threats against Britain, France, and Israel were empty gestures (the Soviets had problems enough in Poland and Hungary at the time), but they were welcomed in Egypt and the rest of the Arab world. The Soviets further strengthened their ties with Egypt, the most populous Arab country, by agreeing to build the Aswan High Dam when the United States pulled out of the project. Soviet influence also grew in Asia. India, looking for a counterweight to China and grateful for Soviet economic aid, proved to be a worthy object of attention. There were also some successes in sub-Saharan Africa as it emerged from European colonial rule. Overall, under Khrushchev the Soviet Union increasingly made its weight felt as a global power.

Khrushchev reached his high-water mark in 1958 and 1959, though by the latter year there were signs the tide was beginning to recede. In January, when the party met at its Twenty-First Congress, Khrushchev, as usual, was full of promises. His new Seven-Year Plan, he assured everyone, would increase both investment in heavy industry and consumer goods and enable the Soviet Union to surpass the United States in per capita production by 1970. What he did *not* say publicly was that the Sixth Five-Year Plan had been scrapped after only one year because widespread shortfalls made it impossible to realize any of its goals. The congress, of course, adopted the Seven-Year Plan, but, significantly, it did not, as Khrushchev wanted, demote some survivors of the "antiparty" group, notably Voroshilov. A far more serious setback occurred later in 1959 when the harvest was poor.

More bad news followed the next year. The long-simmering differences between the Soviet Union and the People's Republic of China finally burst into the open. At the same time relations with the United States were cooling. A planned summit meeting between Khrushchev and President Eisenhower was aborted in June 1960 when the Soviets shot down an American U-2 spy plane deep inside their country just as the summit conference was about to open. When another American plane, this time in the Arctic, was downed that same month, American-Soviet relations cooled further still. They did not improve when Khrushchev, having come to New York to attend the annual meeting of the United Nations General Assembly, shocked everyone by taking a shoe and pounding it on his desk to protest a speech he did not like. He further angered the Americans when he met with his new friend Fidel Castro, who also happened to be in town for the General Assembly meeting.

Khrushchev still had at least one more dramatic gesture to make. At the Twenty-Second Congress of the CPSU in October 1961, the first secretary responded forcefully, almost defiantly, to his various intractable and frustrating domestic and foreign problems. The congress adopted a new party program, only its third in history (the first two were adopted in 1903 and 1919). Khrushchev's program "solemnly" assured the Soviet people that the "present generation will live under communism." By 1980, the "foundations of communism" would be built. The production of everything would be doubled, tripled, quadrupled, etc., by then, and the high road to complete communism would be opened. For the present, Khrushchev informed his comrades that a "state of the whole people" had replaced the "dictatorship of the proletariat" and the party had become a "party of the whole people."

Khrushchev had at least two objectives in mind at the Twenty-Second Congress. Since the late 1950s the Soviet Union in general and he in particular had been under increasing attack from the Chinese Communists for insufficient revolutionary zeal. The Chinese denounced Khrushchev for his concern with material well-being—his so-called goulash communism—and for his attempts to defuse relations with the world's main imperialist dragon, the United States. Khrushchev was determined to reclaim the undisputed leadership of the world communist camp for his country and himself. He also wanted to rekindle mass enthusiasm and idealism at home in the hope that such spirit would help overcome the growing obstacles to economic progress.

These goals demanded, Khrushchev believed, a crushing denunciation of Stalin far beyond anything said in 1956. This would pull the rug from under the Chinese, who were Stalin's staunchest defenders as they railed against the "revisionist" Khrushchev. It would also strike a powerful blow at the various conservatives and bureaucrats at home who were resisting or sabotaging Khrushchev's reform efforts.

This time there was no secret speech; Khrushchev spoke in open session before the world. A chorus of speeches by Khrushchev and his top associates pointed to Malenkov, Kaganovich, Molotov, and Voroshilov as Stalin's accomplices. The crescendo of denunciation apparently reached even the Marxist afterworld, for one venerable delegate rose to announce that she had asked "Illiych," as she fondly called Lenin, for advice, and he had answered that Stalin should be removed from the mausoleum the two dead leaders shared because "I do not like lying beside Stalin, who inflicted so much harm on the party."

An appropriate resolution was passed, and Stalin was removed from the mausoleum the next day and reburied in an area near the Kremlin wall reserved for dignitaries of the second rank. Perhaps Khrushchev and his associates felt like the young poet Yevgeny Yevtushenko, who wrote:

Grimly clenching his embalmed fists,
just pretending to be dead, he watched from inside . . .
He was scheming. Had merely dozed off.
And I, appealing to our government, petition them
to double, and treble, the sentries guarding this slab,
and stop Stalin from ever rising again and, with Stalin, the past.

At any rate, they buried Stalin, not under six feet of earth, but under several truck loads of concrete. A wholesale renaming of places and things followed. Not even Stalingrad, the scene of the tyrant's Civil War adventures and his momentous victory over Hitler in 1943, was spared. It became Volgograd.

Unfortunately for Khrushchev, burying Stalin physically was not enough. The first secretary could not bury many of the problems Stalin had left behind or the new ones that had developed since his death. Probably the most serious was agriculture. Things had been going wrong since 1958. Poor weather reduced the harvest, both in the virgin lands and in the older agricultural regions. Khrushchev's mismanagement and authoritarian methods made things worse. The poor weather in the virgin lands was predictable, since unreliable rainfall was the main reason this area had not been farmed prior to Khrushchev's brainstorms. Even worse, the agricultural methods used in the virgin lands were totally unsuited to the dry climate. In 1963, they combined with dry weather and windstorms to turn large areas into a huge dust bowl. Millions of tons of irreplaceable topsoil were blown away. In the older agricultural regions, Khrushchev's Machine Tractor Station reforms often left the collectives with equipment they could neither afford nor maintain. Khrushchev's corn campaign also took its toll, since at his insistence corn was grown in areas totally unsuited to that crop, such as southern Siberia. Pressures to produce more meat led to excessive slaughtering, which consequently hurt both long-term meat *and* milk production. It also often led to fraud as ambitious or desperate provincial functionaries strove to meet or exceed their targets. Meanwhile, the refusal to let supply-and-demand mechanisms set sensible prices added to the damage. Prices for farm goods set by the state consistently failed to reflect the real costs of production or actual demand. This led to milk and meat being sold at a loss, much to the detriment of the already hard-pressed collective farms. When the peasants turned to their private plots to make up the difference, Khrushchev responded with increased fiscal and other types of pressures, a tactic that reduced productivity on those plots and hence the availability of food.

In 1962 the rising cost of agricultural goods forced the state to raise food prices sharply. This led to numerous protests, riots, and strikes. The worst incident occurred in the city of Novocherkassk, where a procession of strikers carrying portraits of Lenin was fired upon by army troops, who killed seventy demonstrators. The drought of 1963 led to a genuine food shortage because the government had no grain reserves to make up for the resulting shortfall. It also caused a decline in livestock herds. Since the days were gone when the regime could ignore or tolerate widespread hunger, the Soviet Union had to undergo the humiliation of buying grain from the supposedly declining capitalist countries.

By 1963 agriculture was only one of several anchors dragging the Soviet economy down. The centralized planning methods inherited from Stalin were unable to coordinate and manage an increasingly complex economy. Khrushchev's division of the country into 105 *sovnarkhozy* had not helped; instead, it created new webs of conflicting interests, as *sovnarkhozy* competed against one another for resources, and often were unable to get what they needed from distant areas. Khrushchev therefore reduced the number of *sovnarkhozy* to forty-seven. Meanwhile, factories still produced to meet the all-important targets (e.g., producing excessively heavy sheetmetal to meet gross weight requirements) rather than what customers needed. The list of similar difficulties could go on almost endlessly. Increased military expenditures after 1961 added to the strain, with the result that in 1963 and 1964 industrial growth rates registered their worst peacetime performance since 1933.

Foreign policy difficulties, especially vis-a-vis the polar opposites of the United States and the People's Republic, were another area of concern. The dispute with China had deep roots, some going back to nineteenth-century tsarist territorial expansion at the expense of the crumbling Chinese Empire. Other causes were of more recent vintage. The People's Republic of China was a militant, have-not nation, while the Soviet Union, its revolution far in the past, was behaving more like a country with something to lose. In 1958, when China's Mao Zedong launched his "Great Leap Forward," a quixotic attempt to jump directly from backwardness to communism by organizing gigantic "communes," and not incidentally leapfrogging the Soviet Union in the process, he was in effect challenging Khrushchev for leadership in the Communist world. (The Soviets were delighted when the "Great Leap Forward" failed completely.) That same year Khrushchev refused to help Mao drive the Nationalist Chinese from two islands just off the People's Republic's coast for fear of a conflict with the United States. This infuriated Mao, as did Khrushchev's refusal to help the Chinese develop an atomic bomb. In 1960 the Soviet Union suddenly withdrew all its advisors and technicians from China, and in 1962 it refused to support the Chinese in their border war with India. There were other incidents as well, none of which were helped by Khrushchev's bombastic personality. Border incidents began as early as 1960, and in 1963 the

Chinese made their first public call for revisions of the Sino-Soviet borders.

None of this precluded friction with the Americans. The same sour note that closed Soviet relations with the outgoing Eisenhower administration in 1960 sounded again in 1961 with the incoming Kennedy administration. When Khrushchev met Kennedy in Vienna in June 1961, he used the opportunity to demand once again a Western withdrawal from West Berlin (one of eight conditions Khrushchev set regarding the German problem as a whole) and in general attempted to test the young American president. These demands were quickly rejected by the Western powers. For his part, Kennedy came back from Vienna determined never to be bullied by Khrushchev again. As he put it, "If Khrushchev wants to rub my nose in the dirt, it's all over. The son of a bitch won't pay attention to words. He has to see you move."

Kennedy soon had more reasons to show how he could move. The Soviets and their East German puppets acted to stop an accelerating exodus from the German Democratic Republic (East Germany) that had reached thousands of people per week and threatened to cripple that Communist state. The bulk of the exodus was via Berlin, a city divided politically but with no physical barrier separating its Eastern and Western halves. Then, on August 13, 1961, one suddenly appeared, the concrete, barbed-wire-and-broken-glass-topped Berlin Wall that cut through the center of the city. The exodus from East Berlin virtually ceased. In September Khrushchev ended the Soviet Union's voluntary ban on atmospheric nuclear testing, a ban in which the United States had not reciprocated. The subsequent series of Soviet tests included the detonation of a fifty-seven-megaton device, the largest man-made explosion in history.

Then Khrushchev reached too far. His bragging about Soviet military power notwithstanding, the Soviets lagged behind the United States in strategic military capability, in part because under Khrushchev resources had been diverted to nonmilitary priorities in industry and agriculture. As was his wont, Khrushchev tried to make up everything in one stroke. If the Soviet Union could place its intermediate-range ballistic missiles close to the United States, he reasoned, those missiles could hold the line until intercontinental missiles were ready. Such a stroke also would help the first secretary fend off his critics at home and in Peking. Khrushchev's new launching pad was conveniently available in Cuba, where Khrushchev also wanted to protect Fidel Castro's Communist regime in light of the American-backed invasion by Cuban exiles in 1961, the ignominious Bay of Pigs fiasco.

The Cuban Missile Crisis of October 1962 was a disaster for Khrushchev. American intelligence planes spotted the construction sites before the missiles could be installed. President Kennedy then moved boldly (some would say recklessly). He ordered a naval blockade around Cuba and flatly demanded that the missiles on the island be withdrawn. For several days the United States and the USSR stood, as the American Secretary of State Dean Rusk put it, "eyeball to eyeball," and, as Rusk noted, it was the Soviets who "blinked." They had little choice in the face of Kennedy's determination and American military superiority. The face-saving formula that resolved the crisis, under which the Soviets agreed to remove their missiles from Cuba in return for an American guarantee not to invade the island in the future and an unofficial promise to remove obsolete American missiles in Turkey, accomplished Kennedy's announced objectives and gave Castro the security he needed. But the agreement did little for Khrushchev's security. Nor did two important agreements reached later that year: the direct telephone "hot line" between the White House and the Kremlin, and the partial nuclear test-ban treaty (signed by the United States, the USSR, and Great Britain) that banned all above-ground nuclear tests. Despite their value to the Soviet Union and to the United States, they simply were too little and too late for the first secretary in the wake of his defeat in Cuba.

These agreements reflected the chastening effect of a crisis that brought the world to the brink of nuclear war. Both sides now wisely drew back. However, the Cuban Missile Crisis had exposed Khrushchev as a reckless bluffer and added the Soviet military to the growing list of powerful elements inside the Soviet Union dissatisfied with his policies. Along with his difficulties with the economy and with China, the Cuban Missile Crisis added yet another albatross to those already hanging around the neck of the embattled Khrushchev.

Khrushchev carried another albatross—his own ambivalence about how far to go with reform. As much as he hated certain aspects of Stalinism, Khrushchev still *was* a Stalinist in the sense of being committed to the bulk of the system created by the great industrialization drive of the 1930s. Khrushchev the Stalinist constantly constricted or countermanded what Khrushchev the reformer did. When this self-sabotage was added to the resistance to change by large parts of the bureaucracy, Khrushchev's reformist policies were further damaged. This led Khrushchev the reformer to more drastic, desperate, and usually ill-conceived schemes that disrupted more than they solved and made Khrushchev even more opponents. This pattern, which began as early as 1955, had become more pronounced and therefore more damaging by the early 1960s.

The pattern of reform and reaction was clearly visible with regard to cultural policy. Here it was a genuine roller coaster ride, with steep ups and downs sometimes following each other from month to month. One peak, the publication in 1956 of Vladimir Dudintsev's *Not By Bread Alone*, a ringing indictment of party corruption, was followed by a crackdown after the Polish and Hungarian upheavals. Dudintsev fell from grace. Then came Boris Pasternak's *Doctor Zhivago*. This lyrical and sensitive book, which focused on the individual's fate during revolutionary upheavals and raised serious questions about the Bolshevik Revolution, was published in 1957 and won the Nobel Prize for literature in 1958. An avalanche of party-orchestrated abuse fell on Pasternak, who felt compelled not to go to Stockholm to accept his prize for fear of having his citizenship revoked while he was abroad. Yet in 1959 Dudintsev was restored to good standing. Then, in 1961, the young poet and Pasternak admirer Yevgeny Yevtushenko published *Babi Yar*, a stunning denunciation of Soviet anti-Semitism, while in 1962 Khrushchev personally intervened to secure the publication of Aleksandr Solzhenitsyn's *One Day In the Life of Ivan Denisovich*. This literary bombshell exposed the horrors of Stalin's labor camps to public view as never before. By 1963 the cultural chameleon had changed again. That year Khrushchev coldly warned Soviet intellectuals that "My hand will not tremble" if they went too far. December of 1963 witnessed the arrest and trial of poet Joseph Brodsky. At the same time, the Brodsky case produced public and spirited protests from many major Soviet cultural figures, something that would have been suicidal under Stalin.

The same pattern was repeated in other areas. Khrushchev had reversed many of Stalin's Russification policies and permitted some of the national groups Stalin had exiled to return to their homes. There also were legal and judicial reforms and additional limits placed on the powers of the secret police (now called the KGB, the Russian initials for the Committee of State Security). But after 1960 antireligious propaganda and repression were intensified. The Khrushchev regime released millions of political prisoners and attempted to give more authority to popular, non-party bodies in dealing with common crime. Meanwhile, certain crimes became punishable by harsher penalties, including death. Capital punishment became common for so-called economic crimes, such violations as speculation and directing state resources to private ends. The group most singled out for committing alleged "economic crimes" was the Jews, as Khrushchev after 1960 reversed the more tolerant policies of 1953–1957 vis-a-vis that minority.

Khrushchev's reversals of policy did the most harm in economic affairs. He was well aware that industrial policy had to be made more flexible, and there was considerable discussion about what to do, both in terms of expanding the role of market forces and the use of modern mathematical and programming techniques. But very little was done. More damaging were Khrushchev's reversals of policy in agriculture. Some of his policies, such as lower taxes and abolishing the Machine Tractor Stations helped the peasants, but Khrushchev then turned around and curtailed the cultivation of private plots, forced the collectives to buy machinery they did not want, and told the peasants what crops to raise. He also pushed through a program to expand the production of chemical fertilizer, only to see much of it wasted because of inadequate storage and shipping facilities and the lack of machines to spread what did arrive. Khrushchev even restored Lysenko and his discredited theories to prominence. What he did *not* do was allow the peasantry to use its experience and expertise to decide for itself what to grow and when to grow it. His reward was agricultural stagnation. After a 40 percent growth in agricultural output during his early years in power, output rose only about 3 percent between 1958 and 1963. Hunger and massive imports were the disastrous result.

By late 1962 and early 1963, too many of Khrushchev's reforms, campaigns, and inspirational harangues had backfired. He responded in typical fashion by instituting his most radical reform of all: he split the Communist Party in half! Henceforth one branch of the party would be responsible for agriculture and the other for industry. This division of responsibility meant that each half tended to ignore the needs of the other, to the detriment of both. Suddenly it was impossible to tell who was in charge of a locality, since there were now two "first" secretaries, or who had ultimate responsibility for such neutral but vital services as education, police protection, or health care. This administrative nightmare developed at about the same time that Khrushchev ordered the number of *sovnarkhozy* reduced from 105 to forty-seven. Since the new, larger economic boundaries did not conform to the older political-regional ones, the bureaucratic tangle worsened. This tangle came on top of earlier and equally disruptive schemes, such as relocating the National Ministry of Agriculture from Moscow to a rural area sixty miles distant, where it was supposed to set up and run a large model farm. (The agricultural ministries of several national republics also were relocated to state farms.) This may have facilitated Khrushchev's aim of having bureaucrats "dirty their hands" by doing various required farm chores in addition to their regular work, but it was disastrous in terms of efficiency. For example, because of inadequate preparation it was almost impossible to place the telephone calls necessary to coordinate ministry affairs. As for morale, three-quarters of the Ministry's staff quit within a year.

Soon Khrushchev was out of a job as well. He had thoroughly antagonized a majority of the party from top to bottom. The state bureaucracy was equally disenchanted. Khrushchev had few friends left in the military as a result of his earlier limits on military budgets and his failure in the Cuban Missile Crisis. Finally, he had failed by his own standards. He had promised rapid economic progress and delivered far too much chaos. In October 1964, while on vacation, Khrushchev was suddenly called back to Moscow. This time there was no room for maneuvering. His opponents had carefully prepared in both the Presidium and the Central Committee.

Nikita Sergeyevich was informed of his "request" that he be relieved of his duties because of ill health. A terse official announcement followed. Khrushchev then became the latest beneficiary of his own reforms. Although relegated to private life and obscurity (public mention of him ceased), the former first secretary lived in comfort (retaining his Moscow apartment, a nearby country house, the use of a car and a chauffeur, and other luxuries) until his death in 1971. It is in a sense fitting that although no member of the Central Committee attended his funeral, several of those he rescued from the Gulag showed up. The Khrushchev era, so full of sound and fury, ended without a bang or a whimper.

In the end, Khrushchev's fate was that of an idiosyncratic historical figure only partially in touch with his time. His success both in rising to power and exercising it between 1953 and 1958 grew out of an impulse for reform that had broad appeal within the Soviet elite. The drive for reform was powerful because it involved something as basic as personal and professional security and because it had been denied for so long by Stalin's presence. The reform impulse also included a new concern for perceived public desires, specifically a higher standard of living and an easing of general police and bureaucratic controls, as public acquiescence was considered vital to the security of the governing elite. The reform impulse included attempts to ease international tensions because such steps also contributed to that security.

Yet the reform impulse also was a limited one. The Soviet elite did not want to erode or undermine those aspects of the Stalinist system that had provided it with so much status and power. It was also an ambiguous impulse. There was no precise agreement about what should be done beyond dismantling Stalin's terror machine. In these two senses Khrushchev was out of touch with the predominant conservative sentiment among the Soviet elite of his time. Because of his impatience and belief that only through *active* participation of the whole population could the system work, and because of his sympathy for the Soviet people, Khrushchev wanted to change the system more than his colleagues did. This accounts for measures that in a nondictatorial environment would be considered populist. Khrushchev attempted to open up higher education to children of workers and peasants, an effort that met with only marginal success. He invited nonparty members of the intelligentsia to Central Committee meetings. He reformed the party rules at the 22nd Party Congress to require a substantial periodic turnover of leadership at the various levels from the Central Committee on down, a measure that angered many party officials and cost him significant support in powerful circles. Khrushchev even encouraged activity by ordinary people outside the party to make the party more responsive to the population at large. Thus his *sovnarkhozy* reform was discussed at over 500,000 meetings attended

by over 40 million citizens, while almost 1 million meetings attended by
70 million people discussed his proposed Seven-Year Plan. Of course, he
intended that popular pressure would be applied to approve *his* programs.
Instead, his populism got him into trouble with his colleagues. They either
sabotaged his reforms or increasingly turned against him until he fell from his
perch.

Khrushchev lagged behind his colleagues in one respect. Nikita
Sergeyevich acted like a dictator, albeit a generous and paternal one,
with a cult of his own. He was thus *too* Stalinist for his time. He was not
satisfied to act as a representative of the ruling oligarchy, but rather wanted
to bend it to his will. So rather than providing additional security for the
party elite that staffed the upper layers of the nation's vast bureaucracy, as
the times demanded, Khrushchev, the vestigial Stalinist, threatened them.
However, without Stalin's implements of terror, he lacked the power to
overcome them completely. With each passing year that elite became more
deeply entrenched and better able to act cohesively to defend its interests.
And in the end, it, rather than Khrushchev, prevailed.

Both the Soviet elite that removed him and the population at large that
greeted his downfall so indifferently nonetheless owed Nikita Khrushchev
a considerable debt. He did not, needless to say, alter the fundamental
structure of Soviet society. A single party still ruled, the economy
remained highly centralized, censorship and thought control remained
pervasive, and so on. But Khrushchev played a pivotal role in removing
the most unbearable part of the Stalinist inheritance. The secret police
terror was ended, and the bulk of the Gulag slave-labor network was dismantled. A serious and reasonably successful effort was made to raise
the nation's miserably low standard of living. When Stalin in the 1930s said
that life had become "better" and "more joyous," he was lying. Under
Khrushchev Soviet life became better and, if not joyous, at least much
less sorrowful. That accomplishment may not deserve accolades, but there
have been many famous leaders who achieved far less.

17

Brezhnev: The Graying of the Revolution

Order is Heav'n's first law.

——ALEXANDER POPE

Make the Revolution a parent of settlements, and not a nursery for future revolutions.

——EDMUND BURKE

Khrushchev's passing marked the coming of age of the new Soviet ruling class. In 1953, although privileged, it was stunted by Stalin's suffocating terror and therefore lacked the cohesiveness necessary to defend its interests. The tyrant had to die before his court could secure its privileges. In 1964, having thrived on eleven years of political air unpolluted by terror, the governing elite was sufficiently mature to depose Khrushchev, whose Pandoraesque reforms, policy errors, and dictatorial pretensions threatened its security interests, and install a new leadership team headed by Leonid Brezhnev, Khrushchev's successor as first secretary.

That team, which initially included Alexei Kosygin (the new prime minister), Nikolai Podgorny (after 1965 the president of the Soviet Union, or official head of state), and Mikhail Suslov (the most powerful party secretary aside from Brezhnev, and the party's chief ideologist and kingmaker), reflected a new state of affairs. Henceforth the Soviet leaders operated within the parameters of the political consensus that brought it to power. That consensus did not create a democratic Communist Party—the leadership was not responsible to the party as a whole. It *did* mean that both the top leadership and the party as a whole shared a commitment to a specific set of political ground rules that no single person could successfully defy.

Those rules sanctioned efforts to make the economy more efficient and raise the national standard of living, as well as attempts to expand Soviet influence worldwide and overcome Russia's strategic military imbalance vis-à-vis the United States. Above all, however, they guaranteed the security of the state and party bureaucracies from the arbitrary assault that were a constant part of life under Stalin and an occasional unwelcome intrusion under Khrushchev. So intent was the Soviet elite on reinforcing stability that it proved unwilling in the long run to undertake reforms necessary to end stagnation in many key areas, including the economy. Such reforms might have threatened the job security or status of important constituencies of the Soviet party/state.

The prime directive of security and stability influenced the nature of leadership in the Soviet Union. Brezhnev prevailed in a struggle for power over two serious rivals—Nikolai Podgorny and Alexander Shelepin—and emerged as the leading figure on the Presidium. By 1966, he had eclipsed his colleague Kosygin and taken the newly restored title of general secretary, the title Stalin once held. But the new general secretary, though he became the most powerful man in the Soviet Union, used his power and that of his associates to protect the interests of the various branches of the party/state bureaucracy, not to impose policy on them. Rather than being a dictator—by the mid-1970s his accumulated offices and honors put him far above any of his colleagues—Brezhnev was an enormously powerful manager. His long tenure—he remained in office eighteen years, until his death in November 1982—resulted from doing his job well and staying within the new boundaries of power. In short, the Brezhnev years completed the transition from rule by a single dictator to oligarchic rule by the upper layers of the Communist Party bureaucracy.

Brezhnev and his colleagues were well suited to restoring order to the system that Khrushchev had disrupted. Born in the twentieth century (Brezhnev in 1902, Kosygin in 1904, Suslov in 1902), this new generation of leaders spent its formative years in the party under Stalin, not, like Khrushchev and his generation, under Lenin. The son of a metal worker, Brezhnev studied both land surveying and metallurgy and became an engineer. He was admitted to the party as a full member in 1931, at the height of the collectivization drive, when tough recruits were in great demand. From the late 1930s on Brezhnev gained wide experience in a variety of posts in the Ukraine, Moldavia, Moscow, and Kazakhstan. An ethnic Russian, Brezhnev was born in the northern Ukraine, an area of mixed Ukrainian and Russian population. As party chief in Kazakhstan from 1954 to 1956, he was instrumental in carrying out Khrushchev's virgin lands campaign in its critical formative years. A Central Committee member from 1952, Brezhnev became a full member of the Presidium in Khrushchev's triumphant year of 1957. He was considered a Khrushchev supporter, but alienated by both Khrushchev's failures and methods, Brezhnev played a leading role in deposing his benefactor in 1964.

Khrushchev's fall was accompanied by accusations in the Soviet press that he had been guilty of "hare-brained schemes," "hasty decisions divorced from reality," "bragging and bluster," "attraction to rule by fiat" and more, all of which allegedly led to a rash of domestic and foreign difficulties. Not surprisingly, "dekhrushchevization" was not long in coming. It is symptomatic of how isolated Khrushchev had become that aside from a few of his closest cronies, like his son-in-law, none of the party elite followed its leader down the memory hole. By November 1964 what was generally viewed as Khrushchev's most ill-conceived scheme was undone: the sundered party was reassembled. In September 1965 another Khrushchev cornerstone was uprooted when the *sovnarkhozy* were abolished and the centralized ministerial system for running the economy was restored, while in 1966 his rule requiring the regular turnover of party officials was dropped. Destalinization, at least in terms of expanding cultural and literary freedom, also fell victim to dekhrushchevization. An offensive against literary and cultural expression already was well under way by 1965, as was a quiet campaign to restore at least a part of Stalin's battered reputation.

Overall, however, the first priority for Brezhnev and his colleagues was the faltering Soviet economy. Policies to rejuvenate agriculture included easing restrictions on private plots and livestock holding, expanding the markets in which peasants could sell their privately produced foodstuffs, cancelling debts of poorer collective farms, raising prices for required collective farm deliveries to the state, and reducing prices for industrial products (tractors, trucks, electricity, etc.) the farms required. Equally important, in 1966 collective-farm peasants finally were guaranteed a minimum wage and made eligible for pensions. Investment in agriculture increased considerably, eventually rising to about twenty-seven percent of total investment. This was a fifty percent higher share than Khrushchev, supposedly the great friend of agriculture, had permitted.

All this produced mixed results. Grain output climbed from an average of 88 million tons during 1951–1955 to more than 180 million tons during 1971–1975 and over 200 million tons during 1976–1978. The production of milk, meat, vegetables, and eggs approximately doubled between the early 1950s and the late 1970s. But those apparently glittering figures glossed over some serious weaknesses. Production during the early 1950s was appallingly low. Growth after that reflected massive new investments, not the increased productivity that was so desperately needed. The collectivized and state peasants frequently remained lethargic and in-different workers. Centrally planned investment, its size notwithstanding, continued to neglect such problems as poor roads and inadequate local storage facilities in favor of such grandiose projects as irrigation facilities that caught the eye of those in Moscow but did not answer the peasants' needs. As a result waste continued to plague the system during the 1970s: 20 percent of the fruit and vegetables harvested and at least 25 percent of the potato crop spoiled before it was consumed. Equally serious, the initially impressive 21 percent growth in agricultural production achieved under Brezhnev from 1966 to 1970 dropped to 13 percent from 1971 to 1975 and to 9 percent from 1976 to 1980. Poor weather added to the losses and shortfalls in 1965, 1969, 1971, 1972, 1974, 1975, and each year between 1978 to 1982, helping to make massive grain imports a permanent part of Soviet life.

A major reform effort was also made in the industrial sector. The goals were the same as with agriculture: increased productivity and reduced waste and inefficiency. This effort was supervised by Kosygin, an able and experienced administrator who held responsibility for the economy as a whole. Kosygin's reforms reflected discussions that had begun under Khrushchev, particularly concerning the ideas of economist Evsie Liberman. Liberman had advocated that managers of industrial enterprises be allowed to make decisions in such areas as hiring, the percentage of factory resources devoted to wages, and the mix of goods to produce. A manager's performance would be judged by his factory's profitability. Presumably this would lead to improved quality and efficiency, since in order to be profitable a factory would have to produce goods that customers actually wanted, as opposed to the old system under which a factory received production quotas calculated in terms of quantity, weight, and other easily measurable categories (as well as detailed instructions on whom to hire, what wages to pay, what materials to buy, etc.) and was rewarded simply for meeting those quotas, regardless of whether anybody could *use* the goods produced. The traditional system, of course, often led to quotas being met by shirts without buttons, trucks without starter motors, sheets of steel too heavy for many uses, and the like. The Brezhnev team also set lower and more realistic economic growth targets, both for its first five years and for the subsequent decade.

Despite their sensible provisions, the Kosygin reforms never made it off the ground. Because of the conservatism pervading the power structure, the new methods were not introduced in a wide enough scale to acquire what economist Marshall Goldman has called a "critical mass."[1] Without this critical mass, a factory operating according to the new system inevitably became entangled in the old system. For example, it might want to improve its product by using a new material but would be unable to procure it because no factory was either free to produce it under the Kosygin reforms or authorized to produce it by the central planners. Widespread opposition from party bosses concerned over losing much of their authority hamstrung the reforms, as did the central planners' refusal to allow prices to fluctuate according to the dictates of supply and demand.

The Soviet economy nonetheless managed impressive growth, in part because of the Kosygin reforms and because Brezhnev and his central planners continued to favor heavy industry over light and investment over consumption. Soviet industry in the late 1970s produced seven times more than thirty years before, and the Soviets led the world in such basic items as steel, oil, machine tools, and heavy military hardware. The annual rate of increase in the gross national product even grew from 1965 to 1970 as compared to the previous five years (5.2 percent versus 5 percent).

But then an inexorable decline set in, as the annual growth rate slipped to 3.7 percent from 1970 to 1975 and to 2.7 percent from 1975 to 1980. Innovation lagged; much of the Soviet Union's equipment was obsolete. Also, the Soviet Union did not produce many of the finished industrial goods that in Japan, Western Europe, and the United States were the basis for increased productivity and a far higher standard of living than Soviet citizens knew. Even when the Soviet planners gave preference to consumer goods, as in the Ninth Five-Year Plan covering 1971–1975, complications derailed their good intentions.

Economic stagnation occurred in large part because the revolution's past began to catch up with it. The Brezhnev regime made a serious effort to improve lagging agricultural productivity by giving that sector, for so long subject to Stalin's exploitation and Khrushchev's unworkable panaceas, about 25 percent of all investment funds between 1966 and 1975. But that infusion into agriculture by necessity was a drain on the industrial investment pool. Meanwhile, there was no significant structural reform: the *kolkhoz/sovkhoz* system that largely caused the problem remained a sacred cow, and the agricultural sector remained unable to meet the nation's food needs.

Equally important, the central planning system became increasingly unable to cope with the growing complexity of the Soviet Union's industrial economy. The problem was not simply coordinating the requirements of tens of thousands of individual economic units, each with its own schedule and problems; it included managing the competition among these units and among whole industries and entire regions for resources of all kinds. There was also the vexing inability to introduce new products and technologies into an enormous and unwieldy mechanism, particularly when innovation carried the nightmarish risk that haunted most managers and bureaucrats: the failure to produce the number of units, kilograms, square meters, cubic meters, or whatever was required by the master plan. Another shibboleth of the Stalin era—the primacy of the military—continued to absorb vital human and material resources at a prodigious rate, dragging down growth rates for the economy as a whole. Finally, the Soviet economy was being deprived of two formerly abundant resources upon which it had become dependent: cheap labor and cheap natural resources. The huge pool of cheap labor that had fueled Soviet industrialization began to dry up as urbanization and higher levels of education, themselves products of the revolution, drove down birth rates among Slavs and other European peoples who together formed over 80 percent of the USSR's population. Likewise, the cheap and easily exploitable raw materials west of the Urals that had been so vital to both prewar and postwar economic growth were being depleted. The Soviet Union still possessed enormous natural resources, but many of them—including vital oil and natural gas deposits—were deep in Siberia and required large long-term investments to make them exploitable. In the short term, these investments represented another expensive anchor weighing down the economy as a whole.

Despite these problems, the old Stalinist economic structure still had enough momentum to permit the standard of living to rise from its 1964 level. Real wages rose 50 percent between 1965 and 1977. By the late 1970s, the majority of Soviet families owned radios, refrigerators, and even washing machines. Yet, just as the overall economic growth rate declined, so did the growth rate in the standard of living. In 1981 per capita consumption grew by less than 2 percent; the 1982 figure was 1 percent. The housing situation remained unsatisfactory, to say the least; in 1981 the Soviets could not meet minimum standards that had been set by the government in 1928. In 1981 20 percent of all urban families still shared kitchen and bathroom facilities. Repair and personal care services remained exceedingly difficult to obtain. Between 1965 and 1978, the percentage of the budget devoted to health care actually dropped, this in the face of increased need. Soviet infant mortality rates *increased* during the 1970s, and the Soviet Union gained the dubious distinction of being the first industrialized country to see its life expectancy drop. Worst of all, Soviet per capita consumption in the late 1970s remained one-third that of the United States and less than half that of France and West Germany. Another bitter truth was that the economy's best postwar performance in terms of per-year growth was during 1951–1955, *before* most of the reforms, experiments, and efforts of the Khrushchev and Brezhnev years. Finally, what made all the post-1950 consumption figures look so good was the abysmally low standard of living in the immediate postwar era. In short, the performance of the Soviet economy under Brezhnev was impressive for a developing country, but not for an advanced socialist society, which the Soviet Union claimed to be.

If the Brezhnev record was mixed regarding economic performance, it was clear and consistent when it came to intellectual and cultural freedom. Destalinization was over. In 1965 a few ripples of the receding destalinization tide continued to wash up on Soviet shores: a collection of Boris Pasternak's poems; Alexander Nekrich's *June 22, 1941*, an expose of the devastating effects of Stalin's purges on the Soviet military prior to World War II; and the release of poet Joseph Brodsky after having served two years of his five-year sentence. However, these ripples were swamped by a far stronger and growing tide. Several months before Nekrich's book appeared, influential figures in both the military and political bureaucracies, worried that the debunking of Stalin also had undermined the party's authority, began to press for Stalin's rehabilitation. Brezhnev himself was a prime mover in this campaign. At the same time, much of what Khrushchev had washed away could not be restored. Several important intellectuals protested directly to Brezhnev about any further rehabilitation of Stalin, while the party itself was deeply divided on the issue. The result was a typical Brezhnev compromise. Stalin was not rehabilitated at the Twenty-Third Congress (March–April 1966) as had been rumored. The congress did revive two terms from the Stalin era, however, as Brezhnev was designated the *general* secretary and the Presidium became the Politburo. Stalin once again was called an outstanding party leader, albeit one with some faults. Eventually a bust was placed over his grave.

Whatever precise things were done or said about Stalin personally, the most dramatic events that set the limits to destalinization involved other names. In September 1965 two writers, Andrei Siniavsky and Yuli Daniel, were arrested. Their "crime" was having published abroad (under the pseudonyms Abram Tertz and Nikolai Arzhak, respectively) literature critical of the Soviet Union. These arrests sent out a shock wave, as these men were under attack simply for their writing, not for any overt act of defiance. Siniavsky and Daniel followed the dramatic precedent set by Brodsky by refusing to admit any guilt. They were sentenced to seven and five years at hard labor, respectively.

These sentences stunned the intellectual community, but what followed surely must have stunned the Soviet leadership even more. The specter of Stalinism revived was too much for many intellectuals and even ordinary citizens to stand. Despite the fear of harsh reprisals, they engaged in an unheard of response—public protest. Not only such well-known writers as Solzhenitsyn and Yevtushenko, but also prominent figures across the spectrum of Soviet intellectual, cultural, and even scientific life signed petitions of protest. Among them was Andrei Sakharov, the father of the Soviet hydrogen bomb. Many others of humbler status joined in with protests of their own. It mattered little that at the Twenty-Third Congress Brezhnev denounced the protesters, that others soon followed Siniavsky and Daniel into prison or exile, or that the regime quickly added two new articles (190–1 and 190–3) to the criminal code of the Russian Soviet Federated Socialist Republic (RSFSR) to use against dissenters. Soviet intellectuals cherished the small gains that had been made between 1953 and 1964 and hoped to expand them. The end of Stalin's terror meant that those with extraordinary courage might speak out and survive. Vocal dissent certainly exposed its practitioners to the threat of harassment or arrest, but the days of untrammeled secret police arrests for the slightest offense—real, suspected, or imagined—were over. Under these new, if hardly benign, conditions, the attempt to strangle the budding efforts at self-expression gave birth instead to the dissident movement.

This phenomenon has been designated a "movement" for lack of a better word. In reality it was a diffuse, diverse, and disorganized flotilla of largely self-contained vessels, sometimes cooperating, frequently operating independently, often with radically different goals, and sometimes even at odds. Although that flotilla had lacked a flagship, various distinguished intellectuals provided it with a series of beacons, most prominent among them being Sakharov, Solzhenitsyn, and two brothers, Roy and Zhores Medvedev. An important common link among the various dissident groups was the remarkable phenomenon of *samizdat* (literally "self-publication"), the underground publication of materials that developed into an invaluable source of information about the movement, both for the dissidents themselves and for their sympathizers in the West. The most important of these was the *Chronicle of Current Events*. It first came out in 1968 as a bimonthly, was suppressed in 1972 (along with another important journal, the *Ukrainian Herald*) and was successfully revived in 1974. Many other *samizdat* journals appeared across the Soviet Union espousing various causes for varying periods of time, literally thousands of documents. These were supplemented by writings smuggled to the West and published there without official authorization (*tamizdat*) and illegal tape recordings of songs for secret distribution at home (*magnitizdat*).

The two outstanding individuals of the dissident movement were Andrei Sakharov and Aleksandr Solzhenitsyn. Ironically, despite their towering stature as individuals, their deep disagreements and the difficulties they shared in reaching the Russian people made them symbolic of the weakness of dissident movement as a whole. Sakharov, a modern-day "Westerner," advocated reform of Soviet society along Western democratic lines. His 1968 manifesto, "Thoughts on Progress, Peaceful Coexistence, and Intellectual Freedom," called for freedom of thought and expression and a multiparty system in the Soviet Union. Sakharov warned that without these freedoms the Soviet Union would decline into a second-rate power. Two years later he was one of the founders (with Valery Chalidze and Andrei Tverdokhlebov) of the Moscow Committee for Human Rights. He vigorously supported the right of Jews to emigrate from the Soviet Union. In 1975 he was awarded the Nobel Peace Prize, which Soviet authorities prevented him from accepting. Aside from harassment, some of it quite cruel and damaging to both his and his wife's health, Sakharov temporarily remained immune from the more severe punishments generally handed out to other dissidents because of his international reputation. In 1980, however, he was arrested and exiled to Gorky, a city several hundred miles from Moscow and closed to foreigners.

Solzhenitsyn, a towering figure blessed with equal measures of literary talent and personal courage, took it upon himself to assault the entire Soviet system, not just as it stood but all the way down to its Leninist roots. This he did with thunderous power in masterpieces like his novels *The First Circle* and *The Cancer Ward* and his devastating history of the Soviet labor camp system, *The Gulag Archipelago* (none of these works were published in the Soviet Union until the late 1980s). Unlike Sakharov, however, Solzhenitsyn did not look to the West as a model for reform. A classic Slavophile, Solzhenitsyn urged his country to return to what he considered its ancient Russian roots. Western influences, Marxism being the most pernicious, would be banished in favor of values derived from Russia's Orthodox and peasant traditions. Solzhenitsyn, like Sakharov, was protected by his international reputation for a time. Then he became such a painful thorn that the Soviet authorities, while not daring to arrest him, seized him in 1974, put him on a plane, and banished him to the West, a fate that Solzhenitsyn at times may have considered worse than prison in his beloved native land.

Dissent in the multinational Soviet Union inevitably also reflected the suppressed aspirations of non-Russian ethnic nationalities and groups. The deep wellspring of national feeling in the Ukraine again bubbled to the surface in the 1960s. Ukrainian intellectuals protested, among other things, Russification and pervasive discrimination. Given the Ukrainians' status as the Soviet Union's second most populous nationality (after the Great Russians) and the region's immense strategic and economic importance, the regime cracked down hard. Among the many who went to prison between the mid-1960s and the early 1970s were Ivan Dziuba (author of *Internationalism or Russification?*), Viacheslav Chornovil (who chronicled the persecution of Ukrainian dissidents), and Valentin Moroz (author of *A Report from the Beria Reservation*, an expose of the shocking conditions in the post-Stalin labor camps). Higher up the ladder, Piotr Shelest, the Ukrainian party first secretary, was removed from office in 1971 for failing to suppress local nationalist sentiment. The Ukrainian pattern was repeated in other national republics. The problem was the most serious in the Baltic republics (there were a dozen *samizdat* journals at one point in Lithuania alone) and in the Caucasus.

Dissent also took on a religious cast. Roman Catholicism had a number of clashes with the regime, particularly in largely Catholic Lithuania where religious faith was mixed with national feeling. Some Protestant groups pushed for religious freedom, the most active of them being the Baptists.

A few stirrings even occurred within the usually pliant and somewhat privileged Russian Orthodox Church, but these were rather small and easily contained, largely by the Church hierarchy itself.

The most successful of all dissident groups was the Jewish movement. The Jews owed their surprising success to several factors. They received support from Jewish communities abroad, the most influential of which was in the United States, as well as from dissidents at home, like Sakharov. They were unified by the achievements of the state of Israel (first and foremost by its very existence but also due to its triumphs in the 1967 and 1973 wars against far larger, Soviet-supported Arab armies) and because of ever-present anti-Semitic harassment at home. The crucial point, however, is that most Jewish dissidents were not primarily concerned with changing Soviet society; their goal simply was to leave it. Most of the movement's founders and leaders were eager to emigrate to an Israel equally eager to welcome them. Having a country willing to accept them also distinguished the Jews from most groups trying to win the right to emigrate and was another helpful element. Aided especially by United States pressure at a time when the Soviet government wanted improved relations with the West, Soviet Jews succeeded in convincing the Brezhnev regime to let many go. Over 200,000 Jews left the Soviet Union during the 1970s. But even this small success was highly qualified. Hundreds of thousands of others who also wanted to emigrate were either denied permission to leave, prevented from applying, or intimidated from applying in the first place. Meanwhile, renewed difficulties in Soviet-American relations led the Soviets to reduce the emigration flow. A major problem developed in 1974, when the Americans adopted legislation requiring a formal Soviet commitment to continued high levels of Jewish emigration in return for Soviet-desired liberalization of the 1972 American-Soviet trade agreement. The Soviets denounced the trade agreement and curtailed emigration considerably. After a brief revival in the late 1970s (a peak of 50,000 emigrants was reached in 1979), deteriorating Soviet-American relations contributed to Soviet reduction of the flow to a trickle by the early 1980s.

As a whole, the Soviet dissidents had occasional spurts of activity and some small successes. Periodically a dramatic event led to an upsurge in activity. The 1968 Soviet invasion of Czechoslovakia, for example, exerted a powerful influence on Sakharov and others working for democratic reform. Many dissidents interested in democratic reform or in emigration found renewed vigor when the Soviet Union signed the Helsinki Accords in August 1975, which pledged all signatories to guarantee a broad range of human rights to their citizens. "Helsinki Watch Groups" were formed in several Soviet cities after the accords were signed. More frequently, however, state repression debilitated the movement as dissidents were sent to prison, "exported" abroad, or left the Soviet Union by choice.

However, the most fundamental reason for the movement's precarious status was that aside from a few examples where the dissidents had had an ethnic base and a very limited goal (e.g., as with the Jewish movement or the movement of ethnic Germans to immigrate to West Germany), the dissident movement, particularly the segment interested in democratic reform, could not reach a wide audience. The barriers of traditional Russian apathy in the face of authority, the strength of the KGB and other organs of repression, and the enormous social gap separating Soviet intellectuals from the average Soviet citizen were insurmountable. During the early 1980s dissident activity was at a low ebb. By then most of the well-known dissidents were out of commission. Many were in prison or internal exile—people like Sakharov, Yuri Orlov, Alexander Ginzburg, Anatoly Shcharansky, and Yuri Galanskov (who died in a labor camp due to lack of proper medical care). Others were abroad, some having gone directly (such as Solzhenitsyn and Chalidze), some leaving after serving prison terms (Siniavsky, Vladimir Bukovsky, and others).

Yet dissidence continued to exist. Often a nuisance, at times an embarrassment, always a source of discomfiture, the dissident movement under Brezhnev became something like a chronic but narrowly confined case of social psoriasis on the Soviet body politic, unable either to spread outward or bore inward and thereby become an immediate threat, but short of amputation à la Stalin, not subject to complete eradication either.

None of these problems, of course, were reflected in the new Soviet constitution adopted in 1977. It proclaimed that the Soviet Union was a "developed socialist society" in which "All power . . . belongs to the people." The new document, which replaced Stalin's 1936 constitution, also contained a long list of economic and political rights due each Soviet citizen. These included the peasantry's right to farm private plots and the right of all citizens to engage in strictly limited private economic activity. Most significantly, however, the 1977 constitution made the Communist Party the final arbiter of virtually everything of importance, including whether individual Soviet citizens could actually enjoy their constitutionally mandated rights. Unlike the 1936 constitution, which did not emphasize the party, the 1977 document stressed the role of the party as the predominant force in the Soviet Union. Overall, the new constitution, its genuflections to Marxism notwithstanding, did not reflect the Marxist ideal of the state withering away, but the older Russian tradition of the state waxing stronger and controlling society.

While the Soviet state was bringing its power to bear on its citizens, it also was building up its strength against its foreign rivals, particularly the United States. Soviet defense spending grew at an annual rate adjusted for inflation of about 4 percent from 1964 to 1976. Thereafter the rate of growth dropped to a still-impressive 2 percent per year. Despite that decline, approximately 25 percent of the Soviet Union's gross national product was devoted to the military (versus the American figure of 6 percent). About half of all Soviet industrial enterprises and between one-half and three-quarters of their scientific and technical personnel were linked in one way or another to the military effort. By 1981, Soviet defense dollar outlays were 45 percent higher than those of the United States. The result was that Soviet preponderance in conventional arms increased considerably, at least in quantitative terms. In 1981, for example, the Warsaw Pact had more than three times more main battle tanks, three times more artillery and mortars, and over three-and-a-half times more armored personnel carriers and infantry fighting vehicles than did NATO. At the same time, the American strategic nuclear superiority that had loomed so large during the Cuban Missile Crisis was overcome. By the late 1970s, the Soviets led the Americans in the number of ICBMs, submarine-launched missiles, nuclear submarines, and in total nuclear megatonage, although the United States continued to lead in the total number of nuclear warheads and in the accuracy and quality of their missiles. Meanwhile, the Soviet navy developed from an essentially coastal force under Stalin and Khrushchev into a major vehicle for projecting Soviet power worldwide by means of long-range submarines and aircraft carriers.

The direct military effort was complemented by a comprehensive space program. While the Soviets could not match the American achievement of manned lunar landings, their program did manage several impressive "firsts" while providing valuable technological services to the military. Overall, the military sphere was one area where Brezhnev and his colleagues could claim to have achieved a resounding success, although they probably preferred not to mention the burden the military effort placed on the Soviet people and the damage it did to their inefficient and overtaxed economy.

Under Brezhnev, as under Stalin and Khrushchev, the Soviet Union's major foreign policy concern remained the United States. Despite their ideological hostility, other considerations, such as the threat of nuclear catastrophe, the mounting burden of the arms race, and the difficulties each superpower was having with third parties (the Soviets were becoming increasingly worried about Communist China) impelled them to seek some sort of accommodation, or "détente." The path to détente was not a smooth one, and at its best détente did little more than take the edge off a sharp and dangerous rivalry.

Détente actually was the culmination of a period of improving Soviet-American relations. In 1967, after a meeting between President Lyndon Johnson and Premier Kosygin in Glassboro, New Jersey, the superpowers had signed a treaty to prevent the spread of nuclear weapons. In 1969 they began their Strategic Arms Limitation Talks (SALT). These talks bore their first fruit after President Richard M. Nixon's visit to the Soviet Union in 1972. In their 1972 treaty (SALT I) the United States and the USSR agreed to limit the deployment of antiballistic missile systems and to an interim ceiling on strategic nuclear missiles. Other positive signs during 1972 and 1973 included the large Soviet purchases of American wheat, a dramatic increase in overall trade with the West, and Brezhnev's June 1973 visit to the United States.

There nonetheless remained many sources of tension between the two superpowers. The most serious difficulties resulted from the American effort to maintain an anti-Communist government in South Vietnam while the Soviets backed the Communist North Vietnamese regime and Communist insurgency against the American-backed government in the south. The Americans and Soviets also clashed in the strategic and oil-rich Middle East as they backed opposite sides in both the 1967 and 1973 Arab-Israeli wars. Then, in 1973 the Americans, suffering from deep and painful wounds, withdrew from Vietnam, and the pace of détente, which had been progressing slowly for several years, began to quicken.

The next several years marked the high-water mark of détente. In June 1974 President Nixon returned to the Soviet Union, and in November (after Nixon was forced from office by the Watergate scandal), President Gerald Ford and Brezhnev met in the Siberian city of Vladivostok and signed the second phase of the SALT I agreements, which limited each power to 2,400 strategic nuclear missiles and bombers. The two powers even met in space when an American Apollo space vehicle docked with a Soviet Soyuz craft in July 1975. In August, the Soviets and Americans, along with more than thirty other nations, signed the Helsinki Accords. These finalized the post–World War II boundary changes in Europe, a long-time Soviet goal. All signatories also agreed to respect a list of basic human rights, something that would cause the Soviets some subsequent embarrassment but which seemed a small price to pay in return for the legitimization of their postwar expansion.

Détente did not prove to be very durable. The 1974 flap over Jewish emigration and trade led the Soviets to cancel a number of agreements along with the trade agreement in question. Soviet intervention in Angola via its Cuban proxies and, more importantly, its direct 1979 invasion of Afghanistan (which soon tied down over 100,000 troops) left détente in a shambles. Among the casualties were the SALT II agreements initialed by both parties in June 1979 but never ratified by the U.S. Senate. The United States then led a boycott of the 1980 Moscow Olympics, a gesture that provided more insult than injury. Relations reached a new postdétente low in December 1981 when, under immense pressure from Moscow, the Polish government proclaimed martial law and forcibly disbanded the independent labor movement, Solidarity, which in 1980 had grown out of a massive series of strikes to become the first independent union in the history of the Soviet bloc.

Aside from capitalist America, Communist China caused the Soviet Union the most problems. A short-lived Soviet attempt to patch up relations immediately after Khrushchev's fall ended in failure. In 1965 the Soviet Union requested military facilities and air transit rights in China to aid in support of North Vietnam. The Chinese refused. Then came Mao's "Cultural Revolution," a rabid attack on everything Mao felt was hindering China's march to communism. a rogues' gallery that included Soviet "revisionism." China was thrown into bloody turmoil for three years. The Cultural Revolution was framed by China's refusal to attend the Twenty-Third Congress of the CPSU in 1966 and the bloody border incidents that erupted along the Chinese-Soviet frontier in 1969. To make matters worse, the Americans and the Chinese began to develop a détente of their own. Henry Kissinger's secret trip to Peking in July 1971 was followed by the United States dropping its objections to the Peking regime's admission to the United Nations and assumption of the "China" seat in the Security Council formerly held by the Nationalist regime on Taiwan. In 1972 President Nixon made a landmark visit to the People's Republic. In 1979 normal Chinese-American diplomatic relations were established after thirty years of American refusal to recognize the Beijing regime.

Meanwhile, Soviet-Chinese relations had failed to improve. The most successful Soviet effort vis-à-vis the Chinese involved improving relations with China's neighbors. In August 1971, Moscow signed a treaty of friendship with India; in November the Soviets backed India in its successful war against Pakistan. Continued economic aid further solidified Soviet-Indian relations. Moscow also successfully wooed two Communist states that bordered on China—Mongolia and North Korea—and worked to improve relations with Japan. But the Soviet refusal to return four small islands seized from Japan at the end of World War II remained a thorn in their relations, as was the improvement in Sino-Japanese relations that occurred in the late 1970s.

The Sino-Soviet rivalry was further reflected in the intracommunist conflicts that engulfed southeast Asia after the American withdrawal from South Vietnam. The 1975 communist victory in South Vietnam had led to a pro-Soviet regime in all of Vietnam. This was not surprising since Vietnam has traditionally feared China, its huge neighbor to the north. However, the communist victory in Cambodia (renamed Kampuchea) that same year led to a pro-Chinese regime there; the Cambodians feared their traditional rival and powerful neighbor—Vietnam. 1979 witnessed a Vietnamese invasion of Kampuchea in order to oust the pro-Chinese regime (which had slaughtered perhaps one-eighth of the country's population in its campaign to build its own version of utopia). But the Vietnamese soon became bogged down in a guerrilla war—their own "Vietnam"—that continued until 1989. China responded to Vietnam's invasion of Kampuchea by starting a short, bloody war of its own with Vietnam. As the war strained and weakened China and turned the Vietnamese increasingly toward Moscow, the Soviet Union benefited. But these benefits were in part offset by China's development of a nuclear arsenal that included hydrogen bombs and a few medium-range ballistic missiles. By 1980, the Chinese had also begun to test intercontinental missiles.

The Soviet Union's difficulties with Communist China stood in contrast to its successes in capitalist Western Europe. After the French President Charles de Gaulle, chafing under American leadership, took his country out of NATO in 1966, Brezhnev responded by inviting him to visit the Soviet Union and making him the first Western head of state to be permitted to visit a Soviet space facility. This was followed by increased French-Soviet economic cooperation that included the French building of a huge truck factory in the Soviet Union. The Soviets also did reasonably well with West Germany. In a series of treaties beginning in 1970, the West Germans accepted the post–World War II boundaries with Poland, renounced the use of force against the Soviet Union, and recognized East Germany. These improved relations with the two most important capitalist nations in continental Europe and the signing of the Helsinki Accords represented a considerable improvement in the Soviet position in Western Europe. So too did the scrapping of the American plan to deploy in Western Europe the so-called neutron bomb—an effective potential counter to the Warsaw Pact's tank superiority over NATO—and the 1982 decision of several of America's NATO allies, anxious to decrease their dangerous dependence on Middle Eastern oil, to help the Soviet Union build a huge natural gas pipeline to transport Soviet gas to customers in the West.

The Soviets did not, however, succeed in breaking up NATO or weakening the Common Market. Instead, it was their influence over the communist parties of Western Europe that began, if not to unravel, then at least to fray around the edges. Widespread general revulsion to the 1968 Soviet invasion of Czechoslovakia damaged the European communist parties. So too did their continued demeaning subservience to the Soviet Union and their adherence to the Soviet doctrine of "proletarian dictatorship," a euphemism that to many Europeans meant police-state oppression and the destruction of political pluralism. The unpleasant result for the Soviets was Eurocommunism. The major European communist parties—the most important being in France, Italy, and Spain—began to stress the right of each nation to chart its own path toward communism, to assert their independence from

Moscow, and to criticize the suppression of human rights in the Soviet bloc.

Whatever the Soviets' problems in Western Europe, at times it seemed that they had more problems in Communist Eastern Europe. During the Brezhnev years the greatest difficulties were in Czechoslovakia and Poland. Czechoslovakia was the only Eastern European country to maintain a democratic form of government during the period between World War I and World War II. The Soviet Union extinguished that lonely flame in 1948, installing in its place a Communist regime that became one of the most brutal and incompetent in Eastern Europe. It remained rigidly Stalinist even when the Soviet Union was changing under Khrushchev. Rigidity finally turned into brittleness, and in 1968 the system cracked under the pressure of a moribund economy and swelling dissent. In January, Antonin Novotny, the old-line local satrap who was both the Communist Party boss and head of state, was removed from his more important position as party first secretary and replaced by Alexander Dubcek, a leading reform advocate.

What followed thrilled many in the West and horrified the Soviets. The reform impulse, fed by Czechoslovakia's lingering democratic tradition, spread with astonishing speed. Novotny was ousted from the presidency in March and replaced by war-hero General Ludvik Svoboda (the general's last name means "freedom" in both Czech and Russian). The new leadership meanwhile abolished censorship, established freedom of the press, committed itself to civil liberties, and took steps to sanction a genuine multiparty political system. Dubcek, unlike the Hungarian Nagy in 1956, went out of his way to assure the Soviet Union that Czechoslovakia would remain a socialist state and member of the Warsaw Pact. But his "socialism with a human face" was a Medusa to Brezhnev and his Politburo; they worried that Czechoslovakian ideas might spread to other Eastern European satellites or even to the Soviet Union and cause incalculable damage. On August 20, 1968, after neither pressure nor threats could turn Dubcek around, Czechoslovakia was invaded by 400,000 Soviet, East German, Hungarian, Polish, and Bulgarian troops. The West was outraged, as were many European communists and Soviet dissidents. None of that helped Czechoslovakia.

The matter did not stop with the successful invasion. The entire Soviet bloc was promptly informed that the Soviet Union would use force to eliminate any threats to "the course of socialism." This "Brezhnev doctrine" thus proclaimed the impossibility of any fundamental change within the Soviet bloc, as well as the impossibility of secession from it.

The Czechoslovakian episode did not put an end to Soviet problems in Eastern Europe. Communist Albania, a tiny state protected from Soviet military forces by Yugoslavia to its east, continued to support Communist China in the increasingly bitter Sino-Soviet conflict. There also was trouble with Romania. That state, which bordered on the Soviet Union, was ruled by the ruthless Nicolae Ceausescu. Ceausescu maintained an orthodox and repressive Communist dictatorship. No Soviet troops had been stationed in Romania, and Ceausescu refused to permit the Soviets to correct the oversight, using it instead to establish a small measure of independence for his country. Romania was the only Communist state to maintain diplomatic relations with Israel after the 1967 Six-Day War. It refused to participate in the invasion of Czechoslovakia or even to permit Warsaw Pact troops to cross Romanian territory in order to enter Czechoslovakia. The Romanians leaned toward Yugoslavia and China on certain intra-Communist issues and consistently resisted Soviet attempts at closer integration of the Soviet and other Warsaw Pact economies. Romanian intransigence, however, did not prevent the Soviet Union from reinforcing its control over most of its Eastern European satellites. Its main methods were increased integration of various Communist-bloc economies through COMECON (the Council of Mutual Economic Assistance) and increased military integration under the aegis of the Warsaw Pact.

The most notable exception to almost everything was Poland, a country that never accepted tsarist or Soviet domination despite an almost unbroken string of bitter disappointments in numerous attempts to reestablish its independence over the past two centuries. In 1970 incompetence and repression produced food riots that led to Gomulka's dismissal. As the Soviets watched, nervous but menacing, Gomulka was replaced by another functionary, Edward Gierek. Matters stayed under control for a decade, although the Polish government continued to mismanage the economy and alienate its people. In 1980, their poverty standing in ever-starker contrast to the privilege of the utterly corrupted Communist Party, the Polish people could stand no more. Widespread riots centered in the industrial city of Gdansk raged out of control. Eventually they led to something unknown in the Soviet bloc since the earliest days of the Bolshevik Revolution: a genuine trade union. Called "Solidarity," the union was born in the Lenin Shipyards in Gdansk. It was led by Lech Walesa, an electrician who became a national hero. "Solidarity" soon numbered 8 million out of a population of 30 million and clearly had the support of most of the Polish people. Again the Soviets threatened invasion, holding back largely because they feared armed Polish resistance. The Polish Communist Party was virtually paralyzed. The best it could do was replace Gierek with Stanislaw Kania, another undistinguished functionary, and then replace Kania with Wojciech Jaruzelski, an army general who also served as defense minister and prime minister. Soviet pressure finally got Jaruzelski to do the necessary dirty work. In December 1981 he declared martial law, arrested Solidarity's leaders, and drove what was left of the union underground. The best anyone in the West could do was to award Walesa the Nobel Peace Prize in 1983.

Jaruzelski's actions were doubly welcome to the Soviets, for the last thing they needed was a bloody invasion of Poland on their hands. By 1980 they were involved in a costly intervention in Afghanistan, a Moslem country bordering on largely Moslem Soviet Central Asia. The Soviets had sponsored a successful Communist coup in Afghanistan in 1978, but by 1979 popular resistance had put the entire venture in deep trouble. Moscow responded in 1979 by invading. They met such determined resistance that at Brezhnev's death in 1982 an army of over 100,000 Soviet troops (the Afghan "army" was virtually useless, with unwilling recruits deserting faster than they could be replaced) still struggled to prop up a regime seriously lacking in popular support.

Despite its troubles in Poland and Afghanistan, the Soviet Union after 1964 found the resources to engage in a far-ranging foreign policy. The Soviets were active in the Middle East, where their goal was to weaken Western influence in the region containing the world's largest oil reserves. They therefore supported the twenty-one Arab states, authoritarian regimes that ranged from reactionary sheikdoms to radical one-party Marxist dictatorships, and the Palestine Liberation Organization (PLO) against Israel, even though the Soviets, unlike the PLO and the Arab states, recognized Israel's right to exist. Soviet support of the Palestine Liberation Organization and the radical regime of Muammar Kaddafi in Libya strengthened destabilizing forces in the region. This threatened such oil-rich but politically fragile Arab states as Saudi Arabia, Kuwait, and the United Arab Emirates upon which the Western powers and Japan were so dependent for energy supplies. Along with Marxist South Yemen, Soviet influence was particularly strong in Iraq and Syria, the recipients of huge quantities of arms, although both those countries effectively and brutally suppressed local communists. A major setback occurred in Egypt, however, when Egyptian President Anwar Sadat, fearing excessive Soviet influence in his country, reversed his predecessor's policy and expelled 20,000 Soviet advisors in 1972. Sadat then oriented his country toward the West, particularly the United States. After yet another war with Israel in 1973, Sadat in 1979 made Egypt the first (and until Jordan became the second in 1995 the only) Arab state to sign a peace treaty with Israel, further increasing American influence in the region at the Soviets' expense.

The year 1979 did, however, witness a significant gain for the Soviet Union in the Middle East when an Islamic fundamentalist revolution led by the Ayatollah Khomeini overthrew the pro-American regime of the Shah of Iran. The fanatical Khomeini regime was hardly pro-Soviet, but Khomeini's victory in Iran, by replacing the Shah with a virulently anti-American regime, did weaken American influence in the Middle East and along the Soviet Union's southern frontier.

Sub-Saharan Africa, a region of desperately poor countries torn by tribal and ethnic conflict, provided a setting for Soviet advances during the Brezhnev years. The foundations of Soviet policy had been laid by Khrushchev, who established good relations with three rulers of newly independent nations—Kwame Nkrumah of Ghana, Sékou Touré of Guinea, and Modibo Keita of Mali—though Nkrumah (in 1966) and Keita (in 1968) were subsequently overthrown. The region's many conflicts and the dissolution of the Portuguese sub-Saharan empire—the last Western colonial empire in Africa—created new openings for Soviet initiatives. Over 15,000 Cuban troops enabled the pro-Soviet faction to win a three-way civil war in the former Portuguese colony of Angola in 1976, while a Marxist regime established itself in another major former Portuguese colony, Mozambique. The Soviets enjoyed brief influence in Somalia, a Moslem nation on the strategic Horn of Africa, upon the signing of a treaty of friendship and cooperation in 1974. Three years later, however, the Somalian president Siad Barre, upset over Soviet aid to the newly-installed Marxist regime in neighboring Ethiopia, abrogated the treaty. The Soviets thereupon increased aid to Ethiopia, including large numbers of Cuban troops. Moscow also built bridges to several other sub-Saharan countries. Though the rapidly shifting winds of sub-Saharan politics precluded guarantees of longevity for any alliances or agreements, Brezhnev and his colleagues could take credit for making the Soviet Union a significant factor in that region for the first time.

Soviet foreign policy under Brezhnev also found new vistas in Latin America, the United States' backyard. In 1960 the Soviets had relations with three Latin American nations and trade of 70 million dollars; by 1980 this had expanded to diplomatic relations with nineteen nations and trade of over one billion dollars, including large wheat purchases from Argentina that helped minimize the United States grain embargo against Moscow after the 1979 Soviet invasion of Afghanistan. The prize catch remained Cuba, which in return for massive Soviet aid to prop up its sagging economy provided troops and technicians to support pro-Soviet regimes and forces not only in Latin America, but in the Middle East and Africa. Another source of satisfaction was Nicaragua, where Marxist Sandinista rebels deposed the Somoza dictatorship and established a pro-Soviet regime in 1979. The Soviets did suffer two major setbacks in Latin America, however: the failure of Castro's attempt to export his revolution to Bolivia in 1967 and the 1973 United States-sponsored overthrow of the government of Salvador Allende, an independent socialist who had been elected president of Chile with communist support.

During the Brezhnev years, then, the Soviet Union's role in world affairs continued to grow. In its relations with the United States, Moscow could take satisfaction in having overcome America's nuclear superiority, while also signing arms limitation agreements with the Nixon and Ford administrations. However, relations chilled noticeably during the latter part of the Carter administration, and became positively frigid during Brezhnev's last two years, when the Soviets were dealing with the administration of President Ronald Reagan. Overall, Soviet foreign policy under Brezhnev had its successes (improved relations with West Germany and France, the establishment of pro-Soviet regimes in Angola, Mozambique, Ethiopia, South Yemen, and Nicaragua) and failures (continued difficulties with Eastern Europe, Afghanistan, and the People's Republic of China, the anti-Soviet developments in Egypt and Somalia) on a worldwide scale. Only the United States could match the Soviet Union in world influence, an unprecedented achievement in the history of the Russian state. But such grandeur abroad had been bought at a high price at home in terms of unmet human needs, untreated social and economic ills, and unimplemented reforms. Brezhnev left it to his successors to pay that price.

NOTE

1. Marshall Goldman, *USSR in Crisis* (New York: W. W. Norton, 1983), p. 49.

18

Andropov and Chernenko: The Waning of the Old Guard

Wandering between two worlds
one dead,
The other powerless to be born.

————MATTHEW ARNOLD

On November 10, 1982, Leonid Brezhnev, in bad health for years and increasingly enfeebled, died of a heart attack. In what was considered by many in the Soviet Union as a triumph for the system, it took only fifty-four hours for Yuri Andropov to emerge as Brezhnev's successor. But the smooth succession from Brezhnev to Andropov did nothing to solve a far bigger succession crisis—the transfer of power from one generation to another. The generation that had ruled the Soviet Union since Stalin's death had become a gerontocracy as well as an oligarchy, a development that owed much to Brezhnev's stress on stability. Between 1964 and 1982, this meant not only maintaining a coalition of various bureaucratic interests but keeping the same people in their posts. While under Khrushchev 62 percent of the Central Committee was reelected at the Twentieth Congress and only 49 percent at the Twenty-Second Congress, under Brezhnev the figures rose to 79 percent at the Twenty-Third Congress, 76.5 at the Twenty-Fourth Congress, and 83.4 percent at the Twenty-Fifth Congress. By 1980, the average age of the Politburo membership had climbed to seventy years, as against fifty-five in 1952 and sixty-one in 1964. Just before Brezhnev died in office, his septuagenarian colleagues Kosygin and

Suslov died, the former just after his retirement and the latter in office. By 1982 Brezhnev's foreign minister, Andrei Gromyko, his defense minister, Dmitri Ustinov, and his prime minister, Nikolai Tikhonov, were all in their mid- or late seventies.

Andropov, at sixty-eight, was only seven years younger than his predecessor. Nonetheless, the party at least had a tough and intelligent functionary as its new general secretary. An authentic product of the purges, Andropov rose rapidly through the ranks of the Komsomol during the worst years of Stalin's bloodletting and became a member of the Communist Party in 1939. His early years as a local party functionary in Karelia, a region bordering on Finland, were distinguished by a close association with the secret police in managing the Gulag forced-labor system. Andropov subsequently became ambassador to Hungary, where he actively participated in crushing the 1956 uprising. In 1957 he was transferred to Moscow to head the Central Committee's foreign affairs department and in 1962 became a Central Committee secretary, an important increase in power. After supporting Brezhnev in the post-Khrushchev struggle for power, he was appointed head of the KGB in 1967. He served in that post for fifteen years, upgrading its sophistication, the quality of its personnel, and its overall capabilities. It was under Andropov that the KGB first recruited top university students and developed new and less visibly brutal tactics for dealing with dissidents—including "exporting" them abroad instead of resorting to the criminal trials and harsh sentences that often antagonized the West. His entry into the party's ruling circle came in 1973, when he was elected a full member of the Politburo.

During Brezhnev's declining years Andropov used his position at the KGB to undermine the general secretary and his inner circle, mainly by circulating embarrassing stories about corruption in high places. Andropov positioned himself for an eventual bid for power when he gave up his KGB post and took over the powerful ideology portfolio in the Secretariat after Suslov's death early in 1982. Having also cultivated allies in the military and among other important interest groups, Andropov won the top job in November of that year over Konstantin Chernenko, the man Brezhnev preferred as his successor.

Andropov came to power in a Soviet Union suffering from poor leadership and inertia. In his last infirm years Brezhnev could not respond to such problems as an economy and a standard of living that had been stagnant since 1976. He used what energy he had to support the expanding Soviet military establishment and a coalition of bureaucratic interests essential to overall political stability. Corruption grew enormously in those days, reaching even to Brezhnev's own family; his daughter was implicated in schemes involving diamond smuggling, bribery, and currency speculation.

The new general secretary was expected to change all this. One of his first actions was to launch a campaign to prove that a new age of efficiency and honesty had dawned. Shoppers taking time off from work were arrested. Andropov even sent his police into the Moscow public baths and bars to collar delinquent workers. Thousands of people involved in illegal economic activities as well as corrupt officials were arrested, and a number of harsh sentences, including capital punishment, were handed out for corruption. Andropov also started a well-publicized propaganda campaign to spur productivity.

There were a few signs that thought was being given to genuine changes in how to run the country. During 1983 a plan surfaced to allow farmers more freedom to raise livestock on their private plots. An up-and-coming young Politburo member named Mikhail Gorbachev made a speech suggesting the state use long-term contracts to encourage increased peasant productivity. A new law permitted for some worker input in industrial management through so-called workers' collectives. Most far-reaching was a document called the "Novosibirsk Report" put together by a group of academics based in that western Siberian city. The report, which was leaked to an American journalist, was shockingly blunt. It urged a "restructuring that would reflect fundamental changes" in the economy and a greater reliance on "market relations," code words for a free market. Although the report caused a sensation, it produced no immediate policy changes. Andropov continued to stress "socialist discipline," essentially using the old stick rather than a new carrot to get Soviet citizens to increase their efforts at work and to toe the line in all their other pursuits. Repression of dissidents became even more severe than under Brezhnev, while Jewish emigration fell to less than one thousand per year.

The one area where there was significant renewal was in political life. Death and retirement removed some of Brezhnev's old cronies and allowed Andropov to promote to the aged Politburo three younger men who averaged in their spry late fifties. One level down the ladder, Yegor Ligachev, the efficient, reformist-minded Tomsk regional first secretary, became one of several new Central Committee secretaries, while major personnel changes took place in the Secretariat apparatus and the Council of Ministers. One-fifth of the Central Committee was removed. Aided by Gorbachev and Ligachev, who functioned like two political archangels around the general secretary's throne, Andropov replaced about one-fifth of the regional party secretaries, the work proceeding apace even as Andropov's kidneys were failing and he was confined to a sick bed.

Andropov's efforts helped to give the economy a temporary boost in 1983. Industrial output rose by 4 percent, and a large jump in investment in modern technology (including a doubling of investments in industrial robots) testified to a more vigorous campaign to bring the economy up to date. Agriculture showed some improvement from its dismal 1982 performance, as overall output rose by 10 percent and grain output by 20 percent. Yet all this was hardly cause for rejoicing. Most of the increases were attributable to better weather, including a mild winter, rather than to any systematic improvements in the economy. Although grain production rose from 180 million to 200 million metric tons, the total was far short of the official target of 238 million tons. Meanwhile, in the vital oil industry production actually declined during the last quarter of 1983.

Equally troublesome, Andropov's much heralded program designed to increase factory efficiency by giving managers more authority and incentives proved to be quite limited in scope, far more limited, in fact, than the Kosygin reforms of the 1960s. The new workers' collectives that were supposed to participate in industrial management had little power. There was entrenched and powerful opposition to even these limited reforms. It also proved impossible, even for the ubiquitous Soviet police, to end the absenteeism and lax work habits of tens of millions of workers. They soon reverted to their old ways that reflected the motto: "They pretend to pay, we pretend to work."

Much of Andropov's energy was diverted by foreign affairs crises in Afghanistan, Lebanon, Central America and the Caribbean. In Afghanistan, the war against anti-Communist Moslem rebels dragged on as Western commentators began to refer to the Soviet Union's "Vietnam." In the Middle East, the Soviets easily and cheaply checkmated American peacemaking efforts in Lebanon by providing diplomatic and military backing to the Syrians, who desired *de facto* if not *de jure* control of that small country. Another Soviet-American sore point was in Central America, where the United States, troubled by growing Communist influence in its own backyard, stepped up efforts against the activities of Cuba and the Marxist Sandinista regime in Nicaragua. Concerned that the Cubans and Nicaraguans were aiding the pro-Communist rebellion in El Salvador, the United States put increasing pressure on Nicaragua in particular to stop that assistance (pressure that included American support of guerrillas opposed to the Sandinista regime). The United States' frustration in Central America was one factor behind the lightning invasion of the Caribbean island nation of Grenada in October 1983, which overthrew the radical Marxist regime that itself had just seized power in a bloody coup. The large Cuban contingent that had been providing various types of assistance to the deposed regime was expelled and Soviet influence in the area was diminished.

The Kremlin's relations with the White House meanwhile continued to deteriorate. During 1983 the Americans responded to the Soviet deployment of new SS20 intermediate range missiles by beginning their own deployment of new and extremely accurate Pershing II and cruise missiles in Western Europe, the massive Soviet propaganda effort to get America's NATO allies to refuse the missiles having failed. The Soviets then walked out of three sets of arms control negotiations: the talks to limit intermediate range missiles in Europe, the Strategic Arms Reduction Talks (START), and the ten-year-old East-West talks on reducing conventional arms in Central Europe. For the first time in twenty years the Soviet Union and the United States were not even *discussing* the arms race.

Soon it became evident that the sixty-nine-year-old Andropov did not have as much energy as advertised. During the summer of 1983 he allegedly caught a cold, after which he disappeared from view. In fact, Andropov was suffering from kidney failure and was undergoing dialysis treatments. He did not reappear to help quell the international uproar after the Soviets shot down an off-course Korean Air Lines jumbo jet at the cost of 269 lives, an action that helped drive Soviet-American relations to a postdétente low. The official job of explaining Soviet actions went to General Nikolai Ogarkov, the chief of the general staff. Nor could the annual November celebration of the Bolshevik Revolution—an event so important that even Brezhnev staggered through it just days before he died—prompt Andropov's return. In December Andropov missed two other important events: meetings of the Central Committee and the Supreme Soviet, the country's parliament. On February 4, 1984, Yuri Andropov died after only fifteen months in office, the shortest tenure so far of any Soviet leader.

In the second smooth transfer of power in as many years, Andropov was succeeded by Konstantin Chernenko, the bridesmaid in 1982. The seventy-two-year-old Chernenko was the oldest man ever to assume leadership of the Soviet Union; on the day he took power he already had lived ten years longer than the average Soviet male. His health was poor; he suffered from emphysema, was rumored to have heart trouble, and in 1983 had been hospitalized for two months with pneumonia. At Andropov's funeral he looked frail and exhausted, barely able to get through his obligatory speech and unable to raise his hand high enough to give a proper salute, a pathetic exhibition viewed live on television by millions of his fellow citizens. The next several months were no better; it was painfully evident that the new general secretary often needed assistance simply to walk.

Chernenko, rejected by his colleagues barely a year before, made it to the top because Andropov's main protege and heir apparent, Mikhail Gorbachev, was still unable to muster the Politburo votes to win the general secretaryship himself in the face of opposition by conservative Brezhnev-era holdovers. The struggle and indecision was reflected by the four-day lapse between Andropov's death and the announcement of Chernenko's election. The compromise that broke the deadlock

made Chernenko the general secretary but placed enough power in
Gorbachev's hands so that *Pravda* at one point referred to him as the
"second secretary." One sign that Chernenko was viewed purely as a
stop-gap leader was that no changes took place in the Politburo that
strengthened his position during his entire term in office. Chernenko's
tenure in office amounted to a thirteen-month-long pregnant pause. The
reform process slowed and in some cases stopped. Examples of this were
loss of steam by the anticorruption campaign and the failure of a special
Central Committee meeting on agriculture to accomplish anything. A
symbolic stab at reform occurred when Stalin's foreign minister, V. M.
Molotov, well into his nineties, was rehabilitated and restored to the
party membership taken from him by Khrushchev. On several occasions
Gorbachev failed to speak at policy meetings, an indication that in those
cases he was not getting his way.

There was little consistency regarding the poor state of Soviet-American
relations. In the spring of 1984 the Soviets boycotted the Olympics being
held in the United States. A renewed effort was made at limiting contacts
between Soviet citizens and visiting foreigners and emigration rates continued to fall. Yet 1984 also saw the demotion of General Ogarkov, a vocal
advocate for diverting more resources to the military for modernizing Soviet conventional forces facing NATO troops in Europe. At the end of the
year, with Chernenko's health failing and Gorbachev increasingly visible,
the Soviets and Americans reached an agreement to resume suspended
arms negotiations.

In December, while Gorbachev was impressing the West during a tour
of Great Britain, another member of the Brezhnev old guard, Defense
Minister Dmitri Ustinov, died. Three months later, in March of 1985,
Chernenko followed his comrade to the grave. He had been in office
barely a year, even less time than Andropov.

Chernenko's departure finally solved the Soviet Union's larger succession problem by transferring power to a younger and more vigorous
generation. But it still left the Soviet Union with the legacy and leth-
argy of the Brezhnev era largely intact. The Brezhnev regime did have
its accomplishments. The Soviet Union had achieved unprecedented
international power and, most importantly to Soviet citizens, security
from foreign invasion during the 1960s and 1970s. Brezhnev's greatest
domestic success was to maintain satbility while he was in office. He did this
by satisfying the various sectors of the elite that controlled the USSR—the
party's central apparatus; its numerous union republic, provincial, and
local tentacles; the military; the police; and the scientific and technical establishments, among others—while providing at least some improvements
for the population at large. Although housing, availability of consumer
goods, medical care, and many other amenities of life were substandard

by Western standards, the three decades since Stalin's death, including almost two under Brezhnev, had provided a much better life for the average Soviet citizen. Per capita consumption of all goods increased three times between 1950 and 1980. Food consumption doubled over the same period and also improved in quality with the addition of more meat, vegetables, fruit, and dairy products. Clothing consumption rose four-fold, durable goods fourteen-fold. Most citizens enjoyed a broad range of social welfare benefits, from free (if badly flawed) medical care and cheap (although severely cramped) housing to pensions and job security. While the Soviets had not closed the standard of living gap vis-à-vis the West, the elites who were in the best position to compare life at home with that abroad were pampered to minimize dissatisfaction that could prove dangerous.

The social mobility of those decades had given millions a stake in the system. The Communist Party of the Soviet Union (CPSU) alone had over 16 million members, a figure reflecting a forty percent growth during the Brezhnev years. It enrolled about one-third of Soviet citizens with a higher education and forty-four percent of all males with ten years or more of schooling. The Komsomol, the party's youth wing, enrolled about 40 million potential new recruits. Tens of millions more (there were 100,000,000 trade union members) belonged to a dense web of organizations tightly controlled by the party. These organizations were both a means of control and a mechanism to gather and occasionally respond to popular complaints. Stability was further enhanced by the long-standing Soviet and Russian tradition of valuing order and fearing change and chaos, a frame of mind formed by the cruel pressures of Russian history. These pressures also produced a deep mistrust of foreigners and a willingness to accept abuse from the government in return for security from outsiders.

When the regime could not count on popular support, it could count on the KGB, the world's largest security apparatus, employing about 250,000 well-armed troops as well as a million technicians, agents, and informers scattered across the country. The regime also had its Gulag, pared down drastically from Stalin's time, but still a grim nether world into which dissidents and other undesirables could be cast. Finally, despite a host of problems, until the early 1980s the various wellsprings of dissent and discontent remained relatively isolated and therefore manageable currents rather than converging into a single uncontrollable torrent. For example, while workers and intellectuals had their respective complaints, the gap between those two social groups remained unbridged. The economy had faltered, but the memory of harder times lingered. Non-Russian nationalities had their grievances, but they often were directed against each other and were counterbalanced by ethnic Russian nationalism when they were not.

The problem with the Brezhnev era was that stability had turned into stagnation. Unlike Stalin, who threatened everyone with prison or death, or Khrushchev, who rocked the boat with his egalitarianism, appeals to popular sentiment, and utopian or unworkable schemes, Brezhnev guaranteed the elite's status, privileges, and life style. Consequently, the Soviet Union was rendered impervious to reform. Almost two decades of inertia under Brezhnev meant that the Soviet Union entered the 1980s with many serious and festering problems, some of which were becoming critical. The most important domestic ones concerned the faltering economy, pervasive corruption and alienation among the citizenry, and the so-called nationality problem—the increasing percentage of non-Great Russians and non-Slavs in the population. There were also several vexing foreign policy problems. And it took until the death of Chernenko in 1985 to transfer real power from the aging and immobilized Brezhnev men to a new generation of leaders prepared to deal with them.

The post-Stalin but still Stalinist economy of the Brezhnev era may have provided reasonably well for the Soviet population compared to conditions thirty years earlier, but those conditions formed an abysmally low base of comparison. Furthermore, the unreformed Soviet economy entered the 1980s with institutions basically unchanged in fifty years. The Stalinist model with its centralized planning, extreme emphasis on heavy industry, and collectivized agriculture may have been a viable, although utterly cruel and enormously wasteful, method of industrialization; it was not, however, an effective way of running a complex industrial economy. In glaring contrast to the economies of the industrialized capitalist powers, the 1980-vintage Soviet civilian economy generated almost nothing on its own. Hamstrung by central planners, factory managers lacked the authority and incentive to use new methods or technologies or to introduce new products for either factories or consumers. Planners continued to rely almost exclusively on easily computable quantitative standards, rewarding those who met production quotas whether or not the goods themselves were useful. Innovation was stifled because it involved risks that traditionally conservative bureaucrats whose charge was to meet production targets rather than make profits were unwilling to take. The absence of a free market in which products competed for customers, with some succeeding and others failing, meant that there was no way to weed out shoddy goods.

Yet central planning remained untouched by the series of economic reforms introduced under Brezhnev in 1965, 1973, and 1979, and under Andropov in 1983. Strong opposition came from the planning bureaucracy and party bosses whose power blunted or buried every reform impulse. The Soviet economy therefore rang up large output numbers while producing enormous quantities of useless goods. Waves of advances in technology—including the electronic and computer revolution—that generated so much growth in the West and Japan barely touched the Soviet Union's shore, leaving its citizens compelled to buy or steal much of the technology they needed for both civilian and military purposes.

Nor was there improvement in agriculture, the economy's weakest sector. One late 1970s campaign, the "Ipatovo method" developed in the Stavropol region (where Gorbachev was the local first secretary at the time), ended up as a fiasco after initial glowing reports. Brezhnev's last effort, his highly publicized "Food Program," was no better. It was the "largest, most expensive document ever produced on agriculture" according to one expert, who added "it has not worked because it is not a *reform*."[1] After fifty years of collectivization, the failure to build proper storage facilities and adequate rural roads, among other problems, meant that a quarter of the grain and more than half of the fruits and vegetables harvested were lost before reaching the consumer.

Meanwhile, the Soviet Union's traditional methods of overcoming economic difficulties—mass mobilization of cheap labor, exploiting readily available and cheap raw materials, and concentrating on a few key areas—were rendered obsolete in the face of a declining labor supply, scarcer and therefore more expensive raw materials, and an economy increasingly too complex for the old "storming" methods. As a result the standard of living stagnated. This was unwelcome news in a country where despite undeniable improvements the life for the average citizen remained drab. A contemporary witticism summed up what the Soviet people suffered and how frustrated they were becoming:

A man enters a fish store and asks for meat. Upon being told he is in a fish store he stubbornly asks for meat again. Finally he is told: Go to the store across the street. *That* is where there is no meat.[2]

In the mid-1970s the Soviet press reported that its citizens spent 30 billion man-hours each year just buying merchandise, a figure equal to 15 million forty-hour weeks. People walked around with large quantities of cash so they could join a line at a moment's notice if some scarce product were being sold, whether they needed it or not. Many families still shared kitchen and bath facilities, while newlyweds often lived for years with in-laws before securing an apartment of their own. Medical care, though free, was marred by obsolete equipment and shortages of the most basic supplies, so that those among the elite with connections often went abroad for treatment of serious problems.

One of the most scandalous problems in a country that claimed to have achieved "developed socialism" was the persistence of poverty. Estimates in the early 1980s suggested that two-fifths of the nonpeasant labor force earned less than what the Soviets themselves considered the minimum necessary for small urban families. The statistics were worse when larger

families, peasants, and pensioners were included. The peasantry was especially deprived. Although their income varied widely, statistics show
that many collective farm workers in the mid-1970s still made less than
the minimum wages set for state enterprises. Peasants also often worked
unusually long hours, largely because of the time spent on the private plots
so vital to their welfare.

Life obviously offered far greater opportunity for the elite. They did
not eat what they disdainfully called "town stuff"; their food continued
to come from special stores stocked with high-quality meats, fruits, and
vegetables, and a wide range of imported delicacies. A half-century after
an official announcement that the country's exploiting classes had been
eliminated, the Soviet elite's specially built apartment houses, in which
they lived free of charge, were staffed by servants and were complemented by country homes (ranging from cottages to genuine mansions)
and expensive cars (often complete with chauffeurs). (Nobody could
compete with Brezhnev himself, who had a personal automobile fleet
that included, among others, a Mercedes-Benz, a Rolls-Royce, and a
Cadillac.) While the masses coped as best they could, the Soviet elite
enjoyed their own restaurants, ticket agencies, and medical facilities, even
their own graveyards. They received their jobs, the fountainhead from
which all privileges flowed, from a special list controlled by the party,
the secretive *nomenklatura*. The nomenklatura included not only the key
party positions at every level, but the key positions in all important Soviet
institutions. To be eligible for nomenklatura positions required both the
proper political and technical credentials, so that all but posts requiring
the most specialized skills or talents were reserved to party members;
indeed, a nomenklatura position was the first major step in advancing
a party career. Overall, the nomenklatura lists (the term also referred to
the list of individuals filling those posts) included a total of about 750,000
individuals who, along with their families, constituted a social class of approximately three million people that controlled the country and most enjoyed its bounty. Because the Soviet Union supposedly was a "developed
socialist society," as opposed to the capitalist inequality-ridden societies in
the West, efforts were made to enjoy the good Soviet life discreetly. But
most Soviet citizens were aware of the discrepancy between ideology and
reality; as one humorist noted, "We have everything, of course, but not for
everyone."

Because the Soviet economy produced so little of what most people
needed and wanted, especially after the military and heavy industrial
sectors took their hefty shares, a second economy evolved and grew to
enormous proportions. It was here that Soviet citizens exchanged goods
and services under the table on a barter basis; it also was where enormous
corruption developed. Some daring entrepreneurs became millionaires by

operating illicit factories producing goods such as quality clothing right inside state factories. The bribes these people paid at every turn in the production and distribution process did not exhaust their considerable profits; there was no shortage of consumers willing to pay high prices for these so-called left-handed goods, for to do without them meant forgoing fashionable clothing, decent shoes, and other high-quality items. What was diminished as vast quantities of materials and skilled personnel were illicitly siphoned off was the ability of the official economy to do its job. The constraining bureaucratic web that encased the country further encouraged corruption; it simply was virtually impossible to survive without breaking the rules. A factory manager could not get what he needed for his plant without extensive bribery. Those who accepted bribes did so because it was the rule, whether they were policemen who took bribes not to give tickets, professors who charged their students for good grades or just for the right to take examinations, or surgeons who charged for operations supposedly covered by the state's free medical program (this after the patient first bribed his way into a good hospital). Bribery had become a way of life in the Soviet Union. Sooner or later most people got involved in this epidemic of illegality, which is why the lethargic Brezhnev did nothing about it and why the determined but sickly Andropov and the simply sickly Chernenko could not improve very much on Brezhnev's record.

The position of the party was another source of the corruption pervading Soviet society. Party bosses, immune from public control, consistently abused their power. In some places—the Caucasian republics of Georgia and Azerbaijan probably were the most extreme examples— local ministerial posts regularly were bought and sold. Even when central authorities attempted to bring the matter under control, as they did by purging most of the ruling apparatus in Georgia in 1972 and 1973, those removed from office often suffered no further punishment. Prosecuting and jailing large numbers of prominent party leaders would have struck too directly at the myth of party infallibility and hence at its legitimacy. Beyond that, any systematic attack on corruption would have threatened too large a percentage of the party elite to be consistent with Brezhnev's prime directive of maintaining stability. As for Andropov, who was unwilling to accept the status quo, he simply was not around long enough to make more than a dent in the huge problem.

Corruption in turn helped breed demoralization and alienation; the general attitude by the early 1980s was that the system was there to be beaten, not improved. Those who had given up on the system often responded by anesthetizing themselves from it. Chronic drunkenness increasingly was one of the most serious social problems in the Soviet Union; between 1965 and 1979 per capita consumption of alcoholic beverages grew by 50 percent, and alcohol abuse was being linked more frequently to crime, birth defects, automobile accidents, and the like. One important victim of this cynicism and loss of confidence was Marxism itself. Although it was the official ideology of the state, fewer and fewer Soviet citizens took its revolutionary and messianic doctrines seriously. Its predictions about equality and abundance were simply too much at variance with the realities of Soviet life. Popular humor had an ordinary Soviet citizen going to the doctor for ear and eye problems. "I keep seeing one thing and hearing another," he complains. Many party members were no different; they endured the indoctrination sessions in order to safeguard privileges available only to those considered reliable.

Aside from rampant alcoholism, another measure of the drabness and spiritual vacuousness of late 1970s and early 1980s Soviet life was the growth of overt religious expression in a country where religion was condemned and its observance damaging to one's career. One Soviet study concluded that in some regions 25 percent of the population exhibited "religious influence." This disturbing phenomenon was of particular concern when religion and ethnic or national feeling coalesced, as they have among Catholics in Lithuania, Moslems in Central Asia, and Independent Orthodox in Georgia. The regime was further disturbed by the sharp increase in church weddings (a state wedding remained a legal requirement) and the crowds of young people that continued to gather for midnight Easter services.

The greatest threat to the Soviet Union's long-term stability was its nationality problem. For the non-Russian nationalities the "Union of Soviet Socialist Republics" was old Russian wine in a new Soviet bottle. The Soviet Union remained the last of the great European empires forged between the sixteenth and nineteenth centuries. Official ideology to the contrary, the non-Russian nationalities continued to be dominated by the Great Russian majority that held all the levers of power in the "Union." As of 1980, not a single non-Russian served in the party's Secretariat. Only three non-Slavs held any of the top 150 positions in the armed forces. The hope from Lenin to Stalin to their successors was that the Soviet Union's non-Russians would gradually accept the Russian language and culture and be more or less assimilated into a new "Soviet" nationality. In some cases this appeared to be happening, but in most it was not. Despite the thick layer of repression that coated the Brezhnev regime's nationalities policy, ethnic ferment occasionally broke the surface. In 1972 demonstrators in Lithuania openly called for freedom from Moscow, in 1978 angry protests in Georgia forced authorities to back down on a plan to give Russian equal status to Georgian in the southern Soviet republic, and 1980 witnessed street demonstrations against russification in Estonia.

Ironically, Soviet policy had contributed to the persistence of national identities. The federal structure of the state was originally designed to pacify national feeling while gradually encouraging assimilation. Instead, the Soviet Union's formal federal structure reinforced local national identity. Each of the largest national groups was managing many of its own affairs within a clearly defined geographic and political entity. Also, while improved education created local elites that were weaned away from many local traditions, those same elites developed a modern national feeling, much like their counterparts throughout the underdeveloped world.

Demographics added to the nationalities problem. The birth rate in certain non-Russian areas, most notably among the Central Asian Moslems, continued to be far higher than among the Great Russians or their Ukrainian and Belorussian cousins. By 1970, the Great Russians were barely 53 percent of the Soviet Union's overall population; by the year 2000 they were expected to be less than 50 percent, while the Moslem share was projected to rise from 14 to 23 percent. This meant many problems for the new leadership generation, including pressures to divert development resources away from the traditionally favored Slavic parts of the country. More troubling was the projected increase in the percentage of non-Russian and possibly non-Russian-speaking army recruits, a military man's nightmare in terms of both efficiency and reliability.

Finally, Brezhnev and his two immediate successors left the new generation serious problems abroad. Ironically, as it became one of the world's two superpowers, the Soviet Union largely subordinated the worldwide revolutionary ambitions of its founders to the more limited and therefore more attainable goal of expanding the international power and influence of the Soviet state (a process that actually began under Stalin in the 1920s). The Soviets, to be sure, retained an element of their old Marxist heritage, remaining fundamentally hostile to the West and actively trying to undermine Western strength and resolve and to promote the fortunes of like-minded regimes in both hemispheres. However, in its deep mistrust of the outside world and its unrelenting quest for unassailable security guaranteed by superior military power, the post-World War II Soviet Union followed a foreign policy evoking the policies of tsarist Russia. Its confrontation with the West in the 1970s and early 1980s had much in common with the traditional rivalries between great powers. Like its rivals, the Soviet Union had interests and commitments that made it a power with a great deal to lose. This tended to make its foreign policy, despite its pronounced expansionistic component, cautious and pragmatic in general and designed to avoid direct confrontation with the United States in particular. In some parts of the world the Soviet Union even struggled to preserve the status quo, something, as its great rival the United States knew well, that is not easy to do.

By the early 1980s the Soviet Union most of all wanted to preserve the status quo in Eastern Europe. Its dominance there provided a buffer against the West and was an important source of reassurance and confidence at home. But persistent nationalist feeling was an ineradicable source of instability, while economic stagnation turned the region from a source of exploitation to an economic liability. Poland especially remained hostile to everything Russian, at heart a Catholic rather than Communist country, and, despite the suppression of the Solidarity trade union movement late in 1981, was in a state of open, if passive rebellion.

To the east was the People's Republic of China, a hostile power over a billion strong. Fifty Soviet divisions, about one-quarter of the country's ground strength, guarded the long Sino-Soviet border. To the south Afghanistan continued to bleed the Soviets of soldiers (the death toll passing 10,000 in 1984), money (1.7 million dollars per day), and prestige. In the Western hemisphere Cuba, though a valuable ally and a thorn in America's side, was a considerable economic burden. By 1985 Cuba and Vietnam, another strong but expensive Soviet supporter, were costing the Kremlin over 5.7 billion dollars per year. And, of course, the Brezhnev generation left Soviet-American relations worse than they had been for years.

It was against this background that the leadership baton was finally passed. It was passed in neither a timely nor a graceful fashion, but simultaneously dropped to the ground and spasmodically thrust into the hands of the Soviet Union's first leaders to reach adulthood in the post-World War II era. Despite the collective sigh of relief reaching from Moscow to Europe to Washington that this transfer had finally been accomplished, expectations regarding decisive and fundamental change were guarded at best. Soon both the speed and the direction of change made it clear that what had not changed in Russia in more than six decades of Soviet rule was that still-mysterious nation's ability to surprise itself and the entire world.

NOTES

1. Zhores Medvedev, *Soviet Agriculture* (New York and London: W.W. Norton and Company, 1987), pp. 408–409.
2. Cited in David K. Shipler, *Russia: Broken Idols, Solemn Dreams* (New York: *Times* Books, 1983), p. 173.

PART SIX

An End and a Beginning

19

Gorbachev: From Restructuring to Destruction

Our society is ripe for change, and the need for
change has cleared its own road.
　　　　　—MIKHAIL GORBACHEV, 1987

Workers of the world, we're sorry.
　—sign at a counterdemonstration during the seventy-
　　second anniversary celebration of the Bolshevik
　　Revolution in Moscow. November 7, 1989

Half Measures

Half measures
　　can kill
When,
　chafing at the bit in terror
we twitch our ears
　　all lathered in foam
on the brink of precipices,
because we can't jump halfway across.
　　　　　—YEVGENY YEVTUSHENKO[1]

On March 11, 1985, Mikhail Sergeyevich Gorbachev was elected general
secretary of the Communist Party of the Soviet Union. Gorbachev was a
signal that the winds of change which had swirled under Andropov, only to

subside under Chernenko, were again rising in Moscow. The question remained how strong those winds would be and precisely in what direction
they would blow.

Gorbachev was an Andropov protégé, and Andropov had begun making
changes during his brief tenure as general secretary. But there was nothing
in Andropov's program that could be called radical, that promised fundamental changes in any of the major institutions of Soviet life. Gorbachev
was young; he had just celebrated his fifty-fourth birthday. Yet this made
him an exception only to the two sickly senior citizens who had preceded
him in his new job. He was only a few years younger than Khrushchev and
Brezhnev had been when they reached the top and older than both Stalin
and Lenin at similar points in their careers. Gorbachev was, by Soviet
standards at least, an attractive and almost glamorous political figure. Extraordinarily at ease with the media, he cut an especially impressive figure
on television. This also was not entirely new; Andropov, at least before he
was incapacitated, had impressed Western observers as a cultured and
informed man with modern tastes. What Gorbachev would try to do, and to
what degree he would succeed where he tried, therefore were very open
questions. Although there certainly would be change, prudent observers
both inside and outside the Soviet Union understandably were cautious in
their expectations.

If his personality was unusually outgoing and attractive for a Soviet
political leader, Gorbachev's personal background was conventional. Like
any man since the death of Stalin with a serious chance of becoming
general secretary, Gorbachev is an ethnic Russian. He rose, albeit rather
more quickly than usual, through the system along a classic trajectory. He
was born in 1931, at the height of collectivization, in a small village in the
Stavropol region of what is called the North Caucasus, a prime agricultural
region stretching eastward from Ukraine, between the Black and Caspian
Seas. Both his father and maternal grandfather were party members, the
latter having served as the first chairman of a local collective farm during
collectivization. Gorbachev, in effect, therefore was born into the new
Soviet rural elite, which helps explain both his survival at a time when so
many peasant children were dying and the educational opportunities he
subsequently received. Yet like tens of millions of Soviet citizens regardless of their status, Gorbachev did not pass the terror-laden 1930s un-
scathed. Both his paternal and maternal grandfathers were arrested, and
although both somehow survived and returned home, Gorbachev's families
on both sides suffered accordingly.

After his graduation from secondary school in 1950, Gorbachev was
admitted to the law faculty at Moscow State University. Shortly before
receiving his degree in 1955, he married Raisa Titorenko, a bright and

attractive fellow student from a town in the Urals. After graduation Gorbachev returned to Stavropol to take a job as an official in the Komsomol, the Communist Party youth organization. He soon switched to work in the Communist Party apparatus itself, working his way up the ladder over a period of about fifteen years. While in Stavropol he made a number of important friends, including Mikhail Suslov, the behind-the-scenes kingmaker of Soviet politics since the 1960s, and Yuri Andropov, for many years the powerful head of the KGB. Gorbachev's path upward was the beaten one, including the required stints as second and first secretary of the city of Stavropol, and then as second and finally first secretary of the entire Stavropol region, a post he held from 1970 to 1978. His job as Stavropol first secretary also earned him a place on the party's Central Committee in 1971.

In 1978 he was called to Moscow to serve in the powerful Secretariat as the secretary responsible for agriculture. There he presided over a string of poor harvests. His survival must be attributed both to his political skills and to Andropov's protection and patronage. Gorbachev became a candidate member of the Politburo in 1979 and a full voting member in 1980. Under Andropov he emerged as the general secretary's righthand man, often chairing Politburo meetings in the ailing party leader's absence. Under Chernenko, Gorbachev again often stood in for his sick superior and became the de facto second secretary of the party. His election as general secretary reportedly was won by a narrow margin over Viktor Grishin, the chief of the Moscow party organization.

There is nothing concrete in Gorbachev's professional career to suggest that he would turn into the bold and dynamic reformer he became. If there had been, it is safe to say that his career, which was largely made under Brezhnev, would have quickly stalled. Making it in the Soviet system during the Brezhnev era required playing strictly by the rules; initiative was desirable only in quantities large enough to demonstrate a degree of competence. Still, looking backward one can see dim glimmers of originality and faint streaks of independence against the dark gray background of a successful Soviet bureaucrat's career. While a university student, Gorbachev, speaking in confidence to a close friend, challenged the rosy official version of collectivization, no doubt on the basis of his own childhood experiences. In Stavropol he was known for getting out among the people and making on-the-spot visits to farms, factories, and other institutions under his jurisdiction. He was influenced by the reformist spirit of the Khrushchev era when he was just beginning his career and, in fact, referred to his generation as the "children of the Twentieth Party Congress." As the party boss in Stavropol, Gorbachev experimented with methods to improve collective farm efficiency by allowing the peasants increased freedom to organize their work and to sell more of what they earned at market prices rather than at the low prices paid by the state. And once he returned to Moscow in 1978, Gorbachev became part of the reformist group Andropov was collecting around him.

But even all of this would still leave Gorbachev within a mold that he certainly outgrew. The best that one can say about his remarkable political evolution is that prior to 1985 Mikhail Gorbachev had the intelligence and adaptability to transcend conventional Soviet bounds. After 1985 the opportunity to exercise power, the realization of the enormity of the problems his country faced, and the courage to face them catalyzed his potential and made him a political figure of international stature and genuine historic importance.

Actually, the events of March 1985 brought more than a new general secretary to power. They finally ended the Soviet Union's deeper succession crises by bringing a new political generation to the helm of the ship of state. Unlike the older Brezhnev generation, Gorbachev and his colleagues did not work in the industrialization drive, participate in and survive the purges, or, in most cases, fight in World War II. For them industrialization was an established fact; their formative political activities took place during Khrushchev's destalinization era and they were influenced by the spirit and possibilities of those times. They were the first Soviet leaders, with the exception of Lenin and several of his lieutenants, to have a formal university education (Gorbachev, like Lenin, had been trained as a lawyer). The Gorbachev generation also benefited from the rising Soviet standard of living during the 1960s and 1970s. They had the opportunity to visit and learn about the West; Gorbachev and his wife Raisa made two unescorted trips to West European countries—France and Italy—in their younger years. These experiences made them relatively comfortable with Westerners and more ready than previous leaders to borrow both methods and ideas from the United States and Western Europe.

If the party leadership had changed, this is only because the rest of Soviet society underwent a fundamental change in the past generation: the process of urbanization. This process, of course, had been going on since the nineteenth century, when Russian industrialization began in earnest. It accelerated to record levels during the Stalin industrialization drive of the 1930s and maintained a rapid pace after the dictator's death. But although the Soviet Union was becoming increasingly urbanized, it took a very long time for it to become an urban *society,* to overcome what historian Moshe Lewin has called the "rural nexus" of Soviet life.[2] This is true both in terms of raw statistics—i.e., the percentage of Soviet people who actually lived in cities—and even more so in terms of the *quality* of life in those cities. Thus, between 1926 and 1939, the percentage of Soviet citizens living in cities increased from 18 to 32 percent. It took until 1960 to reach 49 percent, which means that despite its industrial growth the Soviet Union remained a rural society until almost the end of the Khrushchev era. By 1972 the urban population reached 58 percent, finally passing the two-thirds mark in 1985, the year Gorbachev came to power. The Soviet Union therefore was not a *predominantly* urban society, comparable to industrially advanced states of Western Europe and the United States, until at least the middle of the 1970s.

The point of all this is not the numbers, but what urbanization has meant for how people live, what they know, and what they are capable of doing and demanding from their government. In this sense urbanization is also a cultural process in which the peasants flooding the Soviet cities abandoned their rural habits and acquired an urban sophistication and state of mind. One important aspect of that transformation was a dramatically increased level of education, which the government for reasons of its own was actively promoting.

Urbanization was pivotal because urban citizens in many ways are more difficult to manage than rural populations. The Stalinist state, for example, was able to mobilize and manipulate peasants and proletarianized peasant workers during the 1930s not only because it used overwhelming force, but also because it was dealing with relatively simple social structures. Another important factor was the kind of work these people were being mobilized to do, which for many years was largely manual labor. But the process of industrialization required highly trained specialists and over the years this led to the creation of a highly educated group of people. They were concentrated in the cities where their work was and their presence gradually began to change the character of Soviet urban life. The number of people with a specialized or technical education increased from about 2.4 million in 1941 and 8 million in 1960 to over 30 million in the mid-1980s. Meanwhile, the millions of ordinary workers in the cities became more highly educated, as, for that matter, did the shrinking minority of Soviet citizens still on the farms; the percentage of workers and peasants with only an elementary education dropped from over 90 percent in 1959 to under 20 percent thirty years later.

Urban society, with its complexity and concentration of people with sophisticated skills and intellectual resources, is not amenable to the same controls that can regulate a rural village. In the anonymity of the modern city, people with special skills easily find their way around governmental attempts to control them as, in the words of one observer, they "rush about like the unplottable electrons in an atom."[3] One example is the state monopoly of information, which from 1917 on was a crucial factor in maintaining the one-party Bolshevik dictatorship. During the 1960s tape recorders, often smuggled in from abroad, became an effective way of transmitting information, either to others in the country or abroad. This information could be a statement from a dissident committed to prison or a rock song the authorities refused to record in their state-controlled studios. Devices like the telephone and automobile also increasingly enabled citizens to slip between the multiple tentacles of the Soviet state. New technologies—such as computers and video cassette recorders—only made the problem for the authorities worse. It is true, of course, that the authorities tried to limit the availability of these and similar devices, but no less true that they had to be made available in ever larger and therefore uncontrollable numbers because without them the increasingly industrialized and complex Soviet state could not function.

It was in the cities that networks of unsanctioned activity multiplied exponentially, beyond the control of even the KGB and other Soviet authorities. And it was not simply a matter of avoiding state control to pass information, but rather asserting what in Russian is called *prava lichnosti*, or the rights of the individual. Millions of urban dwellers of varying degrees of sophistication found niches to pursue private interests. These were as varied as the city dwellers themselves, ranging from small groups who played jazz or rock music or organized unsanctioned art exhibitions, to youths who dodged the draft, and to illegal entrepreneurs in the "second economy" that grew to satisfy the burgeoning wants of Soviet citizens increasingly aware of what the world, both outside and inside the Soviet Union, had to offer. This phenomenon, the direct product of urbanization, itself the product of the Soviet state's industrialization policies, undermined the ability of that state to control society. It produced a nonsocialist nonparty twilight zone in the Soviet universe where individuals made decisions free of official control and formed organizations to implement those decisions. While in the West such activity is considered normal and is the basis of how Western democratic societies purport to function, it ran counter to everything in official Soviet ideology. Still, that did not prevent its evolution in the Soviet Union.

By the late 1970s, legions of skilled specialists—scientists, engineers, economists, and experts in many other fields—had become vital to managing the country. Their existence and essential skills in effect meant that some power had slipped from the party/state bureaucracy and, hence, the Communist Party itself. Stultifying central controls over the economy and gross incompetence and mismanagement became increasingly intolerable to these specialists. They could not suffer a level of censorship that made it difficult to get information vital to their work, not to mention to read, view, or listen to what they wanted in their private time. This phenomenon did not threaten the political power of the Communist Party itself even as late as the first years of the Gorbachev era. But its evolution alongside the Soviet Union's other serious problems created enormous pressure for reform. The frustration this elite felt with the party's incompetence, the country's lagging standard of living, and the limits on its personal aspirations also led to alienation and pessimism, which made the country's problems even worse.

From the outside, as its economic growth slowed and its social problems grew, the Soviet Union during Brezhnev's later years appeared stagnant. But like the barren ice on a frozen lake, the stagnation and lifelessness was only a surface phenomenon. Beneath the sterile surface of the Communist Party was vibrant and growing life. None of this registered with Brezhnev and his aging cohorts. As one observer put it, "The country went through a social revolution while Brezhnev slept."[4] But in the early 1980s that life began to scratch the surface as the Communist Party under Andropov haltingly committed itself to change. It broke through visibly after 1985 with the advent of Gorbachev.

One example of this ferment from below was the emergence of what can be called "public opinion," which even before 1985 was able to influence government policy. An early beneficiary of this was Lake Baikal, the sickle-shaped Siberian sliver of water whose almost six-thousand-foot depth makes it the largest fresh water lake in the world. Pressure from scientists and intellectuals to prevent fouling of the lake by new industries began in the mid-1960s, and was instrumental in getting the government to institute antipollution measures. Public opinion also mobilized during the early 1980s against a plan to divert several Siberian rivers (which flow northward into the Arctic Sea) southward to Central Asia for irrigation purposes, and led to Gorbachev scuttling that plan in 1986.

Gorbachev, then, was not the initiator of change; it had already swept Soviet society in several crucial ways. The problem was that while *society* had changed a great deal, the *party* hardly changed at all, and through its extensive control levers the party was preventing further progress that was necessary to make Soviet society in general and its economy in particular competitive with the West. Gorbachev's job, at least as he first saw it, was to bring the party into sync with that change.

Gorbachev did not arrive as general secretary with a comprehensive program for solving the Soviet Union's problems. Something resembling a strategy with many interrelated programs, albeit with many gaps when it comes to specifics, emerged over time. It can be summarized by four terms. The first was *perestroika,* or "restructuring." While the term was often used to refer to Gorbachev's entire reform program, it most specifically applied to the economy, which from the beginning was the central concern of Gorbachev's reform effort. Perestroika assumed that the Soviet economy would have to be overhauled if it were to become modern and efficient enough to maintain the Soviet Union as a superpower. The key point was to find a way compatible with socialist principles to reduce the role of central planning and administration and allow productive units—the factories and farms—room for initiative and, hopefully, the possibility of increased productivity.

Closely related to perestroika and essential to it was *glasnost*. Glasnost, usually translated as openness, was precisely that: the opening of the Soviet Union to unprecedented limits regarding the availability of information, the parameters of personal and artistic expression, and genuine public debate. It included the drastic reduction of censorship in literature, art, news reporting, and the like. Glasnost was essential to Gorbachev for several reasons. The Soviet Union's educated elite could not work effectively unless it had access to ideas and information, both at home and abroad. Soviet obsession with secrecy, presumably to keep enemies in the West at bay, had led to innumerable absurdities, among them Soviet economists waiting impatiently for the annual publication of *American* estimates on the Soviet economy because Soviet statistics were either unavailable or unreliable. Glasnost also was necessary simply to inform the party leadership properly because so much had been covered up by bureaucrats protecting their fiefs over the years. It was also demanded by the Soviet educated elite who were disgusted by censorship that prevented them from enjoying the best of what both domestic and foreign artists produce, whether it be books, sculpture, paintings, films, or anything else. But glasnost was not an inalienable right of citizens to enjoy the freedom of information and expression as known in the West. Rather it was one of the leadership's instruments of reform, and while the limits on public expression were broadened dramatically, the Gorbachev regime intended to set those limits and made this clear on several occasions. In mid-1987 the general secretary announced that glasnost must "serve the interests of socialism." In October of 1989, in a more menacing attack on glasnost Gorbachev angrily attacked the press for undermining his efforts.

Another key element was a word few people associated with the Soviet Union or its Communist Party: *demokratizatsia,* or democratization. Once again, the term did not mean what it does in the West, at least not to Gorbachev and the Soviet leadership. Gorbachev did not want a multiparty political system in which his Communist Party could be voted out of office or even forced to share power. Demokratizatsia meant that some choice would be allowed in the Soviet system—that in factories, in elections to government bodies, and even in party elections there should be a choice of candidates. The hope was that glasnost and demokratizatsia, even in their limited Soviet version, would entice ordinary citizens to pitch in voluntarily to help the reform effort. This was crucial because Gorbachev understood that without active popular support and help no substantial economic reforms would be possible.

Finally, there was *novoe myshlenie,* or "new thinking." Although this term also could be applied to all of Gorbachev's reforms, it referred most specifically to foreign policy and in particular to the Soviet Union's relationship with the West. New thinking implied a radical change in Soviet-Western relations, which for so long had been marked by hostility. Soviet expansionism in Eastern Europe after World War II had been the key factor in provoking the Cold War with the West and its concomitant arms race. Although "peaceful coexistence" became the official Soviet policy in the 1950s, it existed alongside an aggressive policy of "class struggle" with the capitalist powers which fueled the expensive arms race. For over forty years the Soviets assumed that security could be bought with military power and, therefore, committed huge resources to building the world's largest military establishment. The trouble was that military spending absorbed at least 25 percent of the country's productive resources and was one of the heaviest anchors dragging down the Soviet economy. Gorbachev knew he had to shift resources to the civilian sector in order to rebuild the Soviet economy. This helps to account for the steady stream of arms control proposals, some serious and others for public relations purposes, that flowed from the Kremlin after 1985. At the same time, Gorbachev made clear his conviction that all nations had to work together to solve growing mutual challenges, the chief among them being the world's deteriorating natural environment.

Gorbachev's lack of a comprehensive program when he took office reflected a number of factors. Other than a general agreement that change was necessary, no consensus existed among the new leadership about exactly what to do. Equally important, as one would have expected from a life-long party bureaucrat, Gorbachev initially was committed to the narrow Andropov approach, which focused almost entirely on tightening economic management and combating corruption. That is why calls for *uskorenie,* or acceleration of economic activity, and increased discipline in the work place, both associated with Andropov, dominated Gorbachev's early months as general secretary. In addition, Gorbachev simply did not understand how bad conditions were; he and his colleagues talked only about a "pre-crisis" situation, not one that could in any way threaten the regime. After all, glasnost had not yet shed its bright, searching light on the country's problems. Gorbachev himself affirmed this several times, including in 1988 when he observed, "Frankly speaking, comrades, we have underestimated the extent and gravity of the deformations." Perhaps this accounts for the shocking overconfidence of Gorbachev's first year, when the Soviet leadership seemed to think that some economic tinkering and arresting a few corrupt officials would be enough to turn the economy around and get the situation in hand.

All this made 1985 a year of small deeds and hints of more to come. One of its main virtues from Gorbachev's point of view is that he did not stumble while taking his first steps into the economic, political, cultural, and foreign policy minefields that lay before him. His very modest forays into economic reform included experiments at two factories in which those enterprises retained their profits so they could finance their own development without funds from the central authorities. There were also some administrative reorganizations, the most important being combining six agricultural ministries into one "super ministry." None of these measures did much to loosen the deadening grip of the Moscow central planners on the economy. The agricultural reform did just the opposite, and soon established its reputation as a bureaucratic disaster that had to be undone.

The rest of Gorbachev's 1985 economic program followed Andropov's pattern. It consisted mainly of attempts to tighten discipline in the work place by firing incompetent managers and combating alcohol abuse. Overall, these policies fell into the category of "administrative changes"—that is, attempts to fix the economic machinery that was in place rather than scrap and replace it with something new. As under Andropov, the assumption seems to have been that there was slack in the system and that judicious tightening could make it perform significantly better. When output rose during the second half of the year, this assumption received a short-lived, but totally misleading, boost.

Meanwhile, a glimmer of glasnost was visible on the cultural horizon. The important literary journal *Novyi mir* published a combination prose/poem by Yevgeny Yevtushenko that graphically discussed several sensitive or even forbidden themes from abuses under Stalin, to the fate of Leon Trotsky, to current Soviet neo-Fascists. Yevtushenko also delivered a dramatic speech calling for openness and honesty in Soviet life, while two plays about corruption in the party played to full houses in Moscow.

The most notable domestic initiative by the new Soviet leadership was to attack what the Russians call the "green snake": alcoholism. Once again this policy was a continuation of what Andropov had started, only Gorbachev put teeth into it. He closed down two-thirds of all liquor stores, cut the hours of those that remained, reduced the production of alcoholic beverages, and increased the fine for public drunkenness by *ten* times. During the 1986 new year's celebrations, for the first time in memory soft drinks were sold on Moscow's streets rather than the traditional alcoholic beverages. For his efforts, the public dubbed the new general secretary the "mineral water secretary," a title that probably reflected equal measures of admiration and anger.

But the public did not respond the way Gorbachev hoped. There was considerable support for the campaign among women wearied by their men's drunkenness. Elsewhere enthusiasm waned, as Russia's heavy drinkers displayed an ingenuity for getting around the new rules that Gorbachev would have preferred they reserve for implementing perestroika. There was a huge increase in the number of underground stills, which often produced poisonous brews. Sugar, used in the brewing process, disappeared from store shelves. When home brew was not available, desperate drinkers increasingly consumed brake fluid, after-shave lotion, and similar dangerous and frequently poisonous liquids. Adding financial insult to social injury, the loss of revenue from alcohol sales quickly reached billions of rubles and pushed the Soviet budget further into the red. Such problems eventually forced a reversal of several of these policies, beginning as early as 1986.

Like domestic policy, Soviet foreign policy under the new general secretary initially was marked by slight adjustments that involved more style than substance. Gorbachev announced a unilateral ban on all nuclear tests that lasted from August of 1985 to February of 1987, a measure that raised his stock in West European antinuclear circles when the United States continued its testing. He told Western Europeans about how the Soviet Union shared with them "our common house," in part to try to begin to loosen their ties with the United States, and wooed both Communist and non-Communist Asian nations with references to what he called "our common Asiatic heritage." However, the United States, the world's capitalist superpower, remained the central Soviet foreign policy concern. Even before becoming general secretary, Gorbachev had moved to raise Soviet-American relations from the low point they had reached in the early 1980s. During Chernenko's last months, by which time Gorbachev was making many major decisions, the Soviet Union and the United States agreed to resume arms control negotiations. Once Gorbachev was in power the two sides slowly inched toward each other, not only by sitting down at the negotiating table but by renewing cultural exchanges suspended by the Americans after the 1979 Soviet invasion of Afghanistan. In November of 1985 Gorbachev and Reagan went to their first summit in Geneva. It was a get-acquainted meeting without any serious business on the agenda. The only agreement was that the two leaders accepted invitations to visit the other's country.

Gorbachev's most substantial gain during his first year in power was in the political arena at home. It was, in fact, the logical place to focus attention. Election as general secretary guaranteed neither job security nor the ability to effect significant change. The Politburo only voted for Gorbachev narrowly, and the Central Committee was dominated by holdovers from the Brezhnev era. The party bureaucracy at the middle and lower levels was still staffed by bureaucrats whose status and material well-being depended on the old way of doing things. Against this background, Gorbachev did a remarkable job of consolidating and broadening his power base. The old guard's grip on Soviet political life, loosened under Andropov but slightly retightened under Chernenko, was finally broken. The two highest ranking government officials removed from office were the prime minister (eighty-three-year-old Nikolai Tikhonov) and the foreign minister (the venerable Andrei Gromyko, kicked upstairs to the ceremonial post of President of the Soviet Union). After an intense struggle, Viktor Grishin lost his Politburo seat and his post as Moscow party chief. Grigori Romanov, Gorbachev's other main rival, likewise departed the Politburo under a cloud of personal corruption. This "cold purge" also chilled the next rung down in both the party and state ladders. Among those replaced during Gorbachev's first year were the head of Gosplan (the nation's most important economic planning body), four of the fifteen republic party chiefs, about 40 percent of the Council of Ministers, and close to a third of the regional party secretaries. At lower levels thousands of party and government officials were replaced.

Three new men rose to the Politburo during the spring of 1985, although this did less for reform than first met the eye. The most powerful new face was Yegor Ligachev, who had worked closely with Gorbachev during the Andropov days. Ligachev also became the secretary in charge of party personnel and the politician second in rank to Gorbachev. Most significantly, within a year he also emerged as Gorbachev's main rival as Gorbachev began to explore more radical strategies of reform. Ligachev was not a Brezhnev conservative; he was an Andropov-style reformer ready to continue the type of programs Andropov had started but opposed to going beyond them and overhauling or possibly abolishing any of the basic institutions of Soviet life. Thus, as Gorbachev increasingly began to advocate more radical measures in all areas of Soviet life, Ligachev in effect took on the role of the general secretary's conservative opposition. Joining Ligachev on the Politburo were Nikolai Ryzhkov and Viktor Chebrikov. Ryzhkov, an economic specialist, replaced Tikhonov as prime minister and positioned himself as a moderate reformer somewhere between Gorbachev and Ligachev. Chebrikov, the KGB boss, became Ligachev's close ally and caustic critic of intellectuals trying to expand the parameters of glasnost. Boris Yeltsin, a newcomer to Moscow imported from the provincial city of Sverdlovsk, replaced Grishin as the Moscow Party chief and became a candidate Politburo member. Shortly thereafter Eduard Shevardnadze, a staunch Gorbachev and perestroika supporter, joined the Politburo. Shevardnadze, the former first secretary of Georgia with a reputation as a corruption fighter, also replaced Gromyko as foreign minister. Another important new face was Alexander Yakovlev, the former ambassador to Canada. Although in 1985 he was only head of the Central Committee's propaganda department, he became Gorbachev's closest advisor. Probably the strongest advocate among the Soviet leadership for radical reform during the first two years of Gorbachev's tenure, Yakovlev has been called the architect of perestroika. He rose quickly, becoming a Central Committee secretary in 1986, a candidate Politburo member early in 1987, and a full member by the end of the year.

The Twenty-Seventh Party Congress, which took place in early 1986 according to schedule, saw more political changes. Gorbachev fixed its opening for a significant date: February 25, 1986, thirty years to the day after Nikita Khrushchev gave his secret speech. The house cleaning continued. Almost 40 percent of the Central Committee members elected at the congress were new and several reformers were added to the powerful Secretariat. Among them was Alexandra Biriukova, the first woman since Khrushchev's time to join the top party elite.

The Twenty-Seventh Congress also revised the party's official program. It became far more modest and restrained than the utopian document from the Khrushchev era it replaced. New party rules made it easier to move against corrupt officials, although Gorbachev was thwarted in his attempt to revive Khrushchev's controversial rule no. 25, which limited the tenure of party officials to fifteen years, or three terms. This defeat was symptomatic of a larger division of opinion and lack of consensus at the congress. There was general agreement that reform was necessary, but sharp disagreement on what type of reform and how drastic it should be. This emerged during the congress debates. That there were real debates at all was an historic change; the Twenty-Seventh Congress was the most open party congress since the rise of Stalin. There was a sharp disagreement between Yeltsin and Ligachev, now clearly the number-two man behind Gorbachev, on the extent of corruption and injustice in the Soviet Union. After Gorbachev made a call for radical economic changes, Ryzhkov, presumably a close ally and the logical point man to take on the job, ignored that call in his speech. As a media event the congress was a stunning success and demonstration of change. But it left unanswered Gorbachev's long-term security as general secretary, the degree of unity at the top, and the nature and direction of future reform.

Shortly after the congress closed, another problem literally exploded in the Soviet Union's face. On April 25, 1986, the peaceful spring air of the Ukraine was shattered by thundering noise, roaring flame, and searing heat. What must have seemed to many to be the devil's work was in reality the poorly executed work of man. An explosion had destroyed one of the reactors at the Chernobyl nuclear power plant, sending radioactive poisons in unprecedented and disastrous amounts shooting upward and outward across the countryside.

Chernobyl recalled the 1957 Soviet nuclear disaster in the Urals. The new disaster, however, was far worse. Air currents carried the nuclear poisons into Central and Western Europe. The political fallout for Gorbachev and glasnost was also serious. Both had fallen silent. No announcement of the disaster came until radiation was detected in Western Europe. It took three days for an official response and fifteen more before Gorbachev himself spoke. Meanwhile, the government was painfully slow to respond to the crisis. Only heroic action by local firefighters, of whom many would die from radiation sickness, prevented a greater disaster. Moscow delayed in evacuating the civilian population from around the smoldering reactor. Thirty-six hours after the explosion, children were still playing in the streets of Pripiat, five miles from the stricken reactor. It took a week to evacuate the town of Chernobyl, slightly farther away.

The Soviets soon recovered. After denouncing the Western press for exaggerating the extent of the disaster—a claim that had some validity because the Soviets themselves initially provided no information on what had happened—they issued a long and comprehensive report. Several subsequent disasters, including a cruise ship sinking with the loss of 400 lives, were also fully reported. A few officials directly responsible for the plant later went to jail. Yet nothing could prevent billions of dollars in damage to water, crops, and farm animals, not only in the Soviet Union but in Western Europe. Officially, the immediate death toll—mainly those near the explosion and those who fought the ensuing fire—was put at thirty-one, although reliable unofficial sources put the toll at almost 300. The number of long-term deaths, of course, is unknown, although it will be measured in the thousands. Also unknown but certain to be serious are the environmental effects on Ukraine and Belarus, the regions most contaminated by the fallout from Chernobyl.

As the radioactive and political fallout from Chernobyl cleared, Soviet and American attention shifted to the greater nuclear danger: nuclear arms. Both sides wanted a substantial agreement that would become a real brake on the arms race. In January of 1986, the Soviets had agreed to the American demand that strategic and intermediate arms talks be separated. In the course of the next few months, Gorbachev first linked, then delinked, and then linked again the progress on intermediate range missiles to limits on American research on a space-based antimissile system known as the Strategic Defense Initiative or SDI. This complex maneuvering was yet another lap in the long Soviet-American arms race. The various threads of that contest were so tightly woven as to form a modern-day Gordian knot.

Aside from the mutual intentions, ambitions, suspicions, and fears of the superpowers, the paraphernalia of the arms race included a veritable host of nuclear weapons systems ("weapons systems" has come into vogue to describe means of destruction too powerful and complex simply to be called "weapons"), including intercontinental ballistic missiles, submarine-launched ballistic missiles, cruise missiles, long-range bombers, medium-range ballistic missiles, and short-range missiles; exotic non-nuclear technologies such as chemical and bacteriological weapons; and a bewildering array of conventional weapons. One of the Soviet Union's major concerns was American research on the SDI. The Soviets wanted to limit or derail American research into this complex technology, even while they had been working on similar technology, steadily if unspectacularly, for thirty-five years. Still, reflecting the traditional Russian respect and fear of American technological prowess, stopping SDI was a priority for Gorbachev.

In the fall came the surprising announcement that General Secretary Gorbachev and President Reagan would meet again in Reykjavik, Iceland, to work out a major arms agreement. Amid a whirlpool of near euphoria and serious skepticism, Reagan, Gorbachev and their advisors spent October 11 and 12 in intense negotiations. They reached tentative agreements on several major issues, including a 50 percent mutual cut in strategic weapons. But the agreements and the summit ran aground on the rock of SDI. Gorbachev demanded strict limits on SDI research that Reagan refused to accept. The result, graphically pictured better than words ever could by the grim expressions on Gorbachev's and Reagan's faces when they said farewell, was the worst Soviet-American summit failure in twenty-five years.

When Gorbachev went to Reykjavik, in fact almost wherever he went, along with his usual advisors and security personnel he was accompanied by his wife Raisa. Before 1985 the wives of Soviet leaders stayed in the background, if they were visible at all. Raisa Gorbachev was not only highly visible, she was clearly audible. In effect she became an attractive, modern, educated, and articulate role model for over 50 percent of the Soviet Union's population that had never had one. Persistent rumors that Raisa influenced her husband on matters of policy shocked and offended many Soviet traditionalists in a country where traditional views of a woman's role in society persisted and where women's needs, despite official rhetoric dating from 1917, remained sorely neglected. By the mid-1980s women in the Soviet Union had access to many careers—about 85 percent of all women were in the workforce—but in most fields the prestigious positions were still held by men, while women remained disproportionately concentrated in lower paying jobs. Soviet women did double duty because they received little help at home, either from their husbands or the generally outdated appliances they had to use. Soviet socialism did not provide adequate day care for preschool children, leaving Soviet mothers with yet another burden. Families headed by women received scant extra help from the state, while the number of these families had risen as the Soviet divorce rate soared during the 1970s and 1980s. Soviet women spent endless hours shopping in interminable lines, but found their needs were poorly attended to when their bodies required medical attention. For example, because contraceptives were generally unavailable Soviet women had one of the highest abortion rates in the world, so high that abortions in the Soviet Union exceeded live births. The abortions themselves often took place in clinics that lacked proper anesthetics, a situation that frequently was repeated when Soviet women went to a hospital to give birth. Many women were in the Communist Party—they comprised over a quarter of its total membership—but they became increasingly scarce at the higher ranks. While Raisa Gorbachev's charisma and outspokenness obviously had little immediate impact on all of this, her presence at Gorbachev's side, and Alexandra Biriukova's rise to the Secretariat in 1986 and then to the Politburo as a candidate member in 1988, at least stood as symbols that times were beginning to change.

In truth, despite the considerable political movement, most aspects of Soviet life remained unchanged even after the Twenty-Seventh Party Congress. The economy, Gorbachev's main area of concern, remained stuck in neutral. The greatest movement concerned glasnost, where the pace had picked up considerably during 1986. Censorship of literature was eased as some previously banned works began to reappear on the shelves and reformist-minded editors emerged at a number of newspapers, magazines, and journals. Anatoly Shcharansky, the human rights activist and Jewish movement leader, was released from prison in February and allowed to emigrate to Israel; in December, Andrei Sakharov was freed from internal exile and allowed to return to Moscow.

Meanwhile, the pervasiveness and persistence of social and political problems carried over from the Brezhnev era began to convince Gorbachev that economic progress depended on curing many other ills in Soviet society, that an alienated, demoralized, and frustrated population was not going to make the effort needed to revive the economy, and that what was needed was a program of systemic reform across the full spectrum of Soviet life. It is difficult to gauge precisely how various factors influenced Gorbachev. But he began to grow impatient with the slow pace of progress in the economy, a feeling that was probably reinforced and deepened by the complaints he read in the press and heard directly for himself in his tours around the country. At the beginning of 1986 the furthest Gorbachev had gone was to call vaguely for "radical economic reforms." Then, in August of 1986, Gorbachev indicated the lines of his new thinking when he called for reform of

not only the economy but all other sides of life: social relations, the political
system, the spiritual and ideological sphere, the style and work methods of the
Party and of all our cadres. Restructuring is a capacious word. I would equate
restructuring with revolution . . . a genuine revolution in the hearts and minds of
the people.[5]

The years 1985 and 1986 have been called the "prelude to perestroika."[6]
Gorbachev's summer statement that year and subsequent policy initiatives
in 1987 brought to center stage the main part of the composition.

By 1987 Gorbachev in effect had become radicalized, but he still had to
contend with entrenched opposition before he could move further. One
significant source of resistance was the military leadership, which was
hardly enthusiastic about having its resources diverted elsewhere. In May
of 1987, Gorbachev got some help from an unexpected source that enabled
him to clear out some of the Brezhnev-era military holdovers when a
young West German stunned the Soviet defense establishment by piloting
a single-engine plane through the Soviet Union's vaunted air defenses and
landing in Red Square, right at the Kremlin wall. Gorbachev quickly
launched a major house cleaning. He fired the Minister of Defense and the
air defense commander immediately, quickly following that up with doz-
ens of dismissals. He also passed over about twenty higher-ranking officers
to appoint Dmitri Yazov to head the defense establishment.

A month later the Central Committee endorsed what Gorbachev called a
comprehensive program for economic renewal based on what was called
"market socialism." On paper the changes in Gorbachev's "Enterprise
Law" looked large: limiting central planning to long-range guidelines, cutting the power of the economic ministries, putting factories on a self-
financing basis and requiring them to produce quality goods at a profit,
tying workers' wages to performance, expanding the peasantry's private
plots, etc. However, the key to any economic reform was ending the system in which the government set the prices for most goods. This radical
step was extremely controversial and dangerous because it would eliminate
the subsidies on food and other necessities so vital to ordinary Soviet
consumers. And it was at this key point that Gorbachev, despite his radical
rhetoric, in practice held back; price reform was put off, and with it any
real economic change.

Gorbachev held back again at another Central Committee meeting in
October when Boris Yeltsin, the newly installed Moscow party chief,
stunned his colleagues and the world by publicly denouncing the slow pace
of reform. Yeltsin lashed out at Gorbachev, but reserved his harshest words
for Ligachev, the leading critic of Gorbachev's recent policies and proposals. Faced with a choice between an emerging group of radicals represented

by Yeltsin who would push him into the unknown, and entrenched conservatives symbolized by Ligachev who wanted to keep him within familiar confines, Gorbachev, while staking out the center between the two camps, tilted away from the radicals. He rebuked Yeltsin and removed him from the Politburo and his post in Moscow.

While this obviously made Yeltsin the big loser, the Yeltsin affair also hurt perestroika and the general secretary himself. To Gorbachev's opponents on his conservative flank were added critics on his radical flank. It was at this point that Gorbachev, who previously had been close to the cutting edge among the reformers, moved to a more centrist position, beginning a delicate and sometimes dangerous balancing act between his conservative and radical critics that lasted until the collapse of the Soviet Union in December 1991.

Meanwhile Yeltsin's outburst emboldened the conservatives, who could now raise the specter of perestroika running out of control. Giving substance to that warning was an explosion of ethnic violence in the Caucasus, where Armenians and Azerbaijanis confronted each other over control of Nagorno-Karabakh, a region with an Armenian majority that was part of the Azerbaijan SSR. Gorbachev's performance at the seventieth anniversary celebration of the Bolshevik Revolution in November seemed to reflect a sense of discomfort. His long-awaited speech was expected to fill in some of what he called the "blank pages" of Soviet history. He did so, but with uncharacteristic timidity, attacking Stalin, to be sure, mouthing kind words for Bukharin, as everyone expected, but also repeating standard canards against Trotsky, which blackened those "blank pages" once again, rather than filling them in with enlightening information.

The year 1987 nonetheless ended on a positive note, at least in foreign policy. In December Gorbachev went to Washington for his third summit with President Reagan. The two men signed an agreement to eliminate land-based intermediate-range nuclear missiles from Europe. It was a small step toward ending a long arms race; these missiles represented only about 4 percent of the superpowers' nuclear arsenals. Still, for the first time an entire class of nuclear weapons had been eliminated. The Soviets also accepted what are called asymmetrical reductions: because they had more of these weapons, they had to destroy more than the Americans. They also agreed that British and French missiles would not be counted and therefore need not be removed. Meanwhile, Gorbachev used his four days in Washington to meet representatives of America's elite—artists, scientists, business leaders, and Congressional representatives—in a grinding series of scheduled meetings, making a highly favorable impression on them and, through television and other media, on the American people. He also used an unscheduled meeting to meet a group of ordinary American citizens when, while riding in a motorcade, he ordered his car stopped and forged into a crowd of onlookers gathered at the curb. Before his stunned security guards could react, Gorbachev briefly worked the crowd as well as any American politician.

The next year Gorbachev provided further examples of his "new thinking" in foreign policy. After announcing to a skeptical international reception in February of 1988 that the Soviets would withdraw their troops from Afghanistan, the withdrawal was completed on schedule. On February 15, 1989, the last Soviet soldier, a general, left Afghanistan with the comment, "Our nine-year stay ends with this." That "stay" had cost the Soviets 15,000 lives, tens of thousands of wounded, and a loss of international prestige. The Red Army, the proud victor over Hitler's legions, had been defeated by a collection of poorly armed and quarreling guerrillas. But Gorbachev at last had closed what he called his country's open wound. Eight months later his foreign minister Eduard Shevardnadze denounced the Soviet intervention in Afghanistan as illegal and immoral.

Meanwhile, in December of 1988, Gorbachev came to the United Nations in New York to explain to the world how his "new thinking" applied to the arms race and global peace. In a dramatic and well-received speech, he rejected the old Soviet assumption of security based exclusively on military power. Gorbachev asserted that modern technology made security at the expense of others impossible; rather it could best be achieved by recognizing nations' mutual interdependence and their need for cooperation. He then announced the Soviet Union would unilaterally cut its armed forces by 500,000 men, about 10 percent of its total strength, and by 10,000 tanks. The reductions would be from forces in Eastern Europe, which Gorbachev claimed should reduce the perceived threat the West felt about a potential Soviet invasion. These cuts were not popular everywhere; Sergei Akhromeev, the Soviet Chief of the General Staff, resigned over the issue.

Gorbachev's triumphant U.N./U.S. visit was cut short by a devastating earthquake in the Armenian SSR. But that event, while a massive human tragedy, was only one of the many domestic tremors Gorbachev had to deal with. During 1987 and into 1988 and 1989, the strains caused by the reform effort began to show. One reason for the tension is that the country was being stretched in many ways at once, in part because some areas of reform were advancing faster than others. The fastest pace was in the area of glasnost, where the glimmer of 1985 became a steady beam in 1986 and a glaring beacon thereafter, glowing in many different directions at once. Boris Pasternak's Nobel Prize–winning *Dr. Zhivago* finally was published in his native land. Soviet citizens were able to read Anatoly Rybakov's *Children of the Arbat* and Vasily Grossman's *Life and Fate,* which explicitly compares Stalinism to Nazism. Some of Vladimir Nabokov's writings were published in a magazine. Overall, *Izvestia* reported that by the end of 1988 over six thousand book titles previously confined to "special collections" had become available to the public. In 1989 came the stunning announcement that Solzhenitsyn's *The Gulag Archipelago* was scheduled for publication.

Glasnost let the Soviet people see films like *Repentance* in 1987, three years after it was made. This exposé of Stalin's crimes played to over 700,000 people in Moscow in ten *days,* before being released all over the country. It was only one of 100 formerly banned films released between 1985 and 1988. In 1989 came *Little Vera,* a film about the frustration and hardship of Soviet working class life. While dealing frankly with topics like alcoholism and terrible living conditions, *Little Vera* also focused on youthful sexuality in a number of explicit sex scenes that broke all the rules Soviet censors had once enforced. The film actually was part of a widespread erosion of Soviet puritanical strictures that ranged from the publication of a scholarly text on sexology and a sex manual for young couples (which became an immediate best seller) to occasional nudity on television and a striptease revue playing regularly in Moscow.

Glasnost reverberated in music as well. The liturgical tones of Sergei Rachmaninoff's *Vespers,* smothered for decades by official hostility, filled a Leningrad concert hall during the 1987 Easter season. Rock and roll, once denounced as a "crime," emerged from the underground. Aquarium, the best-known Soviet rock group, finally was allowed to record and release an album. Without a single advertisement, 200,000 copies sold out within hours; its sales soon topped three million. Soviet officials even got together with Paul McCartney, the legendary ex-Beatle, who in 1988 released an album called "Back in the USSR" for distribution exclusively in the Soviet Union.

Religious observance was another beneficiary of glasnost. Public celebrations of the one-thousandth anniversary of Russia's conversion to Christianity in 1988 symbolized the relaxation of restrictions on the Russian Orthodox Church. Roman Catholics, Moslems, and Jews also benefited from the more tolerant atmosphere. Catholics in Lithuania received more bishops and Moslems in Central Asia more mosques. In 1989 the Lithuanian parliament declared Christmas to be an official state holiday in that Baltic republic, a status it had not enjoyed since the Soviet Union annexed Lithuania in 1940. Jews were permitted to open their first rabbinical school since the 1920s, and by 1988 allowed to emigrate to Israel in greatly increased numbers. While these changes did not create genuine religious freedom, they did represent a major improvement from pre-glasnost days.

One of the most sensitive areas glasnost touched was history. Mikhail Shatrov's plays *The Brest Peace* and *Onward, Onward, Onward* portrayed not only Nikolai Bukharin but Leon Trotsky in a favorable light. Bukharin was rehabilitated and posthumously restored to membership in the party, exactly fifty years after his execution in 1938. Bukharin's rehabilitation had a special significance, as the economic ideas he articulated in defending the NEP against Stalin in the late 1920s had resurfaced sixty years later in the economic programs of Mikhail Gorbachev. Restored to grace with Bukharin were Grigory Zinoviev, Lev Kamenev, Alexei Rykov, and hundreds of other old Bolsheviks and purge victims. This process even included Leon Trotsky's son, who was shot in 1937. *The New Course,* Trotsky's 1923 attack on Stalin and increasing authoritarianism in the party, was serialized in a magazine. It joined hundreds of works by political figures as varied as Rykov (who was the Soviet president until purged by Stalin), Provisional Government head Alexander Kerensky, and white guard General Anton Denikin on the long list of political literature restored to open shelves. In 1989 the Soviets even admitted the existence of the notorious secret clauses of the Hitler-Stalin pact of 1939 that divided Poland and the rest of Eastern Europe between Germany and the Soviet Union. That year they also published, for the first time, the text of Nikita Khrushchev's secret speech at the Twentieth Party Congress. These and many other revelations came so quickly that in 1988 history texts in the schools had to be withdrawn and history examinations canceled.

Attacking Stalin, while difficult for many conservatives to stomach, became almost respectable under Gorbachev. More serious difficulties arose when criticism spilled over the limits that Gorbachev wanted maintained and washed over Lenin. It did not take long for a few brave souls to point out Lenin's role in setting up the first Soviet labor camps and his repressive policies that paved the way for Stalin, remarks that virtually no Soviet officials, Gorbachev included, wanted to hear. What turned out to be too much for the general secretary was the suggestion on a popular television show in April of 1989 that Lenin's embalmed remains finally receive a proper funeral. This quickly led to the "retirement" of the head of the state committee for television and radio broadcasting. There were other limits to glasnost as well, such as the continued ban on independent cooperatives publishing and printing books, magazines, and newspapers. Some tried to do so anyway, including a group of dissidents who in 1987 began publishing a journal called, fittingly, *Glasnost.* It found little favor with Soviet officials, who denounced it with the observation that the country needed only one "glasnost." Speaking along broader lines, Yegor Ligachev spoke critically about glasnost a number of times, including issuing a warning that "Western bourgeois values" were infecting the country via the new art and literature.

Glasnost nonetheless continued to cast its probing light on Soviet reality. Soviet citizens, once privy mainly to information about how well their country was doing, instead heard about corruption, poverty, murder, drug addiction, inflation, and prostitution. They read the dreadful story about how AIDS was spread to twenty-seven children when hospital nurses, lacking clean hypodermic needles, gave injections with contaminated ones. They heard immediately about sudden disasters, such as the sinking of a Soviet nuclear submarine in 1989, and long-evolving scandals, such as how an entire peninsula in northern Siberia was so poisoned by nuclear tests that its residents had a life expectancy of only forty-five years. Glasnost also extended to the West. Western military men were permitted to see Soviet bases and weapons, including the controversial radar station at Krasnoyarsk that the United States insisted violated the 1972 treaty banning antimissile defense systems, a fact that Soviets admitted in 1989 shortly after agreeing to dismantle the station. Soviet generals even came to Washington to testify about Soviet capabilities and plans to American legislators. But glasnost, it turned out, also had an underside. It was best symbolized by an organization called *Pamyat,* or Memory. Pamyat expressed the old urgings of extreme Russian nationalism, including a mean streak of anti-Semitism and a pronounced hostility toward the West. Although it operated without official endorsement, Pamyat was rumored to have supporters in high places.

While glasnost brought movement and excitement to the Soviet Union, restructuring of the economy yielded disappointment and frustration. While Gorbachev and his allies tried to implement change, they were resisted by powerful party conservatives, who in turn were backed by the literally hundreds of thousands of bureaucrats whose status and livelihood rested on the status quo. The reformers also were hurt by their own inconsistencies—which included scaling back or even reversing policies—and their own lack of experience or guidance; none had ever tried a thorough overhaul of the Soviet economy. The job was monumental; the basic structure of the Soviet economy, dominated by its massive central planning apparatus, dated from the Stalin era. It was grossly inefficient and would have been hard enough to change had everyone pulled in the same direction. Soviet industry was so technologically backward and inefficient that many leaders worried how it could sustain a military machine modern enough to compete with the West. The country's fifty thousand collective and state farms had become a swamp into which a third of all investment sank without enabling the nation to feed itself. Meanwhile a multibillion-ruble illegal or "second economy" had developed to provide Soviet citizens the necessities of life and even a few luxuries the socialist economy could not.

It did not take long for Gorbachev's initial stress on the "human factor"—firing incompetent managers, attacking alcoholism, replacing ministers, etc., all to promote increased discipline and efficiency within the existing economic institutions—to demonstrate its inadequacy. By 1987 his program was far more radical, the emphasis shifting to changing or even abolishing the Stalinist institutions that simply did not work. Abel Aganbegyan, the economist from Novosibirsk who has been called Gorbachev's economic guru, summed up the change in attitude when he noted that "we tried to solve the most urgent economic problems by a little tinkering, a little improving, whereas what was needed was a series of revolutionary changes."

But what was in theory intended to be radical change, and in fact looked radical on paper, produced many piecemeal, erratic and sometimes contradictory policies in practice. Early in 1987 a series of laws allowed cooperatives and even private businesses to engage in a range of economic activities including restaurants, repair services, taxis, and small-scale manufacturing, although restrictions on private business in matters such as hiring remained stricter than on cooperatives. Later the list of permitted activities for cooperatives was expanded considerably to include activities such as banking and foreign trade. By 1989 there were over 77 thousand cooperatives employing over 1.4 million people in the Soviet Union. But there were many problems, including mixed signals from the government. No sooner had the cooperatives been given the go signal when they were hit with impossibly high taxes—levies that were so high they had to be lowered. This swing in policy occurred in 1988; in 1989 cooperatives and private businesses were hit again by a new set of rules limiting the activities they could engage in and price controls. Cooperatives and private businesses also found they had to struggle to get supplies and materials from a socialist system that could not meet their needs either because of ineptitude or hostility. Some cooperatives and private businesses were quite successful nonetheless. They then ran up against public resentment in a country where equality had been drummed into the national consciousness by seventy years of Soviet rule and centuries of communal peasant life before that. Some businesses were victimized by organized crime that extorted protection money from them.

While these policies only involved a tiny percentage of the Soviet economy, similar problems plagued Gorbachev's Enterprise Law, which covered the bulk of Soviet industry. Although the new law technically precluded economic ministries from telling an industrial enterprise what to produce, they managed to do what amounted to the same thing by using their leverage as *customers* to place orders for as much as 70 to 80 percent of production. In some cases the orders actually exceeded certain firms' *total* output. Another problem arose when the failure of many factories to produce goods of acceptable quality led to lower earnings for many workers. In January of 1987, for example, a tractor factory failed to produce even *one* tractor that met the new standards in place at the time.

A similar pattern of erratic radicalization marked Gorbachev's agricultural reforms. This was an area he knew especially well; he had earned a degree in agronomy in 1967 and had attempted to implement reforms during his term as Stavropol first secretary. A 1986 decree provided for increased incentives for collectives by allowing them to sell part of their production on the free market. By 1989 Gorbachev had moved from tinkering with Stalin's system to preparing to dismantle large parts of it. Declaring that the time had come "to return the man back to the land as its real master," Gorbachev won approval, apparently after a struggle with conservatives led by Ligachev, for a program under which peasants would be permitted to lease land, which in effect would have restored a form of private farming. The key task was finding those people after generations of what Gorbachev himself called "depeasantization," in which government policies drove farmers from the land and destroyed the initiative of many of those who remained. But current policies also were a part of the problem. One reason some peasants refused to step forward into the uncertain field of private farming was the regime's continued prohibition of the right to own land. As late as 1990, Gorbachev himself told *Pravda* that "I . . . do not accept private ownership of land whatever you do with me." It therefore should hardly have been surprising that as of mid-1990, there were only 20,000 private farms in all of the Soviet Union, of which 12,000 were in Georgia and 5700 in Latvia, while all of the RSFSR had 240 and the Ukraine—exactly four private farms.

The Soviets tried many other tactics to jump start their economy. They encouraged foreign companies, with some success, to establish joint ventures with Soviet firms. They negotiated several large loans from Western European banks. Soviet specialists came to the West to study management techniques. A start was made in converting some military factories, generally the best supplied and most efficient in the Soviet Union, to producing goods for civilian use. But the economy simply did not respond. Gorbachev found this out for himself in dramatic fashion during a Siberian tour in the fall of 1988. At a stop in Krasnoyarsk he was surrounded by angry citizens who told him, "Go to the store, Mikhail Sergeyevich, there is nothing there." To his promise to get results came the shout, "That won't happen." And, for the most part, it did not. Soviet harvests continued to be poor; the 1988 harvest was 40 million tons short of the target and the worst in three years, while overall agricultural production fell by 2 percent. A quarter of all grain grown continued to be lost before reaching consumers, as did more than half of the fruits and vegetables. Industrial production rose slightly, but production in key industries continued to lag behind targets. The technological lag in key industries also remained; for example, a 1988 American intelligence report estimated a lag of eight to ten years in microcircuits and nine to fifteen in mainframe computers. Basic consumer goods such as tea, cheese, sausages, and salt were in short supply and some were being rationed. Sugar, in part to prevent its diversion to illegal spirits production, in 1989 was rationed in Moscow for the first time since the end of World War II. The budget deficit, swollen by lost revenues from alcohol sales, soared to 11 percent of the gross national product, a proportion over three times higher than the U.S. deficit. In 1989 the government responded to consumer outrage by setting up an emergency fund to import a range of consumer goods from cassette tapes and soap powder to razor blades and pantyhose. To stem the flow of budget red ink, Prime Minister Ryzhkov announced plans to cut the military budget by 33 percent by 1995, a figure far beyond Gorbachev's earlier proposal of a 14 percent spending cut and one that loomed problematic because the 14 percent cut had not yet been accomplished. The Soviets also announced they were scaling back their manned space program to save money.

Gorbachev's other major domestic concern was the minority nationalities question. While the roots of the Soviet Union's nationalities problem are embedded in the legacy of the multinational empire created by the tsars and preserved by the Bolsheviks, Gorbachev's policies also inadvertently played a role in a burgeoning crisis that became uncontrollable. As glasnost and demokratizatsia made the Soviet Union a more open society, ethnic grievances bottled up for so long by repression soon boiled over. When they did, the new openness allowed them to expand and feed one another in a chain reaction of major and minor incidents that became impossible to control.

Gorbachev's own words provide a good measure for how the situation escalated. His lack of sensitivity and preparation to deal with the question was illustrated shortly after coming to power when he referred to his country as "Russia" during a speech in Kiev, the capital of Ukraine, correcting himself by referring to the "Soviet Union" only after being prompted by an aide. In his book *Perestroika,* written in 1987, Gorbachev penned the utterly incredible remark that the "revolution and socialism had done away with national oppression and inequality" and that in the Soviet Union the nationality question had been "solved in principle." He soon found out how terribly wrong he was. During 1987, when disturbances had already swept the country from the Baltic coast to Central Asia, Gorbachev remained optimistic, expressing his understanding for the notion that "every people wants to understand its roots," and answering "Of course not" to the question of whether this was at variance with socialism. By 1988 a subdued Gorbachev labeled the nationalities problem "a crucially important, vital issue in the USSR" and called for a "very thorough review of our nationalities policy." By 1989 a worried general secretary was denouncing "this multivoiced choir" from which he heard "threats of approaching chaos and talk of a threatened coup, and even of civil war."

The first serious signs of trouble occurred in December of 1986 in Kazakhstan when Gorbachev fired the longtime local party chief Dinmukhamid Kunaev, an ethnic Kazakh known for his corruption, and replaced him with an ethnic Russian. This affront to national pride produced a full-fledged riot, complete with several killings, destruction of property, and attacks on militia troops. Far more serious trouble soon erupted along the Baltic coast and in the Caucasus. In 1987 in the tiny Baltic republics of Latvia, Lithuania, and Estonia, where memories of the short interwar period of independence lingered, there were demonstrations against the Nazi-Soviet pact that ended that era. Soon the spontaneous shouts of "freedom, freedom, freedom" heard in demonstrations evolved into organized political movements called "Popular Fronts" in all three republics. In 1989, Soviet citizens were treated to the spectacle of mutual declarations of invalidity, as the Lithuanian legislators declared the Soviet annexation of their country null and void, while the Soviet Ministry of Justice declared an Estonian voting law that discriminated against ethnic Russians to be unconstitutional. By the fall of that year, the fiftieth anniversary of the notorious pact, calls for economic autonomy and even independence echoed along the entire Baltic coast. In a stunning demonstration of solidarity, two million people linked hands in an unbroken line from Tallinn, Estonia, in the north through Latvia to Vilnius, Lithuania, in the south.

If the situation in the Baltic states was serious, at least it was bloodless. The same cannot be said for the Caucasus, where national hatreds, not for Russians, but for each other, pitted local populations against one another. The most serious problem was in the autonomous region of Nagorno-Karabakh, populated mainly by Christian Armenians but part of the largely Moslem Azerbaijan SSR. Beginning in early 1988 huge demonstrations and riots produced many deaths as Armenians demanded the territory be transferred to the neighboring Armenian SSR. The compromise solution, ruling the region directly from Moscow, satisfied no one. Moscow had to station over fifty thousand troops there to keep the peace. In the summer and fall of 1989, taking advantage of the fact that Armenia received many of its supplies via a railroad line that crosses Azerbaijan, the Azerbaijanis clamped a blockade on their fraternal Soviet republic that lasted for two months. For good measure they blockaded Nagorno-Karabakh and did not lift the blockades until Moscow threatened to use the army to open the rail lines.

In Georgia, yet another Caucasian republic, anti-Russian riots in the spring of 1989 produced several fatalities, and a national scandal, when troops used poison gas against the demonstrators. By the end of 1989, interethnic conflict in the Caucasus and in Central Asia had produced hundreds of deaths and tens of thousands of refugees. In the western part of the country it produced a strong reaction from ethnic Russians living in non-Russian republics. In both Estonia and Moldavia, a region annexed in 1940 and populated by people speaking a Romanian dialect, ethnic Russians went out on strike to protest local legislation making the local language the official language of the republic. Perhaps most disturbing were nationalist stirrings in the Ukraine, home of the largest non-Russian Soviet minority and producer of one-fourth of the nation's food and a third of its heavy industrial production. Russian and Soviet leaders alike always had come down especially hard on Ukrainian nationalism because of the region's strategic importance. In the summer of 1989, when Ukrainians were forming their Ukrainian Popular Movement, they were careful to say their goal was "rebirth" rather than independence, but the entire business caused a collective grimace in the Kremlin reaching from Gorbachev to Ligachev. An old joke has it that the USSR was really the "Union of Silently Swallowed Republics." With the arrival of glasnost, they were not silent any more. As the 1980s waned, minority nationalism rivaled economic troubles on Gorbachev's worry list, having become a threat not only to Gorbachev and perestroika, but to the Soviet Union itself.

These developments took place against continued tension between Gorbachev and his conservative critics. In March of 1988, while Gorbachev was on a foreign visit, a leading Soviet magazine published a letter allegedly written by a Leningrad chemistry teacher, but in fact inspired by Ligachev and other conservatives. The "Andreyeva Letter" was a Stalinist attack, complete with anti-Semitic slanders, against Gorbachev's policies. More disturbing than its appearance was the paralysis in the perestroika camp. Without Gorbachev on the scene, the old fears, supposedly dead since 1985, rose again to haunt Moscow; nobody found the courage to defend perestroika, and the silence continued even after Gorbachev returned home. It took three weeks for Gorbachev's counterattack, but when it came it was a typically vigorous one that included media responses and a rebuke to Ligachev from the Politburo.

Gorbachev's offensive continued at the Nineteenth Party Conference in June of 1988. Party conferences are second in importance only to congresses, although none had been called since 1941. Gorbachev wanted one to push political change, finally getting his way after agreeing not to make any changes in the Central Committee at the conference. The most visible sparks at the stormy meeting came from the open clash between Yeltsin and Ligachev. The real business of the conference, however, concerned the structure of the Soviet government, as Gorbachev had some major political restructuring on his agenda. He wanted to strengthen the state apparatus at the expense of the party, where he continued to face strong opposition to his reforms. After heated debate he got his way. The conference voted to abolish the Supreme Soviet, the old Soviet parliament, and replace it with a 2,250-member Congress of People's Deputies. Elections to this body would feature a radical new innovation: There would be a choice of candidates. The Congress of People's Deputies would then elect a smaller body called the Supreme Soviet, which would conduct the nation's day-to-day business. It would also elect a President of the Soviet Union who would have far more power than the current president. While these changes lay in the future, one innovation was immediate. The open and often angry debate was broadcast on Soviet television for all to see. As Gorbachev understated it, "I think we will not err from the truth by saying nothing of the kind has occurred in the country in six decades."

Gorbachev pressed his advantage at a September Central Committee meeting. He pushed aside Andrei Gromyko, the last powerful Brezhnev era holdover. A few days later Gromyko's post of Soviet president went to Gorbachev. Although this was only a ceremonial post—the resolutions of the Nineteenth Party Congress had not yet been implemented—Gorbachev increased his prestige by becoming head of state. Ligachev meanwhile was weakened by being shifted from his post as Central Committee secretary responsible for ideology to the thankless agriculture slot. A symbolic move was the promotion of Alexandra Biriukova to candidate member of the Politburo, making her the first woman to sit on that body in any capacity since 1961, and only the second since 1917.

In the spring of 1989 Gorbachev led the country into the rough and uncharted waters of multicandidate electoral politics as it chose its new Congress of People's Deputies. The elections were not completely democratic; one-third of the seats were reserved for the party and a variety of party-dominated "social" organizations. With the remaining seats, old line party bosses often kept reformers and dissidents off the ballot, so that almost 400 seats had only one candidate. Nonetheless, it was the most democratic election the country had seen since 1917, complete with literature, large rallies, and frank television debates. The results stunned everybody: 15 percent of the winners were not party members. This tendency was especially pronounced in several non-Russian republics. Outright dissidents won seats, including Andrei Sakharov. Nor did the election of certain party members necessarily give the leadership comfort. In Moscow, Boris Yeltsin, so recently demoted and rejected by the party leadership, did better with the people: he won 89 percent of the vote. Yeltsin now began to emerge as a challenge to Gorbachev in two ways. First, he stood for increasing the pace and expanding the scope of reform. Second, unlike

Gorbachev, who in the selection of the Congress took one of the seats reserved for party officials, Yeltsin was elected directly by the people which gave him a mandate the general secretary lacked. Of more immediate concern and most embarrassing for the party, some of its leaders running *without opposition* managed to lose when they could not win 50 percent of the vote. Among these notable losers were the head of the Leningrad party organization, the mayor of Moscow, and the mayor of Kiev. Whatever he really thought, and his must have been a very mixed reaction, Gorbachev hailed the "people's power" that emerged from the election. Yet he must have been worried lest conservatives again hit him with the club of allowing perestroika to run out of control, as he quickly moved against them. In April, in another "cold purge," Gorbachev engineered the removal of 110 members of the Central Committee, including 74 full members. In their place 24 reformers became full members. Once again the military lost strength, its representation declining by 40 percent.

The new Congress of People's Deputies met in June. Aside from being a historic political event, it was the largest media hit in Soviet history. It was covered live on television across the country's eleven time zones and watched by 200 million people, no less than 70 percent of the population. One American observer compared it to World Series time in the United States. And there was a lot to see. Deputies of varying opinions spoke bluntly; Sakharov, for example, warned lest Gorbachev accumulate too much power, and a former Olympic star lashed out against the KGB. The congress also elected a 542-member Supreme Soviet, the country's new parliament, amid protests by dissidents at the congress that their members were being frozen out. With 95 percent of the vote, the congress elected Gorbachev to the new, more powerful post of President of the Soviet Union, although not before he stood before the delegates to answer hard questions, responded to pointed criticism, and solemnly promised, "I will never allow the things that happened in our past to happen again."

Many others were determined to play their part to realize Gorbachev's promise, even without his approval. During its six-week inaugural session in July and August, the Supreme Soviet showed surprising independence for a body whose membership was 85 percent Communist. It rejected eight of Prime Minister Ryzhkov's nominees for ministerial posts. It set up a committee whose charge was to oversee the KGB, although the committee lacked both the resources and authority to do the job. Toward the end of its session, to Gorbachev's public dismay, a number of dissidents led by Yeltsin set up what they called the "Interregional Group," whose membership also included several hundred delegates from the larger Congress of People's Deputies. That organization, which within two days had established its own newspaper, in effect was the first formal opposition to the party the Soviet Union had seen in over sixty-five years.

These events were paralleled by the revival of another phenomenon not seen since the 1920s: a massive series of labor strikes. Reacting to poor living conditions and shortages of necessities such as a lack of soap for men who spent their days hundreds of feet underground, thousands of coal miners in Siberia put their mark on the summer of 1989 by going on strike. The strikes spread westward to the Ukraine; during a period of two weeks over 500,000 miners struck, seriously threatening the nation's coal supply at a time when economic conditions already were bad enough. Desperate to end a potentially crippling crisis, the government promised a package of improvements including pay increases and increased availability of food, medical supplies, and other consumer goods estimated to cost between five and nine billion dollars. Gorbachev announced that local elections would be moved up from the spring of 1991 to the fall of 1990. While these concessions were enough to get the miners back to work, many mines maintained their strike committees to make sure the government delivered on its promises. In the fall, twenty-five thousand coal miners north of the Arctic Circle again went out on strike, this time in defiance of a partial strike ban enacted by the Supreme Soviet (Gorbachev had wanted a total fifteen-month ban) only two weeks earlier.

Gorbachev meanwhile reinforced his position by striking against conservatives on the Politburo. The blow came at a special Central Committee meeting, finally held in September after being postponed four times, officially devoted to the nationalities problems. The minority republics were promised more autonomy. But Gorbachev's promise of a "radical transformation" in the Soviet federation was vague, and he explicitly rejected any border changes among the republics. The Central Committee's main business was to remove several old-line conservatives from their Politburo posts, including Vladimir Shcherbitsky, the long-time boss of the Ukraine and the only Politburo holdover besides Gorbachev from the Brezhnev era. However, in restaffing the Politburo Gorbachev ran directly into a stumbling block he either overlooked or refused to see: that party regulars who between 1985 and 1987 favored limited Andropov-style reforms were becoming convinced by 1989 and 1990 that change in the Soviet Union was threatening their power and should be stopped and even reversed. This dilemma did not have a better symbol, or more dangerous personification, than Vladimir Kryuchkov, head of the KGB, who with Gorbachev's support vaulted over candidate status to full Politburo membership in September 1989. Almost exactly two years later, Kryuchkov was one of the party leaders, all of whom Gorbachev had promoted or supported, who tried to overthrow him and reverse perestroika.

Gorbachev had more urgent problems with Communist leaders outside the Soviet Union's borders during 1989. The one initiative that went reasonably smoothly was his visit to the People's Republic of China in May, ironically just before authorities there brutally massacred students in Beijing's Tiananmen Square who were demanding the same kinds of political reforms Gorbachev was instituting in the Soviet Union. In Eastern Europe it was Communist governments rather than the people that became the casualties of changes. In Poland, the Communist Party, in a desperate attempt to shore up its popular support, in April legalized Solidarity and agreed to relatively free parliamentary elections; it was promptly routed by Solidarity-backed candidates when the elections were held two months later. This led to the formation of the first non-Communist-dominated government in Eastern Europe since the Communist takeover of Czechoslovakia in 1948, but not until Gorbachev himself pressured his Polish colleagues to take this drastic step in light of their election defeat. Although Soviet divisions were stationed in Poland and local Communists still controlled the country's military and police, the Communist grip on Poland was slipping away. Meanwhile, 1956 began to repeat itself as Hungary once again followed and then outdid Poland. In May hundreds of miles of barbed wire came down as Hungary opened its border with the West. The following month Imre Nagy, the leader of the ill-fated 1956 revolt who was executed by the Soviets along with other leaders of the rebellion, was restored to grace and officially declared a national hero. In the beginning of October the Hungarian Communist Party shocked the world by voting to abolish itself and become a socialist party like those in the West; it correspondingly changed its name to the Hungarian Socialist Party. A few days later the Hungarian People's Republic announced that henceforth it was the Republic of Hungary, a multiparty democracy that intended to hold its first elections the following spring. Within two months, the Hungarians had an agreement in principle from the Soviet Union that Soviet troops, stationed in Hungary since World War II, would be withdrawn. It turned out that the dreams of 1956, once dismissed as dead, had only been deferred.

The Eastern European political earthquake meanwhile hit East Germany, where it brought down Erich Honecker's hard-line regime right in the middle of one of its jack-booted goosesteps. East Germany, a bastion of Teutonic order and Communist orthodoxy, supposedly was the most successful Communist state in Eastern Europe. But no sooner did Hungary open its borders with the West in May than several thousand East Germans, mostly young and educated and, therefore, a critical part of their country's future, in effect punched a gaping hole in the Berlin Wall by crossing the Hungarian frontier into Austria. During the summer of 1989 thousands of East German tourists, temporarily prevented by Hungary from following their countrymen to the West, refused to return home. In

September Hungary again opened its western border to the East Germans. The mass flight resumed, via Czechoslovakia and Poland as well as Hungary, while huge demonstrations on East German soil, the largest since the anti-Soviet uprising of 1953, demanded reforms at home. The fortieth anniversary celebration of East Germany's founding on October 7, with Gorbachev in attendance, did not improve matters. On October 18, Honecker resigned due to "ill health" after eighteen years in office. His replacement was Egon Krenz, at fifty-two the youngest of the old-line leaders and to most East Germans the perfect example of old wine in a new bottle. Krenz's promises of reform—in quick succession he conferred with Gorbachev in Moscow, fired five hard-line members of the Politburo, and then engineered the resignation of the entire cabinet and most of the rest of the Politburo—and his plea to his "dear fellow citizens" that "we need you all" (two weeks earlier the government had called the protesters "neo-Nazi thugs") were greeted with demonstrations that reached half a million strong while tens of thousands continued to stream to the West. Early in November over fifty thousand East Germans reached the West in a few days.

Then what only days before was unthinkable happened. The flood of refugees fleeing abroad, the thunder of protest of those staying put, and quaking political ground underneath the East German leadership combined to topple the Berlin Wall. On November 9, 1989, twenty-eight years after it built the wall to stop an earlier flood of refugees, the East German government announced the end of all travel restrictions to the West, including those via Berlin. The Berlin Wall—singular symbol of the Cold War, scene of spectacular escapes and deadly failed attempts at flight, dead zone of over one hundred miles of concrete, steel, barbed wire, watchtowers, and mine fields surrounding all of West Berlin, place of mourning for over a generation of Germans—suddenly became a place of jubilant celebration with thousands of people crossing back and forth at its checkpoints, drinking champagne, banging at the hated edifice with hammers, chisels, and sledgehammers, and literally dancing atop its concrete blocks. The irony was that at its festive death the wall remained what it was at its funereal birth: a giant monument to the failure of Soviet-style socialism in Eastern Europe.

The day after the Berlin Wall was opened Todor Zhivkov resigned after thirty-five years as the undisputed strongman in Bulgaria. Two weeks later, surrounded by reform in East Germany, Poland, and Hungary and pressured by political forces ranging from huge crowds in Prague's Wenceslas Square to Mikhail Gorbachev and his comrades in Moscow's Red Square, the hard-line Czechoslovakian Politburo resigned. By the end of December, Czechoslovakia had its first non-Communist government since 1948, headed by former dissident Vaclav Havel, while Alexander Dubcek, the tragic hero of his country's ill-fated 1968 precursor to perestroika, emerged in triumph as chairman of the national parliament. Back in East Germany, during December the Communist Party lost its constitutional right to a monopoly of political power, Egon Krenz and his entire Politburo resigned, and several former high-ranking officials, including Erich Honecker himself, were placed under arrest for corruption and abuse of power. Change also finally came to Romania, but unlike elsewhere in Eastern Europe, only after tragic violence. In mid-December Nicolae Ceausescu's secret police forces violently attacked thousands of pro-democracy demonstrators. But the demonstrations continued, and when the Romanian army refused orders to kill the people it was supposed to protect and joined them instead, protest became revolution. Several days of bloody fighting followed, during which Ceausescu and his wife Elena were captured while trying to flee and executed. A quickly formed National Salvation Front then took power and promised a multiparty political system and free elections. By the end of December, the laws in all the presumed Soviet allies in Eastern Europe—Poland, Hungary, Czechoslovakia, Bulgaria, and Romania—had been changed to deprive their respective Communist Parties of a monopoly on political power. As 1989—the "year of the people"—came to an end, ending along with it were the region's Communist regimes and the satellite system and security zone that was the Soviet Union's great prize from World War II and a cornerstone of its foreign policy since 1945.

Moscow, meanwhile, did nothing to slow or stop the continental Communist collapse. In effect, the Gorbachev regime seemed to have quickly calibrated the Soviet Union's security calculus, and written off the control of an increasingly expensive and unreliable Eastern Europe in favor of achieving security through normalized relations with the United States and Western Europe. But if the Soviets now had to restructure their policies in Europe from scratch, at least this time so would the United States and its NATO allies. For not only the Soviets' Eastern European empire but the entire postwar European order had been called into question. That order, whatever its failings regarding national self-determination and democracy as far as Eastern Europe was concerned, had given the continent over forty years of peace. It rested on the division of Germany and Europe and on the NATO and Warsaw Pact alliance system that sheltered the two Germanies and most other European countries. But the end of the Wall undermined the postwar order by reviving the long-dormant issue of German reunification. Not surprisingly, the response to that idea in both Western and Eastern capitals from those who remembered World War II was less than ecstatic. The Soviet Union, while calmly endorsing the Wall's demise, firmly indicated it expected East Germany, where 380,000 Soviet troops were stationed, to remain a separate state and part of the Warsaw Pact, while in Washington talk of unification was called "premature." A promi-

nent French writer certainly spoke for many of his countrymen and other
Europeans as well when he commented that "I like Germany so much that I
want there to be two of them."

The new year, 1990, ushered in a new decade, with new expectations
and concerns. Whereas in 1985 there were few in either the Soviet Union
or the West who thought the Soviet regime, despite its problems, was in
danger, by 1990 it was visibly beginning to totter. The pace of change
clearly was not merely accelerating; it was careening out of control and
turning into chaos, the most dangerous developments being the unraveling
economy and the spreading and increasingly violent ethnic strife.
Gorbachev, the internationally acclaimed master political sorcerer, was
being turned by events into a desperate sorcerer's apprentice, unable to
manage the runaway upheavals his policies had unleashed.

The one area where Gorbachev could still claim success was in foreign
policy, where relations with the West continued to improve. But even
there, Soviet policy, at least to critics at home, was looking more like a
headlong retreat from superpower status and an unending acquiescence to
Western demands. During the early part of the year, the Soviet Union
reached agreements with Czechoslovakia and Hungary for withdrawal of
its troops from those former satellites, and restored relations with the Vati-
can after a break of sixty-seven years. Far more significantly, the fall of
1990 saw the settlement of the German unification problem. But that settlement was on Western, and especially German, terms, not Soviet ones.
There was in fact no great enthusiasm in the West for immediate German
reunification, but both Soviet opposition and Western hesitancy proved
unable to derail the blitzkrieg diplomatic campaign launched by West German Chancellor Helmut Kohl, who lavished assurances about Germany's
peaceful intentions on leaders from Washington to Moscow. In the end,
Gorbachev accepted both German reunification and a united Germany's
membership in NATO, the latter condition representing a repudiation of
Soviet policy that dated to the formation of NATO in 1949. In return, the
Germans agreed to limit the size of their army to 370,000 troops; to re-
nounce chemical, biological, and nuclear weapons; and to provide the Soviet Union with about $8 billion in desperately needed aid. Germany's
formal reunification, and with it the liquidation of the Soviet role in eastern
and central Europe which they won in the carnage and devastation of
World War II, took place on October 3, 1990.

The reunification of Germany was followed within a month by a
NATO/Warsaw Pact arms agreement limiting conventional arms in Europe. Two days later, on November 21, 1990, an event occurred that only a
few years before seemed impossible: the United States, Canada, the Soviet
Union, and every European nation except Albania signed the Charter of

Paris, which, echoing a NATO declaration from the previous June, proclaimed the end of the Cold War. It seemed anticlimactic and not a touch ironic that this titanic struggle, which brought the world to the brink of nuclear destruction, spawned the greatest arms race in history, divided the European continent in two, and consumed one of the world's two superpowers and gravely weakened the other, was concluded with the short, bland understatement that the "era of confrontation and division of Europe has ended." Instead of finishing with the dreaded nuclear bang, the world of the Cold War had ended, if not with a whimper, then with barely a whisper.

The Soviet Union became the first beneficiary of the Cold War's demise when Western European nations and the United States began sending emergency aid to cope with urgent shortages of essentials, including food. Meanwhile, the Soviets were already abandoning old Cold War habits by supporting the international effort to force Iraq, which had invaded and occupied Kuwait in August 1990, to leave its oil-rich neighbor. When economic sanctions failed to budge the Iraqis, the Soviets did not interfere when the U.S.-led coalition used military force early in 1991 to expel their former client from Kuwait. While this development was welcomed in the West, it did not sit very well among Gorbachev's conservative critics in Moscow, who viewed his foreign policy, especially his readiness to give up Eastern Europe, as capitulation rather than cooperation. They remained unimpressed when on October 15, 1990, the Norwegian Nobel Committee announced that the 1990 recipient of the Nobel Peace Prize was Mikhail Sergeyevich Gorbachev. The Soviet old guard suffered another blow, symbolic but still painful, when the Warsaw Pact formally disbanded on July 1, 1991. Nor was Gorbachev's performance a few weeks later at a meeting with the world's seven leading capitalist industrial nations sufficient tonic for his ailing reputation at home, as he failed to win any solid commitments for large-scale economic aid. On July 31, Gorbachev and President Bush signed another breakthrough arms reduction treaty, the START I (Strategic Arms Reduction Talks) agreement calling for the Soviet Union and the United States to reduce their long-range nuclear weapons by 30 percent. But by then, as the world soon found out, time was rapidly running out not only for Gorbachev, but for the Soviet Union itself.

By early 1990, the Soviet political arena provided increasing evidence that Gorbachev was losing control of events at home and becoming unable to respond to them once they occurred. In February and March local elections across large parts of the Soviet Union saw Communist Party candidates rejected en masse. This trouncing included the loss of majorities in the Moscow, Leningrad, and Kiev city councils to non-Communists. Gorbachev's response was contradictory, a classic example of what the long-time dissident poet Yevgeny Yevtushenko called "half measures" in his poem of that name. Shortly after the election, at Gorbachev's urging, the Congress of People's Deputies repealed Article 6 of the Soviet Constitution, which guaranteed the Communist Party a total monopoly on political power. (In February, after a bitter debate, Gorbachev had convinced the party's Central Committee to agree to that change.) However, a few days later, he had retreated back to the old politics. The congress had heeded his call to establish a new executive presidency with even more powers than before, a president who would be elected directly by the people. But rather than risk going to the people for the mandate he so desperately needed, Gorbachev had the congress bypass the new direct election statute and reelect him president of the Soviet Union; a direct election by the people would have to wait until 1995. To be sure, Gorbachev now had even more power than before, but neither he nor the congress could give the presidency the authority and respect that can come from being chosen by the people.

Gorbachev's failure to adjust to the emerging new political culture which increasingly required a direct mandate from the people compared unfavorably with the approach of his new rival Boris Yeltsin. Although humbled by the Communist Party Central Committee when it removed him from the Politburo in 1987, Yeltsin revived his political fortunes in 1989 when he was triumphantly elected with the largest majority of any candidate by the people of Moscow to the Congress of People's Deputies. In the 1990 local elections Yeltsin was elected once again, this time to the new parliament of the Russian Republic. In May 1990 he overcame Gorbachev's backing of a rival candidate and was elected by parliament as the president of the Russian Republic. Yeltsin's best act of political theater occurred in June 1990 at the Communist Party's Twenty-Eighth Congress, when he dramatically announced his resignation from the party after a short speech and strode out of the hall, leaving 4700 stunned delegates and the old Soviet politics behind, thereby planting both feet firmly in the new political arena forming outside the party. He was followed out of the party by a number of other radicals, including Leningrad mayor Anatoly Sobchak and Moscow mayor Gavril Popov.

Gorbachev remained behind, both physically and politically, and continued to manage the party congress. That was not an easy task, as conservative delegates denounced what Yegor Ligachev called General Secretary Gorbachev's "blind radicalism." Still, Gorbachev was able to keep the conservatives in check—he succeeded in pushing Ligachev into retirement—and overhaul the Politburo. Every other prominent party leader, including foreign minister Shevardnadze and Gorbachev's close advisor Alexander Yakovlev, left the Politburo, turning it into what one Soviet observer called a "long list of nobodies." This in effect ended the Politburo's role in governing the country, a role it had played since March of 1919. Gorbachev also had the party faithful create a new post—deputy general secretary—responsible for supervising the day-to-day party operations while General Secretary Gorbachev concentrated on his presidential duties. He thus seemed to be trying to get away with yet another half measure: slowly pushing the party aside and gradually distancing himself from it, but without pushing too fast or far or cutting his ties to what many observers considered a sinking ship.

While these high-level meetings were taking place in Moscow, the regime's authority was crumbling across the country. On March 11, 1990, Lithuania, where anti-Soviet nationalists had won an overwhelming victory in local elections, declared its independence. While the declaration lacked practical significance—it was revoked three months later after immense pressure from Gorbachev that included moving troops into the Lithuanian capital of Vilnius—it was an important symbol of defiance. By December 12, when the small Central Asian republic of Kyrgyzstan made its announcement, all fifteen Soviet republics, including Russia, had declared their "sovereignty," a term sufficiently vague to avoid a reaction from Moscow, but still indicative of how low the Kremlin's authority had sunk.

In the meantime, Gorbachev was retreating from reform. In September 1990 he rejected a radical economic reform program called the Shatalin plan, which would have moved the Soviet Union to a market economy in 500 days. The Soviet president seems to have been motivated by three factors: his perception that growing chaos threatened the country's survival; the fear that the short-term hardship—most notably the sharp rise in the price of food and other necessities—caused by economic reform would lead to dangerous public unrest; and nasty rumblings from powerful conservative forces, including the military. Then on December 2, 1990, Gorbachev stunned and demoralized the proreform camp when he removed reformer Vadim Bakatin, his interior minister (and as such the official in charge of the police), and replaced him with Boris Pugo, a hard-line conservative and apparatchik. Less than three weeks later, Gorbachev's old friend and comrade-in-arms Eduard Shevardnadze resigned as foreign minister with a chilling warning: "The reformers have headed for the hills. Dictatorship is coming." Shevardnadze's warning gained credibility in January 1991, when elite Soviet army troops equipped with tanks and machine guns stormed the central radio station and television station in Vilnius, Lithuania, killing 13 people and injuring over 200. A week later, a similar, though smaller, incident in Latvia cost four lives. Gorbachev denied he knew anything about plans to strike against the Lithuanians, but he also refused to condemn the action. Despite angry public protests—a group of Moscow demonstrators, having let their anger cloud their powers of rational comparison, called Gorbachev the "Saddam Hussein of the Baltics"—he continued his rightward retreat during January and February. He appointed

Valentin Pavlov, a staunch conservative, as prime minister, authorized army patrols of Soviet cities to reinforce local police, and called for a law limiting the freedom of the press. By early 1991, almost all of Gorbachev's old perestroika team—including Shevardnadze, Yakovlev, economic advisor Stanislav Shatalin, and Bakatin—had left or been dropped from Gorbachev's government. They were replaced with conservatives, men like Pugo, Pavlov, Defense Minister Yazov, and KGB chief Vladimir Kryuchkov. Perestroika had become Janus-faced, as it seemed to turn from reform to reaction.

None of these actions had any noticeable effect on the spreading revolt of the minority nationalities and the collapsing economy, twin threats that continued to undermine both Gorbachev and the Soviet Union itself. On the nationalities front, the fifteen declarations of sovereignty of 1990 were followed by two referenda early in 1991, in Lithuania and Georgia, in which local voters overwhelmingly cast their ballots for independence. Interethnic hatred continued to fester and occasionally explode across the country, as in the deadly Armenian/Azerbaijani conflict, rioting in Georgia between Georgians and Ossetians, attacks in the Uzbek republic by the Uzbeks against Meskhetians, and murderous violence in the Kyrgyz republic against Uzbeks.

The economic news for the first half of 1991 was no better. The year began with widespread food shortages as the collapse of the old central distribution system left a large part of the 1990 grain harvest rotting in the fields or on the way to market. Inflation rose, state shops remained empty, national income dropped by about 10 percent, and production fell in key industries from coal and oil to dairy products and meat. The transition to private agriculture, one of the key hopes for economic renewal, proceeded at a snail's pace, and the forecast for the coming harvest was gloomy. In Moscow, the city council began rationing meat, grain, and vodka. One key cause of these difficulties was Gorbachev's search since 1987 for a workable economic program that he hoped could appeal to both the conservatives on his right flank and radicals on his left. He had started dismantling parts of the old Stalinist command system, but refused to take the radical steps necessary to permit the development of a market economy. The result was summed up by one distressed official who observed that "We have completely destroyed the old system and proposed nothing in its place."

It was against this background that Gorbachev tried his last major gambit as Soviet president: he turned away from the conservatives and back to the reformers. In March 1991 the nation held its first-ever referendum on a Gorbachev-inspired question as to whether the Soviet Union should continue to exist as a united country. Gorbachev got the answer he wanted:

three-quarters of those voting on the vaguely worded question answered "yes." However, that figure was less impressive than it looked because six republics, including all three Baltic republics, boycotted the election. The March vote yielded another "yes," but one that Gorbachev did not want: Yeltsin supporters asked voters in the Russian republic if they wanted to elect their president directly instead of via their parliament. After 70 percent of the voters answered affirmatively, Yeltsin swept to victory in June 1991 with over 57 percent of the vote, as compared to 17 percent for Nikolai Ryzhkov, the Communist Party candidate. On July 10, in a ceremony in which he spurned the Communist Party while accepting the blessing of the Russian Orthodox Church, Boris Yeltsin was inaugurated as the first freely elected leader in Russia's history. Once again Yeltsin, whose personal mandate now spanned the Soviet Union's largest republic, had eclipsed Gorbachev.

The Soviet president, however, continued to push forward into the face of a growing storm. In April 1991 he and the leaders of nine Soviet republics, including President Yeltsin, worked out what was called the "nine plus one" agreement for a new union treaty. This was an attempt to hold the union together by giving the individual republics considerable power to run their own affairs. But by the middle of 1991 the center was no longer holding. On the one side, conservatives were denouncing Gorbachev openly and gathering their forces against him, determined to prevent the new union treaty, which would have cut many of the central government's powers, and hence their own, from taking effect. On the other flank, Yeltsin, his supporters, and other radical reformers had given Gorbachev up. Early in August, Alexander Yakovlev, the godfather of Gorbachev's perestroika, resigned from the Communist Party; he also warned of an impending coup against his former colleague. By then Gorbachev had left Moscow for a vacation in the Crimea; his last, it turned out, as president of the Soviet Union.

On the morning of August 19, 1991, the world awoke to the shocking news that Mikhail Gorbachev had been removed from office, presumably "for health reasons." A group of conservative politicians, officially led by the new "president" Gennadi Yanayev, announced that they had taken control of the country. Despite all warnings, the coup, which had been in preparation for months, still came as a shock to most observers, who worried more about food shortages during the coming winter than coups d'état during the summer. As Gorbachev sat stunned under house arrest in the Crimea, he learned that he had been betrayed by the same men he had recently promoted and sponsored. Those men included Pugo and Kryuchkov (the two central conspirators), Defense Minister Yazov, Vladimir Ivashko (the man Gorbachev had just made the party's deputy general secretary), and, most painfully, Anatoly Lukianov, Gorbachev's friend and associate from his university days.

The technical reasons for the failure of the coup are well known. The coup leaders did not begin their coup with mass arrests of potential resistance leaders, notably Russian President Boris Yeltsin. This allowed Yeltsin to rally the resistance from his iron perch atop a tank in the center of Moscow. The coup leaders did not make sure that vital military and KGB troops were prepared to follow orders, and in fact they waited six hours before deploying troops and tanks in Moscow. By the time the conspirators were ready to use force, crowds had gathered around Yeltsin's headquarters. These were not massive crowds by the standards of major historical events, never numbering more than 150,000 in Moscow and 200,000 in Leningrad; the crowds that defied the Eastern European Communist regimes in far smaller cities were several times larger. Most Soviet citizens, in fact, stayed on the sidelines and waited. But like Gideon's hundreds, Yeltsin's hundreds of thousands were enough, even though their barricades were, as one Soviet commander put it, "like toys" that his troops could have overcome in "fifteen minutes." The price, however, would have been a bloodbath, and this the military refused to pay. The soldiers would not defy a sign hanging near Yeltsin's headquarters that told them "Don't Shoot Your Mothers" or shoot at a crowd that stuffed flowers into the gun barrels of their armored vehicles. Individual tanks, paratroopers, and entire units defected to the resistance at the start. The KGB elite troops refused to attack Yeltsin's headquarters. Yeltsin's personal ties with the troops and their commanders paid off when the commander of the air force opposed the coup. Meanwhile, opposition to the coup spread across the country. Leaders of several republics rallied against the coup, and coal miners who struck against it. Finally, support for Gorbachev and Yeltsin came from abroad, most importantly from the United States, which refused to recognize and legitimize the new government. By August 21, 1991, it was all over, and the plotters were under detention. On August 22, though pale and visibly shaken, Mikhail Gorbachev returned to Moscow, once again the president of the Soviet Union.

These are the surface details. The fundamental reasons for the coup's failure lie deeper. It was undertaken to reverse the process of change in the Soviet Union, but failed because the change perestroika had unleashed already had gone too far. For example, by 1991, the conspirators had to base their actions on some sort of legal norms, or risk a potentially dangerous public reaction. One of the reasons the conspirators did not begin with a campaign of massive arrests that would have included Yeltsin is that they wanted to avoid overt illegality. To bolster their legal credentials they cited Article 127 of the Soviet constitution, which justified removing the president if he proved unable to perform his duties because of health problems. In other words, the new conditions in Gorbachev's Soviet Union created what one observer has called the need for "legal cover,"[7] but getting that legal cover helped to undermine the coup and contributed to its failure. At the same time, the country had changed enough so that soldiers refused to fire on their countrymen—this in a country where at one time children were expected to betray their parents. The Soviet Union also had changed to the point where fear no longer could freeze everybody. As recently as 1988, the Andreyeva letter had paralyzed the reformers, until the white knight Mikhail Gorbachev returned from abroad to rally his frightened legions. But in August 1991 there were hundreds of thousands who were not afraid to stand up against dictatorship, little enough in a country of 290 million, but just enough to thwart the coup. They succeeded in part because since 1985 the continual waves of change had hollowed out the Communist Party (about one-fifth of its membership had already quit) and demoralized the army, two crucial pillars of the order the conspirators hoped to save. Those waves also had eroded the foundations of the Soviet Union itself, which was so weakened by the summer of 1991 that it collapsed with barely a shove a few months later.

In short, despite its obvious failings, perestroika had succeeded in its most important task: to make it impossible to turn the clock back. Boris Yeltsin, who at the moment of truth risked his life and demonstrated his capacity to lead, was, to be sure, the hero of that moment. But even under detention and though unable to join the pivotal August battle, Mikhail Gorbachev remained, to paraphrase the Russia's great nineteenth century poet and novelist Mikhail Lermontov, the hero of the time.

Prior to the August coup, Soviet Communism had been dying a slow death; the coup was the blow that killed it once and for all. Yeltsin immediately banned the Communist Party in the Russian Republic, while Gorbachev resigned as its general secretary and ordered that party property be seized. The top leaders of the KGB and army were dismissed, and many of them were arrested. Central ministries of the government were closed down, and their functions transferred to the republics. The Komsomol dissolved itself. A wholesale renaming of cities and towns began, the most symbolic of which was Leningrad's change to St. Petersburg. On November 7, 1991, there was no official celebration of the Bolshevik Revolution.

As Communism collapsed inside the Soviet Union, the union itself disintegrated. Early in September, Lithuania, Latvia, and Estonia won Soviet recognition as independent states. Gorbachev then began a last ditch attempt to hold the Soviet Union together, which collapsed almost as quickly as it began. In a referendum on December 1, 1991, Ukraine voted overwhelmingly for independence. A week later, Boris Yeltsin and the leaders of Ukraine and Belarus banged the last nail into the Soviet Union's coffin when they announced the formation of what would be called the Commonwealth of Independent States (CIS). The Commonwealth was vaguely projected as a loosely organized body of fully independent states. They supposedly would cooperate on matters such as mutual defense and economic problems, although how much the member states genuinely would have in common remained to be answered. Despite Gorbachev's vocal opposition, less than two weeks later the CIS was formally constituted by eleven of the former Soviet republics, the three Baltic states and Georgia remaining outside its rather loose embrace.

On December 25, 1991, Mikhail Gorbachev resigned as the president of the nonexistent Soviet Union. At 7:32 P.M., moments after he finished his resignation speech, the red Soviet flag with its hammer and sickle, the symbol of Soviet Communism Gorbachev had tried to reform and humanize, was lowered from over the Kremlin for the last time. The official end came on December 31, 1991. The Union of Soviet Socialist Republics, the embodiment of a bold and brutal social experiment that once claimed to own the future, now belonged to the past.

Mikhail Gorbachev came to power determined to reform, and thereby to preserve, the Soviet system. He wanted to purge it of what he considered the Stalinist perversions of Leninism, and put the country back on what he believed was the true Leninist path. His objective was to build a humane form of socialism consistent with Marxism and Leninism as he understood them. In these goals he was very much like Khrushchev, and like Khrushchev he failed. Instead of reforming the system, Gorbachev's policies hastened its demise. Gorbachev could not easily accept what had happened; even after the failed coup he argued against both the banning of the Communist Party and the dissolution of the Soviet Union. As late as mid-December 1991, when there was nothing of the old order left for him to save, he warned his countrymen that "We are destroying a state that needs to be reformed."

But in the broader historical sense Gorbachev's achievements dwarf his failures, both in the possibilities his leadership created for the people of the Soviet Union and the example he provided as a statesman. What made Mikhail Gorbachev an outstanding political leader is that he possessed the vision to see farther and wider than other Soviet party leaders and had the courage to try new policies, despite the opposition of powerful entrenched forces and the danger that untested policies could fail and backfire. Trapped with his country in a dark tunnel decades long, Gorbachev had the will and strength to lead his people toward the light. As he did so, often stumbling in the treacherous darkness, sometimes reversing his field, but always returning to the original course, his policies made possible the end of the Cold War. They gradually freed the Soviet people of the fear that had silenced them since Stalin's terror, which is why the conspirators of August 1991 were thwarted by hundreds of thousands of demonstrators, by soldiers who would not kill fellow citizens, and by politicians who were prepared to defend the gains of the previous six years. This process of liberation from fear took time, which Gorbachev provided with his six-year daredevil highwire political balancing act that showcased his remarkable political skills. In short, although in 1991 Gorbachev was unable to break with the old system, his policies created the conditions that allowed others to do so.

Given the realities of the Soviet system, none of the weak and scattered groups of dissidents that pre-dated Gorbachev's election as general secretary could budge or dent the party dictatorship that controlled the country. Only an extraordinary member of the Communist Party power structure could have led the country out of the totalitarian quagmire in which it still was trapped in 1985 to the point where it could finally break free from that system, and do so with a minimum of bloodshed. Mikhail Gorbachev was that man, and therefore a figure of immense historical stature.

Gorbachev also will be remembered as a leader who tried to use his power to accomplish something good for society as a whole and who recognized that his goals precluded the use of certain methods. As political scientist Michael Mandelbaum put it:

> Mikhail Gorbachev's character, however flawed, was marked by a basic decency missing in every previous leader of the Soviet Union and indeed in every ruler of imperial Russia before that. He refused to shoot. He refused—with the exception of several episodes in the Baltics and the Caucasus in which civilians were killed—to countenance the use of violence against the citizens of his country and of Eastern Europe.... For this alone he deserved the Nobel Peace Prize he received ... and deserves as well the place of honor he will occupy in the history of the twentieth century.[8]

Perhaps the most compelling tribute of the many one could cite came from Boris Yeltsin, Gorbachev's rival and the man who eventually pushed him out of the Kremlin:

> What he has achieved will, of course, go down in the history of mankind. I do not like high-sounding praise, yet everything Gorbachev has initiated deserves much praise. He could have gone on just as Brezhnev and Chernenko did before him.... He could have draped himself with orders and medals.... Yet Gorbachev chose another way. He started by climbing a mountain whose summit is not even visible. It is somewhere up in the clouds and no one knows how the ascent will end: Will we all be swept away by an avalanche or will this Everest be conquered?[9]

That said, there are several basic reasons why Gorbachev, his immense political skills notwithstanding, could not save the Soviet system. First of all, he really never fully understood the forces his policies had unleashed, especially how they were affecting the Soviet people and their attitude toward perestroika in general and him in particular. Both his lack of knowledge about economics and his unwillingness to implement essential radical reforms led to policies that killed the old economic system, but could not give birth to a new one. As the old economy collapsed, shortages of food and essential consumer goods hit the general population hard, causing Gorbachev's popularity, so essential to his ability to carry out his program, to plummet. Respected and lionized abroad, especially in the prosperous West, he increasingly was disliked and ridiculed at home by ordinary people whose economic condition rapidly was going from bad to worse. While failing to appreciate fully how dangerous this situation was, Gorbachev also was blind to the nationalities problem for far too long. Even after non-Russians began to raise their voices in the era of glasnost, Gorbachev failed to listen to them and so did not appreciate how resentful they were. As late in the day as December 1991, he was shocked when Ukraine voted to leave the USSR. Gorbachev also had little understanding of freedom and democracy, which is why he thought that he could allow just a little glasnost and democracy, and then perhaps dole out some more bit by bit at times of his own choosing. But, following the logic of openness and freedom, both glasnost and democracy rapidly took on lives of their own and raced ahead beyond the bounds Gorbachev wanted, becoming a radical and uncontrollable genie out of the bottle rather than Gorbachev's desired manageable servant of socialist reform. Gorbachev, ultimately a product of a dictatorial system, reacted to this development with imperious disdain and anger. Each passing day, especially after 1989, left him more and more out of step with the times and therefore unable to respond effectively to new and unfamiliar challenges.

Gorbachev's foreign policy played a major role in undermining Communism at home. As he moved away from the Cold War, he deprived the Soviet system of the implacable outside enemy needed to justify its Marxist ideology, its low standard of living, and the dictatorship it imposed on the people. In addition, when Gorbachev permitted the Communist regimes in Eastern Europe to collapse without a protest, a chain reaction began that did not stop until it reached the Kremlin and shook down its Communist walls. No invader from the west, not even Napoleon or Hitler, ever swept eastward more relentlessly from the Polish frontier into the Russian heartland, brushing aside all opposition as it bore down irresistibly on Moscow and the Kremlin, than did the idea of overthrowing Communism after the revolutions of 1989.

The core reason why Gorbachev failed, and what ultimately rendered his hope of reforming the system futile, lies deeper, however, than any specific policy error or misjudgment. It lies in the totalitarian nature of Soviet society. The Gorbachev era was an education about the Soviet Union for many people, including Western specialists in Soviet affairs. For example, the claims by some revisionist historians that the number of deaths caused by the Stalin regime had been grossly overestimated—one revisionist number-crunching estimate miraculously reduced the toll in Stalin's great terror to "thousands"—and that the fear caused by Stalin's great purge and terror did not hold the entire country in its grip, have been laid to rest and buried under an avalanche of testimony and other evidence that has emerged since the advent of glasnost. Far more widespread among Western scholars by the 1970s was the idea that the Soviet Union after Stalin was not a totalitarian state, but rather an "authoritarian" society where a variety of interest groups shared power. This school of thought also tended to deemphasize Lenin's responsibility for the development of Stalinism, and to draw a sharp distinction between the two regimes. But while the totalitarian view of the Soviet Union did not always account for every twist and turn in Soviet history—what can?—it does explain the essence of Soviet society and what made it different from other systems. As historian Geoffrey Hosking has observed, the concept of totalitarianism

> is capable of affording us a more complete view of Soviet society than any alternative yet propounded.... Remove the term "totalitarian," and it is not obvious how the Soviet Union differs from, say, Spain under Franco or Chile under Pinochet. But these differences are crucial.[10]

These differences certainly were not lost on Soviet leaders and commentators of the post-1985 era, who regularly used the term "totalitarian" to describe the system they were trying to dismantle more than thirty years after Stalin's death. Thus in his resignation speech, Gorbachev summed up his accomplishments by noting that the "totalitarian system that long ago deprived the country of an opportunity to succeed and prosper has been eliminated," while in his autobiography Yeltsin thanked Gorbachev for embarking on reform rather than being satisfied to "have lived the well-fed and happy life of the leader of a totalitarian state."

And it is precisely the totalitarian structure of Soviet society that best explains both how resistant it was to Gorbachev's reforms and why it collapsed so quickly and completely as change finally began to take root. It was not a variety of interest groups, but the Communist Party that ran Soviet society. The party dominated the economy, the state, the political life, and the social institutions of the Soviet Union. As scholar Theodore Draper observed, "this system was held together by the total control of the

Communist Party."[11] Once the party's power began to crumble from the relentless erosion caused by Gorbachev's reforms, the entire Soviet system began to disintegrate. Or, as historian Martin Malia succinctly put it, "such a total collapse could only proceed from a total society."[12]

The collapse was total because it did not stop at the demise of Stalinism —that is, those aspects of Soviet society that could be traced to the Stalin era—as Gorbachev had hoped and as those who would decouple Leninism and Stalinism might have expected. Nor could it, because Leninism, while it did not feature the mad, murderous terror of Stalinism, was the totalitarian foundation upon which Stalinism was built. Lenin, not Stalin, gave the Soviet Union the one-party dictatorship, buttressed by its secret police, that claimed total control over all aspects of life in the new socialist world. To Lenin's work Stalin added the centralized command economy and an expanded secret police apparatus to carry out his terror and consolidate his personal dictatorial rule, parts of which remained in place after his death to serve the party dictatorship of his successors for over three more decades. The institutions created under Lenin's Bolshevik dictatorship of the 1920s and Stalin's personal dictatorship of the 1930s were inextricably fused and part of the same structure, and that is why they collapsed and were swept away together when the tidal wave of freedom washed over them. Nothing could better symbolize that basic fact than what occurred in Moscow and Leningrad—the Soviet Union's two main cities, one for over seventy years the seat of Communist power and the other the site of the Bolshevik Revolution—immediately after the defeat of the August coup. In Moscow, the first thing to come down was the huge statue of Felix Dzerzhinsky, one of Lenin's most loyal supporters and the founder of the secret police, which the Bolsheviks set up barely a month after they came to power and used to entrench and protect their dictatorship. Meanwhile, in Leningrad, the citizens of that city repudiated their city's Bolshevik name and restored the name given to it by its founding tsar, St. Petersburg. The people, to whom Marxists are supposed to appeal as their ultimate authority, were not drawing fine distinctions. When an elderly Moscow woman watching the removal of the hated "Iron Felix" told an American reporter, "We are sick of all Communists. They have been strangling us for seventy years," she was not limiting her critique to Stalinism.

The Russia that emerged from the strangle hold of failed Communism and the debacle of the fallen Soviet Union was still a giant, even a colossus, but a badly wounded one. It was plagued by ominous political, economic, and social problems that required urgent attention. Although still the world's largest country in terms of area and its second-ranking nuclear power, as well as the inheritor of the former Soviet Union's seat on the UN Security Council, Russia was shorn of most of the empire it had ruled for centuries and could no longer be called a superpower. Its future, while potentially more hopeful than before, contained equal potential for turmoil. In short, after more than seven decades, on a road that many Russians bitterly called the "road to nowhere," the country had come full circle. Amid the rubble of a fallen regime and in the face of extremely difficult conditions, Russia faced the unenviable task of beginning again.

NOTES

1. Yevgeny Yevtushenko, "Half Measures," in *Fatal Half Measures: The Cult of Democracy in the Soviet Union* (Boston, Toronto, London: Little Brown, 1991). Translated by Albert C. Todd.

2. Moshe Lewin, *The Gorbachev Phenomenon: A Historical Interpretation* (Berkeley and Los Angeles: University of California Press, 1988), p. 24.

3. S. Frederick Starr, "Soviet Union: A Civil Society," *Foreign Policy*, Number 70, Spring 1988, p. 30.

4. Martin Walker, *The Waking Giant: Gorbachev's Russia* (New York: Pantheon, 1986), p. 175.

5. Cited in Gail W. Lapidus, "State and Society: Toward the Emergence of Civil Society in the Soviet Union," in *Inside Gorbachev's Russia*, Seweryn Bialer, editor (Boulder and London: Westview Press, 1989), p. 122.

6. Seweryn Bialer, "The Changing Soviet Political System," in *Inside Gorbachev's Russia*, p. 193.

7. Robert Kaiser, *Why Gorbachev Happened* (New York: Simon and Schuster, 1992), p. 426.

8. Michael Mandelbaum, "Coup De Grace: The End of the Soviet Union," *Foreign Policy*, Vol. 71, No. 1, 1991, p. 173.

9. Boris Yeltsin, *Against the Grain: An Autobiography,* translated by Michael Glenny (New York: Summit Books, 1990), p. 139.

10. Geoffrey Hosking, *The Awakening of the Soviet Union.* Cambridge: Harvard University Press, 1990, p. 7.

11. Theodore Draper, "Who Killed Soviet Communism?" *The New York Review of Books,* June 11, 1992, p. 12.

12. Martin Malia, "Leninist Endgame," *Daedalus,* Vol. 121, No. 2, Spring 1992, p. 60.

20

Yeltsin and the Birth of Post-Soviet Russia

*And the end man looked for cometh not, and the path
is there that no man thought.*
—EURIPIDES

*There is nothing more difficult to take in hand, more
perilous to conduct, or more uncertain in its success,
than to take the lead in the introduction of a new
order of things.*
—MACHIAVELLI

The king reigns, but does not govern.
—JAN ZAMOYSKI, Polish nobleman, to his country's parliament, 1605

Post-Soviet Russia, which officially began its existence as the Russian Federation on January 1, 1992, was considerably downsized from both the Romanov Empire and its Soviet successor. Gone was Ukraine, taking with it Kiev—the ancient "mother" of Russian cities—as well as about one-fifth of the former Soviet Union's industrial plant, a variety of important mineral resources, a rich belt of black earth that produced about one-fourth of Soviet agricultural goods, and the sunny Black Sea shores of the Crimea. Gone also were the grasslands of Moldova, long contested with Romania; the forests and marshes of Belarus, contested even longer with Poland; most of the Baltic coast, where Lithuania, Latvia, and Estonia—once again free of Russia's imperial grasp—anxiously looked westward; the soaring mountains and picturesque valleys of the Transcaucasus, where the tiny and troubled republics of Georgia, Armenia, and Azerbaijan uneasily calculated their unsettled ethnic scores; and the vast steppe, deserts, and mountains of Central Asia, a politically unstable region divided among sprawling Kazakhstan, arid Uzbekistan and Turkmenistan, and diminutive Kyrgyzstan and Tajikistan. In short, with the collapse of the Soviet Union, Russia lost most of its conquests of the past 250 years. Its borders, with some variations, approximated those of the Russian Empire at the death of Peter the Great.

Yet the Russian Federation was still roughly three-quarters the size of the defunct Russian Empire and Soviet Union, about 6.6 million square miles spread across northern Eurasia, or close to twice the size of any other country on the planet. It retained a vast, if somewhat reduced, treasure trove of natural resources, including oil, gas, iron, rare metals, forests, and coal; its most serious losses were the oil and gas reserves in the Caspian Sea region that fell within the borders of Azerbaijan and Kazakhstan. The reduction was far greater in terms of population: the Russian Federation's 149 million people were barely half of those who had lived in the former Soviet Union. However, over 80 percent of Russia's population, as opposed to barely 50 percent of the Soviet Union's, consisted of ethnic Russians. Another 25 million Russians lived as a minority population scattered throughout the other fourteen independent states that emerged along with Russia from underneath the rubble of the collapsed Soviet Union.

Russia's problems were as immense and complex as the land itself. One of the most costly legacies of seventy years of Soviet totalitarianism was that, once it collapsed, it left so little on which to build. By contrast, when non-Communist authoritarian regimes collapsed in European countries such as Greece, Portugal, and Spain, or in Chile in South America, they left behind social and economic institutions that had been permitted to operate independently of the state as long as they did not interfere with the existing political dictatorship. These institutions, where people functioned autonomously and maintained a variety of skills and self-reliant behavior, traditionally formed the basis for what in the West is known as a civil society, and they provided an invaluable foundation for rebuilding formerly undemocratic societies on a democratic and free market basis once the old authoritarian political regimes were gone. In addition, the former authoritarian countries of Europe and the Americas rarely faced the multiplicity of problems simultaneously confronting Russia. These problems fell into four general categories: making the transition from a socialist to a free market economy; building a democratic political system; crafting a foreign policy that would define Russia's place in the world; and forging a Russian, as opposed to an imperial or Soviet, national identity.

The contrast between Russia and former authoritarian countries, and the

degree of Russia's disadvantage, was especially pronounced when it came
to the economy. Countries such as Greece or Chile began their new eras
with reasonable facsimiles of market economies. Even in the former satellite states of Eastern Europe, where Communism had been imposed only
after World War II, there were people who still retained skills and habits
from the old days. No such legacy existed in Russia, whose economy had
been totally deformed by three generations of Soviet totalitarian socialism.
No Russian entrepreneurial class was available to undertake the countless
activities necessary for the functioning of a market economy. No class of
independent farmers remained from before collectivization to overhaul and
revitalize Russia's moribund agricultural sector. The bulk of the population, including most of the country's elite, looked askance at private
property.

Against this background, building a market economy required taking
several difficult and interdependent steps. First, even though the old centralized socialist economy was falling apart, in late 1991 most prices still
were set by the state. Prices had to be freed from state control and allowed
to fluctuate according to the demands of the marketplace. Second, state-
owned factories, farms, and shops, which amounted to virtually the entire
economy of the country, had to be privatized. This was a monumental task
under any circumstances but was doubly difficult in a country that had not
known private property in over sixty years, and which had no body of law
that conveyed the right of private ownership of economic assets. Third,
Russia needed a stable currency that would enable the domestic economy
to function and permit it to join the world economy, from which it had
been largely isolated since Stalin's First Five-Year Plan. Along with these
tasks, Russia had to start converting its enormously bloated military industries, whose high technology and resource-hungry factories produced little
to meet the needs of the general population, to civilian uses. It had to find a
way of creating competitive market conditions in a country where industrial production was so highly concentrated that a single gigantic factory or
factory complex often produced 100 percent of a given manufactured product. All of this, and more, had to be done while production was falling, the
standard of living was plummeting, and corruption and theft were un-
checked and draining the country of its wealth.

Along with its formidable economic agenda, Russia faced the equally
daunting task of building a new political system. Once again, there was
virtually nothing from the Soviet system that could be retooled for the new
era if Russia's new government was going to be based on democratic
principles. The Soviet-era constitution that the Russian Federation inherited had been a mask for a one-party dictatorship and was useless as a
framework for a workable government. In particular, despite hundreds of

amendments during the Gorbachev years, the constitution left unclear the relationship among the key branches of government, particularly between the president and the parliament, and between them and a third branch, the constitutional court created in July 1991. Russia had no experience with institutions vital to democratic life such as genuine political parties accustomed to legislative give-and-take and compromise. In addition, the collapse of centralized Communist Party control, upon which everything had depended during the Soviet era, threw open the relationship between Russia's new central government and the country's various regions and ethnic republics, while the power vacuum and resultant separatism that emerged threatened the country's unity. This problem was most acute with regard to the several non-Russian ethnic republics that were demanding extensive autonomy or even complete independence, the most militant being Tatarstan and Chechnya.

Russia's relationship to the outside world was one issue where the new regime under President Boris Yeltsin did not have to start from scratch. Between 1985 and 1991 Mikhail Gorbachev's "new thinking" had repudiated the Marxist tenets of Soviet foreign policy and forged a new approach that stressed normalized relations with the West and a mutual concern for dealing with major international problems. One of the architects of the new policy was Andrei Kozyrev, who served in the Soviet foreign ministry until he became the foreign minister of the Russian Federation in October 1990. With Russia's independence, Kozyrev and President Yeltsin continued their pro-Western, or "Atlanticist," policy. Its basic premise was that Russia's national interests were best served by cooperating with the United States and its allies, as this would help integrate Russia into the Western world and, not insignificantly, guarantee a flow of Western aid that would help Russia rebuild. However, it was not long before this approach was challenged by elements less friendly to the West than Yeltsin and his supporters. These groups had deep disagreements: their views about how Russia should be run ranged from traditional Communist to neo-Fascist. At the same time, they generally rejected the Yeltsin-Kozyrev foreign policy because of its alleged subservience to the West and its presumed betrayal or neglect of Russia's national interests, particularly with regard to the states of the former Soviet Union, now known as the "Near Abroad," and the former Soviet satellites in Eastern Europe. These domestic pressures had their effect, as Russia's foreign policy and attitude toward the West hardened noticeably by 1993.

Russia's attitude toward the West and the rest of the world reflected a deeper dilemma that grew out of its unresolved sense of national identity. While there were many conceptions of how post-Soviet Russia should view itself, two core issues stood out. First, for centuries Russia has been associated with empire, first under the tsars and then, for a shorter period, under the Soviets. This association held sway across the political spectrum. Not only unrepentant Communists and neo-Fascists, but moderates and liberals as well, were shaken when the Soviet Union collapsed. The loss of Central Asia may not have been hard to take, but the defection of Ukraine and Belarus, fellow Slavs who were viewed as "brothers," caused shock and dismay. Suddenly it was necessary to accept Russia existing within a much smaller space and playing a far more modest role in the world. Second, a new version of the old Westerner/Slavophile debate reared its head. Russians were asking themselves to what degree Russia was a European nation and how much it should strive to be like Europe. Did Russia have its own uniquely Orthodox Eurasian civilization, and if it did, to what degree should it seek its own path of development? Furthermore, post-Soviet Russia, which presumably aspired to be a democratic society, had to accommodate within its new identity the aspirations and sensibilities of its non-Russian population, a concern unknown during the country's authoritarian past. Nor were these questions strictly academic. How they were answered had direct implications for urgent policy matters, among them how Russia should treat the Near Abroad and how it should build its federal structure at home.

As if all these problems were not enough, Russia emerged from the Soviet era bearing other heavy burdens. The country's environment—its polluted cities, its poisoned rivers, its vast stretches of ruined countryside—amounted to what Yeltsin correctly called an "ecological disaster." Russia also faced a growing health crisis and a swelling crime wave, as well as a host of other severe social problems. Yet somehow there was a feeling of optimism, even euphoria, in the air, an expectation that Russia could make the transition from a socialist dictatorship to a capitalist democratic regime relatively quickly and with a tolerable level of pain. That turned out to be a false hope, a shimmering myth that soon evaporated in the hot glare of Russia's troubled new reality. Russia's post-Soviet era began not with triumph, but with turmoil.

The man at the center as Russia began its post-Soviet era was Boris Yeltsin, the former Communist Party apparatchik turned radical reformer. Yeltsin was the son of generations of peasants, who, he recalled, "had plowed the land, sown wheat, and passed their lives like all other country people," from a village in the Ural Mountains near the city of Ekaterinburg (called Sverdlovsk during the Soviet era), where Europe and Asia meet. He had suffered adversity from the very beginning of his life: as an infant he nearly drowned when a drunken priest dropped him into a baptismal tub, after which the unflustered cleric commented that young Boris's survival indicated he was a "good, tough lad"; he blew off two fingers of his left hand when, with typical Yeltsin finesse, he tried to disassemble a stolen hand grenade with a hammer; and his twisted "boxer's" nose was a permanent reminder of having been hit by a cart axle during a fight. Yeltsin's 1987 Central Committee outburst, which cost him his job as Moscow party chief, was not the first such incident in his life; as a teenager his public denunciation of a teacher at his secondary school graduation for allegedly treating students cruelly nearly derailed his chances for a higher education. Yet Yeltsin landed on his feet time and again after youthful escapades, became a civil engineer, and eventually entered the Communist Party apparatus, where he rose through the ranks to the Moscow post from which he fell with such suddenness in 1987. As 1992 dawned, having just completed his most remarkable comeback yet, Yeltsin now faced the greatest challenge of his life: leading Russia as it struggled to begin building a new social order based on Western political and economic principles.

Yeltsin actually formed Russia's new government in November 1991, while the Soviet Union officially was still in existence. He began by convincing Russia's parliament, elected the year before, to grant him emergency powers for one year, including the right to enact economic reform by decree. (The 1040-member Russian parliament, like the former Soviet parliament, was called the Congress of People's Deputies. It elected a smaller 248-member body called the Supreme Soviet to function as Russia's day-to-day legislature.) President Yeltsin then became his own prime minister and appointed several academics who were advocates of radical economic reform to key government posts. The most important were thirty-five-year-old Egor Gaidar, who had worked with Stanislav Shatalin on his abortive 500-day plan during the Gorbachev era and who became Yeltsin's deputy prime minister responsible for economic affairs, and Gennady Burbulis, the first deputy prime minister. Significantly, two tough and resourceful politicians who had stood prominently with Yeltsin during the August coup now were excluded from the president's inner circle: Aleksandr Rutskoi, Russia's vice president and a highly decorated Afghanistan war hero who had been Yeltsin's running mate in the June 1991 election, and Ruslan Khasbulatov, a former economics professor from Chechnya who had been Yeltsin's ally in Russia's parliament and became chairman of its Supreme Soviet in October 1991 after Yeltsin was elected president. It would not be long before both men emerged as vigorous opponents of Yeltsin and his policies.

Yeltsin and his closest advisors were convinced that they had to move ahead quickly, both because Russia's economy was in such dire straits and because they believed they had to seize the political "window of opportunity" that had opened up with the defeat of conservative forces during the August coup. Devoid of experience with the type of massive economic overhaul they were attempting, as was everybody else both in Russia and abroad, Russia's radical reformers believed that if they moved decisively their country could get its market economy working in the shortest possible time and thereby keep hardship, which they recognized was inevitable, to a minimum. Yeltsin and Gaidar appeared to expect that the worst would be over within a year. Their program of drastic steps was called "shock therapy," an unflattering name from a public relations point of view.

Yeltsin plunged ahead with the crucial first step on January 2, 1992, by doing what Gorbachev had not dared: he ended price controls on most goods. Only a few necessities were exempted to protect low-income people. They included bread, milk, medicines, public transport, and vodka, the last item providing a telling and depressing commentary on the importance of alcoholic beverages in Russian life. Although oil and gas prices were raised, they remained regulated at about 20 to 30 percent of world prices. At the end of January, another Yeltsin decree lifted all restrictions on private trading. For the first time since the 1920s, all Russians legally could engage in the business of buying and selling.

The first stage of shock therapy yielded some modest positive results. It destroyed what was left of the old Soviet central planning system. At the same time, thousands of Russians responded to the price and trading decrees by setting up small stands known as kiosks on the streets of Russia's cities and towns. However, the immediate negative effects of price liberalization appeared to outweigh the positive ones. The kiosks sold mostly imported consumer goods such as liquors, canned foods, and cigarettes, generally at prices ordinary workers and people on fixed incomes could not afford. Uncontrolled prices soared, rising much faster than wages. For example, food prices climbed over 300 percent in January alone and over *2000* percent for 1992 as a whole. Unemployment, unknown during the Soviet era, made its grim appearance; by mid-year almost one million Russians were jobless, as some enterprises and offices tried to cut unnecessary costs. Millions of Russians saw their savings, accumulated over decades of stable prices, wiped out by inflation. Meanwhile, the overall Russian economy, already in decline during the last years of perestroika, continued to contract. Both national income and industrial production shrank by an estimated 20 percent during 1992. By the end of 1993, the decline for both categories passed 30 percent. Not surprisingly, the number of people living in poverty rose; by 1993 over one-third of the population was classified as living beneath the poverty line, with 10 percent classified as "very poor." Among the worst off were the elderly, who generally lived on modest fixed pensions that quickly lost most of their purchasing power. The reaction to shock therapy was not long in coming, particularly from Yeltsin's opponents in parliament, who ranged from moderate centrists to unrepentant Communists and overt neo-Fascists. It contributed to the political tug-of-war already brewing between the parliament and the president, which weakened the Yeltsin government and made it that much more difficult to cope with Russia's enormous problems.

Yeltsin was partly to blame for the political gridlock. Notwithstanding his 1990 resignation from the Communist Party and his 1991 popular election as Russia's president, Yeltsin drew on his experience as a Communist Party boss for much of his political style. Like an old party boss, President Yeltsin intended to govern and introduce his economic and political changes from above. In this regard, he was consistent with Russia's centuries-old tradition of revolution or reform from above that stretched back to Peter the Great. Never having lived in a democratic society, Yeltsin appeared not to appreciate the need to build popular support for his economic reforms. He therefore rejected the idea of early parliamentary and local elections, which, coming in the post-Soviet era, would have strengthened his mandate for change. Yeltsin also specifically placed himself "above politics" and made no effort to organize a political party around himself and to define a clear political platform, which might have helped him to deal with the parliament. Nor did Yeltsin use the prestige he had in late 1991 and early 1992 to press for a new constitution to replace the unworkable Soviet document with its unclear division of powers. The result was a muddle that weakened Yeltsin, who was trying to implement policy, and that bolstered his growing list of opponents, who had the easier task of trying to thwart policy.

The first significant clash occurred in April 1992, when Khasbulatov, already moving closer to hard-line opponents of Yeltsin's policies, led an unsuccessful attempt in parliament to limit Yeltsin's powers. However, Yeltsin had to bow to parliamentary pressure and appoint several moderates to leading posts in his government. The most important, Viktor Chernomyrdin, who had once headed the Soviet natural gas industry, now became one of Yeltsin's deputy prime ministers. At the same time, Yeltsin reaffirmed his economic course by appointing Gaidar acting prime minister. By June, a newly formed group called the Civic Union entered the fray against Yeltsin's economic policies. Led by several centrist politicians including Rutskoi, the Civic Union initially did not support the hard-line conservative opposition to Yeltsin. Yet it strongly advocated a slower approach to economic reform, stressed the necessity of protecting certain key Russian industries from collapse, and, not incidentally, viewed the West with much less enthusiasm than did Yeltsin or Kozyrev.

Rutskoi and Khasbulatov meanwhile moved closer to Yeltsin's hardline opponents in parliament, whose strength was growing along with the country's economic hardship. A sign of that strength was the formation of the National Salvation Front, which brought under one umbrella former Communists still loyal to the cause and hard-line nationalists whose views shaded into neo-Fascism, a combination soon dubbed the "red–brown" alliance. Among the front's goals was the restoration of the Soviet Union with its old borders.

In the meantime, Yeltsin and Gaidar pushed ahead with the second key part of their economic program: privatization of the more than 200,000 state-owned enterprises that dominated the Russian economy. The goal was a transfer of wealth of unprecedented scope and size: the shifting of the ownership of hundreds of thousands of enterprises—not only small shops but also gigantic factories—from the state to individual owners. This was, said Yeltsin, the "ticket to a free economy." Just as important, privatization was to be the vehicle for creating a class of property owners and a strong middle class—"millions of owners, not a small group of millionaires," in Yeltsin's words—that would provide the basis for a democratic society. In effect, it was a modern-day version, albeit in support of a different political regime, of Peter Stolypin's wager on "the sober and the strong."

Progress was extremely slow until October 1992, when Yeltsin, in the face of strong conservative opposition in parliament, inaugurated his "voucher" program. Managed by an energetic reformer named Anatoly Chubais, the program distributed vouchers worth 10,000 rubles to each of Russia's 149 million citizens. The vouchers could be used to buy shares, either on an individual basis or by joining an investment company, in businesses that were being privatized. In deference to conservatives in parliament, the program was modified to enable workers of any given enterprise to gain control of their workplace. While this preference for worker ownership appealed to egalitarian sentiments that were still strong in Russia, it also left many enterprises under the control of people who, in order to protect their jobs and security, were unlikely to take measures— which often included shedding excess workers—that were necessary to make those businesses efficient and profitable. Another problem with Yeltsin's privatization program was that well-placed members of the old nomenklatura were able to use their connections and positions to gain control of valuable state enterprises. They then often sold off assets and turned themselves into instant millionaires, thereby negating Yeltsin's promise that his program would benefit a broad spectrum of the population rather than a privileged or unscrupulous few. A widespread complaint among Russia's hard-pressed masses was that Yeltsin's policy amounted not to genuine privatization, or what had been trumpeted as "people's privatization," but to "nomenklatura privatization."

The results of privatization were most impressive in the area of retail trade, 77 percent of which was outside state control by December 1993.

Progress was much slower in agriculture. Although most collective and state farms officially underwent reorganization, in practice they were little changed. People who withdrew from the collectives to establish private farms faced many difficulties, including getting good land to farm and securing necessary equipment and financing. They also faced resistance from the majority of collective farmers, many of whom were elderly, who considered private farming a threat to the only way of life they knew. By December 1993 Russia had about 270,000 private farmers. However, they farmed only about 6 percent of the land and some of them were failing; over 14,000 private farms went out of business during 1993.

Against this background of rapid change and growing economic hardship, the political conflict between Yeltsin and his opponents in parliament again came to a head in December. Once more the results were inconclusive. Yeltsin thwarted an opposition attempt to limit his powers, but only at the price of sacrificing Gaidar, the architect of his economic program. Gaidar was replaced as prime minister by Chernomyrdin. Both sides agreed that the country would hold a referendum in April 1993 so the people could speak on what should be the basic principles of a new Russian constitution.

Before that could take place, the president and parliament locked horns yet again. On March 12 the Congress of People's Deputies voted to annul the decision to hold the April referendum and, more importantly, to limit the president's powers. Yeltsin retaliated eight days later by announcing what he called a system of "special presidential rule" under which the congress could not overrule presidential decrees. Several days after that Yeltsin's opponents in the congress narrowly lost a vote to impeach him.

Both sides then temporarily drew back from the brink. They agreed to a national referendum in April, although not one about constitutional principles. Instead, voters were asked their views on the president and his economic policies. About 64 percent of the voters turned out; of these, 58 percent said they supported the president and almost 53 percent—a surprisingly high number in light of Russia's economic difficulties—supported his economic policies.

The referendum did not end Russia's political deadlock. By September the tension between Yeltsin and his opponents in parliament was higher than ever. On September 21, declaring that the parliament was making reform impossible, Yeltsin dissolved it and called for new elections in December. The Supreme Soviet, the country's day-to-day legislature, voted to remove Yeltsin from office and ordered security troops not to obey the president. To noisy applause, it swore in Aleksandr Rutskoi as Russia's acting president. Several hundred supporters of the revolt gathered outside the parliament building, known as the White House, where they built bonfires and barricades. This time, neither side drew back from the brink.

On October 2, stone-throwing demonstrators opposed to Yeltsin battled police in the center of Moscow. The well-organized crowd forced police to retreat as Rutskoi, calling himself the "President of the Russian Federation," issued a statement proclaiming a "struggle against dictatorship" that left no doubt an attempt to overthrow Yeltsin was under way. The next day an enormous mob wielding clubs, metal pipes, and wooden planks smashed through police lines to rally at the White House. Armed parliamentary guards seized the office of the mayor of Moscow by driving trucks through plate glass doors. The Russian flag at the office was ripped down and replaced by a red symbol of Communism amid shouts of "It's our October Revolution" (a reference to the Bolshevik Revolution) and "Hang that bastard Yeltsin." At Rutskoi's urging, another crowd tried to storm the building housing Russia's main television complex. By the end of the day at least 20 people were dead. It was the worst street violence in Moscow since the Bolshevik Revolution of 1917.

On October 3, Yeltsin declared a state of emergency. His position was precarious. In August 1991 the military had refused to back the coup against Gorbachev, rallying instead to Yeltsin and helping him to emerge as the hero of the struggle against reaction. In October 1993, aware that the military was demoralized and hurt by cutbacks in funding since 1991, Rutskoi, Khasbulatov, and their allies calculated that this time the army would turn against Yeltsin. They were mistaken. Minister of Defense Pavel Grachev and the troops he commanded remained loyal to Yeltsin. By the early morning of October 4, tanks and troops were in position at several key locations in Moscow, including the White House. So were television crews from around the world, allowing millions of viewers in Russia and abroad to look on in fascination and horror. Near the White House, Muscovites, some perched in trees, watched events unfold with a calmness that seemed out of place for a country on the brink of disaster.

Shortly after 9:00 A.M., pro-Yeltsin troops seized the first two floors of the building. As the battle raged Yeltsin spoke frankly to his "Dear Compatriots," the people of Russia, and told them "I bow to you from my heart." The tone of his speech was a reminder of how, at least in certain respects, Russia had changed since 1985. By noon, clouds of black smoke billowed from the White House as the army's most powerful tanks pounded the building. Soon the top half of the White House was engulfed in flames. The overwhelming firepower was decisive. The rebels inside the White House began to surrender at 5:00 P.M. and an hour later it was all over. A stunned Rutskoi, Khasbulatov, and other rebel leaders were taken from their smoldering headquarters to prison. According to official reports, about 150 people were killed and 600 wounded in the abortive revolt.

With the parliament dispersed and his leading opponents in prison, Yeltsin moved quickly to strengthen his position. He banned eight political parties, including Rutskoi's People's Party of Free Russia and the Communist Party of Russia. Yeltsin also fired several high-ranking government officials who had failed to support him and suspended Russia's regional and town councils, many of which had sided with his opponents. The president then decreed that elections would be held in December for a new parliament to be called the Federal Assembly. Its lower house, called the State Duma, would have 450 seats, half elected from single-seat districts and half according to proportional representation, with each competing party winning over 5 percent of the vote getting seats corresponding to the percentage of votes it received. The upper house—the Federation Council—would consist of 178 members: two representatives from each of Russia's 89 territorial divisions. Another presidential decree announced a vote on a new constitution hastily prepared by Yeltsin's staff, a document that vastly strengthened the power of the presidency at the expense of the parliament.

The short election campaign provided many unpleasant surprises for Yeltsin and his supporters. Yeltsin officially refused to endorse any of the contending political parties, focusing instead on selling his new constitution, although he clearly favored Egor Gaidar's party, known as Russia's Choice (since 1994 as Russia's Democratic Choice). However, Russia's Choice and several other political parties most closely identified with Yeltsin and economic reform policies did poorly. In the party-preference voting for the Duma, a neo-Fascist group misleadingly named the Liberal Democratic Party and headed by a charismatic demagogue named Vladimir Zhirinovsky led the pack with 23 percent of the vote. Zhirinovsky, whose ultra-nationalist rhetoric was liberally laced with anti-Semitism, appealed to a demoralized and weary public with attacks on Yeltsin's economic policies ("Can I do it worse than they have? Can you honestly believe that I can do it worse?" he asked rhetorically) and posters that proclaimed "I will bring Russia off its knees." Another unpleasant surprise for Yeltsin was that a revived Russian Communist Party, led by a former party official named Gennady Zyuganov, won 12 percent of the vote, while a close ally, the Agrarian Party, took another 8 percent. Against these totals, Russia's Choice mustered only 15 percent. Taken together, Russia's Choice and other reform parties took about 34 percent of the party-preference vote, while red–brown parties opposing Yeltsin garnered about 43 percent.

Despite the strong showing of red–brown parties, the December 1993 elections marked an important step forward. For the first time in its history Russia had a freely elected parliament and president as well as a constitution approved by its voters. Moreover, Yeltsin could find some solace in the electoral results from the single-seat districts. Russia's Choice won enough of those seats to become, overall, the largest single party in the State Duma, just ahead of Zhirinovsky's LDP; although the red–brown parties, assuming they could work together, still commanded more Duma votes than the reformers. Yeltsin also won a majority, albeit a narrow one, for his constitution. Russia's new constitution gave the president enormous powers, including the right to appoint the prime minister, issue decrees with the force of law under certain conditions, dismiss the State Duma in specific circumstances, and call for referenda. While the new presidential powers suited Yeltsin's immediate needs, democratic critics worried that those powers could be dangerous in the hands of some future president. They were well aware that one of the strongest supporters of the powerful new presidency was Russia's most prominent would-be dictator, Vladimir Zhirinovsky.

Even with his new powers Yeltsin had to bow to the reality of a public clearly disenchanted with the results of his economic program. Missing from the new cabinet announced in January were Gaidar and the reformist finance minister Boris Fyodorov, both of whom had resigned. Of the pre-election cabinet's leading reformers, only Anatoly Chubais, the man in charge of privatization, remained. In place of the departed reformers were ministers who favored a slower pace toward a free market economy. As Prime Minister Chernomyrdin put it, "the period of market romanticism is over." At the same time, again responding to popular sentiment as expressed in the election, both Yeltsin and Foreign Minister Kozyrev began taking a harder line toward Russia's immediate neighbors in the Near Abroad and toward the United States and its NATO allies. Yeltsin also started talking tougher regarding social issues such as crime. In short, in making policy the Yeltsin regime clearly had an ear tuned to the popular discontent reflected in the parliamentary elections, a sentiment some observers called the "Zhirinovsky factor."

In the Duma itself, a majority of the delegates, mindful of Zhirinovsky's outrageous conduct, which included shouting at those who disagreed with him to "shut up" and "get out of the hall," declined to elect him speaker. The successful candidate for that important post was Ivan Rybkin, an anti-reform communist from the Agrarian Party who ultimately was elected—by one vote—with Zhirinovsky's support. The Duma quickly indicated its attitude toward Yeltsin: in February 1994 it declared an amnesty for all participants in both the August 1991 and October 1993 coups. The Federation Council proved more friendly to the president. It elected a Yeltsin backer, Vladimir Shumeiko, as its chairman, but only after an intense overnight campaign to gather the necessary votes.

One reason Yeltsin wanted a new constitution was to strengthen the central government and assert Moscow's control over the country's territorial divisions. Russia emerged from the wreckage of the fallen Soviet Union officially divided into eighty-nine administrative units, including twenty-one so-called "republics" that were supposed to provide a degree of autonomy for non-Russian ethnic minorities. In reality, in only five of the republics was the titular nationality actually a majority. Ethnic Russians made up about 45 percent of the total population of the republics and constituted a majority in nine of them. Nonetheless, the Yeltsin government was immediately faced with demands for genuine autonomy from several of the republics with large non-Russian populations, and three of them—Tatarstan, Bashkortostan, and Chechnya—openly threatened secession. Yeltsin also had plenty of trouble with nonethnic administrative units, several of which echoed demands for autonomy and even withheld tax revenues they were supposed to send to Moscow.

The new constitution legally strengthened the central government vis-à-vis the country's eighty-nine administrative units. While by itself this did not solve any practical problems with the restive republics and regions, during 1994 most of them at least accepted Russia's new constitutional order. The exception was the republic of Chechnya, a strategically located territory near the Caspian Sea and Caucasus Mountains with a population of about 1.3 million, most of them Moslem Chechens. The president of Chechnya was a ruthless and recklessly ambitious former Soviet air force officer named Dzhokhar Dudaev. After seizing power in Chechnya in the fall of 1991 and confirming his status in a rigged election, Dudaev declared the territory independent. Unlike the leaders of Russia's other republics and regions, Dudaev defiantly resisted any agreement with Moscow short of genuine independence. He further kicked sand in Moscow's face by allowing Chechen gangs to base their illegal operations in what one Russian official called Dudaev's "free economic-criminal zone." Among these illicit activities were arms smuggling and narcotics trafficking.

However, Yeltsin did not move against Chechnya because it was a hub for criminal activity or because it represented a potential threat to Russian territorial integrity. Certainly these were real problems, but not so acutely menacing that they demanded immediate massive military action. In fact, by 1994 there were signs that Dudaev's grip on Chechnya was weakening. Yeltsin had other imperatives. He was convinced by advisors on his National Security Council that he needed to steal some of Zhirinovsky's nationalist thunder if he expected to be reelected president in 1996. These advisors—who included the minister of the interior, the head of the Federal Security Service (the former KGB), and Defense Minister Pavel Grachev —guaranteed Yeltsin a quick victory in a matter of weeks. Grachev suggested that Chechnya, which in the nineteenth century had resisted Russian conquest for no less than forty years, could be disposed of "in two hours by a single paratroop regiment."

That boast, as well as the rest of the prognostications Yeltsin received from the small group of advisors that the Russian press called the "party of war," turned out to be empty. The invasion of Chechnya began on December 11, 1994, and immediately turned into a bloody and humiliating fiasco for the Russian army and for Yeltsin's government. The operation was poorly planned and the first inexperienced and unprepared troops sent into the Chechen capital of Grozny—which means "terrible" in Russian—were slaughtered. Eventually 40,000 Russian troops fought in Chechnya. Although Grozny was bombarded and shelled until it was a shattered hulk, the city did not fall for eight weeks. By then over 4,000 Russian soldiers, thousands of Chechen fighters, and 25,000 civilians in the city, including Russian residents, were dead. By mid-1995 Russian forces held every major Chechen town but faced a protracted guerrilla war against Chechen fighters holding out in their mountain bastions.

The war in Chechnya was a disaster for the Yeltsin regime in virtually every way. Its enormous financial cost drained Russia's budget and fueled inflation, thereby undermining Yeltsin's economic reforms. It embarrassed Russia internationally and humiliated its army, which still bore deep scars from the Soviet military's disastrous experience in Afghanistan. Sold to Yeltsin by his advisors as a way of rescuing his presidency, instead the war in Chechnya badly undermined Yeltsin's popularity at home, further weakening his ability to govern. It also drove a deep wedge between Russia's president and his former supporters in Russia's democratic camp, most of whom opposed the war. In particular, the war against Chechnya severely damaged Yeltsin's relationship with Gaidar and Russia's Choice and further estranged him from Yabloko, Russia's other major reform party led by the respected liberal economist Grigory Yavlinsky, best known as the co-author of the stillborn "500 Day" economic reform plan of the Gorbachev era.

The war in Chechnya ultimately came home to Russia in disastrous fashion in June 1995, when a band of 100 Chechen fighters crossed the border into Russia's Stavropol region and entered the city of Budyonnovsk. They then killed over 100 people and seized more than 1,000 hostages. With Yeltsin out of the country, Prime Minister Chernomyrdin conducted negotiations that led to the release of the hostages and the Chechens' unmolested withdrawal to their homeland. While the negotiations, which were carried live on television, enhanced Chernomyrdin's reputation with the general public, the Budyonnovsk episode led to a bitter clash between the Yeltsin government and the parliament that forced the president to dismiss three ministers blamed for mishandling the crisis and who were closely identified with the war policy.

Against this background of wrenching economic change and political turmoil, in its first post-Soviet years Russia also was beset by a crime wave of staggering proportions. Yeltsin called Russia's criminal element a "superpower," adding that "crime has become problem number one for us."[1] Millions of ordinary Russians agreed with him. One opinion poll in 1993 found that almost half of those surveyed feared crime more than unemployment. A 1994 poll found that 91 percent of all Muscovites feared for their lives and that one in three had been in a life-threatening situation involving criminals during the past year. They had good reason for their fears: in 1994 Moscow, once considered an extremely safe city, experienced over 1,800 murders, over 200 more than violence-plagued New York City.

By far the most dangerous aspect of Russia's new lawlessness was organized crime. Russia's organized criminal gangs had their origins in the Brezhnev era, when the illegal "second economy" developed to supply the people with goods the Communist system did not provide. Hundreds of criminal gangs dominated large parts of that economy, often in collusion with corrupt government officials. It was during this period that Russians first began to talk about their "Mafiya." These gangs grew stronger during the Gorbachev era, as government controls over everything weakened. They took over many of the new small businesses that sprang up during the 1980s. After 1991, as Moscow's ability to control the country diminished further, criminal gangs flourished as never before. By 1994, there were 5,000 gangs in Russia, ten times as many as in 1990. The Russian government estimated that these gangs controlled one-third of all goods and services sold in the country, while the CIA reported that criminal organizations controlled 40,000 Russian enterprises. Criminals dominated as much as 50 percent of all private business. Organized crime also played a major role in the transfer of billions of dollars of vitally needed capital from Russia to Western banks. It discouraged foreign investment in Russia and hampered the expansion of legitimate private business.

Making matters worse, as criminal gangs spread their net throughout Russia's emerging market economy, they extended their tentacles to government officials at every level. Among the most terrifying prospects involving Russian organized crime was its potential involvement in the trade of stolen nuclear material that could be used to make atomic weapons. It was no secret that there were eager buyers for these materials in aggressive Middle Eastern countries such as Iran and Iraq and Islamic terrorist organizations linked to them. This illegal trade, of course, was not only Russia's problem. As one FBI official put it, the spread of nuclear weapons through thefts by organized crime was "the greatest long-term threat to the security of the United States." As for Russia itself, in 1994 one Western expert observed that "Russia's crime syndicate constitutes a serious threat to post-Soviet democracy."[2]

While juggling all these domestic problems, the Yeltsin regime simultaneously struggled to formulate a post-Soviet foreign policy. The challenge for the Russian government was to emerge from the shadow of seven decades of Soviet hostility toward the West while maintaining what it regarded as its vital security interests as a great power. Foreign Minister Kozyrev summed up that goal when he said he expected Russia to play the international role of a "normal great power."

Despite its territorial losses, Russia still had a legitimate claim to great-power status. It inherited the defunct Soviet Union's place in many international bodies, including its permanent seat and veto on the United Nations Security Council. It also inherited most of the Soviet Union's nuclear arsenal, which left it, along with the United States, one of the world's two dominant nuclear powers. The remaining Soviet nuclear arms were located in the territories of Ukraine, Belarus, and Kazakhstan.

One of Yeltsin's most urgent objectives was to continue the progress on nuclear arms reduction that began with the landmark Soviet–United States START I agreement of 1991. In January 1993 Russia and the United States signed START II, which stipulated yet deeper cuts. However, before the Yeltsin government would implement even START I, it wanted guarantees that Ukraine, Belarus, and Kazakhstan, which possessed arsenals that included both short-range and long-range (strategic) weapons, would give up their nuclear weapons. After difficult negotiations and under heavy pressure from the United States and its NATO allies, Ukraine, Belarus, and Kazakhstan transferred all short-range weapons to Russia in 1992. But it proved more difficult to resolve the question of strategic weapons. This required that the three nations sign and ratify both START I and the Nuclear Non-Proliferation Treaty (NPT). Belarus accepted both treaties in 1993 and Kazakhstan ratified START I in 1992 and the NPT in 1994. Ukraine, ever suspicious of Russian intentions, held out longer, despite pressure from both Russia and the United States. It finally ratified START I in November 1993 and the NPT in November 1994.

Another major Russian foreign policy goal was to assert its power, and often its hegemony, in as much of the Near Abroad as possible. It could do little with the westward-looking Baltic countries, the only former Soviet states that remained outside the new Commonwealth of Independent States (CIS), and from which all Russian troops were withdrawn by the summer of 1994. The CIS itself remained a rather ill-defined organization without significant operational substance, other than indicating by its existence that most of its members remained within Russia's orbit, despite 300 documents signed by its members between 1991 and 1995.

Russia's relations with Ukraine, the most populous and economically important of the Near Abroad states, were generally tense. Russian–Ukrainian relations had several sore points, the most serious being the status of the Crimea, a predominantly Russian peninsula that Nikita Khrushchev transferred from Russia to Ukraine as a "gift" in 1954, ten years after Stalin deported the region's Tatar population to Central Asia. Despite continued threats of secession, which found considerable sympathy in Russia, as of mid-1995 the Crimea remained a part of Ukraine, albeit an unwilling one and a source of continued tension between Ukraine and Russia. In June of that year the two nations reached an agreement on the division of the former Soviet Black Sea fleet, a bone of contention since 1991. While Ukraine held Russia at arms length, the Yeltsin government was more successful in drawing Belarus more closely into its orbit, as demonstrated by a May 1995 agreement that established a Russian–Belarusian customs union.

Elsewhere in the Near Abroad, ethnic turmoil helped Russia assert its influence in both the Caucasus and Central Asia. After Azerbaijan left the CIS in 1992, Russia took advantage of that country's defeat in its struggle with Armenia over Nagorno-Karabakh to pressure it to rejoin the organization in 1993. A similar strategy brought Georgia, which was being torn apart by two secessionist movements, including a successful military uprising in its westernmost province of Abkhazia, into the CIS fold. More importantly, the agreement allowed Russia to maintain military bases in Georgia. In Central Asia, thousands of Russian troops sent to defend Tajikistan's dictatorial government of ex-Communist functionaries against a rebellion by Islamic fundamentalists turned that troubled country into a Russian protectorate. By 1994, Russia had a total of 16,000 troops stationed throughout the Near Abroad and plans to establish about thirty permanent bases there.

Russia was less able to assert its influence on its former satellite states in Eastern Europe. The Yeltsin government was especially disturbed about the prospect of an expansion of NATO that would include some of those states. Russian objections initially had limited success; in 1994 NATO created a compromise program called the Partnership for Peace that allowed the East European states to be associated with the alliance and cooperate with it militarily, but denied them full-fledged membership. However, as talk of NATO expansion continued, in December Yeltsin angrily asked the sixteen NATO members, "Why are you sowing the seeds of mistrust?" and warned them that despite the end of the Cold War, "Europe is in danger of plunging into a cold peace." When Russia finally agreed to become an active member in the Partnership in May 1995, Yeltsin warned that NATO expansion would end Moscow's participation in the program. Inside Russia nationalist politicians used the issue of NATO expansion to lambaste the government and especially Foreign Minister Kozyrev, the leading advocate of a conciliatory approach to the West.

Another source of tension between Russia and the West was Moscow's decision to sell light-water nuclear reactors to Iran, which could help that militant Islamic state build nuclear weapons. Further problems arose in 1995 over NATO bombing attacks against the Serbs of war-torn Bosnia in the former Yugoslavia. Although Yeltsin generally supported U.S.-led peace efforts in Bosnia, Moscow also saw the NATO bombings as an intrusion into what had once been a Soviet sphere of influence and an attack on a people, the Serbs, who shared Russia's Orthodox Christian heritage. Yeltsin's denunciation of the bombings also was linked to domestic politics; he understood that angry and growing nationalist sentiment at home was strengthening opponents of his government. In September 1995, the Duma reacted to the NATO bombing attacks by passing a resolution calling on the government to suspend its Partnership for Peace agreement with NATO and demanding that Yeltsin fire Foreign Minister Kozyrev. Communist Party leader Gennady Zyuganov denounced Kozyrev as the "minister of national disgrace," while Vladimir Zhirinovsky, not to be outdone in militancy by any Russian politician, announced the time had come to "start the motors of Russian tanks and bombers" and send them to the war zone.

Zhirinovsky's proposal was not only outlandish politically, it was impossible to execute militarily. By mid-1995 Russia's military was severely limited in what it could do. Its total strength of 1.2 to 1.5 million men was only one-quarter of the former Soviet Union's armed force. It received an even smaller fraction of the resources it consumed during the Soviet era, leaving it with few funds for research and development or the procurement of new weapons. Only the Strategic Forces that controlled Russia's nuclear weapons were at full authorized strength; the army, navy, and air force lacked the necessary recruits to fill their units.

Overall, Russia's first four post-Soviet years brought very mixed news and little shelter from the cold winds of change. On the positive side, there was considerable economic change and progress. By the middle of 1995 the spread of privatization (over 100,000 enterprises when the first stage ended in mid-1994) and the sprouting of over 1 million new businesses meant that two-thirds of the labor force worked in the private sector. Russia's major cities sported new shops, restaurants, and renovated buildings. Some newly privatized industrial enterprises, including large military firms, were producing for the consumer market, sometimes in joint ventures with foreign companies. Inflation, while still a problem, had dropped significantly from the stratospheric levels of 1992 and 1993. Individual consumption appeared to have hit bottom in 1993 and slowly begun to recover, while the number of people living in poverty also slowly started to decline. The ruble, which early in 1995 dropped below 5,000 to the dollar, recovered and appeared to have stabilized in the mid-4,000s by the fall. While experts predicted the economy would shrink by another 3 percent in 1995, they projected 2 percent growth in 1996 and 3 percent in 1997. Increasing numbers of Russians, especially younger people, were making money as entrepreneurs of various sorts and enjoying the luxuries, generally imported, their new wealth could buy.

However, Russia's post-Soviet economy was rife with discouraging statistics and pictures. Between 1991 and 1994 Russia's gross domestic product dropped by almost 40 percent. Production in light industry, which produces goods for consumers, slumped particularly sharply; by 1995 it was only 25 percent of what it had been in early 1991, with large chunks of that drop coming in 1994 and the first half of 1995. Overall industrial production by mid-1995 was about half that of 1990, although it seemed to have finally hit bottom, and signs pointed to the beginning of a recovery. Making matters worse, investment in production—which defines the future for any society—was sharply down, leading one Russian economist to worry that "there is a very strong tendency of growing deindustrialization of the country and irreversible degradation of our scientific and industrial potential."[3] Of particular concern was the fate of the high-technology factories of the military-industrial complex, which employed many of Russia's best engineers and scientists and produced its most advanced civilian as well as military products. Part of the problem was that foreign investors, deterred by crime, corruption, and instability, continued to shun Russia. Foreign investment in Russia by 1994 not only trailed far behind China, but even behind small states such as Poland, Hungary, and the Czech Republic.

The picture in agriculture also was worrisome. The grain harvest of 1994 was the lowest in a decade, while overall food production continued to drop in both 1993 and 1994. Private farming remained stuck around 5 percent of total farmland. Thus, while a small minority of Russia's people thrived under the new conditions and managed to prosper and even become rich, overall after 1991 the country's standard of living fell drastically and the inequality between the rich and the poor grew. A reasonable estimate was that by mid-1995, 10 million Russians were unemployed.

There were many other serious structural problems as well. Privatization notwithstanding, the existence of so many huge factory complexes meant that Russia remained what one local economist called a "country of monopolies," and these monopolies remained oblivious to market forces that were supposed to make Russian industry more efficient. Market forces were further hamstrung because the state continued to own a controlling interest in many officially "privatized" industrial enterprises. In addition, Russia lacked a social safety net for its workers, to replace the collapsed Soviet system, and a body of law and tax policies necessary for a market economy to function. By 1995 about $130 billion in capital had been sent abroad by Russia's rapacious new rich, while foreign aid fell billions short of expectations. Criminal elements became increasingly entrenched in many sectors of the new economy. As one Western financial journal observed, "Moscow's roads are busy with flashy foreign cars, driven by men in dark glasses, whose profession is invariably 'trade' or 'banking.' " As political scientist Peter Reddaway put it, the defunct state-run economy had been replaced "not by a true market economy, but by an unstable semi-market system preyed on by a growing army of parasites—mafiosi and bribe-taking officials."[4] Or, as economist Marshall Goldman observed, Russia's "bastard" capitalism "may be a market, but not one that most societies would tolerate."[5]

Russia's political situation likewise was problematical. Russia no longer had a totalitarian regime, but despite its popularly elected president and parliament and its voter-approved constitution it did not have a fully democratic one either. Enormous power was concentrated in the presidency, which commanded a bureaucracy so swollen that by 1995 the Russian government actually was larger than the Soviet government had been in 1991. An important part of that bureaucracy was the presidential security service under Yeltsin's crony General Aleksandr Korzhakov. With Yeltsin's health increasingly more fragile—he was hospitalized in December 1994, June 1995, and October–November 1995—he relied more and more on Korzhakov, whom Yeltsin called his most loyal friend and trusted advisor and who controlled both the president's schedule and access to him. A concern among democrats in Russia was the revitalized Federal Security Service (FSB), the successor to the domestic parts of the KGB, which in early 1995, as part of Yeltsin's efforts to battle crime, received extensive new powers to spy on Russian citizens. A Moscow newspaper spoke for many when it complained that the new law "allows Lubyanka [the infamous KGB headquarters] to cover the entire country with a network of secret agents again." Meanwhile, theft by government officials and the bribes they demanded from businessmen discredited the government in the eyes of the people and probably caused greater harm to the economy than organized crime. Adding insult to injury, the perks and privileges of Russia's ruling elite—which included special access to cars, apartments, quality medical care, vacation spots, and the like—increasingly recalled the life style of the old Soviet nomenklatura.

Despite its size, Russia's government was not effective. The central government was so inefficient that it was able to collect only one-fourth of the taxes it imposed. Russia's social safety net was full of holes, and its schools, roads, and many other public facilities and services were in disrepair or disarray. As one Western observer put it, the "reality of Russia in 1995 is that it is *undergoverned*. And an undergoverned Russia is dangerous both to itself and to others."[6]

Yeltsin's poor health was another shadow across post-Soviet Russian politics. It remained an open question whether he would be a candidate in the scheduled June 1996 presidential elections. A possible replacement for Yeltsin was Prime Minister Chernomyrdin, in office since December 1992, whose public stature benefited from his increasingly steady hand in running the economy and his handling of the Budyonnovsk hostage crisis. Whether Yeltsin ran or not, potential opponents were not hard to find. One, of course, was Zhirinovsky, the best known of a growing group of politicians on the far right of Russia's political spectrum. A far more formidable potential presidential candidate in the nationalist camp was General Aleksandr Lebed, a hero of the Afghanistan war and, until his resignation in June 1995, commander of Russia's Fourteenth Army stationed in Moldova. Extremely popular in the military and respected for his honesty, Lebed was a harsh critic of Defense Minister Grachev and the war in Chechnya. The most popular reformist politican was Grigory Yavlinsky of Yabloko. Other potential candidates included Moscow Mayor Yurii Luzhkov and the reformist governor of Nizhny Novgorod, Boris Nemtsov. Also in the wings was Gennady Zyuganov, leader of the resurgent Communist Party.

Russia's struggle to overcome its staggering array of problems was made all the more difficult because it was losing many of its most capable people. By 1994 it was estimated that 10 percent of the country's scientists and engineers had emigrated, among them many with international reputations and the most valuable skills. This brain drain abroad was compounded by an internal brain drain as scientific personnel abandoned their research institutes to make a living wherever they could. A typical example was a talented theoretical physicist from a major institute in Novosibirsk who gave up physics to become an officer in a bank. The man was doing well and could afford a new car, but as his former colleague asked with a touch of both sadness and contempt, "What's he producing in a bank?"

Even more debilitating and dangerous in the long term, the physical health of the Russian people was deteriorating with shocking speed. Between 1990 and 1994, the life expectancy for Russian men fell from 63.8 to 57.3 years, a plunge unprecedented in modern industrial countries. Life expectancy for women also fell, although at a slower rate. Fed by epidemic rates of heart disease, cancer, infectious diseases, and accidents, Russia's death rate doubled in a decade and by 1994 was almost twice the birth rate. As a result, the country's population declined by 1 million between 1991 and 1995. The birth rate fell to an all-time low; Russia's 1.4 million births in 1994 were less than half the number of abortions. Even more alarming, of the children that were born about 10 percent suffered from serious birth defects and about 50 percent of those in school suffered from chronic diseases. Whether the cause of these developments was the collapse of the country's health-care system from lack of funding or, more alarmingly, the result of decades of irresponsible ecological policies that poisoned many parts of the county with radioactive wastes and toxic chemicals, or a combination of these and other factors, it was hard to disagree with one expert who said, simply: "What we have here is a disaster." It was more difficult to conceive of how to cope with the situation.

Russia's problems during the first years of the post-Soviet era parallel the country's experiences earlier in the century. The twentieth century has not been kind to Russia. It has brought Russia's people world war and civil war, revolution and totalitarian tyranny, famine and ecological destruction. Now once again Russia finds itself in the midst of a revolution, albeit initially a remarkably peaceful one, but nevertheless a phenomenon comparable in depth and breadth to the Bolshevik Revolution and other modern revolutionary upheavals. However, unlike during the Bolshevik Revolution, the goal in Russia today is not to build a utopian society. That would sit well with Soviet-era writer and dissident Andrei Siniavsky, who after six years in a Soviet labor camp had this to say about utopias: "The fact is that ideal societies cannot be—they only cause the blood to flow." Instead the objective of Russia's current leaders appears to be a practical social order in which people are free to prosper by their own efforts and participate in the governance of their country. The extent to which today's efforts succeed will do much to determine how well future Russian generations will be able to address the unfavorable balance between what their country has enjoyed and what it has had to endure.

NOTES

1. Cited in Stephen Handelman, "The Russian 'Mafiya,' " *Foreign Affairs*, Vol. 73, No. 2 (March/April 1994), p. 88.
2. *Ibid.*, p. 83.
3. Cited in Lynn D. Nelson and Irina Y. Kuzes, *Radical Reform in Yeltsin's Russia: Political, Social, and Economic Dimensions* (Armonk and London: M.E. Sharpe, 1995), p. 103.
4. Peter Reddaway, "Desperation Time for Yeltsin's Clique," *The New York Times*, January 3, 1995.
5. Marshall Goldman, "Is This Any Way to Create a Market Economy?" *Current History*, October 1995, p. 310.
6. S. Frederick Starr, "The Paradox of Yeltsin's Russia," *The Wilson Quarterly*, Summer 1995, p. 73.

Selected
Readings

Selected Readings

PART ONE

Billingston, James H. *The Icon and the Axe.* New York: Vintage. 1970.

Blum, Jerome. *Lord and Peasant in Russia.* New York: Atheneum. 1965.

Pipes, Richard. *Russia Under the Old Regime.* New York: Scribners, 1974.

Pomper, Philip. *The Russian Revolutionary Intelligentsia.* New York: Crowen, 1970.

Robinson, Geroid Tanquary. *Rural Russia Under the Old Regime.* Berkeley: University of California Press, 1967.

Seton-Watson, Hugh. *The Russian Empire 1801–1917.* Oxford, Eng.: Clarendon Press, 1967.

Sumner, B. H. *A Short History of Russia.* New York: Harcourt, 1949.

Szamuely, Tibor. *The Russian Tradition.* New York: McGraw-Hill, 1974.

Venturi, Franco. *Roots of Revolution.* Francis Haskell, trans. New York: Grosset and Dunlap, 1966.

Vucinich, Wayne S., ed. *The Peasant in Nineteenth-Century Russia.* Stanford: Stanford University Press, 1968.

PART TWO

Charques, Richard. *The Twilight of Imperial Russia.* New York: Oxford University Press, 1958.

Crankshaw, Edward. *The Shadow of the Winter Palace.* New York: Penguin, 1978.

Florinsky, Michael. *The End of the Russian Empire*. New York: Collier, 1961.

Harcave, Sidney. *First Blood: The Russian Revolution of 1905*. New York: Macmillan, 1964.

Kochan, Lionel. *Russia in Revolution 1890–1918*. London: Granada Publishing Ltd., 1970.

Kolakowski, Leszek. *Main Currents of Marxism, Vol. 2: The Golden Age*. F. S. Fella, trans. Oxford: Oxford University Press, 1978.

Meyer, Alfred G. *Leninism*. Cambridge, MA: Harvard University Press, 1955.

Oberländer, Edwin, et al., eds. *Russia Enters the Twentieth Century*. New York, Schocken, 1971.

Ulam, Adam. *The Bolsheviks*. New York: Collier, 1965.

Von Laue, Theodore H. *Sergei Witte and the Industrialization of Russia*. New York: Atheneum, 1969.

PART THREE

Chamberlin, William Henry. *The Russian Revolution, vols. I and II*. New York: Grosset and Dunlap, 1965.

Daniels, Robert V. *The Conscience of the Revolution*. Cambridge, MA: Harvard University Press, 1965.

Deutscher, Isaac. *The Prophet Armed, Trotsky: 1879–1921, vol. I*. New York: Vintage, 1965.

———. *The Prophet Unarmed, Trotsky: 1921–1929, vol. II*. New York: Vintage, 1965.

Gerson, Leonard. *The Secret Police in Lenin's Russia*. Philadelphia: Temple University Press, 1976.

Lewin, Moshe. *Lenin's Last Struggle*. A. M. Sheridan Smith, trans. New York: Pantheon, 1968.

Pipes, Richard. *The Russian Revolution*. New York: Knopf, 1990.

———. *Russia Under the Bolshevik Regime*. New York: Knopf, 1993.

Rabinowitch, Alexander. *The Bolsheviks Come to Power*. New York: W. W. Norton, 1976.

Schapiro, Leonard. *The Origin of the Communist Autocracy*. New York: Praeger, 1965.

———. *The Russian Revolutions of 1917: The Origins of Modern Communism*. New York: Basic Books, 1984.

Service, Robert. *The Bolshevik Party in Revolution*. New York: Barnes and Noble, 1979.

Theen, Rolf H. W. *Lenin*. Princeton, NJ: Princeton University Press, 1973.

Thompson, John M. *Revolutionary Russia, 1917*. New York: Scribners, 1981.

Volkogonov, Dmitri. *Lenin: A New Biography*. Harold Shukman, ed. and trans. New York: The Free Press, 1994.

PART FOUR

Blackwell, William L. *The Industrialization of Russia*. New York: Crowell, 1970.

Conquest, Robert. *The Great Terror*. New York: Macmillan, 1968.

Dallin, David J. and Nicolaevsky, Boris I. *Forced Labor in Soviet Russia.* New Haven, CT: Yale University Press, 1947.

Jasny, Haum. *Soviet Industrialization 1928–1952.* Chicago: University of Chicago Press, 1961.

McNeal, Robert A. *Stalin: Man and Ruler,* New York: New York University Press, 1988.

Medvedev, Roy A. *Let History Judge.* Colleen Taylor, trans. New York: Vintage, 1971.

Nove, Alec. *An Economic History of the U.S.S.R.* Middlesex, Eng.: Penguin, 1969.

Solzhenitsyn, Aleksandr. *The Gulag Archipelago.* Thomas P. Whitney, trans. New York: Harper & Row, 1973.

————. *The Gulag Archipelago Two.* Thomas P. Whitney, trans. New York: Harper & Row, 1975.

————. *The Gulag Archipelago Three.* Thomas P. Whitney, trans. New York: Harper & Row; 1978.

Tucker, Robert C., ed. *Stalinism: Essays in Historical Interpretation.* New York: W. W. Norton, 1976.

Tolstoy, Nikolai. *Stalin's Secret War.* George Saunders, trans. New York: Holt, Rinehart and Winston, 1981.

Ulam, Adam. *Stalin.* New York: Viking, 1973.

PART FIVE

Breslauer, George W. *Khrushchev and Brezhnev as Leaders.* London: George, Allen & Unwin, 1982.

Burlatsky, Fedor. *Khrushchev and the First Russian Spring: The Era of Khrushchev Through the Eyes of His Advisor.* Daphne Skillen, trans. New York: Charles Scribner's Sons, 1988.

Cohen, Stephen, et al., eds. *The Soviet Union Since Stalin.* Bloomington, Ind.: University of Indiana Press, 1980.

d'Encausse, Helene. *Confiscated Power.* George Holoch, trans. New York: Harper & Row, 1982.

Dornberg, John. *Brezhnev: The Masks of Power.* New York: Basic Books, 1974.

McCauley, Martin, editor. *Khrushchev and Khrushchevism.* Bloomington and Indianapolis: Indiana University Press, 1987.

McNeal, Robert A. *Stalin: Man and Ruler.* New York: New York University Press, 1988.

Medvedev, Roy A. and Medvedev, Zhores A. *Khrushchev: The Years in Power.* Andrew R. Durkin, trans. New York: Columbia University Press, 1975.

Rubinstein, Joshua. *Soviet Dissidents.* Boston: Beacon Press, 1980.

Smith, Hedrick. *The Russians.* New York: Ballantine Books, 1976.

Thompson, William J. *Khrushchev: A Political Life.* New York: St. Martin's Press, 1995.

Voslensky, Michael. *Nomenklatura: The Soviet Ruling Class.* Erich Mosbacher, trans. New York and Garden City: Doubleday, 1984.

Yanov, Alexander. *The Drama of the Soviet 1960s: A Lost Reform.* Stephen P. Dunn, trans. Berkeley: Institute of International Studies, 1984.

PART SIX

Adelman, Deborah. *The "Children of Perestroika" Come of Age: Young People of Moscow Talk about Life in the New Russia*, Armonk and London: M.E. Sharpe, 1994.

Desai, Padma. *Perestroika in Perspective: The Design and Dilemmas of Soviet Reform*. Princeton: Princeton University Press, 1989.

Feshbach, Murray and Friendly, Jr., Alfred. *Ecocide in the USSR: Health and Nature under Siege*. New York: Basic Books, 1992.

Goldman, Marshall. *What Went Wrong with Perestroika*. New York and London: Norton, 1992.

Hosking, Geoffrey. *The Awakening of the Soviet Union*, Cambridge: Harvard University Press, 1990.

Jones, Anthony, ed. *Education and Society in the New Russia*, Armonk and London: M.E. Sharpe, 1994.

Kaiser, Robert. *Why Gorbachev Happened: His Triumphs, His Failure, and His Fall*. New York: Simon and Schuster, 1992.

Lewin, Moshe. *The Gorbachev Phenomenon: A Historical Interpretation*. Berkeley: University of California Press, 1988.

Lapidus, Gail, ed. *The New Russia: Troubled Transformation*. Boulder: Westview Press, 1995.

Lowenhardt, John. *The Reincarnation of Russia: Struggling With the Legacy of Communism, 1990–1994*. Durham: Duke University Press, 1994.

Nelson, Lynn D., and Kuzes, Irina. *Radical Reform in Yeltsin's Russia: Political, Economic, and Social Dimensions*. Armonk: M.E. Sharpe, 1995.

Remnick, David. *Lenin's Tomb: The Last Days of the Soviet Empire*. New York: Random House, 1993.

White, Stephen; Pravda, Alex; and Gittleman, Zvi, eds. *Developments in Russian and Post-Soviet Politics*. Durham: Duke University Press, 1994.

Yeltsin, Boris. *Against the Grain: An Autobiography*. Michael Glenny, trans. New York: Summit Books, 1990.

"Overviews of the Soviet Era"

Daniels, Robert V. *The End of the Communist Revolution*. London and New York: Routledge, 1993.

Laqueur, Walter. *The Dream that Failed: Reflections on the Soviet Union*. New York and Oxford: Oxford University Press, 1994.

Malia, Martin. *The Soviet Tragedy: A History of Socialism in Russia, 1917–1991*. New York: The Free Press, 1994.

Index

Index

MICHAEL KORT, educated at the John Hopkins University and New York University, is a professor of social science in the College of General Studies at Boston University and has been a fellow of the Russian Research Center at Harvard University. He writes frequently about Soviet history and politics and is the author of the books *Russia and The Commonwealth; Nikita Khrushchev;* and *Mikhail Gorbachev;* and co-author of *Modernization and Revolution in China.* The first edition of *The Soviet Colossus,* published in 1985, was an alternate selection of the Book-of-the-Month Club.

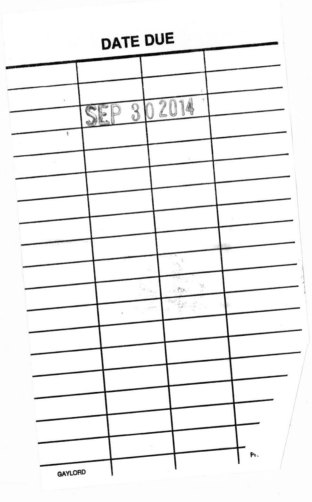

DATE DUE

	SEP 30 2014		
			Pr.